THE HARVARD CLASSICS

The Five-Foot Shelf of Books

Sir Thomas Browne

Sir Thomas Browne

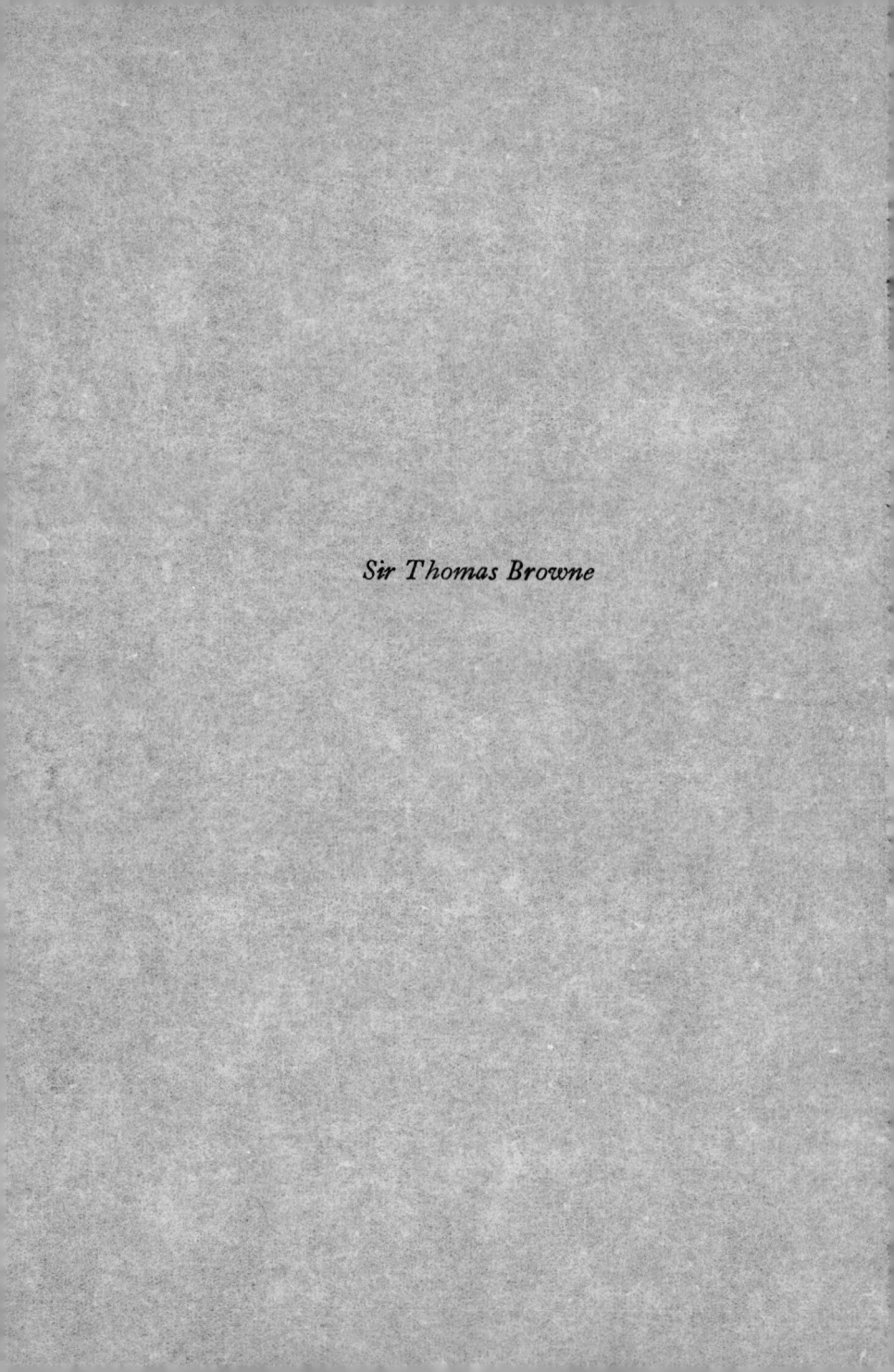

THE HARVARD CLASSICS
EDITED BY CHARLES W. ELIOT, LL.D.

Essays, Civil and Moral
AND
The New Atlantis
By Francis Bacon

Areopagitica
AND
Tractate on Education
By John Milton

Religio Medici
By Sir Thomas Browne

With *Introductions and* Notes
Volume 3

P. F. Collier & Son Corporation
NEW YORK

Copyright, 1937
By P. F. Collier & Son Corporation

Copyright, 1909
By P. F. Collier & Son

MANUFACTURED IN U. S. A.

CONTENTS

	PAGE
ESSAYS OR COUNSELS—CIVIL AND MORAL	7
I. Of Truth	7
II. Of Death	9
III. Of Unity in Religion	11
IV. Of Revenge	15
V. Of Adversity	16
VI. Of Simulation and Dissimulation	17
VII. Of Parents and Children	19
VIII. Of Marriage and Single Life	21
IX. Of Envy	22
X. Of Love	26
XI. Of Great Place	28
XII. Of Boldness	31
XIII. Of Goodness and Goodness of Nature	32
XIV. Of Nobility	34
XV. Of Seditions and Troubles	36
XVI. Of Atheism	42
XVII. Of Superstition	45
XVIII. Of Travel	46
XIX. Of Empire	48
XX. Of Counsel	52
XXI. Of Delays	56
XXII. Of Cunning	57
XXIII. Of Wisdom for a Man's Self	60
XXIV. Of Innovations	61
XXV. Of Dispatch	62
XXVI. Of Seeming Wise	64
XXVII. Of Friendship	65
XXVIII. Of Expense	72
XXIX. Of the True Greatness of Kingdoms and Estates	73
XXX. Of Regiment of Health	81
XXXI. Of Suspicion	82
XXXII. Of Discourse	83
XXXIII. Of Plantations	85
XXXIV. Of Riches	87
XXXV. Of Prophecies	90

CONTENTS

	PAGE
XXXVI. Of Ambition	93
XXXVII. Of Masques and Triumphs	95
XXXVIII. Of Nature in Men	96
XXXIX. Of Custom and Education	98
XL. Of Fortune	99
XLI. Of Usury	101
XLII. Of Youth and Age	104
XLIII. Of Beauty	106
XLIV. Of Deformity	107
XLV. Of Building	108
XLVI. Of Gardens	112
XLVII. Of Negotiating	117
XLVIII. Of Followers and Friends	119
XLIX. Of Suitors	120
L. Of Studies	122
LI. Of Faction	123
LII. Of Ceremonies and Respects	124
LIII. Of Praise	126
LIV. Of Vain-glory	127
LV. Of Honor and Reputation	129
LVI. Of Judicature	130
LVII. Of Anger	134
LVIII. Of Vicissitude of Things	136
LIX. Of Fame	140

THE NEW ATLANTIS 145

AREOPAGITICA 183
   Order of the Long Parliament for the Regulating of Printing,
      14 June, 1643 185
   A Speech for the Liberty of Unlicensed Printing 189

MILTON'S TRACTATE ON EDUCATION 233

RELIGIO MEDICI 249
   The First Part 253
   The Second Part 310

INTRODUCTORY NOTE

FRANCIS BACON, son of Sir Nicholas Bacon, Lord Keeper of the Great Seal to Queen Elizabeth, was born in London on January 22, 1561. He entered Trinity College, Cambridge, at the age of twelve, and in 1576 he interrupted the law studies he had begun in that year, to go to France in the train of the English Ambassador, Sir Amyas Paulet. He was called home in 1579 by the death of his father; and, having been left with but a small income, he resumed the study of law, and became a barrister in 1582. Two years later he entered the House of Commons, and began to take an active part in politics.

From an early age Bacon had been interested in science, and it was in the pursuit of scientific truth that his heart lay. He conceived, however, that for the achievement of the great results at which he aimed, money and prestige were necessary; and he worked hard for both. He was a candidate for several offices of state during Elizabeth's reign, but gained no substantial promotion, and was often in hard straits for money. He received aid from influential patrons, notably the Earl of Essex; and his desertion of this nobleman, with the part he took in his prosecution for treason, is regarded as one of the chief blots on his personal record.

Shortly after the accession of James I, Bacon was knighted; in 1606 he married the daughter of an alderman; and in the following year he received the appointment of Solicitor-General, the first important step in the career which culminated in the Lord Chancellorship in 1618. In the latter year he was raised to the peerage as Baron Verulam, and in 1621 he became Viscount St. Albans. He was now at the summit of his public career; but within four months the crash came, and he was convicted of bribery, and sentenced by the House of Lords to the loss of all his offices, to imprisonment, and to the payment of a large fine. He died in retirement on April 9, 1626, leaving no children.

Bacon's most important writings in science and philosophy are parts of a vast work which he left unfinished, his "Magna Instauratio." The first part of this, the "De Augmentis," is an enlargement in Latin of his book on "The Advancement of Learning," in which he takes account of the progress in human knowledge to his own day. The second part is the famous "Novum Organum," or "New Instrument"; a description of the method of induction based on observation and experiment, by which he believed future progress was to be made. The later parts consist chiefly of fragmentary collections of natural phenomena, and tentative suggestions of the philosophy which was to result from the application of his method to the facts of the physical world.

Bacon's own experiments are of slight scientific value, nor was he very familiar with some of the most important discoveries of his own day; but the fundamental principles laid down by him form the foundation of modern scientific method.

Bacon's writings are by no means confined to the field of natural philosophy. He wrote a notable "History of Henry VII"; many pamphlets on current political topics; "The New Atlantis," an unfinished account of an ideal state; "The Wisdom of the Ancients," a series of interpretations of classical myths in an allegorical sense; legal "Maxims"; and much else.

But by far his most popular work is his "Essays," published in three editions in his lifetime, the first containing ten essays, in 1597; the second, with thirty-eight, in 1612; and the third, as here printed, in 1625. These richly condensed utterances on men and affairs show in the field of conduct something of the same stress on the useful and the expedient as appears in his scientific work. But it is unjust to regard the "Essays" as representing Bacon's ideal of conduct. They are rather a collection of shrewd observations as to how, in fact, men do get on in life; human nature, not as it ought to be, but as it is. Sometimes, but by no means always, they consider certain kinds of behavior from a moral standpoint; oftener they are frankly pieces of worldly wisdom; again, they show Bacon's ideas of state policy; still again, as in the essay "Of Gardens," they show us his private enthusiasms. They cover an immense variety of topics; they are written in a clear, concise, at times almost epigrammatic, style; they are packed with matter; and now, as when he wrote them, they, to use his own words of them, "come home to men's business and bosoms."

THE EPISTLE DEDICATORY

To the Right Honorable my very good Lo. the DUKE OF BUCKINGHAM his Grace, Lo. High Admiral of England.

EXCELLENT LO.

SOLOMON says, *A good name is as a precious ointment;* and I assure myself, such will your Grace's name be with posterity. For your fortune and merit both have been eminent. And you have planted things that are like to last. I do now publish my Essays; which, of all my other works, have been most current; for that, as it seems, they come home to men's business and bosoms. I have enlarged them both in number and weight; so that they are indeed a new work. I thought it therefore agreeable to my affection and obligation to your Grace, to prefix your name before them, both in English and in Latin. For I do conceive that the Latin volume of them (being in the universal language) may last as long as books last. My Instauration I dedicated to the King; my History of Henry the Seventh (which I have now also translated into Latin), and my portions of Natural History, to the Prince; and these I dedicate to your Grace; being of the best fruits that by the good increase which God gives to my pen and labors I could yield. God lead your Grace by the hand.

Your Grace's most obliged and
faithful servant,
FR. ST. ALBAN.

ESSAYS OR COUNSELS
CIVIL AND MORAL

I

OF TRUTH

WHAT *is truth?* said jesting Pilate, and would not stay for an answer. Certainly there be that delight in giddiness, and count it a bondage to fix a belief; affecting[1] free-will in thinking, as well as in acting. And though the sects of philosophers, of that kind[2] be gone, yet there remain certain discoursing[3] wits which are of the same veins, though there be not so much blood in them as was in those of the ancients. But it is not only the difficulty and labor which men take in finding out of truth, nor again that when it is found it imposeth upon[4] men's thoughts, that doth bring lies in favor; but a natural though corrupt love of the lie itself. One of the later school[5] of the Grecians examineth the matter and is at a stand to think what should be in it, that men should love lies, where neither they make for pleasure, as with poets, nor for advantage, as with the merchant; but for the lie's sake. But I cannot tell; this same truth is a naked and open day-light, that doth not show the masks and mummeries and triumphs of the world, half so stately and daintily as candle-lights. Truth may perhaps come to the price of a pearl, that showeth best by day; but it will not rise to the price of a diamond or carbuncle, that showeth best in varied lights. A mixture of a lie doth ever add pleasure. Doth any man doubt, that if there were taken out of men's minds vain opinions, flattering hopes, false valuations, imaginations as one would, and the like, but it would leave the minds of a number of men poor shrunken things, full of melancholy and indisposition, and unpleasing to themselves?

[1] Loving.   [2] The Skeptics.   [3] Latin, windy and rambling.
[4] Restricts.   [5] Lucian.

One of the fathers, in great severity, called poesy *vinum dæmonum* [devils'-wine], because it filleth the imagination; and yet it is but with the shadow of a lie. But it is not the lie that passeth through the mind, but the lie that sinketh in and settleth in it, that doth the hurt; such as we spake of before. But howsoever these things are thus in men's depraved judgments and affections, yet truth, which only doth judge itself, teacheth that the inquiry of truth, which is the love-making or wooing of it, the knowledge of truth, which is the presence of it, and the belief of truth, which is the enjoying of it, is the sovereign good of human nature. The first creature of God, in the works of the days, was the light of the sense; the last was the light of reason; and his sabbath work ever since is the illumination of his Spirit. First he breathed light upon the face of the matter or chaos; then he breathed light into the face of man; and still he breatheth and inspireth light into the face of his chosen. The poet[6] that beautified the sect[7] that was otherwise inferior to the rest, saith yet excellently well: *It is a pleasure to stand upon the shore and to see ships tossed upon the sea; a pleasure to stand in the window of a castle and to see a battle and the adventures thereof below: but no pleasure is comparable to the standing upon the vantage ground of truth* (a hill not to be commanded, and where the air is always clear and serene), *and to see the errors and wanderings and mists and tempests in the vale below;* so always that this prospect be with pity, and not with swelling or pride. Certainly, it is heaven upon earth, to have a man's mind move in charity, rest in providence, and turn upon the poles of truth.

To pass from theological and philosophical truth to the truth of civil business; it will be acknowledged even by those that practise it not, that clear and round dealing is the honor of man's nature; and that mixture of falsehood is like alloy in coin of gold and silver, which may make the metal work the better, but it embaseth it. For these winding and crooked courses are the goings of the serpent; which goeth basely upon the belly, and not upon the feet. There is no vice that doth so cover a man with shame as to be found false and perfidious. And therefore Montaigne saith prettily, when he inquired the reason why the word of the lie should be such a dis-

[6] Lucretius.   [7] Epicureans.

grace and such an odious charge. Saith he, *If it be well weighed, to say that a man lieth, is as much to say, as that he is brave towards God and a coward towards men.* For a lie faces God, and shrinks from man. Surely the wickedness of falsehood and breach of faith cannot possibly be so highly expressed, as in that it shall be the last peal to call the judgments of God upon the generations of men; it being foretold that when Christ cometh, *he shall not find faith upon the earth.*

II

OF DEATH

MEN fear death, as children fear to go in the dark; and as that natural fear in children is increased with tales, so is the other. Certainly, the contemplation of death, as the wages of sin and passage to another world, is holy and religious; but the fear of it, as a tribute due unto nature, is weak. Yet in religious meditations there is sometimes mixture of vanity and of superstition. You shall read in some of the friars' books of mortification, that a man should think with himself what the pain is if he have but his finger's end pressed or tortured, and thereby imagine what the pains of death are, when the whole body is corrupted and dissolved; when many times death passeth with less pain than the torture of a limb; for the most vital parts are not the quickest of sense. And by him that spake[1] only as a philosopher and natural man, it was well said, *Pompa mortis magis terret, quam mors ipsa* [It is the accompaniments of death that are frightful rather than death itself]. Groans and convulsions, and a discolored face, and friends weeping, and blacks,[2] and obsequies, and the like, show death terrible. It is worthy the observing, that there is no passion in the mind of man so weak, but it mates[3] and masters the fear of death; and therefore death is no such terrible enemy when a man hath so many attendants about him that can win the combat of him. Revenge triumphs over death; love slights it; honor aspireth to it; grief flieth to it; fear pre-occupateth[4] it; nay, we read,[5] after Otho the emperor had slain himself, pity (which is

---
[1] Seneca.   [2] Mourning garments.   [3] Conquers.
[4] Anticipates.   [5] In Plutarch's "Lives."

the tenderest of affections) provoked many to die, out of mere compassion to their sovereign, and as the truest sort of followers. Nay, Seneca adds niceness[6] and satiety: *Cogita quamdiu eadem feceris; mori velle, non tantum fortis aut miser, sed etiam fastidiosus potest* [Think how long thou hast done the same thing; not only a valiant man or a miserable man, but also a fastidious man is able to wish for death]. A man would die, though he were neither valiant nor miserable, only upon a weariness to do the same thing so oft over and over. It is no less worthy to observe, how little alteration in good spirits the approaches of death make; for they appear to be the same men till the last instant. Augustus Cæsar died in a compliment; *Livia, conjugii nostri memor, vive et vale* [Farewell, Livia; and forget not the days of our marriage]. Tiberius in dissimulation; as Tacitus saith of him, *Jam Tiberium vires et corpus, non dissimulatio, deserebant* [His powers of body were gone, but his power of dissimulation still remained]. Vespasian in a jest, sitting upon the stool; *Ut puto deus fio* [As I think, I am becoming a god]. Galba with a sentence; *Feri, si ex re sit populi Romani* [Strike, if it be for the good of Rome]; holding forth his neck. Septimius Severus in despatch; *Adeste si quid mihi restat agendum* [Be at hand, if there is anything more for me to do]. And the like. Certainly the Stoics bestowed too much cost upon death, and by their great preparations made it appear more fearful. Better saith he,[7] *qui finem vitæ extremum inter munera ponat naturæ* [who accounts the close of life as one of the benefits of nature]. It is as natural to die as to be born; and to a little infant, perhaps, the one is as painful as the other. He that dies in an earnest pursuit, is like one that is wounded in hot blood; who, for the time, scarce feels the hurt; and therefore a mind fixed and bent upon somewhat that is good doth avert the dolers of death. But, above all, believe it, the sweetest canticle is, *Nunc dimittis* [Now lettest thou ... depart]; when a man hath obtained worthy ends and expectations. Death hath this also; that it openeth the gate to good fame, and extinguisheth envy. *Extinctus amabitur idem* [The same man that was envied while he lived, shall be loved when he is gone].

[6] Fastidiousness. [7] Juvenal.

III

OF UNITY IN RELIGION

RELIGION being the chief band of human society, it is a happy thing when itself is well contained within the true band of unity. The quarrels and divisions about religion were evils unknown to the heathen. The reason was because the religion of the heathen consisted rather in rites and ceremonies than in any constant belief. For you may imagine what kind of faith theirs was, when the chief doctors and fathers of their church were the poets. But the true God hath this attribute, that he is a *jealous God;* and therefore his worship and religion will endure no mixture nor partner. We shall therefore speak a few words concerning the unity of the church; what are the fruits thereof; what the bounds; and what the means.

The fruits of unity (next unto the well pleasing of God, which is all in all) are two: the one towards those that are without the church, the other towards those that are within. For the former; it is certain that heresies and schisms are of all others the greatest scandals; yea, more than corruption of manners. For as in the natural body a wound or solution of continuity is worse than a corrupt humor; so in the spiritual. So that nothing doth so much keep men out of the church, and drive men out of the church, as breach of unity. And therefore, whensoever it cometh to that pass, that one saith *Ecce in deserto* [Lo! in the desert], another saith *Ecce in penetralibus*[1] [Lo! in the sanctuary]; that is, when some men seek Christ in the conventicles of heretics, and others in an outward face of a church, that voice had need continually to sound in men's ears, *Nolite exire,*[1]—*Go not out.* The doctor of the Gentiles[2] (the propriety of whose vocation drew him to have a special care of those without) saith, *If an heathen come in, and hear you speak with several tongues, will he not say that you are mad?* And certainly it is little better, when atheists and profane persons do hear of so many discordant and contrary opinions in religion; it doth avert them from the church, and maketh them *to sit down in the chair of the scorners.* It is but a light thing to be vouched in so serious a

---
[1] Matthew xxiv. 26. [2] St. Paul.

matter, but yet it expresseth well the deformity. There is a master of scoffing,[3] that in his catalogue of books of a feigned library sets down this title of a book, *The Morris-Dance of Heretics.* For indeed every sect of them hath a diverse posture or cringe by themselves, which cannot but move derision in worldlings and depraved politics,[4] who are apt to contemn holy things.

As for the fruit towards those that are within; it is peace; which containeth infinite blessings. It establisheth faith; it kindleth charity; the outward peace of the church distilleth into peace of conscience; and it turneth the labors of writing and reading of controversies into treaties[5] of mortification and devotion.

Concerning the bounds of unity; the true placing of them importeth exceedingly. There appear to be two extremes. For to certain zealants[6] all speech of pacification is odious. *Is it peace, Jehu? What hast thou to do with peace? turn thee behind me.*[7] Peace is not the matter, but following and party. Contrariwise, certain Laodiceans and lukewarm persons think they may accommodate points of religion by middle ways, and taking part of both, and witty[8] reconcilements; as if they would make an arbitrament between God and man. Both these extremes are to be avoided; which will be done, if the league of Christians penned by our Savior himself were in the two cross clauses thereof soundly and plainly expounded: *He that is not with us is against us;* and again, *He that is not against us is with us;* that is, if the points fundamental and of substance in religion were truly discerned and distinguished from points not merely of faith, but of opinion, order, or good intention. This is a thing may seem to many a matter trivial,[9] and done already. But if it were done less partially, it would be embraced more generally.

Of this I may give only this advice, according to my small model. Men ought to take heed of rending God's church by two kinds of controversies. The one is, when the matter of the point controverted is too small and light, not worth the heat and strife about it, kindled only by contradiction. For as it is noted by one of the fathers, *Christ's coat indeed had no seam, but the church's vesture was of divers colors;* whereupon he saith, *In veste varietas sit, scissura non*

[3] Rabelais.   [4] Politicians.   [5] Treatises.   [6] Zealots.   [7] 2 Kings ix. 18, 19.
[8] Ingenious.   [9] Commonplace.

OF UNITY IN RELIGION

sit[10] [Let there be variety in the garment, but let there be no division]; they be two things, unity and uniformity. The other is, when the matter of the point controverted is great, but it is driven to an over-great subtilty and obscurity; so that it becometh a thing rather ingenious than substantial. A man that is of judgment and understanding shall sometimes hear ignorant men differ, and know well within himself that those which so differ mean one thing, and yet they themselves would never agree. And if it come so to pass in that distance of judgment which is between man and man, shall we not think that God above, that knows the heart, doth not discern that frail men in some of their contradictions intend the same thing; and accepteth of both? The nature of such controversies is excellently expressed by St. Paul in the warning and precept that he giveth concerning the same, *Devita profanas vocum novitates, et oppositiones falsi nominis scientiæ* [Avoid profane novelties of terms, and oppositions of science falsely so called]. Men create oppositions which are not; and put them into new terms so fixed, as whereas the meaning ought to govern the term, the term in effect governeth the meaning. There be also two false peaces or unities: the one, when the peace is grounded but upon an implicit[11] ignorance; for all colors will agree in the dark: the other, when it is pieced up upon a direct admission of contraries in fundamental points. For truth and falsehood, in such things, are like the iron and clay in the toes of Nebuchadnezzar's image; they may cleave, but they will not incorporate.

Concerning the means of procuring unity; men must beware, that in the procuring or muniting[12] of religious unity they do not dissolve and deface the laws of charity and of human society. There be two swords amongst Christians, the spiritual and temporal; and both have their due office and place in the maintenance of religion. But we may not take up the third sword, which is Mahomet's sword, or like unto it; that is, to propagate religion by wars or by sanguinary persecutions to force consciences; except it be in cases of overt scandal, blasphemy, or intermixture of practice[13] against the state; much less to nourish seditions; to authorize conspiracies and rebellions; to put the sword into the people's hands; and the like;

[10] St. Augustine.   [11] Entangled.   [12] Fortifying.   [13] Plotting.

tending to the subversion of all government, which is the ordinance of God. For this is but to dash the first table[14] against the second; and so to consider men as Christians, as we forget that they are men. Lucretius the poet, when he beheld the act of Agamemnon, that could endure the sacrificing of his own daughter, exclaimed:

"Tantum Religio potuit suadere malorum"

[To such ill actions Religion could persuade a man]. What would he have said, if he had known of the massacre in France,[15] or the powder treason of England? He would have been seven times more Epicure and atheist than he was. For as the temporal sword is to be drawn with great circumspection in cases of religion; so it is a thing monstrous to put it into the hands of the common people. Let that be left unto the Anabaptists, and other furies. It was great blasphemy when the devil said, *I will ascend and be like the Highest;* but it is greater blasphemy to personate God, and bring him in saying, *I will descend, and be like the prince of darkness:* and what is better, to make the cause of religion to descend to the cruel and execrable actions of murthering princes, butchery of people, and subversion of states and governments? Surely this is to bring down the Holy Ghost, instead of the likeness of a dove, in the shape of a vulture or raven; and set out of the bark of a Christian church a flag of a bark of pirates and assassins. Therefore it is most necessary that the church by doctrine and decree, princes by their sword, and all learnings, both Christian and moral, as by their Mercury rod,[16] do damn and send to hell for ever those facts[17] and opinions tending to the support of the same; as hath been already in good part done. Surely in counsels concerning religion, that counsel of the apostle[18] would be prefixed, *Ira hominis non implet justitiam Dei* [The wrath of man worketh not the righteousness of God]. And it was a notable observation of a wise father, and no less ingenuously confessed; *that those which held and persuaded pressure of consciences, were commonly interested therein themselves for their own ends.*

[14] Of the commandments. Exodus xxxii. 15, 16; xxxiv. 1-5, 29. [15] On St. Bartholomew's Day, 1572. [16] With which Mercury summoned souls to the other world. [17] Deeds. [18] St. James.

IV

OF REVENGE

REVENGE is a kind of wild justice; which the more man's nature runs to, the more ought law to weed it out. For as for the first wrong, it doth but offend the law; but the revenge of that wrong putteth the law out of office. Certainly, in taking revenge, a man is but even with his enemy; but in passing it over, he is superior; for it is a prince's part to pardon. And Solomon, I am sure, saith, *It is the glory of a man to pass by an offence.* That which is past is gone, and irrevocable; and wise men have enough to do with things present and to come; therefore they do but trifle with themselves, that labor in past matters. There is no man doth a wrong for the wrong's sake; but thereby to purchase himself profit, or pleasure, or honor, or the like. Therefore why should I be angry with a man for loving himself better than me? And if any man should do wrong merely out of ill-nature, why, yet it is but like the thorn or briar, which prick and scratch, because they can do no other. The most tolerable sort of revenge is for those wrongs which there is no law to remedy; but then let a man take heed the revenge be such as there is no law to punish; else a man's enemy is still before hand, and it is two for one. Some, when they take revenge, are desirous the party should know whence it cometh. This is the more generous. For the delight seemeth to be not so much in doing the hurt as in making the party repent. But base and crafty cowards are like the arrow that flieth in the dark. Cosmus, duke of Florence, had a desperate saying against perfidious or neglecting friends, as if those wrongs were unpardonable; *You shall read* (saith he) *that we are commanded to forgive our enemies; but you never read that we are commanded to forgive our friends.* But yet the spirit of Job was in a better tune: *Shall we* (saith he) *take good at God's hands, and not be content to take evil also?* And so of friends in a proportion. This is certain, that a man that studieth revenge keeps his own wounds green, which otherwise would heal and do well. Public revenges are for the most part fortunate; as that for the death of Cæsar; for the death of Pertinax; for the death of Henry the Third of France; and many more. But in private revenges it is not so. Nay rather, vindictive persons live the life of witches; who, as they are mischievous, so end they infortunate.

V

OF ADVERSITY

It was a high speech of Seneca (after the manner of the Stoics), *that the good things which belong to prosperity are to be wished; but the good things that belong to adversity are to be admired. Bona rerum secundarum optabilia; adversarum mirabilia.* Certainly if miracles be the command over nature, they appear most in adversity. It is yet a higher speech of his than the other (much too high for a heathen), *It is true greatness to have in one the frailty of a man, and the security of a God. Vere magnum habere fragilitatem hominis, securitatem Dei.* This would have done better in poesy, where transcendences are more allowed. And the poets indeed have been busy with it; for it is in effect the thing which figured in that strange fiction of the ancient poets, which seemeth not to be without mystery; nay, and to have some approach to the state of a Christian; that *Hercules, when he went to unbind Prometheus* (by whom human nature is represented), *sailed the length of the great ocean in an earthen pot or pitcher;* lively describing Christian resolution, that saileth in the frail bark of the flesh through the waves of the world. But to speak in a mean.[1] The virtue of prosperity is temperance; the virtue of adversity is fortitude; which in morals is the more heroical virtue. Prosperity is the blessing of the Old Testament; adversity is the blessing of the New; which carrieth the greater benediction, and the clearer revelation of God's favor. Yet even in the Old Testament, if you listen to David's harp, you shall hear as many hearse-like airs as carols; and the pencil of the Holy Ghost hath labored more in describing the afflictions of Job than the felicities of Solomon. Prosperity is not without many fears and distastes; and adversity is not without comforts and hopes. We see in needleworks and embroideries, it is more pleasing to have a lively work upon a sad[2] and solemn ground, than to have a dark and melancholy work upon a lightsome ground: judge therefore of the

[1] In moderation.   [2] Dark-colored.

pleasure of the heart by the pleasure of the eye. Certainly virtue is like precious odors, most fragrant when they are incensed or crushed: for prosperity doth best discover[3] vice, but adversity doth best discover virtue.

VI

OF SIMULATION AND DISSIMULATION

DISSIMULATION is but a faint kind of policy or wisdom; for it asketh a strong wit and a strong heart to know when to tell truth, and to do it. Therefore it is the weaker sort of politics that are the great dissemblers.

Tacitus saith, *Livia sorted well with the arts of her husband and dissimulation of her son;* attributing arts or policy to Augustus, and dissimulation to Tiberius. And again, when Mucianus encourageth Vespasian to take arms against Vitellius, he saith, *We rise not against the piercing judgment of Augustus, nor the extreme caution or closeness of Tiberius.* These properties, of arts or policy and dissimulation or closeness, are indeed habits and faculties several, and to be distinguished. For if a man have that penetration of judgment as he can discern what things are to be laid open, and what to be secreted, and what to be showed at half lights, and to whom and when (which indeed are arts of state and arts of life, as Tacitus well calleth them), to him a habit of dissimulation is a hinderance and a poorness. But if a man cannot obtain to that judgment, then it is left to him generally to be close, and a dissembler. For where a man cannot choose or vary in particulars, there it is good to take the safest and wariest way in general; like the going softly by one that cannot well see. Certainly the ablest men that ever were have had all an openness and frankness of dealing; and a name of certainty and veracity; but then they were like horses well managed;[1] for they could tell passing well when to stop or turn; and at such times when they thought the case indeed required dissimulation, if then they used it, it came to pass that the former opinion spread abroad of their good faith and clearness of dealing made them almost invisible.

[3] Display. [1] Trained.

There be three degrees of this hiding and veiling of a man's self. The first, closeness, reservation, and secrecy; when a man leaveth himself without observation, or without hold to be taken, what he is. The second, dissimulation, in the negative; when a man lets fall signs and arguments, that he is not that he is. And the third, simulation, in the affirmative; when a man industriously and expressly feigns and pretends to be that he is not.

For the first of these, secrecy; it is indeed the virtue of a confessor. And assuredly the secret man heareth many confessions. For who will open himself to a blab or a babbler? But if a man be thought secret, it inviteth discovery; as the more close air sucketh in the more open; and as in confession the revealing is not for worldly use, but for the ease of a man's heart, so secret men come to the knowledge of many things in that kind; while men rather discharge their minds than impart their minds. In few words, mysteries are due to secrecy. Besides (to say truth) nakedness is uncomely, as well in mind as body; and it addeth no small reverence to men's manners and actions, if they be not altogether open. As for talkers and futile[2] persons, they are commonly vain and credulous withal. For he that talketh what he knoweth, will also talk what he knoweth not. Therefore set it down, *that an habit of secrecy is both politic and moral*. And in this part it is good that a man's face give his tongue leave to speak. For the discovery of a man's self by the tracts[3] of his countenance is a great weakness and betraying; by how much it is many times more marked and believed than a man's words.

For the second, which is dissimulation; it followeth many times upon secrecy by a necessity; so that he that will be secret must be a dissembler in some degree. For men are too cunning to suffer a man to keep an indifferent carriage between both, and to be secret, without swaying the balance on either side. They will so beset a man with questions, and draw him on, and pick it out of him, that, without an absurd silence, he must show an inclination one way; or if he do not, they will gather as much by his silence as by his speech. As for equivocations, or oraculous speeches, they cannot hold out long. So that no man can be secret, except he give himself a little scope of dissimulation; which is, as it were, but the skirts or train of secrecy.   [2] Babbling.   [3] Lines, expression.

But for the third degree, which is simulation and false profession; that I hold more culpable, and less politic; except it be in great and rare matters. And therefore a general custom of simulation (which is this last degree) is a vice, rising either of a natural falseness or fearfulness, or of a mind that hath some main faults, which because a man must needs disguise, it maketh him practise simulation in other things, lest his hand should be out of ure.[4]

The great advantages of simulation and dissimulation are three. First, to lay asleep opposition, and to surprise. For where a man's intentions are published, it is an alarum to call up all that are against them. The second is, to reserve to a man's self a fair retreat. For if a man engage himself by a manifest declaration, he must go through or take a fall. The third is, the better to discover the mind of another. For to him that opens himself men will hardly show themselves adverse; but will (fair[5]) let him go on, and turn their freedom of speech to freedom of thought. And therefore it is a good shrewd proverb of the Spaniard, *Tell a lie and find a troth*. As if there were no way of discovery but by simulation. There be also three disadvantages, to set it even. The first, that simulation and dissimulation commonly carry with them a show of fearfulness, which in any business doth spoil the feathers of round[6] flying up to the mark. The second, that it puzzleth and perplexeth the conceits of many, that perhaps would otherwise co-operate with him; and makes a man walk almost alone to his own ends. The third and greatest is, that it depriveth a man of one of the most principal instruments for action; which is trust and belief. The best composition and temperature[7] is to have openness in fame and opinion; secrecy in habit; dissimulation in seasonable use; and a power to feign, if there be no remedy.

VII

OF PARENTS AND CHILDREN

THE joys of parents are secret; and so are their griefs and fears. They cannot utter the one; nor they will not utter the other. Chil-

---

[4] Practise.   [5] Rather.   [6] Straight.   [7] Combination of qualities, temperament.

dren sweeten labors; but they make misfortunes more bitter. They increase the cares of life; but they mitigate the remembrance of death. The perpetuity by generation is common to beasts; but memory, merit, and noble works are proper to men. And surely a man shall see the noblest works and foundations have proceeded from childless men; which have sought to express the images of their minds, where those of their bodies have failed. So the care of posterity is most in them that have no posterity. They that are the first raisers of their houses are most indulgent towards their children; beholding them as the continuance not only of their kind but of their work; and so both children and creatures.

The difference in affection of parents towards their several children is many times unequal; and sometimes unworthy; especially in the mother; as Solomon saith, *A wise son rejoiceth the father, but an ungracious son shames the mother*. A man shall see, where there is a house full of children, one or two of the eldest respected, and the youngest made wantons;[1] but in the midst some that are as it were forgotten, who many times nevertheless prove the best. The illiberality of parents in allowance towards their children is an harmful error; makes them base; acquaints them with shifts; makes them sort[2] with mean company; and makes them surfeit more when they come to plenty. And therefore the proof is best, when men keep their authority towards their children, but not their purse. Men have a foolish manner (both parents and schoolmasters and servants) in creating and breeding an emulation between brothers during childhood, which many times sorteth[3] to discord when they are men, and disturbeth families. The Italians make little difference between children and nephews or near kinsfolks; but so they be of the lump, they care not though they pass not through their own body. And, to say truth, in nature it is much a like matter; insomuch that we see a nephew sometimes resembleth an uncle or a kinsman more than his own parent; as the blood happens. Let parents choose betimes the vocations and courses they mean their children should take; for then they are most flexible; and let them not too much apply themselves to the disposition of their children, as thinking they will take best to that which they have most mind to.

[1] Spoiled.   [2] Associate.   [3] Turns out.

It is true, that if the affection or aptness of the children be extraordinary, then it is good not to cross it; but generally the precept is good, *optimum elige, suave et facile illud faciet consuetudo* [choose the best—custom will make it pleasant and easy]. Younger brothers are commonly fortunate, but seldom or never where the elder are disinherited.

VIII

OF MARRIAGE AND SINGLE LIFE

HE that hath wife and children hath given hostages to fortune; for they are impediments to great enterprises, either of virtue or mischief. Certainly the best works, and of greatest merit for the public, have proceeded from the unmarried or childless men; which both in affection and means have married and endowed the public. Yet it were great reason that those that have children should have greatest care of future times; unto which they know they must transmit their dearest pledges. Some there are, who though they lead a single life, yet their thoughts do end with themselves, and account future times impertinences.[1] Nay, there are some other that account wife and children but as bills of charges. Nay more, there are some foolish rich covetous men, that take a pride in having no children, because they may be thought so much the richer. For perhaps they have heard some talk, *Such an one is a great rich man,* and another except to it, *Yea, but he hath a great charge of children;* as if it were an abatement to his riches. But the most ordinary cause of a single life is liberty, especially in certain self-pleasing and humorous[2] minds, which are so sensible of every restraint, as they will go near to think their girdles and garters to be bonds and shackles. Unmarried men are best friends, best masters, best servants; but not always best subjects; for they are light to run away; and almost all fugitives are of that condition. A single life doth well with churchmen; for charity will hardly water the ground where it must first fill a pool. It is indifferent for judges and magistrates; for if they be facile and corrupt, you shall have a servant five times worse than a wife. For soldiers, I find the generals commonly in their hortatives put men in mind of their wives and children; and I think the despising of mar-

---

[1] Not their affair.   [2] Capricious.

riage amongst the Turks maketh the vulgar soldier more base. Certainly wife and children are a kind of discipline of humanity; and single men, though they may be many times more charitable, because their means are less exhaust, yet, on the other side, they are more cruel and hardhearted (good to make severe inquisitors), because their tenderness is not so oft called upon. Grave natures, led by custom, and therefore constant, are commonly loving husbands, as was said of Ulysses, *vetulam suam prætulit immortalitati* [he preferred his old wife to immortality]. Chaste women are often proud and froward, as presuming upon the merit of their chastity. It is one of the best bonds both of chastity and obedience in the wife, if she think her husband wise; which she will never do if she find him jealous. Wives are young men's mistresses; companions for middle age; and old men's nurses. So as a man may have a quarrel[3] to marry when he will. But yet he[4] was reputed one of the wise men, that made answer to the question, when a man should marry,—*A young man not yet, an elder man not at all.* It is often seen that bad husbands have very good wives; whether it be that it raiseth the price of their husband's kindness when it comes; or that the wives take a pride in their patience. But this never fails, if the bad husbands were of their own choosing, against their friends' consent; for then they will be sure to make good their own folly.

IX

OF ENVY

There be none of the affections which have been noted to fascinate or bewitch, but love and envy. They both have vehement wishes; they frame themselves readily into imaginations and suggestions; and they come easily into the eye, especially upon the presence of the objects; which are the points that conduce to fascination, if any such thing there be. We see likewise the Scripture calleth envy an *evil eye;* and the astrologers call the evil influences of the stars *evil aspects;* so that still there seemeth to be acknowledged, in the act of envy, an ejaculation[1] or irradiation of the eye. Nay some have been so curious as to note that the times when the

[3] Pretext.   [4] Thales.   [1] Darting out.

stroke or percussion of an envious eye doth most hurt are when the party envied is beheld in glory or triumph; for that sets an edge upon envy: and besides, at such times the spirits of the person envied do come forth most into the outward parts, and so meet the blow.

But leaving these curiosities (though not unworthy to be thought on in fit place), we will handle, what persons are apt to envy others; what persons are most subject to be envied themselves; and what is the difference between public and private envy.

A man that hath no virtue in himself, ever envieth virtue in others. For men's minds will either feed upon their own good or upon others' evil; and who wanteth the one will prey upon the other; and whoso is out of hope to attain to another's virtue, will seek to come at even hand by depressing another's fortune.

A man that is busy and inquisitive is commonly envious. For to know much of other men's matters cannot be because all that ado may concern his own estate; therefore it must needs be that he taketh a kind of play-pleasure in looking upon the fortunes of others. Neither can he that mindeth but his own business find much matter for envy. For envy is a gadding passion, and walketh the streets, and doth not keep home: *Non est curiosus, quin idem sit malevolus* [There is no curious man but has some malevolence to quicken his curiosity].

Men of noble birth are noted to be envious towards new men when they rise. For the distance is altered, and it is like a deceit of the eye, that when others come on they think themselves go back.

Deformed persons, and eunuchs, and old men, and bastards, are envious. For he that cannot possibly mend his own case will do what he can to impair another's; except these defects light upon a very brave and heroical nature, which thinketh to make his natural wants part of his honor; in that it should be said, that an eunuch, or a lame man, did such great matters; affecting the honor of a miracle; as it was in Narses the eunuch, and Agesilaus and Tamberlanes, that were lame men.

The same is the case of men that rise after calamities and misfortunes. For they are as men fallen out with the times; and think other men's harms a redemption of their own sufferings.

They that desire to excel in too many matters, out of levity and vain glory, are ever envious. For they cannot want work; it being impossible but many in some one of those things should surpass them. Which was the character of Adrian the Emperor; that mortally envied poets and painters and artificers, in works wherein he had a vein to excel.

Lastly, near kinsfolks, and fellows in office, and those that have been bred together, are more apt to envy their equals when they are raised. For it doth upbraid unto them their own fortunes, and pointeth at them, and cometh oftener into their remembrance, and incurreth[2] likewise more into the note of others; and envy ever redoubleth from speech and fame. Cain's envy was the more vile and malignant towards his brother Abel, because when his sacrifice was better accepted there was no body to look on. Thus much for those that are apt to envy.

Concerning those that are more or less subject to envy: First, persons of eminent virtue, when they are advanced, are less envied. For their fortune seemeth but due unto them; and no man envieth the payment of a debt, but rewards and liberality rather. Again, envy is ever joined with the comparing of a man's self; and where there is no comparison, no envy; and therefore kings are not envied but by kings. Nevertheless it is to be noted that unworthy persons are most envied at their first coming in, and afterwards overcome it better; whereas contrariwise, persons of worth and merit are most envied when their fortune continueth long. For by that time, though their virtue be the same, yet it hath not the same lustre; for fresh men grow up that darken it.

Persons of noble blood are less envied in their rising. For it seemeth but right done to their birth. Besides, there seemeth not much added to their fortune; and envy is as the sunbeams, that beat hotter upon a bank or steep rising ground, than upon a flat. And for the same reason those that are advanced by degrees are less envied than those that are advanced suddenly and *per saltum* [at a bound].

Those that have joined with their honor great travels,[3] cares, or perils, are less subject to envy. For men think that they earn their honors hardly, and pity them sometimes; and pity ever healeth envy. Wherefore you shall observe that the more deep and sober sort of

[2] Runneth into.   [3] Travails, labors.

politic persons,[4] in their greatness, are ever bemoaning themselves, what a life they lead; chanting a *quanta patimur* [how great things do we suffer!]. Not that they feel it so, but only to abate the edge of envy. But this is to be understood of business that is laid upon men, and not such as they call unto themselves. For nothing increaseth envy more than an unnecessary and ambitious engrossing of business. And nothing doth extinguish envy more than for a great person to preserve all other inferior officers in their full rights and pre-eminences of their places. For by that means there be so many screens between him and envy.

Above all, those are most subject to envy, which carry the greatness of their fortunes in an insolent and proud manner; being never well but while they are showing how great they are, either by outward pomp, or by triumphing over all opposition or competition; whereas wise men will rather do sacrifice to envy, in suffering themselves sometimes of purpose to be crossed and overborne in things that do not much concern them. Notwithstanding, so much is true, that the carriage of greatness in a plain and open manner (so it be without arrogancy and vain glory) doth draw less envy than if it be in a more crafty and cunning fashion. For in that course a man doth but disavow fortune; and seemeth to be conscious of his own want in worth; and doth but teach others to envy him.

Lastly, to conclude this part; as we said in the beginning that the act of envy had somewhat in it of witchcraft, so there is no other cure of envy but the cure of witchcraft; and that is, to remove the *lot*[5] (as they call it) and to lay it upon another. For which purpose, the wiser sort of great persons bring in ever upon the stage somebody upon whom to derive[6] the envy that would come upon themselves; sometimes upon ministers and servants; sometimes upon colleagues and associates; and the like; and for that turn there are never wanting some persons of violent and undertaking natures, who, so they may have power and business, will take it at any cost.

Now, to speak of public envy. There is yet some good in public envy, whereas in private there is none. For public envy is as an ostracism, that eclipseth men when they grow too great. And therefore it is a bridle also to great ones, to keep them within bounds.

[4] Politicians. [5] Spell. [6] Divert.

This envy, being in the Latin word *invidia,* goeth in the modern languages by the name of *discontentment;* of which we shall speak in handling sedition. It is a disease in a state like to infection. For as infection spreadeth upon that which is sound, and tainteth it; so when envy is gotten once into a state, it traduceth even the best actions thereof, and turneth them into an ill odor. And therefore there is little won by intermingling of plausible[7] actions. For that doth argue but a weakness and fear of envy, which hurteth so much the more, as it is likewise usual in infections; which if you fear them, you call them upon you.

This public envy seemeth to beat chiefly upon principal officers or ministers, rather than upon kings and estates themselves. But this is a sure rule, that if the envy upon the minister be great, when the cause of it in him is small; or if the envy be general in a manner upon all the ministers of an estate; then the envy (though hidden) is truly upon the state itself. And so much of public envy or discontentment, and the difference thereof from private envy, which was handled in the first place.

We will add this in general, touching the affection of envy; that of all other affections it is the most importune and continual. For of other affections there is occasion given but now and then; and therefore it was well said, *Invidia festos dies non agit* [Envy keeps no holidays]: for it is ever working upon some or other. And it is also noted that love and envy do make a man pine, which other affections do not, because they are not so continual. It is also the vilest affection, and the most depraved; for which cause it is the proper attribute of the devil, who is called *the envious man, that soweth tares amongst the wheat by night;* as it always cometh to pass, that envy worketh subtilly, and in the dark, and to the prejudice of good things, such as is the wheat.

X

OF LOVE

THE stage is more beholding to love, than the life of man. For as to the stage, love is ever matter of comedies, and now and then of

[7] Praiseworthy.

tragedies; but in life it doth much mischief; sometimes like a siren, sometimes like a fury. You may observe that amongst all the great and worthy persons (whereof the memory remaineth, either ancient or recent) there is not one that hath been transported to the mad degree of love: which shows that great spirits and great business do keep out this weak passion. You must except nevertheless Marcus Antonius, the half partner of the empire of Rome, and Appius Claudius, the decemvir and lawgiver; whereof the former was indeed a voluptuous man, and inordinate; but the latter was an austere and wise man: and therefore it seems (though rarely) that love can find entrance not only into an open heart, but also into a heart well fortified, if watch be not well kept. It is a poor saying of Epicurus, *Satis magnum alter alteri theatrum sumus* [Each is to another a theatre large enough]; as if man, made for the contemplation of heaven and all noble objects, should do nothing but kneel before a little idol, and make himself a subject, though not of the mouth (as beasts are), yet of the eye; which was given him for higher purposes. It is a strange thing to note the excess of this passion, and how it braves the nature and value of things, by this; that the speaking in a perpetual hyperbole is comely in nothing but in love. Neither is it merely in the phrase; for whereas it hath been well said that the arch-flatterer, with whom all the petty flatterers have intelligence, is a man's self; certainly the lover is more. For there was never proud man thought so absurdly well of himself as the lover doth of the person loved; and therefore it was well said, *That it is impossible to love and to be wise*. Neither doth this weakness appear to others only, and not to the party loved; but to the loved most of all, except the love be reciproque.[1] For it is a true rule, that love is ever rewarded either with the reciproque or with an inward and secret contempt. By how much the more men ought to beware of this passion, which loseth not only other things, but itself! As for the other losses, the poet's relation doth well figure them: that he that preferred Helena quitted the gifts of Juno and Pallas. For whosoever esteemeth too much of amorous affection quitteth both riches and wisdom. This passion hath his floods in very times of weakness; which are great prosperity and great adversity; though this latter hath been less

[1] Mutual.

observed: both which times kindle love, and make it more fervent, and therefore show it to be the child of folly. They do best, who if they cannot but admit love, yet make it keep quarter;[2] and sever it wholly from their serious affairs and actions of life; for if it check[3] once with business, it troubleth men's fortunes, and maketh men that they can no ways be true to their own ends. I know not how, but martial men are given to love: I think it is but as they are given to wine; for perils commonly ask to be paid in pleasures. There is in man's nature a secret inclination and motion towards love of others, which if it be not spent upon some one or a few, doth naturally spread itself towards many, and maketh men become humane and charitable; as it is seen sometime in friars. Nuptial love maketh mankind; friendly love perfecteth it; but wanton love corrupteth and embaseth it.

XI

OF GREAT PLACE

MEN in great place are thrice servants: servants of the sovereign or state; servants of fame; and servants of business. So as they have no freedom; neither in their persons, nor in their actions, nor in their times. It is a strange desire, to seek power and to lose liberty: or to seek power over others and to lose power over a man's self. The rising unto place is laborious; and by pains men come to greater pains; and it is sometimes base; and by indignities men come to dignities. The standing is slippery, and the regress is either a downfall, or at least an eclipse, which is a melancholy thing. *Cum non sis qui fueris, non esse cur velis vivere* [When a man feels that he is no longer what he was, he has no reason to live longer]. Nay, retire men cannot when they would, neither will they when it were reason; but are impatient of privateness, even in age and sickness, which require the shadow; like old townsmen, that will be still sitting at their street door, though thereby they offer age to scorn. Certainly great persons had need to borrow other men's opinions, to think themselves happy; for if they judge by their own feeling, they cannot find it; but if they think with themselves what other men think of them, and that other men would fain be as they are, then

[2] Its own place. [3] Interfere.

they are happy as it were by report; when perhaps they find the contrary within. For they are the first that find their own griefs, though they be the last that find their own faults. Certainly men in great fortunes are strangers to themselves, and while they are in the puzzle of business they have no time to tend their health either of body or mind. *Illi mors gravis incubat, qui notus nimis omnibus, ignotus moritur sibi* [It is a sad fate for a man to die too well known to everybody else, and still unknown to himself]. In place there is license to do good and evil; whereof the latter is a curse: for in evil the best condition is not to will; the second, not to can. But power to do good is the true and lawful end of aspiring. For good thoughts (though God accept them) yet towards men are little better than good dreams, except they be put in act; and that cannot be without power and place, as the vantage and commanding ground. Merit and good works is the end of man's motion; and conscience of the same is the accomplishment of man's rest. For if a man can be partaker of God's theatre,[1] he shall likewise be partaker of God's rest. *Et conversus Deus, ut aspiceret opera quæ fecerunt manus suæ, vidit quod omnia essent bona nimis* [And God turned to look upon the works which his hands had made, and saw that all were very good]; and then the sabbath. In the discharge of thy place set before thee the best examples; for imitation is a globe[2] of precepts. And after a time set before thee thine own example; and examine thyself strictly whether thou didst not best at first. Neglect not also the examples of those that have carried themselves ill in the same place; not to set off thyself by taxing[3] their memory, but to direct thyself what to avoid. Reform therefore, without bravery[4] or scandal of former times and persons; but yet set it down to thyself as well to create good precedents as to follow them. Reduce things to the first institution, and observe wherein and how they have degenerate; but yet ask counsel of both times; of the ancient time, what is best; and of the latter time, what is fittest. Seek to make thy course regular, that men may know beforehand what they may expect; but be not too positive and peremptory; and express thyself well when thou digressest from thy rule. Preserve the right of thy place; but stir not questions of jurisdiction; and rather assume thy right in silence and

[1] What God saw.   [2] Complete body.   [3] Censuring.   [4] Boastfulness.

de facto [from the fact], than voice it with claims and challenges. Preserve likewise the rights of inferior places; and think it more honor to direct in chief than to be busy in all. Embrace and invite helps and advices touching the execution of thy place; and do not drive away such as bring thee information, as meddlers; but accept of them in good part. The vices of authority are chiefly four: delays, corruption, roughness, and facility.[5] For delays: give easy access; keep times appointed; go through with that which is in hand, and interlace not business but of necessity. For corruption: do not only bind thine own hands or thy servants' hands from taking, but bind the hands of suitors also from offering. For integrity used doth the one; but integrity professed, and with a manifest detestation of bribery, doth the other. And avoid not only the fault, but the suspicion. Whosoever is found variable, and changeth manifestly without manifest cause, giveth suspicion of corruption. Therefore always when thou changest thine opinion or course, profess it plainly, and declare it, together with the reasons that move thee to change; and do not think to steal[6] it. A servant or a favorite, if he be inward, and no other apparent cause of esteem, is commonly thought but a by-way to close[7] corruption. For roughness: it is a needless cause of discontent: severity breedeth fear, but roughness breedeth hate. Even reproofs from authority ought to be grave, and not taunting. As for facility:[5] it is worse than bribery. For bribes come but now and then; but if importunity or idle respects[8] lead a man, he shall never be without. As Solomon saith, *To respect persons is not good; for such a man will transgress for a piece of bread*. It is most true that was anciently spoken, *A place showeth the man*. And it showeth some to the better, and some to the worse. *Omnium consensu capax imperii, nisi imperasset* [A man whom every body would have thought fit for empire if he had not been emperor], saith Tacitus of Galba; but of Vespasian he saith, *Solus imperantium, Vespasianus mutatus in melius* [He was the only emperor whom the possession of power changed for the better]; though the one was meant of sufficiency, the other of manners and affection. It is an assured sign of a worthy and generous spirit, whom honor amends. For honor

[5] Being easily led. [6] Do secretly. [7] Secret. [8] Considerations.

is, or should be, the place of virtue; and as in nature things move violently to their place and calmly in their place, so virtue in ambition is violent, in authority settled and calm. All rising to great place is by a winding stair; and if there be factions, it is good to side a man's self whilst he is in the rising, and to balance himself when he is placed. Use the memory of thy predecessor fairly and tenderly; for if thou dost not, it is a debt will sure be paid when thou art gone. If thou have colleagues, respect them, and rather call them when they look not for it, than exclude them when they have reason to look to be called. Be not too sensible or too remembering of thy place in conversation and private answers to suitors; but let it rather be said, *When he sits in place he is another man.*

XII

OF BOLDNESS

IT is a trivial grammar-school text, but yet worthy a wise man's consideration. Question was asked of Demosthenes, *what was the chief part of an orator?* he answered, *action;* what next? *action;* what next again? *action.* He said it that knew it best, and had by nature himself no advantage in that he commended. A strange thing, that that part of an orator which is but superficial, and rather the virtue of a player, should be placed so high, above those other noble parts of invention, elocution, and the rest; nay almost alone, as if it were all in all. But the reason is plain. There is in human nature generally more of the fool than of the wise; and therefore those faculties by which the foolish part of men's minds is taken are most potent. Wonderful like is the case of boldness in civil business: what first? boldness; what second and third? boldness. And yet boldness is a child of ignorance and baseness, far inferior to other parts. But nevertheless it doth fascinate and bind hand and foot those that are either shallow in judgment or weak in courage, which are the greatest part; yea and prevaileth with wise men at weak times. Therefore we see it hath done wonders in popular states; but with senates and princes less; and more ever upon the first entrance of bold persons into action than soon after; for boldness is an ill keeper of promise. Surely as there are mountebanks[1] for the natural body, so are there mountebanks for the politic body; men that undertake great cures, and perhaps have been lucky in two or three experiments, but want the grounds of science, and therefore cannot hold out. Nay, you shall see a bold fellow many times do Mahomet's miracle. Mahomet made the people believe that he would call an hill to him, and from the top of it offer up his prayers, for the observers of his law. The people assembled; Mahomet called the hill to come to him, again and again; and when the hill stood still, he was never a whit abashed, but said, *If the hill will not come to Mahomet, Mahomet will go to the hill.* So these men, when they have promised great matters and failed most shamefully, yet (if they have the perfection of boldness) they will but slight it over, and make a turn, and no more ado. Certainly to men of great judgment, bold persons are a sport to behold; nay and to the vulgar also, boldness has somewhat of the ridiculous. For if absurdity be the subject of laughter, doubt you not but great boldness is seldom without some absurdity. Especially it is a sport to see, when a bold fellow is out of countenance; for that puts his face into a most shrunken and wooden posture; as needs it must; for in bashfulness the spirits do a little go and come; but with bold men, upon like occasion, they stand at a stay; like a stale at chess, where it is no mate, but yet the game cannot stir. But this last were fitter for a satire than for a serious observation. This is well to be weighed; that boldness is ever blind; for it seeth not dangers and inconveniences. Therefore it is ill in counsel, good in execution; so that the right use of bold persons is, that they never command in chief, but be seconds, and under the direction of others. For in counsel it is good to see dangers; and in execution not to see them, except they be very great.

XIII

OF GOODNESS AND GOODNESS OF NATURE

I TAKE goodness in this sense, the affecting of the weal of men, which is that the Grecians call *philanthropia;* and the word *humanity* (as it is used) is a little too light to express it. Goodness I call

[1] Quacks.

the habit, and goodness of nature the inclination. This of all virtues and dignities of the mind is the greatest; being the character of the Deity: and without it man is a busy, mischievous, wretched thing; no better than a kind of vermin. Goodness answers to the theological virtue charity, and admits no excess, but error. The desire of power in excess caused the angels to fall; the desire of knowledge in excess caused man to fall: but in charity there is no excess; neither can angel nor man come in danger by it. The inclination to goodness is imprinted deeply in the nature of man; insomuch that if it issue not towards men, it will take unto other living creatures; as it is seen in the Turks, a cruel people, who nevertheless are kind to beasts, and give alms to dogs and birds; insomuch as Busbechius reporteth, a Christian boy in Constantinople had like to have been stoned for gagging in a waggishness a long-billed fowl. Errors indeed in this virtue of goodness or charity may be committed. The Italians have an ungracious proverb, *Tanto buon che val niente* [*So good, that he is good for nothing*]. And one of the doctors of Italy, Nicholas Machiavel, had the confidence to put in writing, almost in plain terms, *That the Christian faith had given up good men in prey to those that are tyrannical and unjust.* Which he spake, because indeed there was never law or sect or opinion did so much magnify goodness as the Christian religion doth. Therefore, to avoid the scandal and the danger both, it is good to take knowledge of the errors of an habit so excellent. Seek the good of other men, but be not in bondage to their faces or fancies; for that is but facility or softness; which taketh an honest mind prisoner. Neither give thou Æsop's cock a gem, who would be better pleased and happier if he had had a barley-corn. The example of God teacheth the lesson truly: *He sendeth his rain and maketh his sun to shine upon the just and unjust;* but he doth not rain wealth nor shine honor and virtues, upon men equally. Common benefits are to be communicate with all; but peculiar benefits with choice. And beware how in making the portraiture thou breakest the pattern. For divinity maketh the love of ourselves the pattern; the love of our neighbors but the portraiture. *Sell all thou hast, and give it to the poor, and follow me:* but sell not all thou hast, except thou come and follow me; that is, except thou have a vocation wherein thou mayest do as much good with little means as with great; for otherwise in feeding the streams thou driest the fountain. Neither is there only a habit of goodness, directed by right reason; but there is in some men, even in nature, a disposition towards it; as on the other side there is a natural malignity. For there be that in their nature do not affect the good of others. The lighter sort of malignity turneth but to a crossness, or frowardness, or aptness to oppose, or difficilness,[1] or the like; but the deeper sort to envy and mere mischief. Such men in other men's calamities are, as it were, in season, and are ever on the loading part: not so good as the dogs that licked Lazarus' sores; but like flies that are still buzzing upon any thing that is raw; *misanthropi* [haters of men], that make it their practice to bring men to the bough,[2] and yet never a tree for the purpose in their gardens, as Timon had. Such dispositions are the very errors of human nature; and yet they are the fittest timber to make great politics of; like to knee timber, that is good for ships, that are ordained to be tossed; but not for building houses, that shall stand firm. The parts and signs of goodness are many. If a man be gracious and courteous to strangers, it shows he is a citizen of the world, and that his heart is no island cut off from other lands, but a continent that joins to them. If he be compassionate towards the afflictions of others, it shows that his heart is like the noble tree that is wounded itself when it gives the balm. If he easily pardons and remits offences, it shows that his mind is planted above injuries; so that he cannot be shot. If he be thankful for small benefits, it shows that he weighs men's minds, and not their trash. But above all, if he have St. Paul's perfection, that he would wish to be *anathema*[3] from Christ for the salvation of his brethren, it shows much of a divine nature, and a kind of conformity with Christ himself.

XIV

OF NOBILITY

WE will speak of nobility first as a portion of an estate,[1] then as a condition of particular persons. A monarchy where there is no

---
[1] Moroseness.   [2] To hang themselves.   [3] Accused.   [1] State.

nobility at all is ever a pure and absolute tyranny; as that of the Turks. For nobility attempers sovereignty, and draws the eyes of the people somewhat aside from the line royal. But for democracies, they need it not; and they are commonly more quiet and less subject to sedition, than where there are stirps[2] of nobles. For men's eyes are upon the business, and not upon the persons; or if upon the persons, it is for the business' sake, as fittest, and not for flags and pedigree. We see the Switzers last well, notwithstanding their diversity of religion and of cantons. For utility is their bond, and not respects.[3] The united provinces of the Low Countries in their government excel; for where there is an equality, the consultations are more indifferent, and the payments and tributes more cheerful. A great and potent nobility addeth majesty to a monarch, but diminisheth power; and putteth life and spirit into the people, but presseth their fortune. It is well when nobles are not too great for sovereignty nor for justice; and yet maintained in that height, as the insolency of inferiors may be broken upon them before it come on too fast upon the majesty of kings. A numerous nobility causeth poverty and inconvenience in a state; for it is a surcharge[4] of expense; and besides, it being of necessity that many of the nobility fall in time to be weak in fortune, it maketh a kind of disproportion between honor and means.

As for nobility in particular persons; it is a reverend thing to see an ancient castle or building not in decay; or to see a fair timber tree sound and perfect. How much more to behold an ancient noble family, which hath stood against the waves and weathers of time! For new nobility is but the act of power, but ancient nobility is the act of time. Those that are first raised to nobility are commonly more virtuous,[5] but less innocent, than their descendants; for there is rarely any rising but by a commixture of good and evil arts. But it is reason the memory of their virtues remain to their posterity, and their faults die with themselves. Nobility of birth commonly abateth industry; and he that is not industrious, envieth him that is. Besides, noble persons cannot go much higher; and he that standeth at a stay when others rise, can hardly avoid motions of envy. On the other side, nobility extinguisheth the passive envy from others

[2] Families.   [3] Considerations of rank.   [4] Excess.   [5] Able.

towards them; because they are in possession of honor. Certainly, kings that have able men of their nobility shall find ease in employing them, and a better slide into their business; for people naturally bend to them, as born in some sort to command.

XV

OF SEDITIONS AND TROUBLES

SHEPHERDS of people had need know the calendars[1] of tempests in state; which are commonly greatest when things grow to equality; as natural tempests are greatest about the *Equinoctia*. And as there are certain hollow blasts of wind and secret swellings of seas before a tempest, so are there in states:

> —— Ille etiam cæcos instare tumultus
> Sæpe monet, fraudesque et operta tumescere bella.
>
> [Of troubles imminent and treasons dark
> Thence warning comes, and wars in secret gathering. *Virgil*]

Libels and licentious discourses against the state, when they are frequent and open; and in like sort, false news often running up and down to the disadvantage of the state, and hastily embraced; are amongst the signs of troubles. Virgil, giving the pedigree of Fame, saith *she was sister to the Giants*:

> Illam Terra parens, irâ irritata deorum,
> Extremam (ut perhibent) Cœo Enceladoque sororem
> Progenuit.

[Her, Parent Earth, furious with the anger of the gods, brought forth, the youngest sister (as they affirm) of Cœus and Enceladus.] As if fames[2] were the relics of seditions past; but they are no less indeed the preludes of seditions to come. Howsoever he noteth it right, that seditious tumults and seditious fames differ no more but as brother and sister, masculine and feminine; especially if it come to that, that the best actions of a state, and the most plausible, and which ought to give greatest contentment, are taken in ill sense, and traduced: for that shows the envy great, as Tacitus saith; *conflata*

---
[1] Weather predictions.   [2] Rumors.

OF SEDITIONS AND TROUBLES

magna invidia, seu bene seu male gesta premunt [when dislike prevails against the government, good actions and bad offend alike]. Neither doth it follow, that because these fames are a sign of troubles that the suppressing of them with too much severity should be a remedy of troubles. For the despising of them many times checks them best; and the going about to stop them doth but make a wonder long-lived. Also that kind of obedience which Tacitus speaketh of, is to be held suspected: *Erant in officio, sed tamen qui mallent mandata imperantium interpretari quam exequi* [Ready to serve, and yet more disposed to construe commands than execute them]; disputing, excusing, cavilling upon mandates and directions, is a kind of shaking off the yoke, and assay of disobedience; especially if in those disputings they which are for the direction speak fearfully and tenderly, and those that are against it audaciously.

Also, as Machiavel noteh well, when princes, that ought to be common parents, make themselves as a party, and lean to a side, it is as a boat that is overthrown by uneven weight on the one side; as was well seen in the time of Henry the Third of France; for first himself entered league for the extirpation of the Protestants; and presently after the same league was turned upon himself. For when the authority of princes is made but an accessory to a cause, and that there be other bands that tie faster than the band of sovereignty, kings begin to be put almost out of possession.

Also, when discords, and quarrels, and factions are carried openly and audaciously, it is a sign the reverence of government is lost. For the motions of the greatest persons in a government ought to be as the motions of the planets under *primum mobile;*[3] (according to the old opinion), which is, that every of them is carried swiftly by the highest motion, and softly in their own motion. And therefore, when great ones in their own particular motion move violently, and, as Tacitus expresseth it well, *liberius quam ut imperantium meminissent* [unrestrained by reverence for the government], it is a sign the orbs are out of frame. For reverence is that wherewith

---

[3] In the old astronomy, the *primum mobile* (first moving) was the outer sphere, whose motion from east to west dominated the motions of the inner spheres of the planets.

princes are girt from God; who threateneth the dissolving thereof; *Solvam cingula regum* [I will unbind the girdles of kings].

So when any of the four pillars of government are mainly shaken or weakened (which are religion, justice, counsel, and treasure), men had need to pray for fair weather. But let us pass from this part of predictions (concerning which, nevertheless, more light may be taken from that which followeth); and let us speak first of the materials of seditions; then of the motives of them; and thirdly of the remedies.

Concerning the materials of seditions. It is a thing well to be considered; for the surest way to prevent seditions (if the times do bear it) is to take away the matter of them. For if there be fuel prepared, it is hard to tell whence the spark shall come that shall set it on fire. The matter of seditions is of two kinds: much poverty and much discontentment. It is certain, so many overthrown estates, so many votes for troubles. Lucan noteth well the state of Rome before the Civil War,

> Hinc usura vorax, rapidumque in tempore fœnus,
> Hinc concussa fides, et multis utile bellum.

[Hence estates eaten up by usurious rates of interest, and interest greedy of time, hence credit shaken, and war a gain to many.]

This same *multis utile bellum* is an assured and infallible sign of a state disposed to seditions and troubles. And if this poverty and broken estate in the better sort be joined with a want and necessity in the mean people, the danger is imminent and great. For the rebellions of the belly[4] are the worst. As for discontentments, they are in the politic body like to humors in the natural, which are apt to gather a preternatural heat and to inflame. And let no prince measure the danger of them by this, whether they be just or unjust: for that were to imagine people to be too reasonable; who do often spurn at their own good: nor yet by this, whether the griefs whereupon they rise be in fact great or small: for they are the most dangerous discontentments where the fear is greater than the feeling. *Dolendi modus, timendi non item* [Suffering has its limit, but fears are endless]. Besides, in great oppressions, the same things that provoke the

[4] From hunger.

patience, do withal mate[5] the courage; but in fears it is not so. Neither let any prince or state be secure[6] concerning discontentments, because they have been often, or have been long, and yet no peril hath ensued: for as it is true that every vapor or fume doth not turn into a storm; so it is nevertheless true that storms, though they blow over divers times, yet may fall at last; and, as the Spanish proverb noteth well, *The cord breaketh at the last by the weakest pull.*

The causes and motives of seditions are, innovation in religion; taxes; alteration of laws and customs; breaking of privileges; general oppression; advancement of unworthy persons; strangers; dearths; disbanded soldiers; factions grown desperate; and whatsoever, in offending people, joineth and knitteth them in a common cause.

For the remedies; there may be some general preservatives, whereof we will speak: as for the just cure, it must answer to the particular disease; and so be left to counsel rather than rule.

The first remedy or prevention is to remove by all means possible that material cause of sedition whereof we spake; which is, want and poverty in the estate. To which purpose serveth the opening and well-balancing of trade; the cherishing of manufactures; the banishing of idleness; the repressing of waste and excess by sumptuary[7] laws; the improvement and husbanding of the soil; the regulating of prices of things vendible; the moderating of taxes and tributes; and the like. Generally, it is to be foreseen[8] that the population of a kingdom (especially if it be not mown down by wars) do not exceed the stock of the kingdom which should maintain them. Neither is the population to be reckoned only by number; for a smaller number that spend more and earn less do wear out an estate sooner than a greater number that live lower and gather more. Therefore the multiplying of nobility and other degrees of quality in an over proportion to the common people doth speedily bring a state to necessity; and so doth likewise an overgrown clergy; for they bring nothing to the stock; and in like manner, when more are bred scholars than preferments can take off.

It is likewise to be remembered, that forasmuch as the increase of

---

[5] Confound.　　[6] Free from care.　　[7] Against extravagance.
[8] Guarded against beforehand.

any estate must be upon the foreigner (for whatsoever is somewhere gotten is somewhere lost), there be but three things which one nation selleth unto another; the commodity as nature yielded it; the manufacture; and the vecture, or carriage. So that if these three wheels go, wealth will flow as in a spring tide. And it cometh many times to pass, that *materiam superabit opus;* that the work and carriage is more worth than the material, and enricheth a state more; as is notably seen in the Low-Countrymen, who have the best mines above ground in the world.

Above all things, good policy is to be used that the treasure and moneys in a state be not gathered into few hands. For otherwise a state may have a great stock, and yet starve. And money is like muck, not good except it be spread. This is done chiefly by suppressing or at least keeping a strait hand upon the devouring trades of usury, ingrossing[9] great pasturages, and the like.

For removing discontentments, or at least the danger of them; there is in every state (as we know) two portions of subjects; the noblesse and the commonalty. When one of these is discontent, the danger is not great; for common people are of slow motion, if they be not excited by the greater sort; and the greater sort are of small strength, except the multitude be apt and ready to move of themselves. Then is the danger, when the greater sort do but wait for the troubling of the waters amongst the meaner, that then they may declare themselves. The poets feign that the rest of the gods would have bound Jupiter; which he hearing of, by the counsel of Pallas, sent for Briareus, with his hundred hands, to come in to his aid. An emblem, no doubt, to show how safe it is for monarchs to make sure of the good will of common people. To give moderate liberty for griefs and discontentments to evaporate (so it be without too great insolency or bravery), is a safe way. For he that turneth the humors back, and maketh the wound bleed inwards, endangereth malign ulcers and pernicious imposthumations.[10]

The part of Epimetheus[11] mought well become Prometheus[12] in the case of discontentments: for there is not a better provision against them. Epimetheus, when griefs and evils flew abroad, at last shut the lid, and kept hope in the bottom of the vessel. Certainly, the

[9] "Cornering."   [10] Abscesses.   [11] Afterthought.   [12] Forethought.

politic and artificial nourishing and entertaining of hopes, and carrying men from hopes to hopes, is one of the best antidotes against the poison of discontentments. And it is a certain sign of a wise government and proceeding, when it can hold men's hearts by hopes, when it cannot by satisfaction; and when it can handle things in such manner, as no evil shall appear so peremptory but that it hath some outlet of hope; which is the less hard to do, because both particular persons and factions are apt enough to flatter themselves, or at least to brave that which they believe not.

Also the foresight and prevention, that there be no likely or fit head whereunto discontented persons may resort, and under whom they may join, is a known, but an excellent point of caution. I understand a fit head to be one that hath greatness and reputation; that hath confidence with the discontented party, and upon whom they turn their eyes; and that is thought discontented in his own particular: which kind of persons are either to be won and reconciled to the state, and that in a fast and true manner; or to be fronted with some other of the same party, that may oppose them, and so divide the reputation. Generally, the dividing and breaking of all factions and combinations that are adverse to the state, and setting them at distance, or at least distrust, amongst themselves, is not one of the worst remedies. For it is a desperate case, if those that hold with the proceeding of the state be full of discord and faction, and those that are against it be entire and united.

I have noted that some witty and sharp speeches which have fallen from princes have given fire to seditions. Cæsar did himself infinite hurt in that speech, *Sylla nescivit literas, non potuit dictare* [Sylla was no scholar, he could not dictate]; for it did utterly cut off that hope which men had entertained, that he would at one time or other give over his dictatorship. Galba undid himself by that speech, *legi a se militem, non emi* [that he did not buy his soldiers, but levied them]; for it put the soldiers out of hope of the donative.[13] Probus likewise, by that speech, *Si vixero, non opus erit amplius Romano imperio militibus* [If I live, the Roman empire shall have no more need of soldiers]; a speech of great despair for the soldiers. And many the like. Surely princes had need, in tender matters and

[13] Gifts of money.

ticklish times, to beware what they say; especially in these short speeches, which fly abroad like darts, and are thought to be shot out of their secret intentions. For as for large discourses, they are flat things, and not so much noted.

Lastly, let princes, against all events, not be without some great person, one or rather more, of military valor, near unto them, for the repressing of seditions in their beginnings. For without that, there useth to be more trepidation in court upon the first breaking out of troubles than were fit. And the state runneth the danger of that which Tacitus saith; *Atque is habitus animorum fuit, ut pessimum facinus auderent pauci, plures vellent, omnes paterentur* [A few were in a humor to attempt mischief, more to desire, all to allow it]. But let such military persons be assured, and well reputed of, rather than factious and popular; holding also good correspondence with the other great men in the state; or else the remedy is worse than the disease.

XVI

OF ATHEISM

I HAD rather believe all the fables in the Legend,[1] and the Talmud,[2] and the Alcoran,[3] than that this universal frame is without a mind. And therefore God never wrought miracle to convince[4] atheism, because his ordinary works convince it. It is true, that a little philosophy inclineth man's mind to atheism; but depth in philosophy bringeth men's minds about to religion. For while the mind of man looketh upon second causes scattered, it may sometimes rest in them, and go no further; but when it beholdeth the chain of them, confederate and linked together, it must needs fly to Providence and Deity. Nay, even that school which is most accused of atheism doth most demonstrate religion; that is, the school of Leucippus and Democritus and Epicurus. For it is a thousand times more credible, that four mutable elements, and one immutable fifth essence, duly and eternally placed, need no God, than that an army of infinite small portions or seeds unplaced, should have produced this order and

---

[1] "The Golden Legend," a 13th century collection of saints' lives.
[2] The body of Jewish traditional law.   [3] "The Koran," the sacred book of the Mohammedans.   [4] Refute.

beauty without a divine marshal. The Scripture saith, *The fool hath said in his heart, there is no God;* it is not said, *The fool hath thought in his heart;* so as he rather saith it by rote to himself, as that he would have, than that he can thoroughly believe it, or be persuaded of it. For none deny there is a God, but those for whom it maketh[5] that there were no God. It appeareth in nothing more, that atheism is rather in the lip than in the heart of man, than by this; that atheists will ever be talking of that their opinion, as if they fainted in it within themselves, and would be glad to be strengthened by the consent of others. Nay more, you shall have atheists strive to get disciples, as it fareth with other sects. And, which is most of all, you shall have of them that will suffer for atheism, and not recant; whereas if they did truly think that there were no such thing as God, why should they trouble themselves? Epicurus is charged that he did but dissemble for his credit's sake, when he affirmed there were blessed natures, but such as enjoyed themselves without having respect to the government of the world. Wherein they say he did temporize; though in secret he thought there was no God. But certainly he is traduced; for his words are noble and divine: *Non deos vulgi negare profanum; sed vulgi opiniones diis applicare profanum* [There is no profanity in refusing to believe in the gods of the people: the profanity is in believing of the gods what the people believe of them]. Plato could have said no more. And although he had the confidence to deny the administration, he had not the power to deny the nature. The Indians of the West have names for their particular gods, though they have no name for God: as if the heathens should have had the names Jupiter, Apollo, Mars, etc. but not the word *Deus;* which shows that even those barbarous people have the notion, though they have not the latitude and extent of it. So that against atheists the very savages take part with the very subtlest philosophers. The contemplative atheist is rare: a Diagoras, a Bion, a Lucian perhaps, and some others; and yet they seem to be more than they are; for that all that impugn a received religion or superstition are by the adverse part branded with the name of atheists. But the great atheists indeed are hypocrites; which are ever handling holy things, but without feeling; so as they must needs be

[5] Profiteth.

cauterized in the end. The causes of atheism are: divisions in religion, if they be many; for any one main division addeth zeal to both sides; but many divisions introduce atheism. Another is, scandal of priests; when it is come to that which St. Bernard saith, *Non est jam dicere, ut populus sic sacerdos; quia nec sic populus ut sacerdos* [One cannot now say the priest is as the people, for the truth is that the people are not so bad as the priest]. A third is, custom of profane scoffing in holy matters; which doth by little and little deface the reverence of religion. And lastly, learned times, specially with peace and prosperity; for troubles and adversities do more bow men's minds to religion. They that deny a God destroy man's nobility; for certainly man is of kin to the beasts by his body; and, if he be not of kin to God by his spirit, he is a base and ignoble creature. It destroys likewise magnanimity, and the raising of human nature; for take an example of a dog, and mark what a generosity and courage he will put on when he finds himself maintained by a man; who to him is instead of a God, or *melior natura* [better nature]; which courage is manifestly such as that creature, without that confidence of a better nature than his own, could never attain. So man, when he resteth and assureth himself upon divine protection and favor, gathered a force and faith which human nature in itself could not obtain. Therefore, as atheism is in all respects hateful, so in this, that it depriveth human nature of the means to exalt itself above human frailty. As it is in particular persons, so it is in nations. Never was there such a state for magnanimity as Rome. Of this state hear what Cicero saith: *Quam volumus licet, patres conscripti, nos amemus, tamen nec numero Hispanos, nec robore Gallos, nec calliditate Pœnos, nec artibus Græcos, nec denique hoc ipso hujus gentis et terræ domestico nativoque sensu Italos ipsos et Latinos; sed pietate, ac religione, atque hac una sapientia, quod deorum immortalium numine omnia regi gubernarique perspeximus, omnes gentes nationesque superavimus* [Pride ourselves as we may upon our country, yet are we not in number superior to the Spaniards, nor in strength to the Gauls, nor in cunning to the Carthaginians, not to the Greeks in arts, nor to the Italians and Latins themselves in the homely and native sense which belongs to this nation and land; it is in piety only and religion, and the wisdom of regarding the providence of the immortal gods as that which rules and governs all things, that we have surpassed all nations and peoples].

XVII

OF SUPERSTITION

It were better to have no opinion of God at all, than such an opinion as is unworthy of him. For the one is unbelief, the other is contumely; and certainly superstition is the reproach of the Deity. Plutarch saith well to that purpose: *Surely* (saith he) *I had rather a great deal men should say there was no such man at all as Plutarch, than that they should say that there was one Plutarch that would eat his children as soon as they were born;* as the poets speak of Saturn. And as the contumely is greater towards God, so the danger is greater towards men. Atheism leaves a man to sense, to philosophy, to natural piety, to laws, to reputation; all which may be guides to an outward moral virtue, though religion were not; but superstition dismounts all these, and erecteth an absolute monarchy in the minds of men. Therefore atheism did never perturb states; for it makes men wary of themselves, as looking no further: and we see the times inclined to atheism (as the time of Augustus Cæsar) were civil[1] times. But superstition hath been the confusion of many states, and bringeth in a new *primum mobile*,[2] that ravisheth all the spheres of government. The master of superstition is the people; and in all superstition wise men follow fools; and arguments are fitted to practice, in a reversed order. It was gravely said by some of the prelates in the Council of Trent, where the doctrine of the Schoolmen bare great sway, *that the Schoolmen were like astronomers, which did feign eccentrics and epicycles,[3] and such engines[4] of orbs, to save[5] the phenomena; though they knew there were no such things;* and in like manner, that the Schoolmen had framed a number of subtle and intricate axioms and theorems, to save the practice of the church. The causes of superstition are: pleasing and sensual rites and cere-

[1] Peaceful.   [2] See Essay xv., n. 3.
[3] According to the Ptolemaic astronomy, the planets moved in circles called epicycles, the centers of which also moved in circles called eccentrics, because their centers were outside the earth.   [4] Machinery.   [5] Account for.

monies; excess of outward and pharisaical holiness; over-great reverence of traditions, which cannot but load the church; the stratagems of prelates for their own ambition and lucre; the favoring too much of good intentions, which openeth the gate to conceits and novelties; the taking an aim at divine matters by human, which cannot but breed mixture of imaginations; and, lastly, barbarous times, especially joined with calamities and disasters. Superstition, without a veil, is a deformed thing; for as it addeth deformity to an ape to be so like a man, so the similitude of superstition to religion makes it the more deformed. And as wholesome meat corrupteth to little worms, so good forms and orders corrupt into a number of petty observances. There is a superstition in avoiding superstition, when men think to do best if they go furthest from the superstition formerly received; therefore care would be had that (as it fareth in ill purgings) the good be not taken away with the bad; which commonly is done when the people is the reformer.

XVIII

OF TRAVEL

TRAVEL, in the younger sort, is a part of education; in the elder, a part of experience. He that travelleth into a country before he hath some entrance into the language, goeth to school, and not to travel. That young men travel under some tutor, or grave servant, I allow[1] well; so that he be such a one that hath the language, and hath been in the country before; whereby he may be able to tell them what things are worthy to be seen in the country where they go; what acquaintances they are to seek; what exercises or discipline the place yieldeth. For else young men shall go hooded, and look abroad little. It is a strange thing, that in sea voyages, where there is nothing to be seen but sky and sea, men should make diaries; but in land-travel, wherein so much is to be observed, for the most part they omit it; as if chance were fitter to be registered than observation. Let diaries therefore be brought in use. The things to be seen and observed are: the courts of princes, especially when they give audience to ambas-

[1] Approve.

sadors; the courts of justice, while they sit and hear causes; and so of consistories ecclesiastic; the churches and monasteries, with the monuments which are therein extant; the walls and fortifications of cities and towns, and so the havens and harbors; antiquities and ruins; libraries; colleges, disputations, and lectures, where any are; shipping and navies; houses and gardens of state and pleasure, near great cities; armories; arsenals; magazines; exchanges; burses; warehouses; exercises of horsemanship, fencing, training of soldiers, and the like; comedies, such whereunto the better sort of persons do resort; treasuries of jewels and robes; cabinets and rarities; and, to conclude, whatsoever is memorable in the places where they go. After all which the tutors or servants ought to make diligent inquiry. As for triumphs, masks, feasts, weddings, funerals, capital executions, and such shows, men need not to be put in mind of them; yet are they not to be neglected. If you will have a young man to put his travel into a little room, and in short time to gather much, this you must do. First, as was said, he must have some entrance into the language before he goeth. Then he must have such a servant or tutor as knoweth the country, as was likewise said. Let him carry with him also some card[2] or book describing the country where he travelleth; which will be a good key to his inquiry. Let him keep also a diary. Let him not stay long in one city or town; more or less as the place deserveth, but not long; nay, when he stayeth in one city or town, let him change his lodging from one end and part of the town to another; which is a great adamant[3] of acquaintance. Let him sequester himself from the company of his countrymen, and diet in such places where there is good company of the nation where he travelleth. Let him, upon his removes from one place to another, procure recommendation to some person of quality residing in the place whither he removeth; that he may use his favor in those things he desireth to see or know. Thus he may abridge his travel with much profit. As for the acquaintance which is to be sought in travel; that which is most of all profitable is acquaintance with the secretaries and employed men of ambassadors: for so in travelling in one country he shall suck the experience of many. Let him also see and visit eminent persons in all kinds, which are of great name

[2] Map. [3] Loadstone.

abroad; that he may be able to tell how the life agreeth with the fame. For quarrels, they are with care and discretion to be avoided. They are commonly for mistresses, healths, place, and words. And let a man beware how he keepeth company with choleric and quarrelsome persons; for they will engage him into their own quarrels. When a traveller returneth home, let him not leave the countries where he hath travelled altogether behind him; but maintain a correspondence by letters with those of his acquaintance which are of most worth. And let his travel appear rather in his discourse than his apparel or gesture; and in his discourse let him be rather advised in his answers, than forward to tell stories; and let it appear that he doth not change his country manners for those of foreign parts; but only prick in some flowers of that he hath learned abroad into the customs of his own country.

XIX

OF EMPIRE

IT is a miserable state of mind to have few things to desire, and many things to fear; and yet that commonly is the case of kings; who, being at the highest, want matter of desire, which makes their minds more languishing; and have many representations of perils and shadows, which makes their minds the less clear. And this is one reason also of that effect which the Scripture speaketh of, *That the king's heart is inscrutable.* For multitude of jealousies, and lack of some predominant desire that should marshal and put in order all the rest, maketh any man's heart hard to find or sound. Hence it comes likewise, that princes many times make themselves desires, and set their hearts upon toys; sometimes upon a building; sometimes upon erecting of an order; sometimes upon the advancing of a person; sometimes upon obtaining excellency in some art or feat of the hand; as Nero for playing on the harp, Domitian for certainty of the hand with the arrow, Commodus for playing at fence, Caracalla for driving chariots, and the like. This seemeth incredible unto those that know not the principle *that the mind of man is more cheered and refreshed by profiting in small things, than by standing at a stay in great.* We see also that kings that have been fortunate conquerors in their first years, it being not possible for them to go forward infinitely, but that they must have some check or arrest in their fortunes, turn in their latter years to be superstitious and melancholy; as did Alexander the Great; Diocletian; and in our memory, Charles the Fifth; and others: for he that is used to go forward, and findeth a stop, falleth out of his own favor, and is not the thing he was.

To speak now of the true temper[1] of empire, it is a thing rare and hard to keep; for both temper and distemper consist of contraries. But it is one thing to mingle contraries, another to interchange them. The answer of Apollonius to Vespasian is full of excellent instruction. Vespasian asked him, *What was Nero's overthrow?* He answered, *Nero could touch and tune the harp well; but in government sometimes he used to wind the pins too high, sometimes to let them down too low.* And certain it is that nothing destroyeth authority so much as the unequal and untimely interchange of power pressed too far, and relaxed too much.

This is true, that the wisdom of all these latter times in princes' affairs is rather fine deliveries and shiftings of dangers and mischiefs when they are near, than solid and grounded courses to keep them aloof. But this is but to try masteries with fortune. And let men beware how they neglect and suffer matter of trouble to be prepared; for no man can forbid the spark, nor tell whence it may come. The difficulties in princes' business are many and great; but the greatest difficulty is often in their own mind. For it is common with princes (saith Tacitus) to will contradictories, *Sunt plerumque regum voluntates vehementes, et inter se contrariæ* [Their desires are commonly vehement and incompatible one with another]. For it is the solecism[2] of power, to think to command the end, and yet not to endure the mean.

Kings have to deal with their neighbors, their wives, their children, their prelates or clergy, their nobles, their second-nobles or gentlemen, their merchants, their commons, and their men of war; and from all these arise dangers, if care and circumspection be not used.

First for their neighbors; there can no general rule be given (the occasions are so variable), save one, which ever holdeth; which is, that princes do keep due sentinel, that none of their neighbors do

---
[1] Proportion.   [2] Absurd mistake.

ever grow so (by increase of territory, by embracing of trade, by approaches, or the like), as they become more able to annoy them than they were. And this is generally the work of standing counsels to foresee and to hinder it. During that triumvirate of kings, King Henry the Eighth of England, Francis the First King of France, and Charles the Fifth Emperor, there was such a watch kept, that none of the three could win a palm of ground, but the other two would straightways balance it, either by confederation, or, if need were, by a war; and would not in any wise take up peace at interest. And the like was done by that league (which Guicciardini saith was the security of Italy) made between Ferdinando King of Naples, Lorenzius Medici, and Ludovicus Sforza, potentates, the one of Florence, the other of Milan. Neither is the opinion of some of the Schoolmen to be received, *that a war cannot justly be made but upon a precedent injury or provocation*. For there is no question but a just fear of an imminent danger, though there be no blow given, is a lawful cause of a war.

For their wives; there are cruel examples of them. Livia is infamed for the poisoning of her husband; Roxalana, Solyman's wife, was the destruction of that renowned prince Sultan Mustapha, and otherwise troubled his house and succession; Edward the Second of England his queen had the principal hand in the deposing and murther of her husband. This kind of danger is then to be feared chiefly, when the wives have plots for the raising of their own children; or else that they be advoutresses.[3]

For their children; the tragedies likewise of dangers from them have been many. And generally, the entering of fathers into suspicion of their children hath been ever unfortunate. The destruction of Mustapha (that we named before) was so fatal to Solyman's line, as the succession of the Turks from Solyman until this day is suspected to be untrue, and of strange blood; for that Selymus the Second was thought to be suppositious. The destruction of Crispus, a young prince of rare towardness, by Constantinus the Great, his father, was in like manner fatal to his house; for both Constantinus and Constance, his sons died violent deaths; and Constantius, his other son, did little better; who died indeed of sickness, but after

[3] Adulteresses.

that Julianus had taken arms against him. The destruction of Demetrius, son to Philip the Second of Macedon, turned upon the father, who died of repentance. And many like examples there are; but few or none where the fathers had good by such distrust; except it were where the sons were up in open arms against them; as was Selymus the First against Bajazet; and the three sons of Henry the Second, King of England.

For their prelates; when they are proud and great, there is also danger from them; as it was in the times of Anselmus and Thomas Becket, Archbishops of Canterbury; who with their croziers did almost try it with the king's sword; and yet they had to deal with stout and haughty kings, William Rufus, Henry the First, and Henry the Second. The danger is not from that state, but where it hath a dependence of foreign authority; or where the churchmen come in and are elected, not by the collation of the king, or particular patrons, but by the people.

For their nobles; to keep them at a distance, it is not amiss; but to depress them, may make a king more absolute, but less safe; and less able to perform any thing that he desires. I have noted it in my History of King Henry the Seventh of England, who depressed his nobility; whereupon it came to pass that his times were full of difficulties and troubles; for the nobility, though they continued loyal unto him, yet did they not co-operate with him in his business. So that in effect he was fain to do all things himself.

For their second-nobles; there is not much danger from them, being a body dispersed. They may sometimes discourse high, but that doth little hurt; besides, they are a counterpoise to the higher nobility, that they grow not too potent; and, lastly, being the most immediate in authority with the common people, they do best temper popular commotions.

For their merchants; they are *vena porta;*[4] and if they flourish not, a kingdom may have good limbs, but will have empty veins, and nourish little. Taxes and imposts upon them do seldom good to the king's revenue; for that that he wins in the hundred he leeseth[5] in the shire; the particular rates being increased, but the total bulk of trading rather decreased.

[4] The "gate-vein," which Bacon regarded as distributing nourishment to the body.
[5] Loseth.

For their commons; there is little danger from them, except it be where they have great and potent heads; or where you meddle with the point of religion, or their customs, or means of life.

For their men of war; it is a dangerous state where they live and remain in a body; and are used to donatives; whereof we see examples in the janizaries,[6] and pretorian bands[7] of Rome; but trainings of men, and arming them in several places, and under several commanders, and without donatives, are things of defence, and no danger.

Princes are like to heavenly bodies, which cause good or evil times; and which have much veneration, but no rest. All precepts concerning kings are in effect comprehended in those two remembrances: *memento quod es homo;* and *memento quod es Deus,* or *vice Dei* [Remember that you are a man; and remember that you are a God, or God's lieutenant]; the one bridleth their power, and the other their will.

XX

OF COUNSEL

THE greatest trust between man and man is the trust of giving counsel. For in other confidences men commit the parts of life; their lands, their goods, their children, their credit, some particular affair; but to such as they make their counsellors, they commit the whole: by how much the more they are obliged to all faith and integrity. The wisest princes need not think it any diminution to their greatness, or derogation to their sufficiency, to rely upon counsel. God himself is not without, but hath made it one of the great names of his blessed Son: *The Counsellor.* Solomon hath pronounced that *in counsel is stability.* Things will have their first or second agitation: if they be not tossed upon the arguments of counsel, they will be tossed upon the waves of fortune; and be full of inconstancy, doing and undoing, like the reeling of a drunken man. Solomon's son found the force of counsel, as his father saw the necessity of it. For the beloved kingdom of God was first rent and broken by ill counsel; upon which counsel there are set for our instruction the two marks whereby bad counsel is for ever best dis-

[6] Bodyguard of the Sultan. [7] Bodyguard of the Roman emperors.

cerned; that it was young counsel, for the persons; and violent counsel, for the matter.

The ancient times do set forth in figure both the incorporation and inseparable conjunction of counsel with kings, and the wise and politic use of counsel by kings: the one, in that they say Jupiter did marry Metis, which signifieth counsel; whereby they intend that Sovereignty is married to Counsel: the other in that which followeth, which was thus: They say, after Jupiter was married to Metis, she conceived by him and was with child, but Jupiter suffered her not to stay till she brought forth, but eat her up; whereby he became himself with child, and was delivered of Pallas armed, out of his head. Which monstrous fable containeth a secret of empire; how kings are to make use of their counsel of state. That first they ought to refer matters unto them, which is the first begetting or impregnation; but when they are elaborate, moulded, and shaped in the womb of their counsel, and grow ripe and ready to be brought forth, that then they suffer not their counsel to go through with the resolution and direction, as if it depended on them; but take the matter back into their own hands, and make it appear to the world that the decrees and final directions (which, because they come forth with prudence and power, are resembled to Pallas armed) proceeded from themselves; and not only from their authority, but (the more to add reputation to themselves) from their head and device.

Let us now speak of the inconveniences of counsel, and of the remedies. The inconveniences that have been noted in calling and using counsel are three. First, the revealing of affairs, whereby they become less secret. Secondly, the weakening of the authority of princes, as if they were less of themselves. Thirdly, the danger of being unfaithfully counselled, and more for the good of them that counsel than of him that is counselled. For which inconveniences, the doctrine of Italy, and practice of France, in some kings' times, hath introduced *cabinet*[1] counsels; a remedy worse than the disease.

As to secrecy; princes are not bound to communicate all matters with all counsellors; but may extract and select. Neither is it necessary that he that consulteth what he should do, should declare what he will do. But let princes beware that the unsecreting of their affairs comes not from themselves. And as for cabinet counsels, it may be

[1] Secret.

their motto, *plenus rimarum sum* [I am full of leaks]: one futile[2] person that maketh it his glory to tell, will do more hurt than many that know it their duty to conceal. It is true there be some affairs which require extreme secrecy, which will hardly go beyond one or two persons besides the king: neither are those counsels unprosperous; for, besides the secrecy, they commonly go on constantly in one spirit of direction, without distraction. But then it must be a prudent king, such as is able to grind with a hand-mill; and those inward counsellors had need also be wise men, and especially true and trusty to the king's ends; as it was with King Henry the Seventh of England, who in his greatest business imparted himself to none, except it were to Morton and Fox.

For weakening of authority; the fable showeth the remedy. Nay, the majesty of kings is rather exalted than diminished when they are in the chair of counsel; neither was there ever prince bereaved of his dependences by his counsel; except where there hath been either an over-greatness in one counsellor or an over-strict combination in divers; which are things soon found and holpen.[3]

For the last inconvenience, that men will counsel with an eye to themselves; certainly, *non inveniet fidem super terram* [he will not find faith on the earth] is meant of the nature of times, and not of all particular persons. There be that are in nature faithful, and sincere, and plain, and direct; not crafty and involved; let princes, above all, draw to themselves such natures. Besides, counsellors are not commonly so united, but that one counsellor keepeth sentinel over another; so that if any do counsel out of faction or private ends, it commonly comes to the king's ear. But the best remedy is, if princes know their counsellors, as well as their counsellors know them:

Principis est virtus maxima nosse suos.

[It is the greatest virtue of a prince to know his own.] And on the other side, counsellors should not be too speculative[4] into their sovereign's person. The true composition of a counsellor is rather to be skilful in their master's business, than in his nature; for then he is like to advise him, and not feed his humor. It is of singular use to princes if they take the opinions of their counsel both separately

[2] Babbling.   [3] Helped.   [4] Inquisitive.

OF COUNSEL

and together. For private opinion is more free; but opinion before others is more reverent. In private, men are more bold in their own humors; and in consort, men are more obnoxious[5] to others' humors; therefore it is good to take both; and of the inferior sort rather in private, to preserve freedom; of the greater rather in consort, to preserve respect. It is in vain for princes to take counsel concerning matters, if they take no counsel likewise concerning persons; for all matters are as dead images; and the life of the execution of affairs resteth in the good choice of persons. Neither is it enough to consult concerning persons *secundum genera* [according to classes], as in an idea, or mathematical description, what the kind and character of the person should be; for the greatest errors are committed, and the most judgment is shown, in the choice of individuals. It was truly said, *optimi consiliarii mortui* [the best counsellors are the dead]: books will speak plain when counsellors blanch.[6] Therefore it is good to be conversant in them, especially the books of such as themselves have been actors upon the stage.

The counsels at this day in most places are but familiar meetings, where matters are rather talked on than debated. And they run too swift to the order or act of counsel. It were better that in causes of weight, the matter were propounded one day and not spoken to till the next day; *in nocte consilium* [night is the season for counsel]. So was it done in the Commission of Union between England and Scotland; which was a grave and orderly assembly. I commend set days for petitions; for both it gives the suitors more certainty for their attendance, and it frees the meetings for matters of estate, that they may *hoc agere* [do this]. In choice of committees for ripening business for the counsel, it is better to choose indifferent[7] persons, than to make an indifferency by putting in those that are strong on both sides. I commend also standing commissions; as for trade, for treasure, for wars, for suits, for some provinces; for where there be divers particular counsels and but one counsel of estate (as it is in Spain), they are, in effect, no more than standing commissions: save that they have greater authority. Let such as are to inform counsels out of their particular professions (as lawyers, seamen, mintmen, and the like) be first heard before committees; and then, as occasion

[5] Subservient [6] Flatter. [7] Impartial.

serves, before the counsel. And let them not come in multitudes, or in a tribunitious manner;[8] for that is to clamor counsels, not to inform them. A long table and a square table, or seats about the walls, seem things of form, but are things of substance; for at a long table a few at the upper end, in effect, sway all the business; but in the other form there is more use of the counsellors' opinions that sit lower. A king, when he presides in counsel, let him beware how he opens his own inclination too much in that which he propoundeth; for else counsellors will but take the wind of him, and instead of giving free counsel, sing him a song of *placebo*[9] [I shall please].

XXI

OF DELAYS

FORTUNE is like the market; where many times, if you can stay a little, the price will fall. And again, it is sometimes like Sibylla's offer; which at first offereth the commodity at full, then consumeth part and part, and still holdeth up the price. For occasion (as it is in the common verse) *turneth a bald noddle, after she hath presented her locks in front, and no hold taken;* or at least turneth the handle of the bottle first to be received, and after the belly, which is hard to clasp. There is surely no greater wisdom than well to time the beginnings and onsets of things. Dangers are no more light, if they once seem light; and more dangers have deceived men than forced them. Nay, it were better to meet some dangers half way, though they come nothing near, than to keep too long a watch upon their approaches; for if a man watch too long, it is odds he will fall asleep. On the other side, to be deceived with too long shadows (as some have been when the moon was low and shone on their enemies' back), and so to shoot off before the time; or to teach dangers to come on, by over early buckling towards them; is another extreme. The ripeness or unripeness of the occasion (as we said) must ever be well weighed; and generally it is good to commit the beginnings of all great actions to Argus with his hundred eyes, and the ends to Briareus with his hundred hands; first to watch, and then to speed. For the helmet of Pluto, which maketh the politic man[1]

[8] As demagogues.   [9] Flattery.   [1] Politician.

go invisible, is secrecy in the counsel and celerity in the execution. For when things are once come to the execution, there is no secrecy comparable to celerity; like the motion of a bullet in the air, which flieth so swift as it outruns the eye.

XXII

OF CUNNING

We take cunning for a sinister or crooked wisdom. And certainly there is a great difference between a cunning man and a wise man; not only in point of honesty, but in point of ability. There be that can pack the cards, and yet cannot play well; so there are some that are good in canvasses and factions, that are otherwise weak men. Again, it is one thing to understand persons, and another thing to understand matters; for many are perfect in men's humors, that are not greatly capable of the real part of business; which is the constitution of one that hath studied men more than books. Such men are fitter for practice than for counsel; and they are good but in their own alley:[1] turn them to new men, and they have lost their aim; so as the old rule to know a fool from a wise man, *Mitte ambos nudos ad ignotos, et videbis* [Send them both naked to those they know not, and you will see], doth scarce hold for them. And because these cunning men are like haberdashers of small wares, it is not amiss to set forth their shop.

It is a point of cunning, to wait upon him with whom you speak, with your eye; as the Jesuits give it in precept: for there be many wise men that have secret hearts and transparent countenances. Yet this would be done with a demure abasing of your eye sometimes, as the Jesuits also do use.

Another is, that when you have anything to obtain of present despatch, you entertain and amuse the party with whom you deal with some other discourse; that he be not too much awake to make objections. I knew a counsellor and secretary, that never came to Queen Elizabeth of England with bills to sign, but he would always first put her into some discourse of estate, that she mought[2] the less mind the bills.

[1] Bowling-alley.   [2] Might.

The like surprise may be made by moving things when the party is in haste, and cannot stay to consider advisedly of that is moved.

If a man would cross a business that he doubts some other would handsomely and effectually move, let him pretend to wish it well, and move it himself in such sort as may foil it.

The breaking off in the midst of that one was about to say, as if he took himself up, breeds a greater appetite in him with whom you confer, to know more.

And because it works better when anything seemeth to be gotten from you by question, than if you offer it of yourself, you may lay a bait for a question, by showing another visage and countenance than you are wont; to the end to give occasion for the party to ask what the matter is of the change? As Nehemias did; *And I had not before that time been sad before the king.*

In things that are tender and unpleasing, it is good to break the ice by some whose words are of less weight, and to reserve the more weighty voice to come in as by chance, so that he may be asked the question upon the other's speech: as Narcissus did, relating to Claudius the marriage of Messalina and Silius.

In things that a man would not be seen in himself, it is a point of cunning to borrow the name of the world; as to say, *The world says,* or *There is a speech abroad.*

I knew one that, when he wrote a letter, he would put that which was most material in the postscript, as if it had been a by-matter.

I knew another that, when he came to have speech, he would pass over that that he intended most; and go forth, and come back again, and speak of it as of a thing that he had almost forgot.

Some procure themselves to be surprised at such times as it is like the party that they work upon will suddenly come upon them; and to be found with a letter in their hand, or doing somewhat which they are not accustomed; to the end they may be apposed[3] of those things which of themselves they are desirous to utter.

It is a point of cunning, to let fall those words in a man's own name, which he would have another man learn and use, and thereupon take advantage. I knew two that were competitors for the

[3] Questioned.

secretary's place in Queen Elizabeth's time, and yet kept good quarter[4] between themselves; and would confer one with another upon the business; and the one of them said, That to be a secretary in the *declination of a monarchy* was a ticklish thing, and that he did not affect[5] it: the other straight caught up those words and discoursed with divers of his friends, that he had no reason to desire to be secretary in the *declination of a monarchy,* The first man took hold of it, and found means it was told the Queen; who hearing of a *declination of a monarchy,* took it so ill as she would never after hear of the other's suit.

There is a cunning, which we in England call *the turning of the cat*[6] *in the pan;* which is, when that which a man says to another, he lays it as if another had said it to him. And to say truth, it is not easy, when such a matter passed between two, to make it appear from which of them it first moved and began.

It is a way that some men have, to glance and dart at others by justifying themselves by negatives; as to say, *This I do not;* as Tigellinus did towards Burrhus, *Se non diversas spes, sed incolumitatem imperatoris simpliciter spectare* [That he had not several hopes to rest on, but looked simply to the safety of the Emperor.]

Some have in readiness so many tales and stories, as there is nothing they would insinuate, but they can wrap it into a tale; which serveth both to keep themselves more in guard, and to make others carry it with more pleasure.

It is a good point of cunning for a man to shape the answer he would have in his own words and propositions; for it makes the other party stick the less.

It is strange how long some men will lie in wait to speak somewhat they desire to say; and how far about they will fetch; and how many other matters they will beat over, to come near it. It is a thing of great patience, but yet of much use.

A sudden, bold, and unexpected question doth many times surprise a man, and lay him open. Like to him that, having changed his name and walking in Paul's,[7] another suddenly came behind him and called him by his true name, whereat straightways he looked back.

[4] Relations. [5] Desire. [6] Cate or cake.
[7] St. Paul's Cathedral, then a fashionable promenade.

But these small wares and petty points of cunning are infinite; and it were a good deed to make a list of them; for that nothing doth more hurt in a state than that cunning men pass for wise.

But certainly some there are that know the resorts and falls[8] of business, that cannot sink into the main of it; like a house that hath convenient stairs and entries, but never a fair room. Therefore you shall see them find out pretty looses[9] in the conclusion, but are no ways able to examine or debate matters. And yet commonly they take advantage of their inability, and would be thought wits of direction.[10] Some build rather upon the abusing of others, and (as we now say) *putting tricks upon them,* than upon soundness of their own proceedings. But Solomon saith, *Prudens advertit ad gressus suos; stultus divertit ad dolos* [The wise taketh heed to his steps; the fool turneth aside to deceits.]

XXIII

OF WISDOM FOR A MAN'S SELF

AN ant is a wise creature for itself, but it is a shrewd[1] thing in an orchard or garden. And certainly men that are great lovers of themselves waste the public. Divide with reason between self-love and society; and be so true to thyself, as thou be not false to others; specially to thy king and country. It is a poor centre of a man's actions, *himself*. It is right earth.[2] For that only stands fast upon his own centre; whereas all things that have affinity with the heavens move upon the centre of another, which they benefit. The referring of all to a man's self is more tolerable in a sovereign prince; because themselves are not only themselves but their good and evil is at the peril of the public fortune. But it is a desperate evil in a servant to a prince, or a citizen in a republic. For whatsoever affairs pass such a man's hands, he crooketh them to his own ends; which must needs be often eccentric to[3] the ends of his master or state. Therefore let princes, or states, choose such servants as have not this

---

[8] Entrances and exits. [9] Shots. [10] Clever at directing others. [1] Mischievous.
[2] Precisely like the earth. Bacon here is thinking of the old astronomy, according to which all the heavenly bodies moved round the earth.
[3] Have a different center from.

mark; except they mean their service should be made but the accessory. That which maketh the effect more pernicious is that all proportion is lost. It were disproportion enough for the servant's good to be preferred before the master's; but yet it is a greater extreme, when a little good of the servant shall carry things against a great good of the master's. And yet that is the case of bad officers, treasurers, ambassadors, generals, and other false and corrupt servants; which set a bias[4] upon their bowl, of their own petty ends and envies, to the overthrow of their master's great and important affairs. And for the most part, the good such servants receive is after the model[5] of their own fortune; but the hurt they sell for that good is after the model of their master's fortune. And certainly it is the nature of extreme self-lovers, as they will set an house on fire, and it were but to roast their eggs; and yet these men many times hold credit with their masters, because their study is but to please them and profit themselves; and for either respect they will abandon the good of their affairs.

Wisdom for a man's self is, in many branches thereof, a depraved thing. It is the wisdom of rats, that will be sure to leave a house somewhat before it fall. It is the wisdom of the fox, that thrusts out the badger, who digged and made room for him. It is the wisdom of crocodiles, that shed tears when they would devour. But that which is specially to be noted is, that those which (as Cicero says of Pompey) are *sui amantes, sine rivali* [lovers of themselves without a rival] are many times unfortunate. And whereas they have all their times sacrificed to themselves, they become in the end themselves sacrifices to the inconstancy of fortune, whose wings they sought by their self-wisdom to have pinioned.

XXIV

OF INNOVATIONS

As the births of living creatures at first are ill-shapen, so are all innovations, which are the births of time. Yet notwithstanding, as those that first bring honor into their family are commonly more

---

[4] A weight let into one side, to make the bowl describe a curve.   [5] Scale.

worthy than most that succeed, so the first precedent (if it be good) is seldom attained by imitation. For ill, to man's nature as it stands perverted, hath a natural motion, strongest in continuance; but good, as a forced motion, strongest at first. Surely every medicine is an innovation; and he that will not apply new remedies must expect new evils; for time is the greatest innovator; and if time of course[1] alter things to the worse, and wisdom and counsel shall not alter them to the better, what shall be the end? It is true, that what is settled by custom, though it be not good, yet at least it is fit; and those things which have long gone together are as it were confederate within themselves; whereas new things piece not so well; but though they help by their utility, yet they trouble by their inconformity. Besides, they are like strangers; more admired and less favored. All this is true, if time stood still; which contrariwise moveth so round, that a froward[2] retention of custom is as turbulent a thing as an innovation; and they that reverence too much old times are but a scorn to the new. It were good therefore that men in their innovations would follow the example of time itself; which indeed innovateth greatly, but quietly, by degrees scarce to be perceived. For otherwise, whatsoever is new is unlooked for; and ever it mends some, and pairs[3] other; and he that is holpen takes it for a fortune, and thanks the time; and he that is hurt, for a wrong, and imputeth it to the author. It is good also not to try experiments in states, except the necessity be urgent, or the utility evident; and well to beware that it be the reformation that draweth on the change, and not the desire of change that pretendeth the reformation. And lastly, that the novelty, though it be not rejected, yet be held for a suspect; and, as the Scripture saith, *that we make a stand upon the ancient way, and then look about us, and discover what is the straight and right way, and so to walk in it.*

XXV

OF DISPATCH

AFFECTED[1] dispatch is one of the most dangerous things to business that can be. It is like that which the physicians call *predigestion,*

[1] By its course.   [2] Stubborn.   [3] Impairs.   [1] Excessively desired.

or hasty digestion; which is sure to fill the body full of crudities and secret seeds of diseases. Therefore measure not dispatch by the times of sitting, but by the advancement of the business. And as in races it is not the large stride or high lift that makes the speed; so in business, the keeping close to the matter, and not taking of it too much at once, procureth dispatch. It is the care of some only to come off speedily for the time; or to contrive some false periods[2] of business, because they may seem men of dispatch. But it is one thing to abbreviate by contracting, another by cutting off. And business so handled at several sittings or meetings goeth commonly backward and forward in an unsteady manner. I knew a wise man that had it for a by-word, when he saw men hasten to a conclusion, *Stay a little, that we may make an end the sooner.*

On the other side, true dispatch is a rich thing. For time is the measure of business, as money is of wares; and business is bought at a dear hand where there is small dispatch. The Spartans and Spaniards have been noted to be of small dispatch; *Mi venga la muerte de Spagna; Let my death come from Spain;* for then it will be sure to be long in coming.

Give good hearing to those that give the first information in business; and rather direct them in the beginning than interrupt them in the continuance of their speeches; for he that is put out of his own order will go forward and backward, and be more tedious while he waits upon his memory, than he could have been if he had gone on in his own course. But sometimes it is seen that the moderator is more troublesome than the actor.

Iterations are commonly loss of time. But there is no such gain of time as to iterate often the state of the question; for it chaseth away many a frivolous speech as it is coming forth. Long and curious[3] speeches are as fit for dispatch, as a robe or mantle with a long train is for race. Prefaces and passages,[4] and excusations, and other speeches of reference to the person, are great wastes of time; and though they seem to proceed of modesty, they are bravery.[5] Yet beware of being too material[6] when there is an impediment or obstruction in men's wills; for pre-occupation of mind ever

---

[2] Only apparently finished. [3] Elaborate. [4] Transitions. [5] Showing off.
[6] Coming too soon to the point.

requireth preface of speech; like a fomentation to make the unguent enter.

Above all things, order, and distribution, and singling out of parts, is the life of dispatch; so as the distribution be not too subtle: for he that doth not divide will never enter well into business; and he that divideth too much will never come out of it clearly. To choose time is to save time; and an unseasonable motion is but beating the air. There be three parts of business; the preparation, the debate or examination, and the perfection. Whereof, if you look for dispatch, let the middle only be the work of many, and the first and last the work of few. The proceeding upon somewhat conceived in writing doth for the most part facilitate dispatch: for though it should be wholly rejected, yet that negative is more pregnant of direction than an indefinite; as ashes are more generative than dust.

XXVI

OF SEEMING WISE

It hath been an opinion that the French are wiser than they seem, and the Spaniards seem wiser than they are. But howsoever it be between nations, certainly it is so between man and man. For as the Apostle[1] saith of godliness, *Having a show of godliness, but denying the power thereof;* so certainly there are in point of wisdom and sufficiency, that do nothing or little very solemnly: *magno conatu nugas* [with great effort, trifles]. It is ridiculous thing and fit for a satire to persons of judgment, to see what shifts these formalists have, and what prospectives[2] to make *superficies* [a surface] to seem body that hath depth, and bulk. Some are so close and reserved, as they will not show their wares but by a dark light; and seem always to keep back somewhat; and when they know within themselves they speak of that they do not well know, would nevertheless seem to others to know of that which they may not well speak. Some help themselves with countenance and gesture, and are wise by signs; as Cicero saith of Piso, that when he answered him, he fetched one of his brows up to his forehead, and bent the

[1] St. Paul.   [2] Stereoscopes.

other down to his chin; *Respondes, altero ad frontem sublato, altero ad mentum depresso supercilio, crudelitatem tibi non placere* [You answer, with one eyebrow lifted to the forehead and the other lowered to the chin, that cruelty does not please you]. Some think to bear it[3] by speaking a great word, and being peremptory; and go on, and take by admittance that which they cannot make good.[4] Some, whatsoever is beyond their reach, will seem to despise or make light of it as impertinent[5] or curious;[6] and so would have their ignorance seem judgment. Some are never without a difference, and commonly by amusing men with a subtility, blanch[7] the matter; of whom A. Gellius saith, *Hominem delirum, qui verborum minutiis rerum frangit pondera* [A foolish man, that with verbal points and niceties breaks up the mass of matter]. Of which kind also, Plato in his Protagoras bringeth in Prodius in scorn, and maketh him make a speech that consisteth of distinctions from the beginning to the end. Generally, such men in all deliberations find ease to be of the negative side, and affect a credit to object and foretell difficulties; for when propositions are denied, there is an end of them; but if they be allowed, it requireth a new work; which false point of wisdom is the bane of business. To conclude, there is no decaying merchant, or inward[8] beggar, hath so many tricks to uphold the credit of their wealth, as these empty persons have to maintain the credit of their sufficiency. Seeming wise men may make shift to get opinion; but let no man choose them for employment; for certainly you were better take for business a man somewhat absurd[9] than over-formal.

XXVII

OF FRIENDSHIP

It had been hard for him that spake[1] it to have put more truth and untruth together in few words, than in that speech, *Whatsoever is delighted in solitude is either a wild beast or a god.* For it is most true that a natural and secret hatred and aversation towards

---

[3] Carry it off.   [4] Assume what they can not prove.   [5] Irrelevant.
[6] Uselessly elaborate.   [7] Evade.   [8] Secretly bankrupt.   [9] Rough.   [1] Aristotle.

society in any man, hath somewhat of the savage beast; but it is most untrue that it should have any character at all of the divine nature; except it proceed, not out of a pleasure in solitude, but out of a love and desire to sequester a man's self for a higher conversation:[2] such as is found to have been falsely and feignedly in some of the heathen; as Epimenides the Candian, Numa the Roman, Empedocles the Sicilian, and Apollonius of Tyana; and truly and really in divers of the ancient hermits and holy fathers of the church. But little do men perceive what solitude is, and how far it extendeth. For a crowd is not company; and faces are but a gallery of pictures; and talk but a tinkling cymbal, where there is no love. The Latin adage meeteth with it a little: *Magna civitas, magna solitudo* [A great town is a great solitude]; because in a great town friends are scattered; so that there is not that fellowship, for the most part, which is in less neighborhoods. But we may go further, and affirm most truly that it is a mere and miserable solitude to want true friends; without which the world is but a wilderness; and even in this sense also of solitude, whosoever in the frame of his nature and affections is unfit for friendship, he taketh it of the beast, and not from humanity.

A principal fruit of friendship is the ease and discharge of the fulness and swellings of the heart, which passions of all kinds do cause and induce. We know diseases of stoppings and suffocations are the most dangerous in the body; and it is not much otherwise in the mind; you may take sarza[3] to open the liver, steel to open the spleen, flowers of sulphur for the lungs, castoreum for the brain; but no receipt openeth the heart, but a true friend; to whom you may impart griefs, joys, fears, hopes, suspicions, counsels, and whatsoever lieth upon the heart to oppress it, in a kind of civil shrift or confession.

It is a strange thing to observe how high a rate great kings and monarchs do set upon this fruit of friendship whereof we speak: so great, as they purchase it many times at the hazard of their own safety and greatness. For princes, in regard of the distance of their fortune from that of their subjects and servants, cannot gather this

[2] Intercourse.   [3] Sarsaparilla.

fruit, except (to make themselves capable thereof) they raise some persons to be as it were companions and almost equals to themselves, which many times sorteth to inconvenience. The modern languages give unto such persons the name of favorites, or privadoes; as if it were matter of grace, or conversation. But the Roman name attaineth the true use and cause thereof, naming them *participes curarum* [partners of cares]; for it is that which tieth the knot. And we see plainly that this hath been done, not by weak and passionate princes only, but by the wisest and most politic that ever reigned; who have oftentimes joined to themselves some of their servants; whom both themselves have called friends, and allowed others likewise to call them in the same manner; using the word which is received between private men.

L. Sylla, when he commanded Rome, raised Pompey (after surnamed the Great) to that height, that Pompey vaunted himself for Sylla's over-match. For when he had carried the consulship for a friend of his, against the pursuit of Sylla, and that Sylla did a little resent thereat, and began to speak great, Pompey turned upon him again, and in effect bade him be quiet; *for that more men adored the sun rising than the sun setting*. With Julius Cæsar, Decimus Brutus had obtained that interest, as he set him down in his testament for heir in remainder after his nephew. And this was the man that had power with him to draw him forth to his death. For when Cæsar would have discharged the senate, in regard of some ill presages, and specially a dream of Calpurnia; this man lifted him gently by the arm out of his chair, telling him he hoped he would not dismiss the senate till his wife had dreamt a better dream. And it seemeth his favor was so great, as Antonius, in a letter which is recited *verbatim* in one of Cicero's Philippics, calleth him *venefica, witch;* as if he had enchanted Cæsar. Augustus raised Agrippa (though of mean birth) to that height, as when he consulted with Mæcenas about the marriage of his daughter Julia, Mæcenas took the liberty to tell him, *that he must either marry his daughter to Agrippa, or take away his life; there was no third way, he had made him so great*. With Tiberius Cæsar, Sejanus had ascended to that height, as they two were termed and reckoned as a pair of friends. Tiberius in a letter to him saith, *Hæc pro amicitiâ nostrâ non occultavi* [These things, as our friendship required, I have not concealed from you]; and the whole senate dedicated an altar to Friendship, as to a goddess, in respect of the great dearness of friendship between them two. The like or more was between Septimius Severus and Plautianus. For he forced his eldest son to marry the daughter of Plautianus; and would often maintain Plautianus in doing affronts to his son; and did write also in a letter to the senate, by these words: *I love the man so well, as I wish he may over-live me.* Now if these princes had been as a Trajan or a Marcus Aurelius, a man might have thought that this had proceeded of an abundant goodness of nature; but being men so wise, of such strength and severity of mind, and so extreme lovers of themselves, as all these were, it proveth most plainly that they found their own felicity (though as great as ever happened to mortal men) but as an half piece,[4] except they mought have a friend to make it entire; and yet, which is more, they were princes that had wives, sons, nephews; and yet all these could not supply the comfort of friendship.

It is not to be forgotten what Comineus observeth of his first master, Duke Charles the Hardy; namely, that he would communicate his secrets with none; and least of all, those secrets which troubled him most. Whereupon he goeth on and saith that towards his latter time *that closeness*[5] *did impair and a little perish his understanding.* Surely Comineus mought have made the same judgment also, if it had pleased him, of his second master, Lewis the Eleventh, whose closeness was indeed his tormentor. The parable[6] of Pythagoras is dark, but true; *Cor ne edito; Eat not the heart.* Certainly, if a man would give it a hard phrase, those that want friends to open themselves unto are cannibals of their own hearts. But one thing is most admirable (wherewith I will conclude this first fruit of friendship), which is, that this communicating of a man's self to his friend works two contrary effects; for it redoubleth joys, and cutteth griefs in halves. For there is no man that imparteth his joys to his friend, but he joyeth the more; and no man that imparteth his griefs to his friend, but he grieveth the less. So that it is in truth of operation

---

[4] Coin cut in two.   [5] Secretiveness.   [6] Proverb.

OF FRIENDSHIP

upon a man's mind, of like virtue as the alchemists use to attribute to their stone[7] for man's body; that it worketh all contrary effects, but still to the good and benefit of nature. But yet without praying in aid of alchemists, there is a manifest image of this in the ordinary course of nature. For in bodies, union strengthened and cherisheth any natural action; and on the other side weakeneth and dulleth any violent impression: and even so it is of minds.

The second fruit of friendship is healthful and sovereign for the understanding, as the first is for the affections. For friendship maketh indeed a fair day in the affections, from storm and tempests; but it maketh daylight in the understanding, out of darkness and confusion of thoughts. Neither is this to be understood only of faithful counsel, which a man receiveth from his friend; but before you come to that, certain it is that whosoever hath his mind fraught with many thoughts, his wits and understanding do clarify and break up, in the communicating and discoursing with another; he tosseth his thoughts more easily; he marshalleth them more orderly; he seeth how they look when they are turned into words: finally, he waxeth wiser than himself; and that more by an hour's discourse than by a day's meditation. It was well said by Themistocles to the king of Persia, *That speech was like cloth of Arras, opened and put abroad; whereby the imagery doth appear in figure;*[8] *whereas in thoughts they lie but as in packs.* Neither is this second fruit of friendship, in opening the understanding, restrained only to such friends as are able to give a man counsel; (they indeed are best;) but even without that, a man learneth of himself, and bringeth his own thoughts to light, and whetteth his wits as against a stone, which itself cuts not. In a word, a man were better relate himself to a statua or picture, than to suffer his thoughts to pass in smother.[9]

Add now, to make this second fruit of friendship complete, that other point which lieth more open and falleth within vulgar observation; which is faithful counsel from a friend. Heraclitus saith well in one of his enigmas, *Dry light is ever the best.* And certain it is, that the light that a man receiveth by counsel from another is drier

---

[7] The "philosopher's stone."   [8] Fully displayed.   [9] Suppressed.

and purer than that which cometh from his own understanding and judgment; which is ever infused and drenched in his affections and customs. So as there is as much difference between the counsel that a friend giveth, and that a man giveth himself, as there is between the counsel of a friend and of a flatterer. For there is no such flatterer as is a man's self; and there is no such remedy against flattery of a man's self as the liberty of a friend. Counsel is of two sorts: the one concerning manners, the other concerning business. For the first, the best preservative to keep the mind in health is the faithful admonition of a friend. The calling of a man's self to a strict account is a medicine, sometime, too piercing and corrosive. Reading good books of morality is a little flat and dead. Observing our faults in others is sometimes improper for our case. But the best receipt (best, I say, to work, and best to take) is the admonition of a friend. It is a strange thing to behold what gross errors and extreme absurdities many (especially of the greater sort) do commit, for want of a friend to tell them of them; to the great damage both of their fame and fortune: for, as St. James saith, they are as men *that look sometimes into a glass, and presently forget their own shape and favor.* As for business, a man may think, if he will, that two eyes see no more than one; or that a gamester seeth always more than a looker-on; or that a man in anger is as wise as he that hath said over the four and twenty letters; or that a musket may be shot off as well upon the arm as upon a rest; and such other fond and high imaginations, to think himself all in all. But when all is done, the help of good counsel is that which setteth business straight. And if any man think that he will take counsel, but it shall be by pieces; asking counsel in one business of one man, and in another business of another man; it is well (that is to say, better perhaps than if he asked none at all); but he runneth two dangers: one, that he shall not be faithfully counselled; for it is a rare thing, except it be from a perfect and entire friend, to have counsel given, but such as shall be bowed and crooked to some ends which he hath that giveth it. The other, that he shall have counsel given, hurtful and unsafe (though with good meaning), and mixed partly of mischief and partly of remedy; even as if you would call a physician that is thought good for the cure of the disease you complain of, but is unacquainted with your body; and therefore may put you in way for a present cure, but overthroweth your health in some other kind; and so cure the disease and kill the patient. But a friend that is wholly acquainted with a man's estate will beware, by furthering any present business, how he dasheth upon other inconvenience. And therefore rest not upon scattered counsels; they will rather distract and mislead, than settle and direct.

After these two noble fruits of friendship (peace in the affections, and support of the judgment), followeth the last fruit; which is like the pomegranate, full of many kernels; I mean aid and bearing a part in all actions and occasions. Here the best way to represent to life the manifold use of friendship is to cast and see how many things there are which a man cannot do himself; and then it will appear that it was a sparing speech of the ancients, to say, *that a friend is another himself;* for that a friend is far more than himself. Men have their time, and die many times in desire of some things which they principally take to heart; the bestowing[10] of a child, the finishing of a work, or the like. If a man have a true friend, he may rest almost secure that the care of those things will continue after him. So that a man hath, as it were, two lives in his desires. A man hath a body, and that body is confined to a place; but where friendship is, all offices of life are as it were granted to him and his deputy. For he may exercise them by his friend. How many things are there which a man cannot, with any face or comeliness, say or do himself? A man can scarce allege his own merits with modesty, much less extol them; a man cannot sometimes brook to supplicate or beg; and a number of the like. But all these things are graceful in a friend's mouth, which are blushing in a man's own. So again, a man's person hath many proper relations which he cannot put off. A man cannot speak to his son but as a father; to his wife but as a husband; to his enemy but upon terms: whereas a friend may speak as the case requires, and not as it sorteth with the person. But to enumerate these things were endless; I have given the rule, where a man cannot fitly play his own part; if he have not a friend, he may quit the stage.

[10] Settling in life.

XXVIII

OF EXPENSE

RICHES are for spending, and spending for honor and good actions. Therefore extraordinary expense must be limited by the worth of the occasion; for voluntary undoing may be as well for a man's country as for the kingdom of heaven. But ordinary expense ought to be limited by a man's estate; and governed with such regard, as it be within his compass; and not subject to deceit and abuse[1] of servants; and ordered to the best show, that the bills may be less than the estimation abroad. Certainly, if a man will keep but of even hand, his ordinary expenses ought to be but to the half of his receipts; and if he think to wax rich, but to the third part. It is no baseness for the greatest to descend and look into their own estate. Some forbear it, not upon negligence alone, but doubting to bring themselves into melancholy, in respect they shall find it broken.[2] But wounds cannot be cured without searching. He that cannot look into his own estate at all, had need both choose well those whom he employeth, and change them often; for new are more timorous and less subtle. He that can look into his estate but seldom, it behooveth him to turn all to certainties. A man had need, if he be plentiful in some kind of expense, to be as saving again in some other. As if he be plentiful in diet, to be saving in apparel; if he be plentiful in the hall, to be saving in the stable; and the like. For he that is plentiful in expenses of all kinds will hardly be preserved from decay. In clearing of a man's estate, he may as well hurt himself in being too sudden, as in letting it run on too long. For hasty selling is commonly as disadvantageable as interest. Besides, he that clears at once will relapse; for finding himself out of straits, he will revert to his customs: but he that cleareth by degrees induceth a habit of frugality, and gaineth as well upon his mind as upon his estate. Certainly, who hath a state to repair, may not despise small things; and commonly it is less dishonorable to abridge petty charges, than to stoop to petty gettings. A man ought warily to begin charges which once begun will continue; but in matters that return not he may be more magnificent.

[1] Cheating.   [2] Bankrupt.

XXIX

OF THE TRUE GREATNESS OF KINGDOMS AND ESTATES

THE speech of Themistocles the Athenian, which was haughty and arrogant in taking so much to himself, had been a grave and wise observation and censure, applied at large to others. Desired at a feast to touch a lute, he said, *He could not fiddle, but yet he could make a small town a great city.* These words (holpen a little with a metaphor) may express two differing abilities in those that deal in business of estate. For if a true survey be taken of counsellors and statesmen, there may be found (though rarely) those which can make a small state great, and yet cannot fiddle; as on the other side, there will be found a great many that can fiddle very cunningly, but yet are so far from being able to make a small state great, as their gift lieth the other way; to bring a great and flourishing estate to ruin and decay. And certainly those degenerate arts and shifts, whereby many counsellors and governors gain both favor with their masters and estimation with the vulgar, deserve no better name than fiddling; being things rather pleasing for the time, and graceful to themselves only, than tending to the weal and advancement of the state which they serve. There are also (no doubt) counsellors and governors which may be held sufficient (*negotiis pares* [equals in business]), able to manage affairs, and to keep them from precipices and manifest inconveniences; which nevertheless are far from the ability to raise and amplify an estate in power, means, and fortune. But be the workmen what they may be, let us speak of the work; that is, the true greatness of kingdoms and estates, and the means thereof. An argument fit for great and mighty princes to have in their hand; to the end that neither by over-measuring their forces, they leese[1] themselves in vain enterprises; nor on the other side, by undervaluing them, they descend to fearful and pusillanimous counsels.

The greatness of an estate in bulk and territory doth fall under measure; and the greatness of finances and revenue doth fall under computation. The population may appear by musters; and the number and greatness of cities and towns by cards[2] and maps. But yet

---
[1] Lose. [2] Charts.

there is not any thing amongst civil affairs more subject to error than the right valuation and true judgment concerning the power and forces of an estate. The kingdom of heaven is compared, not to any great kernel or nut, but to a grain of mustard-seed: which is one of the least grains, but hath in it a property and spirit hastily to get up and spread. So are there states great in territory, and yet not apt to enlarge or command; and some that have but a small dimension of stem, and yet apt to be the foundations of great monarchies.

Walled towns, stored arsenals and armories, goodly races of horse, chariots of war, elephants, ordnance, artillery, and the like; all this is but a sheep in a lion's skin, except the breed and disposition of the people be stout and warlike. Nay, number (itself) in armies importeth not much, where the people is of weak courage; for (as Virgil saith) *It never troubles a wolf how many the sheep be.* The army of the Persians in the plains of Arbela was such a vast sea of people, as it did somewhat astonish the commanders in Alexander's army; who came to him therefore, and wished him to set upon them by night; but he answered, *He would not pilfer the victory.* And the defeat was easy. When Tigranes the Armenian, being encamped upon a hill with four hundred thousand men, discovered the army of the Romans, being not above fourteen thousand, marching towards him, he made himself merry with it, and said, *Yonder men are too many for an embassage, and too few for a fight.* But before the sun set, he found them enow to give him the chase with infinite slaughter. Many are the examples of the great odds between number and courage; so that a man may truly make a judgment, that the principal point of greatness in any state is to have a race of military men. Neither is money the sinews of war (as it is trivially[3] said), where the sinews of men's arms, in base and effeminate people, are failing. For Solon said well to Crœsus (when in ostentation he showed him his gold), *Sir, if any other come that hath better iron than you, he will be master of all this gold.* Therefore let any prince or state think soberly of his forces, except his militia of natives be of good and valiant soldiers. And let princes, on the other side, that have subjects of martial disposition, know their own strength;

[3] Commonly.

unless they be otherwise wanting unto themselves. As for mercenary forces (which is the help in this case), all examples show that whatsoever estate or prince doth rest upon them, *he may spread his feathers for a time, but he will mew them soon after.*

The blessing of Judah and Issachar will never meet; *that the same people or nation should be both the lion's whelp and the ass between burthens;* neither will it be, that a people overlaid with taxes should ever become valiant and martial. It is true that taxes levied by consent of the estate do abate men's courage less: as it hath been seen notably in the excises of the Low Countries; and, in some degree, in the subsidies of England. For you must note that we speak now of the heart and not of the purse. So that although the same tribute and tax, laid by consent or by imposing, be all one to the purse, yet it works diversely upon the courage. So that you may conclude, *that no people overcharged with tribute is fit for empire.*

Let states that aim at greatness take heed how their nobility and gentlemen do multiply too fast. For that maketh the common subject grow to be a peasant and base swain, driven out of heart, and in effect but the gentleman's laborer. Even as you may see in coppice woods; if you leave your staddles[4] too thick, you shall never have clean underwood, but shrubs and bushes. So in countries, if the gentlemen be too many, the commons will be base; and you will bring it to that, that not the hundred poll[5] will be fit for an helmet; especially as to the infantry, which is the nerve[6] of an army; and so there will be great population and little strength. This which I speak of hath been nowhere better seen than by comparing of England and France; whereof England, though far less in territory and population, hath been (nevertheless) an over-match; in regard the middle people of England make good soldiers, which the peasants of France do not. And herein the device of king Henry the Seventh (whereof I have spoken largely in the *History of his Life*) was profound and admirable; in making farms and houses of husbandry of a standard; that is, maintained with such a proportion of land unto them, as may breed a subject to live in convenient plenty and no servile condition; and to keep the plough in the hands of the owners,

[4] Young trees left standing.   [5] Hundredth head.   [6] Sinew.

and not mere hirelings. And thus indeed you shall attain to Virgil's character which he gives to ancient Italy:

> Terra potens armis atque ubere glebæ.

[A land powerful in arms and in productiveness of soil.] Neither is that state (which, for any thing I know, is almost peculiar to England, and hardly to be found anywhere else, except it be perhaps in Poland) to be passed over; I mean the state of free servants and attendants upon noblemen and gentlemen; which are no ways inferior unto the yeomanry for arms. And therefore out of all question, the splendor and magnificence and great retinues and hospitality of noblemen and gentlemen, received into custom, doth much conduce unto martial greatness. Whereas, contrariwise, the close and reserved living of noblemen and gentlemen causeth a penury of military forces.

By all means it is to be procured, that the trunk of Nebuchadnezzar's tree[7] of monarchy be great enough to bear the branches and the boughs; that is, that the natural subjects of the crown or state bear a sufficient proportion to the stranger subjects that they govern. Therefore all states that are liberal of naturalization towards strangers are fit for empire. For to think that an handful of people can, with the greatest courage and policy in the world, embrace too large extent of dominion, it may hold for a time, but it will fail suddenly. The Spartans were a nice[8] people in point of naturalization; whereby, while they kept their compass, they stood firm; but when they did spread, and their boughs were becomen too great for their stem, they became a windfall upon the sudden. Never any state was in this point so open to receive strangers into their body as were the Romans. Therefore it sorted with them accordingly; for they grew to the greatest monarchy. Their manner was to grant naturalization (which they called *jus civitatis* [the right of citizenship]), and to grant it in the highest degree; that is, not only *jus commercii* [the right to commercial trade], *jus connubii* [the right to intermarry], *jus hæreditatis* [the right of inheritance]; but also *jus suffragii* [the right of suffrage], and *jus honorum* [the right of holding office]. And this not to singular persons alone, but like-

[7] Daniel iv. 10.   [8] Particular.

wise to whole families; yea to cities, and sometimes to nations. Add to this their custom of plantation of colonies; whereby the Roman plant was removed into the soil of other nations. And putting both constitutions together, you will say that it was not the Romans that spread upon the world, but it was the world that spread upon the Romans; and that was the sure way of greatness. I have marvelled sometimes at Spain, how they clasp and contain so large dominions with so few natural Spaniards; but sure the whole compass of Spain is a very great body of a tree; far above Rome and Sparta at the first. And besides, though they have not had that usage to naturalize liberally, yet they have that which is next to it; that is, to employ almost indifferently all nations in their militia of ordinary soldiers; yea and sometimes in their highest commands. Nay it seemeth at this instant they are sensible of this want of natives; as by the Pragmatical Sanction,[9] now published, appeareth.

It is certain that sedentary and within-door arts, and delicate manufactures (that require rather the finger than the arm), have in their nature a contrariety to a military disposition. And generally, all warlike people are a little idle and love danger better than travail. Neither must they be too much broken of it, if they shall be preserved in vigor. Therefore it was great advantage in the ancient states of Sparta, Athens, Rome, and others, that they had the use of slaves, which commonly did rid those manufactures. But that is abolished, in greater part, by the Christian law. That which cometh nearest to it is to leave those arts chiefly to strangers (which for that purpose are the more easily to be received), and to contain the principal bulk of the vulgar natives within those three kinds,—tillers of the ground; free servants; and handicraftsmen of strong and manly arts, as smiths, masons, carpenters, etc.; not reckoning professed soldiers.

But above all, for empire and greatness, it importeth most, that a nation do profess arms as their principal honor, study, and occupation. For the things which we formerly have spoken of are but habilitations towards arms; and what is habilitation without intention and act? Romulus, after his death (as they report or feign), sent

[9] A decree "which gave certain privileges to persons who married, and further immunities to those who had six children."

a present to the Romans, that above all they should intend[10] arms; and then they should prove the greatest empire of the world. The fabric of the state of Sparta was wholly (though not wisely) framed and composed to that scope and end. The Persians and Macedonians had it for a flash. The Gauls, Germans, Goths, Saxons, Normans, and others, had it for a time. The Turks have it at this day, though in great declination. Of Christian Europe, they that have it are, in effect, only the Spaniards. But it is so plain *that every man profiteth in that he most intendeth,* that it needeth not to be stood upon. It is enough to point at it; that no nation which doth not directly profess arms may look to have greatness fall into their mouths. And on the other side, it is a most certain oracle of time, that those states that continue long in that profession (as the Romans and Turks principally have done) do wonders. And those that have professed arms but for an age, have notwithstanding commonly attained that greatness in that age which maintained them long after, when their profession and exercise of arms hath grown to decay.

Incident to this point is, for a state to have those laws or customs which may reach forth unto them just occasions (as may be pretended) of war. For there is that justice imprinted in the nature of men, that they enter not upon wars (whereof so many calamities do ensue) but upon some, at the least specious, grounds and quarrels. The Turk hath at hand, for cause of war, the propagation of his law or sect; a quarrel that he may always command. The Romans, though they esteemed the extending the limits of their empire to be great honor to their generals when it was done, yet they never rested upon that alone to begin a war. First therefore, let nations that pretend to greatness have this; that they be sensible of[11] wrongs, either upon borderers, merchants, or politic ministers; and that they sit not too long upon a provocation. Secondly, let them be prest[12] and ready to give aids and succors to their confederates; as it ever was with the Romans; insomuch, as if the confederate had leagues defensive with divers other states, and, upon invasion offered, did implore their aids severally, yet the Romans would ever be the foremost, and leave it to none other to have the honor. As for the wars which were anciently made on the behalf of a kind of party, or

[10] Pay attention to.   [11] Sensitive to.   [12] Prepared.

tacit conformity of estate, I do not see how they may be well justified: as when the Romans made a war for the liberty of Grecia; or when the Lacedæmonians and Athenians made wars to set up or pull down democracies and oligarchies; or when wars were made by foreigners, under the pretence of justice or protection, to deliver the subjects of others from tyranny and oppression; and the like. Let it suffice, that no estate expect to be great, that is not awake upon any just occasion of arming.

No body can be healthful without exercise, neither natural body nor politic; and certainly to a kingdom or estate, a just and honorable war is the true exercise. A civil war, indeed, is like the heat of a fever; but a foreign war is like the heat of exercise, and serveth to keep the body in health; for in a slothful peace, both courages will effeminate and manners corrupt. But howsoever it be for happiness, without all question, for greatness it maketh, to be still for the most part in arms; and the strength of a veteran army (though it be a chargeable business) always on foot is that which commonly giveth the law, or at least the reputation, amongst all neighbor states; as may well be seen in Spain, which hath had, in one part or other, a veteran army almost continually, now by the space of six score years.

To be master of the sea is an abridgment[13] of a monarchy. Cicero, writing to Atticus of Pompey his preparation against Cæsar, saith, *Consilium Pompeii plane Themistocleum est; putat enim, qui mari potitur, eum rerum potiri* [Pompey is going upon the policy of Themistocles; thinking that he who commands the sea commands all]. And, without doubt, Pompey had tired out Cæsar, if upon vain confidence he had not left that way. We see the great effects of battles by sea. The battle of Actium decided the empire of the world. The battle of Lepanto arrested the greatness of the Turk. There be many examples where sea-fights have been final to the war; but this is when princes or states have set up their rest upon the battles. But thus much is certain, that he that commands the sea is at great liberty, and may take as much and as little of the war as he will. Whereas those that be strongest by land are many times nevertheless in great straits. Surely, at this day, with us of Europe,

[13] "A monarchy in miniature."

the vantage of strength at sea (which is one of the principal dowries of this kingdom of Great Britain) is great; both because most of the kingdoms of Europe are not merely inland, but girt with the sea most part of their compass; and because the wealth of both Indies seems in great part but an accessory to the command of the seas.

The wars of latter ages seem to be made in the dark, in respect of the glory and honor which reflected upon men from the wars in ancient time. There be now, for martial encouragement, some degrees and orders of chivalry; which nevertheless are conferred promiscuously upon soldiers and no soldiers; and some remembrance perhaps upon the scutcheon; and some hospitals for maimed soldiers; and such like things. But in ancient times, the trophies erected upon the place of the victory; the funeral laudatives and monuments for those that died in the wars; the crowns and garlands personal; the style of emperor, which the great kings of the world after borrowed; the triumphs of the generals upon their return; the great donatives and largesses upon the disbanding of the armies; were things able to inflame all men's courages. But above all, that of the triumph, amongst the Romans, was not pageants or gaudery, but one of the wisest and noblest institutions that ever was. For it contained three things: honor to the general; riches to the treasury out of the spoils; and donatives to the army. But that honor perhaps were not fit for monarchies; except it be in the person of the monarch himself, or his sons; as it came to pass in the times of the Roman emperors, who did impropriate the actual triumphs to themselves and their sons, for such wars as they did achieve in person; and left only, for wars achieved by subjects, some triumphal garments and ensigns to the general.

To conclude: no man can *by care taking* (as the Scripture saith) *add a cubit to his stature,* in this little model of a man's body; but in the great frame of kingdoms and commonwealths, it is in the power of princes or estates to add amplitude and greatness to their kingdoms; for by introducing such ordinances, constitutions, and customs, as we have now touched, they may sow greatness to their posterity and succession. But these things are commonly not observed, but left to take their chance.

XXX

OF REGIMENT OF HEALTH

THERE is a wisdom in this beyond the rules of physic: a man's own observation, what he finds good of, and what he finds hurt of, is the best physic to preserve health. But it is a safer conclusion to say, *This agreeth not well with me, therefore I will not continue it;* than this, *I find no offence of this, therefore I may use it.* For strength of nature in youth passeth over many excesses, which are owing a man till his age. Discern of the coming on of years, and think not to do the same things still; for age will not be defied. Beware of sudden change in any great point of diet, and if necessity inforce it, fit the rest to it. For it is a secret both in nature and state, that it is safer to change many things than one. Examine thy customs of diet, sleep, exercise, apparel, and the like; and try, in any thing thou shalt judge hurtful, to discontinue it by little and little; but so, as if thou dost find any inconvenience by the change, thou come back to it again: for it is hard to distinguish that which is generally held good and wholesome, from that which is good particularly, and fit for thine own body. To be free-minded and cheerfully disposed at hours of meat and of sleep and of exercise, is one of the best precepts of long lasting. As for the passions and studies of the mind; avoid envy; anxious fears; anger fretting inwards; subtle and knotty inquisitions; joys and exhilarations in excess; sadness not communicated. Entertain hopes; mirth rather than joy; variety of delights, rather than surfeit of them; wonder and admiration, and therefore novelties; studies that fill the mind with splendid and illustrious objects, as histories, fables, and contemplations of nature. If you fly physic in health altogether, it will be too strange for your body when you shall need it. If you make it too familiar, it will work no extraordinary effect when sickness cometh. I commend rather some diet for certain seasons, than frequent use of physic, except it be grown into a custom. For those diets alter the body more and trouble it less. Despise no new accident in your body, but ask opinion of it. In sickness, respect health principally; and in health, action. For those that put their bodies to endure in health, may in most sicknesses, which are not very sharp, be cured only with diet and tendering.[1] Celsus could never have spoken it as a physician, had he not been a wise man withal, when he giveth it for one of the great precepts of health and lasting, that a man do vary and interchange contraries, but with an inclination to the more benign extreme: use fasting and full eating, but rather full eating; watching and sleep, but rather sleep; sitting and exercise, but rather exercise; and the like. So shall nature be cherished, and yet taught masteries. Physicians are some of them so pleasing and conformable to the humor of the patient, as they press not the true cure of the disease; and some other are so regular in proceeding according to art for the disease, as they respect not sufficiently the condition of the patient. Take one of a middle temper; or if it may not be found in one man, combine two of either sort; and forget not to call as well the best acquainted with your body, as the best reputed of for his faculty.[2]

XXXI

OF SUSPICION

Suspicions amongst thoughts are like bats amongst birds, they ever fly by twilight. Certainly they are to be repressed, or at least well guarded: for they cloud the mind; they leese[1] friends; and they check with business, whereby business cannot go on currently and constantly. They dispose kings to tyranny, husbands to jealousy, wise men to irresolution and melancholy. They are defects, not in the heart, but in the brain; for they take place in the stoutest[2] natures; as in the example of Henry the Seventh of England. There was not a more suspicious man, nor a more stout. And in such a composition they do small hurt. For commonly they are not admitted, but with examination, whether they be likely or no. But in fearful natures they gain ground too fast. There is nothing makes a man suspect much, more than to know little; and therefore men should remedy suspicion by procuring to know more, and not to keep their suspicions in smother.[3] What would men have? Do they think those they employ and deal with are saints? Do they not

[1] Nursing.   [2] Ability.   [1] Lose.   [2] Bravest.   [3] Suppressed.

think they will have their own ends, and be truer to themselves than to them? Therefore there is no better way to moderate suspicions, than to account upon such suspicions as true and yet to bridle them as false. For so far a man ought to make use of suspicions, as to provide, as if that should be true that he suspects, yet it may do him no hurt. Suspicions that the mind of itself gathers are but buzzes; but suspicions that are artificially nourished, and put into men's heads by the tales and whisperings of others, have stings. Certainly, the best mean to clear the way in this same wood of suspicions is frankly to communicate them with the party that he suspects; for thereby he shall be sure to know more of the truth of them than he did before; and withal shall make that party more circumspect not to give further cause of suspicion. But this would not be done to men of base natures; for they, if they find themselves once suspected, will never be true. The Italian says, *Sospetto licentia fede*;[4] as if suspicion did give a passport to faith; but it ought rather to kindle it to discharge itself.

XXXII

OF DISCOURSE

SOME in their discourse desire rather commendation of wit, in being able to hold all arguments, than of judgment, in discerning what is true; as if it were a praise to know what might be said, and not what should be thought. Some have certain common places and themes wherein they are good, and want variety; which kind of poverty is for the most part tedious, and when it is once perceived, ridiculous. The honorablest part of talk is to give the occasion; and again to moderate[1] and pass to somewhat else; for then a man leads the dance. It is good, in discourse and speech of conversation, to vary and intermingle speech of the present occasion with arguments, tales with reasons, asking of questions with telling of opinions, and jest with earnest: for it is a dull thing to tire, and, as we say now, to jade,[2] any thing too far. As for jest, there be certain things which ought to be privileged from it; namely, religion, matters of state,

---

[4] *I. e.*, suspicion justifies breaking faith.   [1] Guide the discussion.
[2] Tire with overdriving.

great persons, any man's present business of importance, and any case that deserveth pity. Yet there be some that think their wits have been asleep, except they dart out somewhat that is piquant, and to the quick. That is a vein which would be bridled:

> Parce, puer, stimulis, et fortius utere loris.

[Spare, boy, the whip and tighter hold the reins.] And generally, men ought to find the difference between saltness and bitterness. Certainly, he that hath a satirical vein, as he maketh others afraid of his wit, so he had need be afraid of others' memory. He that questioneth much shall learn much, and content much; but especially if he apply his questions to the skill of the persons whom he asketh; for he shall give them occasion to please themselves in speaking, and himself shall continually gather knowledge. But let his questions not be troublesome; for that is fit for a poser.[3] And let him be sure to leave other men their turns to speak. Nay, if there be any that would reign and take up all the time, let him find means to take them off, and to bring others on; as musicians use to do with those that dance too long galliards. If you dissemble sometimes your knowledge of that you are thought to know, you shall be thought another time to know that you know not. Speech of a man's self ought to be seldom, and well chosen. I knew one was wont to say in scorn, *He must needs be a wise man, he speaks so much of himself:* and there is but one case wherein a man may commend himself with good grace; and that is in commending virtue in another; especially if it be such a virtue whereunto himself pretendeth. Speech of touch[4] towards others should be sparingly used; for discourse ought to be as a field, without coming home to any man. I knew two noblemen, of the west part of England, whereof the one was given to scoff, but kept ever royal cheer in his house; the other would ask of those that had been at the other's table, *Tell truly was there never a flout or dry blow[5] given?* To which the guest would answer, *Such and such a thing passed*. The lord would say, *I thought he would mar a good dinner*. Discretion of speech is more than eloquence; and to speak agreeably to him with whom we deal, is more than to speak in good words or in good order. A good

[3] Examiner.   [4] Personal, touching a sore spot.   [5] Scornful jest.

continued speech, without a good speech of interlocution, shows slowness: and a good reply or second speech, without a good settled speech, showeth shallowness and weakness. As we see in beasts, that those that are weakest in the course are yet nimblest in the turn; as it is betwixt the greyhound and the hare. To use too many circumstances ere one come to the matter, is wearisome; to use none at all, is blunt.

XXXIII

OF PLANTATIONS[1]

PLANTATIONS are amongst ancient, primitive, and heroical works. When the world was young it begat more children; but now it is old it begets fewer: for I may justly account new plantations to be the children of former kingdoms. I like a plantation in a pure soil; that is, where people are not displanted to the end to plant in others. For else it is rather an extirpation than a plantation. Planting of countries is like planting of woods; for you must make account to leese[2] almost twenty years' profit, and expect your recompense in the end. For the principal thing that hath been the destruction of most plantations, hath been the base and hasty drawing of profit in the first years. It is true, speedy profit is not to be neglected, as far as may stand with the good of the plantation, but no further. It is a shameful and unblessed thing to take the scum of people, and wicked condemned men, to be the people with whom you plant; and not only so, but it spoileth the plantation; for they will ever live like rogues, and not fall to work, but be lazy, and do mischief, and spend victuals, and be quickly weary, and then certify[3] over to their country to the discredit of the plantation. The people wherewith you plant ought to be gardeners, ploughmen, laborers, smiths, carpenters, joiners, fishermen, fowlers, with some few apothecaries, surgeons, cooks, and bakers. In a country of plantation, first look about what kind of victual the country yields of itself to hand; as chestnuts, walnuts, pineapples, olives, dates, plums, cherries, wild honey, and the like; and make use of them. Then consider what victual or esculent things there are, which grow speedily, and within the year; as parsnips, carrots, turnips, onions, radish, artichokes of Hierusalem,

[1] Colonies.　　[2] Lose.　　[3] Send word.

maize, and the like. For wheat, barley, and oats, they ask too much labor; but with pease and beans you may begin, both because they ask less labor, and because they serve for meat as well as for bread. And of rice likewise cometh a great increase, and it is a kind of meat. Above all, there ought to be brought store of biscuit, oat-meal, flour, meal, and the like, in the beginning, till bread may be had. For beasts, or birds, take chiefly such as are least subject to diseases, and multiply fastest; as swine, goats, cocks, hens, turkeys, geese, house-doves, and the like. The victual in plantations ought to be expended almost as in a besieged town; that is, with certain allowance. And let the main part of the ground employed to gardens or corn, be to a common stock; and to be laid in, and stored up, and then delivered out in proportion; besides some spots of ground that any particular person will manure for his own private. Consider likewise what commodities the soil where the plantation is doth naturally yield, that they may some way help to defray the charge of the plantation (so it be not, as was said, to the untimely prejudice of the main business), as it hath fared with tobacco in Virginia. Wood commonly aboundeth but too much; and therefore timber is fit to be one. If there be iron ore, and streams whereupon to set the mills, iron is a brave[4] commodity where wood aboundeth. Making of bay-salt, if the climate be proper for it, would be put in experience. Growing silk likewise, if any be, is a likely commodity. Pitch and tar, where store of firs and pines are, will not fail. So drugs and sweet woods, where they are, cannot but yield great profit. Soap-ashes likewise, and other things that may be thought of. But moil[5] not too much under ground; for the hope of mines is very uncertain, and useth to make the planters lazy in other things. For government, let it be in the hands of one, assisted with some counsel; and let them have commission to exercise martial laws, with some limitation. And above all, let men make that profit of being in the wilderness, as they have God always, and his service, before their eyes. Let not the government of the plantation depend upon too many counsellors and undertakers in the country that planteth, but upon a temperate number; and let those be rather noblemen and gentlemen, than merchants; for they look ever to the present gain. Let there be

[4] Fine. [5] Drudge.

freedom from custom,[6] till the plantation be of strength; and not only freedom from custom, but freedom to carry their commodities where they may make their best of them, except there be some special cause of caution. Cram not in people, by sending too fast company after company; but rather harken how they waste, and send supplies proportionably; but so as the number may live well in the plantation, and not by surcharge[7] be in penury. It hath been a great endangering to the health of some plantations, that they have built along the sea and rivers, in marish and unwholesome grounds. Therefore, though you begin there, to avoid carriage and other like discommodities, yet build still rather upwards from the streams than along. It concerneth likewise the health of the plantation that they have good store of salt with them, that they may use it in their victuals, when it shall be necessary. If you plant where savages are, do not only entertain them with trifles and gingles, but use them justly and graciously, with sufficient guard nevertheless; and do not win their favor by helping them to invade their enemies, but for their defence it is not amiss; and send oft of them over to the country that plants, that they may see a better condition than their own, and commend it when they return. When the plantation grows to strength, then it is time to plant with women as well as with men; that the plantation may spread into generations, and not be ever pieced from without. It is the sinfullest thing in the world to forsake or destitute a plantation once in forwardness; for besides the dishonor, it is the guiltiness of blood of many commiserable[8] persons.

XXXIV

OF RICHES

I CANNOT call riches better than the baggage of virtue. The Roman word is better, *impedimenta*. For as the baggage is to an army, so is riches to virtue. It cannot be spared nor left behind, but it hindereth the march; yea, and the care of it sometimes loseth or disturbeth the victory. Of great riches there is no real use, except it be in the distribution; the rest is but conceit. So saith Solomon, *Where much is, there are many to consume it; and what hath the owner*

[6] Duties on imports and exports.   [7] Overloading.   [8] Deserving pity.

but the sight of it with his eyes? The personal fruition in any man cannot reach to feel great riches: there is a custody of them; or a power of dole and donative of them; or a fame of them; but no solid use to the owner. Do you not see what feigned prices are set upon little stones and rarities? and what works of ostentation are undertaken, because there might seem to be some use of great riches? But then you will say, they may be of use to buy men out of dangers or troubles. As Solomon saith, *Riches are as a strong hold, in the imagination of the rich man.* But this is excellently expressed, that it is in imagination, and not always in fact. For certainly great riches have sold more men than they have bought out. Seek not proud riches, but such as thou mayest get justly, use soberly, distribute cheerfully, and leave contentedly. Yet have no abstract nor friarly contempt of them. But distinguish, as Cicero saith well of Rabirius Posthumus, *In studio rei amplificandæ apparebat, non avaritiæ prædam, sed instrumentum bonitati quæri* [In seeking to increase his estate it was apparent that he sought not a prey for avarice to feed on, but an instrument for goodness to work with]. Harken also to Solomon, and beware of hasty gathering of riches; *Qui festinat ad divitias, non erit insons* [He that maketh haste to be rich shall not be innocent]. The poets feign, that when Plutus (which is Riches) is sent from Jupiter, he limps and goes slowly; but when he is sent from Pluto, he runs and is swift of foot. Meaning that riches gotten by good means and just labor pace slowly; but when they come by the death of others (as by the course of inheritance, testaments, and the like), they come tumbling upon a man. But it mought be applied likewise to Pluto, taking him for the devil. For when riches come from the devil (as by fraud and oppression and unjust means), they come upon speed. The ways to enrich are many, and most of them foul. Parsimony is one of the best, and yet is not innocent; for it withholdeth men from works of liberality and charity. The improvement of the ground is the most natural obtaining of riches; for it is our great mother's blessing, the earth's; but it is slow. And yet where men of great wealth do stoop to husbandry, it multiplieth riches exceedingly. I knew a nobleman in England, that had the greatest audits[1] of any man in my time; a great grazier,

[1] Revenues.

a great sheep-master, a great timber man, a great collier, a great corn-master, a great lead-man, and so of iron, and a number of the like points of husbandry. So as the earth seemed a sea to him, in respect of the perpetual importation. It was truly observed by one, that himself came very hardly to a little riches, and very easily to great riches. For when a man's stock is come to that, that he can expect the prime of markets, and overcome those bargains which for their greatness are few men's money, and be partner in the industries of younger men, he cannot but increase mainly. The gains of ordinary trades and vocations are honest; and furthered by two things chiefly: by diligence, and by a good name for good and fair dealing. But the gains of bargains are of a more doubtful nature; when men shall wait upon[2] others' necessity, broke[3] by servants and instruments to draw them on, put off others cunningly that would be better chapmen,[4] and the like practices, which are crafty and naught. As for the chopping of bargains, when a man buys not to hold but to sell over again, that commonly grindeth double, both upon the seller and upon the buyer. Sharings do greatly enrich, if the hands be well chosen that are trusted. Usury is the certainest means of gain, though one of the worst; as that whereby a man doth eat his bread *in sudore vultus alieni* [in the sweat of another man's face]; and besides, doth plough upon Sundays. But yet certain though it be, it hath flaws; for that the scriveners and brokers do value[5] unsound men to serve their own turn. The fortune in being the first in an invention or in a privilege doth cause sometimes a wonderful overgrowth in riches; as it was with the first sugar man in the Canaries. Therefore if a man can play the true logician, to have as well judgment as invention, he may do great matters; especially if the times be fit. He that resteth upon gains certain shall hardly grow to great riches; and he that puts all upon adventures doth oftentimes break and come to poverty: it is good therefore to guard adventures with certainties, that may uphold losses. Monopolies, and coemption of[6] wares for re-sale, where they are not restrained, are great means to enrich; especially if the party have intelligence what things are like to come into request, and so store himself beforehand. Riches gotten by

[2] Watch for. [3] Deal. [4] Traders. [5] Represent as sound.
[6] Buying up.

service, though it be of the best rise,[7] yet when they are gotten by flattery, feeding humors, and other servile conditions, they may be placed amongst the worst. As for fishing for testaments and executorships (as Tacitus saith of Seneca, *testamenta et orbos tamquam indagine capi* [he took testaments and wardships as with a net]), it is yet worse; by how much men submit themselves to meaner persons than in service. Believe not much them that seem to despise riches; for they despise them that despair of them; and none worse when they come to them. Be not penny-wise; riches have wings, and sometimes they fly away of themselves, sometimes they must be set flying to bring in more. Men leave their riches either to their kindred, or to the public; and moderate portions prosper best in both. A great state left to an heir, is as a lure to all the birds of prey round about to seize on him, if he be not the better stablished in years and judgment. Likewise glorious[8] gifts and foundations are like *sacrifices without salt;* and but the painted sepulchres of alms, which soon will putrefy and corrupt inwardly. Therefore measure not thine advancements by quantity, but frame them by measure: and defer not charities till death; for, certainly, if a man weigh it rightly, he that doth so is rather liberal of another man's than of his own.

XXXV

OF PROPHECIES

I MEAN not to speak of divine prophecies; nor of heathen oracles; nor of natural predictions; but only of prophecies that have been of certain memory, and from hidden causes. Saith the Pythonissa[1] to Saul, *To-morrow thou and thy son shall be with me.* Homer hath these verses:

> At domus Æneæ cunctis dominabitur oris,
> Et nati natorum, et qui nascentur ab illis.

[But the house of Æneas shall reign in all lands, and his children's children, and their generations.] A prophecy, as it seems, of the Roman empire. Seneca the tragedian hath these verses:

---

[7] Latin, though it have a certain dignity.   [8] Showy.   [1] Witch of Endor.

OF PROPHECIES

———— Venient annis
Sæcula seris, quibus Oceanus
Vincula rerum laxet, et ingens
Pateat Tellus, Tiphysque novos
Detegat orbes; nec sit terris
Ultima Thule

[There shall come a time when the bands of ocean shall be loosened, and the vast earth shall be laid open; another Tiphys shall disclose new worlds, and lands shall be seen beyond Thule]: a prophecy of the discovery of America. The daughter of Polycrates dreamed that Jupiter bathed her father, and Apollo anointed him; and it came to pass that he was crucified in an open place, where the sun made his body run with sweat, and the rain washed it. Philip of Macedon dreamed he sealed up his wife's belly; whereby he did expound it, that his wife should be barren; but Aristander the soothsayer told him his wife was with child, because men do not use to seal vessels that are empty. A phantasm that appeared to M. Brutus in his tent, said to him, *Philippis iterum me videbis* [Thou shall see me again at Philippi]. Tiberius said to Galba, *Tu quoque, Galba, degustabis imperium* [Thou likewise, Galba, shall taste of empire]. In Vespasian's time, there went a prophecy in the East, that those that should come forth of Judea should reign over the world: which though it may be was meant of our Savior; yet Tacitus expounds it of Vespasian. Domitian dreamed, the night before he was slain, that a golden head was growing out of the nape of his neck: and indeed the succession that followed him for many years, made golden times. Henry the Sixth of England said of Henry the Seventh, when he was a lad, and gave him water, *This is the lad that shall enjoy the crown for which we strive.* When I was in France, I heard from one Dr. Pena, that the Queen Mother, who was given to curious arts, caused the King her husband's nativity to be calculated, under a false name; and the astrologer gave a judgment, that he should be killed in a duel; at which the Queen laughed, thinking her husband to be above challenges and duels: but he was slain upon a course at tilt, the splinters of the staff of Montgomery going in at his beaver.[2] The trivial[3] prophecy, which I heard when I was

[2] The movable face part of a helmet.   [3] Common.

a child, and Queen Elizabeth was in the flower of her years, was,

> When hempe is spun
> England's done:

whereby it was generally conceived, that after the princes had reigned which had the principal letters of that word *hempe* (which were Henry, Edward, Mary, Philip, and Elizabeth), England should come to utter confusion; which, thanks be to God, is verified only in the change of the name; for that the King's style[4] is now no more of England, but of Britain. There was also another prophecy, before the year of '88, which I do not well understand.

> There shall be seen upon a day,
> Between the Baugh and the May,
> The black fleet of Norway.
> When that that is come and gone,
> England build houses of lime and stone,
> For after wars shall you have none.

It was generally conceived to be meant of the Spanish fleet that came in '88: for that the king of Spain's surname, as they say, is Norway. The prediction of Regiomontanus,

> Octogesimus octavus mirabilis annus

[The eighty-eighth, a year of wonders], was thought likewise accomplished in the sending of that great fleet, being the greatest in strength, though not in number, of all that ever swam upon the sea. As for Cleon's dream, I think it was a jest. It was, that he was devoured of a long dragon; and it was expounded of a maker of sausages, that troubled him exceedingly. There are numbers of the like kind; especially if you include dreams, and predictions of astrology. But I have set down these few only of certain credit, for example. My judgment is, that they ought all to be despised; and ought to serve but for winter talk by the fireside. Though when I say *despised,* I mean it as for belief; for otherwise, the spreading or publishing of them is in no sort to be despised. For they have done much mischief; and I see many severe laws made to suppress them. That that hath given them grace, and some credit, consisteth in three things. First, that men mark when they hit, and never mark when

---
[4] Title.

they miss; as they do generally also of dreams. The second is, that probable conjectures, or obscure traditions, many times turn themselves into prophecies; while the nature of man, which coveteth divination, thinks it no peril to foretell that which indeed they do but collect.[5] As that of Seneca's verse. For so much was then subject to demonstration, that the globe of the earth had great parts beyond the Atlantic, which mought be probably conceived not to be all sea: and adding thereto the tradition in Plato's Timæus, and his Atlanticus, it mought encourage one to turn it to a prediction. The third and last (which is the great one) is, that almost all of them, being infinite in number, have been impostures, and by idle and crafty brains merely contrived and feigned after the event past.

XXXVI

OF AMBITION

AMBITION is like choler; which is an humor[1] that maketh men active, earnest, full of alacrity, and stirring, if it be not stopped. But if it be stopped, and cannot have his way, it becometh adust,[2] and thereby malign and venomous. So ambitious men, if they find the way open for their rising, and still get forward, they are rather busy than dangerous; but if they be checked in their desires, they become secretly discontent, and look upon men and matters with an evil eye, and are best pleased when things go backward; which is the worst property in a servant of a prince or state. Therefore it is good for princes, if they use ambitious men, to handle it so as they be still progressive and not retrograde; which because it cannot be without inconvenience, it is good not to use such natures at all. For if they rise not with their service, they will take order to make their service fall with them. But since we have said it were good not to use men of ambitious natures, except it be upon necessity, it is fit we speak in what cases they are of necessity. Good commanders in the wars must be taken, be they never so ambitious; for the use of their service dispenseth with the rest; and to take a soldier without

[5] Infer. [1] According to the old physiology, the body contained four humors—blood, phlegm, choler (red bile), melancholy (black bile)—the varying combination of which determined the individual temperament. [2] Scorched, overheated.

ambition is to pull off his spurs. There is also great use of ambitious men in being screens to princes in matters of danger and envy; for no man will take that part, except he be like a seeled[3] dove, that mounts and mounts because he cannot see about him. There is use also of ambitious men in pulling down the greatness of any subject that overtops; as Tiberius used Macro in the pulling down of Sejanus. Since therefore they must be used in such cases, there resteth to speak how they are to be bridled, that they may be less dangerous. There is less danger of them if they be of mean birth, than if they be noble; and if they be rather harsh of nature, than gracious and popular: and if they be rather new raised, than grown cunning and fortified in their greatness. It is counted by some a weakness in princes to have favorites; but it is of all others the best remedy against ambitious great-ones. For when the way of pleasuring and displeasuring lieth by the favorite, it is impossible any other should be over-great. Another means to curb them is to balance them by others as proud as they. But then there must be some middle counsellors, to keep things steady; for without that ballast the ship will roll too much. At the least, a prince may animate and inure[4] some meaner persons, to be as it were scourges to ambitious men. As for the having of them obnoxious[5] to ruin; if they be of fearful natures, it may do well; but if they be stout and daring, it may precipitate their designs, and prove dangerous. As for the pulling of them down, if the affairs require it, and that it may not be done with safety suddenly, the only way is the interchange continually of favors and disgraces; whereby they may not know what to expect, and be as it were in a wood.[6] Of ambitions, it is less harmful, the ambition to prevail in great things, than that other, to appear in every thing; for that breeds confusion, and mars business. But yet it is less dangerous to have an ambitious man stirring in business, than great in dependences. He that seeketh to be eminent amongst able men hath a great task; but that is ever good for the public. But he that plots to be the only figure amongst ciphers is the decay of a whole age. Honor hath three things in it: the vantage ground to do good; the approach to kings and principal persons; and the raising of a man's own fortunes. He that hath the

---

[3] With the eyelids sewed together.   [4] Accustom.   [5] Liable.   [6] Maze.

best of these intentions, when he aspireth, is an honest man; and that prince that can discern of these intentions in another that aspireth, is a wise prince. Generally, let princes and states choose such ministers as are more sensible of duty than of rising; and such as love business rather upon conscience than upon bravery,[7] and let them discern a busy nature from a willing mind.

XXXVII

OF MASQUES AND TRIUMPHS

THESE things are but toys, to come amongst such serious observations. But yet, since princes will have such things, it is better they should be graced with elegancy than daubed with cost. Dancing to song is a thing of great state and pleasure. I understand it, that the song be in quire, placed aloft, and accompanied with some broken music;[1] and the ditty fitted to the device. Acting in song, especially in dialogues, hath an extreme good grace; I say acting, not dancing (for that is a mean and vulgar thing); and the voices of the dialogue would be strong and manly (a base and a tenor; no treble); and the ditty high and tragical; not nice or dainty. Several quires, placed one over against another, and taking the voice by catches, anthem-wise, give great pleasure. Turning dances into figure is a childish curiosity. And generally let it be noted, that those things which I here set down are such as do naturally take the sense, and not respect petty wonderments. It is true, the alterations of scenes, so it be quietly and without noise, are things of great beauty and pleasure; for they feed and relieve the eye, before it be full of the same object. Let the scenes abound with light, specially colored and varied; and let the masquers, or any other, that are to come down from the scene, have some motions upon the scene itself before their coming down; for it draws the eye strangely, and makes it with great pleasure to desire to see that it cannot perfectly discern. Let the songs be loud and cheerful, and not chirpings or pulings. Let the music likewise be sharp and loud, and well placed. The colors that show best by candle-light are white, carnation, and

[7] Ostentation.   [1] Part music, for different instruments.

a kind of sea-water-green; and oes,[2] or spangs, as they are of no great cost, so they are of most glory. As for rich embroidery, it is lost and not discerned. Let the suits of the masquers be graceful, and such as become the person when the vizors are off; not after examples of known attires; Turks, soldiers, mariners, and the like. Let anti-masques not be long; they have been commonly of fools, satyrs, baboons, wild-men, antics,[3] beasts, sprites, witches, Ethiops, pigmies, turquets,[4] nymphs, rustics, Cupids, statuas moving, and the like. As for angels, it is not comical enough to put them in anti-masques; and anything that is hideous, as devils, giants, is on the other side as unfit. But chiefly, let the music of them be recreative, and with some strange changes. Some sweet odors suddenly coming forth, without any drops falling, are, in such a company as there is steam and heat, things of great pleasure and refreshment. Double masques, one of men, another of ladies, addeth state and variety. But all is nothing except the room be kept clear and neat.

For justs, and tourneys, and barriers; the glories of them are chiefly in the chariots, wherein the challengers make their entry; especially if they be drawn with strange beasts: as lions, bears, camels, and the like; or in the devices of their entrance; or in the bravery of their liveries; or in the goodly furniture of their horses and armor. But enough of these toys.

XXXVIII

OF NATURE IN MEN

Nature is often hidden; sometimes overcome; seldom extinguished. Force maketh nature more violent in the return;[1] doctrine and discourse maketh nature less importune; but custom only doth alter and subdue nature. He that seeketh victory over his nature, let him not set himself too great nor too small tasks; for the first will make him dejected by often failings; and the second will make him a small proceeder, though by often prevailings. And at the first let him practise with helps, as swimmers do with bladders or rushes; but after a time let him practise with disadvantages, as

[2] Round spangles.   [3] Clowns.   [4] Turkish dwarfs.   [1] Reaction.

dancers do with thick shoes. For it breeds great perfection, if the practice be harder than the use. Where nature is mighty, and therefore the victory hard, the degrees had need be, first to stay and arrest nature in time; like to him that would say over the four and twenty letters when he was angry; then to go less in quantity; as if one should, in forbearing wine, come from drinking healths to a draught at a meal; and lastly, to discontinue altogether. But if a man have the fortitude and resolution to enfranchise himself at once, that is the best:

> Optimus ille animi vindex lædentia pectus
> Vincula qui rupit, dedoluitque semel.

> [Wouldst thou be free? The chains that gall thy breast
> With one strong effort burst, and be at rest.]

Neither is the ancient rule amiss, to bend nature as a wand to a contrary extreme, whereby to set it right, understanding it, where the contrary extreme is no vice. Let not a man force a habit upon himself with a perpetual continuance, but with some intermission. For both the pause reinforceth the new onset; and if a man that is not perfect be ever in practice, he shall as well practise his errors as his abilities, and induce one habit of both; and there is no means to help this but by seasonable intermissions. But let not a man trust his victory over his nature too far; for nature will lay buried a great time, and yet revive upon the occasion or temptation. Like as it was with Æsop's damsel, turned from a cat to a woman, who sat very demurely at the board's end, till a mouse ran before her. Therefore let a man either avoid the occasion altogether; or put himself often to it, that he may be little moved with it. A man's nature is best perceived in privateness, for there is no affectation; in passion, for that putteth a man out of his precepts; and in a new case or experiment, for there custom leaveth him. They are happy men whose natures sort with their vocations; otherwise they may say, *multum incola fuit anima mea* [my soul hath been long a sojourner]; when they converse in those things they do not affect. In studies, whatsoever a man commandeth upon himself, let him set hours for it; but whatsoever is agreeable to his nature, let him take no care for any set times; for his thoughts will fly to it of themselves; so as the spaces of other business or studies will suffice. A man's nature runs either to herbs or weeds; therefore let him seasonably water the one, and destroy the other.

XXXIX

OF CUSTOM AND EDUCATION

M EN's thoughts are much according to their inclination; their discourse and speeches according to their learning and infused opinions; but their deeds are after as they have been accustomed. And therefore, as Machiavel well noteth (though in an evil-favored instance), there is no trusting to the force of nature nor to the bravery of words, except it be corroborate[1] by custom. His instance is, that for the achieving of a desperate conspiracy, a man should not rest upon the fierceness of any man's nature, or his resolute undertakings; but take such an one as hath had his hands formerly in blood. But Machiavel knew not of a Friar Clement, nor a Ravillac, nor a Jaureguy, nor a Baltazar Gerard; yet his rule holdeth still that nature, nor the engagement of words, are not so forcible as custom. Only superstition is now so well advanced, that men of the first blood are as firm as butchers by occupation; and votary[2] resolution is made equipollent[3] to custom even in matter of blood. In other things the predominancy of custom is everywhere visible; insomuch as a man would wonder to hear men profess, protest, engage, give great words, and then do just as they have done before; as if they were dead images, and engines moved only by the wheels of custom. We see also the reign or tyranny of custom, what it is. The Indians (I mean the sect of their wise men) lay themselves quietly upon a stack of wood, and so sacrifice themselves by fire. Nay the wives strive to be burned with the corpses of their husbands. The lads of Sparta, of ancient time, were wont to be scourged upon the altar of Diana, without so much as queching.[4] I remember, in the beginning of Queen Elizabeth's time of England, an Irish rebel condemned, put up a petition to the deputy that he might be

[1] Strengthened.   [2] Based on a vow.   [3] Equally powerful.   [4] Flinching.

hanged in a withe, and not in an halter; because it had been so used with former rebels. There be monks in Russia, for penance, that will sit a whole night in a vessel of water, till they be engaged with hard ice. Many examples may be put of the force of custom, both upon mind and body. Therefore, since custom is the principal magistrate of man's life, let men by all means endeavor to obtain good customs. Certainly custom is most perfect when it beginneth in young years: this we call education; which is, in effect, but an early custom. So we see, in languages the tongue is more pliant to all expressions and sounds, the joints are more supple to all feats of activity and motions, in youth than afterwards. For it is true that late learners cannot so well take the ply; except it be in some minds that have not suffered themselves to fix, but have kept themselves open and prepared to receive continual amendment, which is exceeding rare. But if the force of custom simple and separate be great, the force of custom copulate and conjoined and collegiate is far greater. For there example teacheth, company comforteth, emulation quickeneth, glory raiseth: so as in such places the force of custom is in his exaltation.[5] Certainly the great multiplication of virtues upon human nature resteth upon societies well ordained and disciplined. For commonwealths and good governments do nourish virtue grown, but do not much mend the seeds. But the misery is, that the most effectual means are now applied to the ends least to be desired.

XL

OF FORTUNE

IT cannot be denied, but outward accidents conduce much to fortune; favor, opportunity, death of others, occasion fitting virtue. But chiefly, the mould of a man's fortune is in his own hands. *Faber quisque fortunæ suæ* [Every one is the architect of his own fortune], saith the poet. And the most frequent of external causes is, that the folly of one man is the fortune of another. For no man prospers so suddenly as by others' errors. *Serpens nisi serpentem*

[5] At its height.

comederit non fit draco [A serpent must have eaten another serpent before he can become a dragon]. Overt and apparent virtues bring forth praise; but there be secret and hidden virtues that bring forth fortune; certain deliveries of a man's self, which have no name. The Spanish name, *desemboltura* [facility in expression], partly expresseth them; when there be not stonds[1] nor restiveness in a man's nature; but that the wheels of his mind keep way with the wheels of his fortune. For so Livy (after he had described Cato Major in these words, *In illo viro tantum robur corporis et animi fuit, ut quocunque loco natus esset, fortunam sibi facturus videretur* [Such was his strength of body and mind, that wherever he had been born he could have made himself a fortune]) falleth upon that, that he had *versatile ingenium* [a wit that could turn well]. Therefore if a man look sharply and attentively, he shall see Fortune: for though she be blind, yet she is not invisible. The way of fortune is like the Milken Way in the sky; which is a meeting or knot of a number of small stars; not seen asunder, but giving light together. So are there a number of little and scarce discerned virtues, or rather faculties and customs, that make men fortunate. The Italians note some of them, such as a man would little think. When they speak of one that cannot do amiss, they will throw in into his other conditions, that he hath *Poco di matto* [a little out of his senses]. And certainly there be not two more fortunate properties, than to have a little of the fool, and not too much of the honest. Therefore extreme lovers of their country or masters were never fortunate, neither can they be. For when a man placeth his thoughts without himself, he goeth not his own way. An hasty fortune maketh an enterpriser and remover (the French hath it better, *entreprenant*, or *remuant*); but the exercised fortune maketh the able man. Fortune is to be honored and respected, and it be but for her daughters, Confidence and Reputation. For those two Felicity breedeth; the first within a man's self, the latter in others towards him. All wise men, to decline the envy of their own virtues, use to ascribe them to Providence and Fortune; for so they may the better assume them: and, besides, it is greatness in a man to be the care of the higher powers. So Cæsar said to the pilot in the

[1] Stops.

tempest, *Cæsarem portas, et fortunam ejus* [You carry Cæsar and his fortune]. So Sylla chose the name of *Felix* [the Fortunate], and not of *Magnus* [the Great]. And it hath been noted, that those who ascribe openly too much to their own wisdom and policy end infortunate. It is written that Timotheus the Athenian, after he had, in the account he gave to the state of his government, often interlaced this speech, *and in this Fortune had no part,* never prospered in anything he undertook afterwards. Certainly there be, whose fortunes are like Homer's verses, that have a slide and easiness more than the verses of other poets; as Plutarch saith of Timoleon's fortune, in respect of that of Agesilaus or Epaminondas. And that this should be, no doubt it is much in a man's self.

XLI

OF USURY

MANY have made witty invectives against usury.[1] They say that it is a pity the devil should have God's part, which is the tithe. That the usurer is the greatest Sabbath-breaker, because his plough goeth every Sunday. That the usurer is the drone that Virgil speaketh of;

> Ignavum fucos pecus a præsepibus arcent.

[They drive away the drones, a slothful race, from the hives.] That the usurer breaketh the first law that was made for mankind after the fall, which was, *in sudore vultus tui comedes panem tuum;* not, *in sudore vultus alieni* [in the sweat of thy face shalt thou eat bread—not in the sweat of another's face]. That usurers should have orange-tawny[2] bonnets, because they do judaize. That it is against nature for money to beget money; and the like. I say this only, that usury is a *concessum propter duritiem cordis* [a thing allowed by reason of the hardness of men's hearts]; for since there must be borrowing and lending, and men are so hard of heart as they will not lend freely, usury must be permitted. Some others have made suspicious and cunning propositions of banks, discovery[3] of men's estates, and other inventions. But few have spoken of usury usefully. It is good to set before us the incommodities and

---
[1] Interest, not necessarily excessive.   [2] The color the Jews used to be required to wear.
[3] Revealing.

commodities of usury, that the good may be either weighed out or culled out; and warily to provide, that while we make forth to that which is better, we meet not with that which is worse.

The discommodities of usury are, First, that it makes fewer merchants. For were it not for this lazy trade of usury, money would not lie still, but would in great part be employed upon merchandizing; which is the *vena porta*[4] of wealth in a state. The second, that it makes poor merchants. For as a farmer cannot husband his ground so well if he sit at a great rent; so the merchant cannot drive his trade so well, if he sit at great usury. The third is incident to the other two; and that is the decay of customs of kings or states, which ebb or flow with merchandizing. The fourth, that it bringeth the treasure of a realm or state into a few hands. For the usurer being at certainties, and others at uncertainties, at the end of the game most of the money will be in the box; and ever a state flourisheth when wealth is more equally spread. The fifth, that it beats down the price of land; for the employment of money is chiefly either merchandizing or purchasing; and usury waylays both. The sixth, that it doth dull and damp all industries, improvements, and new inventions, wherein money would be stirring, if it were not for this slug. The last, that it is the canker and ruin of many men's estates; which in process of time breeds a public poverty.

On the other side, the commodities of usury are, first, that howsoever usury in some respect hindereth merchandizing, yet in some other it advanceth it; for it is certain that the greatest part of trade is driven by young merchants, upon borrowing at interest; so as if the usurer either call in or keep back his money, there will ensue presently a great stand of trade. The second is, that were it not for this easy borrowing upon interest, men's necessities would draw upon them a most sudden undoing; in that they would be forced to sell their means (be it lands or goods) far under foot;[5] and so, whereas usury doth but gnaw upon them, bad markets would swallow them quite up. As for mortgaging or pawning, it will little mend the matter: for either men will not take pawns without use; or if they do, they will look precisely for the forfeiture. I remember a cruel moneyed man in the country, that would say, The devil

---

[4] Essay xix. n. 4.   [5] Below the real value.

take this usury, it keep us from forfeitures of mortgages and bonds. The third and last is, that it is a vanity to conceive that there would be ordinary borrowing without profit; and it is impossible to conceive the number of inconveniences that will ensue, if borrowing be cramped. Therefore to speak of the abolishing of usury is idle. All states have ever had it, in one kind or rate, or other. So as that opinion must be sent to Utopia.[6]

To speak now of the reformation and reiglement[7] of usury; how the discommodities of it may be best avoided, and the commodities retained. It appears by the balance of commodities and discommodities of usury, two things are to be reconciled. The one, that the tooth of usury be grinded, that it bite not too much; the other, that there be left open a means to invite moneyed men to lend to the merchants, for the continuing and quickening of trade. This cannot be done, except you introduce two several sorts of usury, a less and a greater. For if you reduce usury to one low rate, it will ease the common borrower, but the merchant will be to seek for money. And it is to be noted, that the trade of merchandize, being the most lucrative, may bear usury at a good rate; other contracts not so.

To serve both intentions, the way would be briefly thus. That there be two rates of usury: the one free, and general for all; the other under license only, to certain persons and in certain places of merchandizing. First, therefore, let usury in general be reduced to five in the hundred; and let that rate be proclaimed to be free and current; and let the state shut itself out to take any penalty for the same. This will preserve borrowing from any general stop or dryness. This will ease infinite borrowers in the country. This will, in good part, raise the price of land, because land purchased at sixteen years' purchase will yield six in the hundred, and somewhat more; whereas this rate of interest yields but five. This by like reason will encourage and edge industrious and profitable improvements; because many will rather venture in that kind than take five in the hundred, especially having been used to greater profit. Secondly, let there be certain persons licensed to lend to known merchants upon usury at a higher rate; and let it be with the cau-

[6] Sir Thomas More's imaginary ideal commonwealth.   [7] Regulation.

tions following. Let the rate be, even with the merchant himself, somewhat more easy than that he used formerly to pay; for by that means all borrowers shall have some ease by this reformation, be he merchant, or whosoever. Let it be no bank or common stock, but every man be master of his own money. Not that I altogether mislike banks, but they will hardly be brooked, in regard of certain suspicions. Let the state be answered some small matter for the license, and the rest left to the lender; for if the abatement be but small, it will no whit discourage the lender. For he, for example, that took before ten or nine in the hundred, will sooner descend to eight in the hundred than give over his trade of usury, and go from certain gains to gains of hazard. Let these licensed lenders be in number indefinite, but restrained to certain principal cities and towns of merchandizing; for then they will be hardly able to color other men's moneys in the country: so as the license of nine will not suck away the current rate of five; for no man will lend his moneys far off, nor put them into unknown hands.

If it be objected that this doth in a sort authorize usury, which before was in some places but permissive; the answer is, that it is better to mitigate usury by declaration, than to suffer it to rage by connivance.

XLII

OF YOUTH AND AGE

A MAN that is young in years may be old in hours, if he have lost no time. But that happeneth rarely. Generally, youth is like the first cogitations, not so wise as the second. For there is a youth in thoughts, as well as in ages. And yet the invention of young men is more lively than that of old; and imaginations stream into their minds better, and as it were more divinely. Natures that have much heat and great and violent desires and perturbations are not ripe for action till they have passed the meridian of their years; as it was with Julius Cæsar and Septimius Severus. Of the latter of whom it is said, *Juventutem egit erroribus, imo furoribus, plenam* [He passed a youth full of errors, yea of madnesses]. And yet he was the ablest emperor, almost, of all the list. But reposed natures may do well in youth. As it is seen in Augustus Cæsar, Cosmus Duke of Florence, Gaston de Foix, and others. On the other side, heat and vivacity in age is an excellent composition for business. Young men are fitter to invent than to judge; fitter for execution than for counsel; and fitter for new projects than for settled business. For the experience of age, in things that fall within the compass of it, directeth them; but in new things, abuseth[1] them. The errors of young men are the ruin of business; but the errors of aged men amount but to this, that more might have been done, or sooner. Young men, in the conduct and manage of actions, embrace more than they can hold; stir more than they can quiet; fly to the end, without consideration of the means and degrees; pursue some few principles which they have chanced upon absurdly; care not to[2] innovate, which draws unknown inconveniences; use extreme remedies at first; and that which doubleth all errors will not acknowledge or retract them; like an unready[3] horse, that will neither stop nor turn. Men of age object too much, consult too long, adventure too little, repent too soon, and seldom drive business home to the full period,[4] but content themselves with a mediocrity of success. Certainly it is good to compound employments of both; for that will be good for the present, because the virtues of either age may correct the defects of both; and good for succession, that young men may be learners, while men in age are actors; and, lastly, good for extern accidents, because authority followeth old men, and favor and popularity youth. But for the moral part, perhaps youth will have the pre-eminence, as age hath for the politic. A certain rabbin, upon the text, *Your young men shall see visions, and your old men shall dream dreams*, inferreth that young men are admitted nearer to God than old, because vision is a clearer revelation than a dream. And certainly, the more a man drinketh of the world, the more it intoxicateth; and age doth profit rather in the powers of understanding, than in the virtues of the will and affections. There be some have an over-early ripeness in their years, which fadeth betimes. These are, first, such as have brittle wits, the edge whereof is soon turned; such as was Hermogenes the rhetorician, whose books are

[1] Deceiveth. [2] Are reckless in innovating. [3] Badly trained. [4] Completion.

exceeding subtle; who afterwards waxed stupid. A second sort is of those that have some natural dispositions which have better grace in youth than in age; such as is a fluent and luxuriant speech; which becomes youth well, but not age: so Tully saith of Hortensius, *Idem manebat, neque idem decebat* [He continued the same, when the same was not becoming]. The third is of such as take too high a strain at the first, and are magnanimous more than tract of years can uphold. As was Scipio Africanus, of whom Livy saith in effect, *Ultima primis cedebant* [His last actions were not equal to his first].

XLIII

OF BEAUTY

VIRTUE is like a rich stone, best plain set; and surely virtue is best in a body that is comely, though not of delicate features; and that hath rather dignity of presence than beauty of aspect. Neither is it almost seen, that very beautiful persons are otherwise of great virtue; as if nature were rather busy not to err, than in labor to produce excellency. And therefore they prove accomplished, but not of great spirit; and study rather behavior than virtue. But this holds not always: for Augustus Cæsar, Titus Vespasianus, Philip le Bel of France, Edward the Fourth of England, Alcibiades of Athens, Ismael the Sophy of Persia, were all high and great spirits; and yet the most beautiful men of their times. In beauty, that of favor[1] is more than that of color; and that of decent[2] and gracious motion more than that of favor. That is the best part of beauty, which a picture cannot express; no nor the first sight of the life. There is no excellent beauty that hath not some strangeness in the proportion. A man cannot tell whether Apelles or Albert Durer were the more trifler; whereof the one would make a personage by geometrical proportions; the other, by taking the best parts out of divers faces, to make one excellent. Such personages, I think, would please nobody but the painter that made them. Not but I think a painter may make a better face than ever was; but he must do it by a kind of felicity (as a musician that maketh an excellent air in

[1] Feature.   [2] Becoming.

music), and not by rule. A man shall see faces, that if you examine them part by part, you shall find never a good; and yet altogether do well. If it be true that the principal part of beauty is in decent motion, certainly it is no marvel though persons in years seem many times more amiable; *pulchrorum autumnus pulcher* [beautiful persons have a beautiful autumn]; for no youth can be comely but by pardon,[3] and considering the youth as to make up the comeliness. Beauty is as summer fruits, which are easy to corrupt, and cannot last; and for the most part it makes a dissolute youth, and an age a little out of countenance; but yet certainly again, if it light well, it maketh virtue shine, and vices blush.

XLIV

OF DEFORMITY

DEFORMED persons are commonly even with nature; for as nature hath done ill by them, so do they by nature; being for the most part (as the Scripture saith) *void of natural affection;* and so they have their revenge of nature. Certainly there is a consent[1] between the body and the mind; and where nature erreth in the one, she ventureth in the other. *Ubi peccat in uno, periclitatur in altero.* But because there is in man an election touching the frame of his mind, and a necessity in the frame of his body, the stars of natural inclination are sometimes obscured by the sun of discipline and virtue. Therefore it is good to consider of deformity, not as a sign, which is more deceivable; but as a cause, which seldom faileth of the effect. Whosoever hath anything fixed in his person that doth induce contempt, hath also a perpetual spur in himself to rescue and deliver himself from scorn. Therefore all deformed persons are extreme bold. First, as in their own defence, as being exposed to scorn; but in process of time by a general habit. Also it stirreth in them industry, and especially of this kind, to watch and observe the weakness of others, that they may have somewhat to repay. Again, in their superiors, it quencheth jealousy towards them, as persons that they think they may at pleasure despise: and it layeth their competitors

[3] Making special allowance.   [1] Agreement.

and emulators asleep; as never believing they should be in possibility of advancement, till they see them in possession. So that upon the matter,[2] in a great wit, deformity is an advantage to rising. Kings in ancient times (and at this present in some countries) were wont to put great trust in eunuchs; because they that are envious towards all are more obnoxious[3] and officious towards one. But yet their trust towards them hath rather been as to good spials[4] and good whisperers, than good magistrates and officers. And much like is the reason of deformed persons. Still the ground is, they will, if they be of spirit, seek to free themselves from scorn; which must be either by virtue or malice; and therefore let it not be marvelled if sometimes they prove excellent persons; as was Agesilaus, Zanger the son of Solyman, Æsop, Gasca, President of Peru; and Socrates may go likewise amongst them; with others.

XLV

OF BUILDING

Houses are built to live in, and not to look on; therefore let use be preferred before uniformity, except where both may be had. Leave the goodly fabrics of houses, for beauty only, to the enchanted palaces of the poets; who build them with small cost. He that builds a fair house upon an ill seat, committeth himself to prison. Neither do I reckon it an ill seat only where the air is unwholesome; but likewise where the air is unequal; as you shall see many fine seats set upon a knap[1] of ground, environed with higher hills round about it; whereby the heat of the sun is pent in, and the wind gathereth as in troughs; so as you shall have, and that suddenly, as great diversity of heat and cold as if you dwelt in several places. Neither is it ill air only that maketh an ill seat, but ill ways, ill markets; and, if you will consult with Momus,[2] ill neighbors. I speak not of many more; want of water; want of wood, shade, and shelter; want of fruitfulness, and mixture of grounds of several natures; want of prospect; want of level grounds; want of places at some near distance for sports of hunting, hawking, and races; too

[2] On the whole.   [3] Subservient.   [4] Spies.   [1] Knoll.   [2] The God of fault-finding.

near the sea, too remote; having the commodity[3] of navigable rivers, or the discommodity of their overflowing; too far off from great cities, which may hinder business, or too near them, which lurcheth[4] all provisions, and maketh everything dear; where a man hath a great living laid together, and where he is scanted: all which, as it is impossible perhaps to find together, so it is good to know them, and think of them, that a man may take as many as he can; and if he have several dwellings, that he sort them so, that what he wanteth in the one he may find in the other. Lucullus answered Pompey well; who, when he saw his stately galleries, and rooms so large and lightsome, in one of his houses, said, *Surely an excellent place for summer, but how do you in winter?* Lucullus answered, *Why, do you not think me as wise as some fowl are, that ever change their abode towards the winter?*

To pass from the seat to the house itself; we will do as Cicero doth in the orator's art; who writes books *De Oratore,* and a book he entitles *Orator;* whereof the former delivers the precepts of the art, and the latter the perfection. We will therefore describe a princely palace, making a brief model thereof. For it is strange to see, now in Europe, such huge buildings as the Vatican and Escurial and some others be, and yet scarce a very fair room in them.

First, therefore, I say you cannot have a perfect palace except you have two several sides; a side for the banquet, as it is spoken of in the book of Hester, and a side for the household; the one for feasts and triumphs, and the other for dwelling. I understand both these sides to be not only returns,[5] but parts of the front; and to be uniform without, though severally partitioned within; and to be on both sides of a great and stately tower in the midst of the front, that, as it were, joineth them together on either hand. I would have on the side of the banquet, in front, one only goodly room above stairs, of some forty foot high; and under it a room for a dressing or preparing place at times of triumphs. On the other side, which is the household side, I wish it divided at the first into a hall and a chapel (with a partition between); both of good state and bigness; and those not to go all the length, but to have at the

---

[3] Lat., no commodity or convenience, which gives better sense.
[4] Intercepts.   [5] Wings running back from the front.

further end a winter and a summer parlor, both fair. And under these rooms, a fair and large cellar sunk under ground; and likewise some privy kitchens, with butteries and pantries, and the like. As for the tower, I would have it two stories, of eighteen foot high apiece, above the two wings; and a goodly leads upon the top, railed with statuas interposed; and the same tower to be divided into rooms, as shall be thought fit. The stairs likewise to the upper rooms, let them be upon a fair open newel,[6] and finely railed in with images of wood, cast into a brass color; and a very fair landing-place at the top. But this to be, if you do not point any of the lower rooms for a dining place of servants. For otherwise you shall have the servants' dinner after your own: for the steam of it will come up as in a tunnel. And so much for the front. Only I understand the height of the first stairs to be sixteen foot, which is the height of the lower room.

Beyond this front is there to be a fair court, but three sides of it, of a far lower building than the front. And in all the four corners of that court fair staircases, cast into turrets, on the outside, and not within the row of buildings themselves. But those towers are not to be of the height of the front, but rather proportionable to the lower building. Let the court not be paved, for that striketh up a great heat in summer, and much cold in winter. But only some side alleys, with a cross, and the quarters to graze, being kept shorn, but not too near shorn. The row of return on the banquet side, let it be all stately galleries: in which galleries let there be three, or five, fine cupolas in the length of it, placed at equal distance; and fine colored windows of several works. On the household side, chambers of presence[7] and ordinary entertainments, with some bed-chambers; and let all three sides be a double house, without thorough lights on the sides, that you may have rooms from the sun, both for forenoon and afternoon. Cast[8] it also, that you may have rooms both for summer and winter; shady for summer, and warm for winter. You shall have sometimes fair houses so full of glass that one cannot tell where to become to be out of the sun or cold. For inbowed windows, I hold them of good use (in cities, indeed, upright do better,

---

[6] The center pillar, or, when "open," the well, of a winding stair.
[7] Reception-rooms.   [8] Plan.

in respect of the uniformity towards the street); for they be pretty retiring places for conference; and besides, they keep both the wind and sun off; for that which would strike almost through the room doth scarce pass the window. But let them be but few, four in the court, on the sides only.

Beyond this court, let there be an inward court, of the same square and height; which is to be environed with the garden on all sides; and in the inside, cloistered on all sides, upon decent and beautiful arches, as high as the first story. On the under story, towards the garden, let it be turned to a grotto, or place of shade, or estivation.[9] And only have opening and windows towards the garden; and be level upon the floor, no whit sunken under ground, to avoid all dampishness. And let there be a fountain, or some fair work of statuas in the midst of this court; and to be paved as the other court was. These buildings to be for privy lodgings on both sides; and the end for privy galleries. Whereof you must foresee that one of them be for an infirmary, if the prince or any special person should be sick, with chambers, bed-chamber, ante-camera, and recamera[10] joining to it. This upon the second story. Upon the ground story, a fair gallery, open, upon pillars; and upon the third story likewise, an open gallery, upon pillars, to take the prospect and freshness of the garden. At both corners of the further side, by way of return, let there be two delicate or rich cabinets, daintily paved, richly hanged, glazed with crystalline glass, and a rich cupola in the midst; and all other elegancy that may be thought upon. In the upper gallery too, I wish that there may be, if the place will yield it, some fountains running in divers places from the wall, with some fine avoidances.[11] And thus much for the model of the palace; save that you must have, before you come to the front, three courts. A green court plain, with a wall about it; a second court of the same, but more garnished, with little turrets, or rather embellishments, upon the wall; and a third court, to make a square with the front, but not to be built, nor yet enclosed with a naked wall, but enclosed with terraces, leaded aloft, and fairly garnished, on the three sides; and cloistered on the inside, with pillars, and not with arches be-

---

[9] For summer use. [10] Retiring-room.
[11] Secret outlets.

low. As for offices, let them stand at distance, with some low galleries, to pass from them to the palace itself.

XLVI

OF GARDENS

God Almighty first planted a garden. And indeed it is the purest of human pleasures. It is the greatest refreshment to the spirits of man; without which buildings and palaces are but gross handiworks; and a man shall ever see that when ages grow to civility and elegancy, men come to build stately sooner than to garden finely; as if gardening were the greater perfection. I do hold it, in the royal ordering of gardens, there ought to be gardens for all the months in the year; in which severally things of beauty may be then in season. For December, and January, and the latter part of November, you must take such things as are green all winter: holly; ivy; bays; juniper; cypress-trees; yew; pine-apple-trees;[1] fir-trees; rosemary; lavender; periwinkle, the white, the purple, and the blue; germander; flags; orange-trees; lemon-trees; and myrtles, if they be stoved;[2] and sweet marjoram, warm set. There followeth, for the latter part of January and February, the mezereon-tree, which then blossoms; crocus vernus,[3] both the yellow and the grey; primroses; anemones; the early tulippa; hyacinthus orientalis; chamaïris; fritellaria.[4] For March, there come violets, specially the single blue, which are the earliest; the yellow daffodil; the daisy; the almond-tree in blossom; the peach-tree in blossom; the cornelian-tree in blossom; sweet-briar. In April follow the double white violet; the wall-flower; the stock-gilliflower; the cowslip; flower-delices, and lilies of all natures; rosemary-flowers; the tulippa; the double peony; the pale daffodil; the French honeysuckle; the cherry-tree in blossom; the damson and plum-trees in blossom; the white thorn in leaf; the lilac-tree. In May and June come pinks of all sorts, specially the blush-pink; roses of all kinds, except the musk, which comes later; honeysuckles; strawberries; bugloss; columbine; the French marigold, flos Africanus; cherry-tree in fruit; ribes;[5] figs in fruit; rasps;

---

[1] Pine trees. The cones were called pineapples. [2] Kept in a hothouse. [3] Spring crocus. [4] A kind of lily. [5] Currants or gooseberries.

OF GARDENS

vine-flowers; lavender in flowers; the sweet satyrian, with the white flower; herba muscaria;[6] lilium convallium;[7] the apple-tree in blossom. In July come gilliflowers of all varieties; musk-roses; the lime-tree in blossom; early pears and plums in fruit; jennetings,[8] codlins.[8] In August come plums of all sorts in fruit; pears; apricocks; berberries; filberds; musk-melons; monks-hoods, of all colors. In September come grapes; apples; poppies of all colors; peaches; melocotones;[9] nectarines; cornelians; wardens;[10] quinces. In October and the beginning of November come services; medlars; bullaces;[11] roses cut or removed to come late; holly-hocks; and such like. These particulars are for the climate of London; but my meaning is perceived, that you may have *ver perpetuum* [perpetual spring], as the place affords.

And because the breath of flowers is far sweeter in the air (where it comes and goes like the warbling of music) than in the hand, therefore nothing is more fit for that delight, than to know what be the flowers and plants that do best perfume the air. Roses, damask and red, are fast flowers[12] of their smells; so that you may walk by a whole row of them, and find nothing of their sweetness; yea though it be in a morning's dew. Bays likewise yield no smell as they grow. Rosemary little; nor sweet marjoram. That which above all others yields the sweetest smell in the air is the violet, specially the white double violet, which comes twice a year; about the middle of April, and about Bartholomew-tide.[13] Next to that is the musk-rose. Then the strawberry-leaves dying, which [yield] a most excellent cordial smell. Then the flower of the vines; it is a little dust, like the dust of a bent,[14] which grows upon the cluster in the first coming forth. Then sweet-briar. Then wall-flowers, which are very delightful to be set under a parlor or lower chamber window. Then pinks and gilliflowers,[15] especially the matted pink and clove gilliflower. Then the flowers of the lime-tree. Then the honeysuckles, so they be somewhat afar off. Of bean-flowers I speak not, because they are field flowers. But those which perfume the air most delightfully, not passed by as the rest, but being trodden upon and crushed,

[6] Grape-hyacinth. [7] Lily of the valley. [8] Kinds of apples. [9] A kind of peach. [10] Large baking pears. [11] A sort of plum. [12] Not yielding odor freely. [13] August 24. [14] A kind of grass. [15] Carnations.

are three; that is, burnet, wild-thyme, and watermints. Therefore you are to set whole alleys of them, to have the pleasure when you walk or tread.

For gardens (speaking of those which are indeed prince-like, as we have done of buildings), the contents ought not well to be under thirty acres of ground; and to be divided into three parts; a green in the entrance; a heath or desert in the going forth; and the main garden in the midst; besides alleys on both sides. And I like well that four acres of ground be assigned to the green; six to the heath; four and four to either side; and twelve to the main garden. The green hath two pleasures: the one, because nothing is more pleasant to the eye than green grass kept finely shorn; the other, because it will give you a fair alley in the midst, by which you may go in front upon a stately hedge, which is to enclose the garden. But because the alley will be long, and, in great heat of the year or day, you ought not to buy the shade in the garden by going in the sun through the green, therefore you are, of either side the green, to plant a covert alley upon carpenter's work, about twelve foot in height, by which you may go in shade into the garden. As for the making of knots or figures, with divers colored earths, that they may lie under the windows of the house on that side which the garden stands, they be but toys; you may see as good sights many times in tarts. The garden is best to be square, encompassed on all the four sides with a stately arched hedge. The arches to be upon pillars of carpenter's work, of some ten foot high, and six foot broad; and the spaces between of the same dimension with the breadth of the arch. Over the arches let there be an entire hedge of some four foot high, framed also upon carpenter's work; and upon the upper hedge, over every arch, a little turret, with a belly, enough to receive a cage of birds: and over every space between the arches some other little figure, with broad plates of round colored glass gilt, for the sun to play upon. But this hedge I intend to be raised upon a bank, not steep, but gently slope, of some six foot, set all with flowers. Also I understand, that this square of the garden should not be the whole breadth of the ground, but to leave on either side ground enough for diversity of side alleys; unto which the two covert alleys of the green may deliver you. But there must be no alleys with hedges at either end of this great enclosure; not at the hither end, for letting[16] your prospect upon this fair hedge from the green; nor at the further end, for letting your prospect from the hedge, through the arches upon the heath.

For the ordering of the ground within the great hedge, I leave it to variety of device; advising nevertheless that whatsoever form you cast it into, first, it be not too busy, or full of work. Wherein I, for my part, do not like images cut out in juniper or other garden stuff; they be for children. Little low hedges, round, like welts, with some pretty pyramids, I like well; and in some places, fair columns upon frames of carpenter's work. I would also have the alleys spacious and fair. You may have closer alleys upon the side grounds, but none in the main garden. I wish also, in the very middle, a fair mount, with three ascents, and alleys, enough for four to walk abreast; which I would have to be perfect circles, without any bulwarks or embossments; and the whole mount to be thirty foot high; and some fine banqueting-house, with some chimneys neatly cast, and without too much glass.

For fountains, they are a great beauty and refreshment; but pools mar all, and make the garden unwholesome, and full of flies and frogs. Fountains I intend to be of two natures: the one that sprinkleth or spouteth water; the other a fair receipt of water, of some thirty or forty foot square, but without fish, or slime, or mud. For the first, the ornaments of images gilt, or of marble, which are in use, do well: but the main matter is so to convey the water, as it never stay, either in the bowls or in the cistern; that the water be never by rest discolored, green or red or the like; or gather any mossiness or putrefaction. Besides that, it is to be cleansed every day by the hand. Also some steps up to it, and some fine pavement about it, doth well. As for the other kind of fountain, which we may call a bathing pool, it may admit much curiosity and beauty; wherewith we will not trouble ourselves: as, that the bottom be finely paved, and with images; the sides likewise; and withal embellished with colored glass, and such things of lustre; encompassed also with fine rails of low statuas. But the main point is the same which we mentioned in the former kind of fountain; which is, that the water be in

[16] Hindering.

perpetual motion, fed by a water higher than the pool, and delivered into it by fair spouts, and then discharged away under ground by some equality of bores, that it stay little. And for fine devices, of arching water without spilling, and making it rise in several forms (of feathers, drinking glasses, canopies, and the like), they be pretty things to look on, but nothing to health and sweetness.

For the heath, which was the third part of our plot, I wish it to be framed, as much as may be, to a natural wildness. Trees I would have none in it, but some thickets made only of sweet-briar and honeysuckle, and some wild vine amongst; and the ground set with violets, strawberries, and primroses. For these are sweet, and prosper in the shade. And these to be in the heath, here and there, not in any order. I like also little heaps, in the nature of mole-hills (such as are in wild heaths), to be set, some with wild thyme; some with pinks; some with germander, that gives a good flower to the eye; some with periwinkle; some with violets; some with strawberries; some with cowslips; some with daisies; some with red roses; some with lilium convallium; some with sweet-williams red; some with bear's-foot: and the like low flowers, being withal sweet and sightly. Part of which heaps are to be with standards of little bushes pricked[17] upon their top, and part without. The standards to be roses; juniper; holly; berberries (but here and there, because of the smell of their blossom); red currants; gooseberries; rosemary; bays; sweet-briar; and such like. But these standards to be kept with cutting, that they grow not out of course.

For the side grounds, you are to fill them with variety of alleys, private, to give a full shade, some of them, wheresoever the sun be. You are to frame some of them likewise for shelter, that when the wind blows sharp you may walk as in a gallery. And those alleys must be likewise hedged at both ends, to keep out the wind; and these closer alleys must be ever finely gravelled, and no grass, because of going wet. In many of these alleys, likewise, you are to set fruit-trees of all sorts; as well upon the walls as in ranges. And this would be generally observed, that the borders wherein you plant your fruit-trees be fair and large, and low, and not steep; and set with fine flowers, but thin and sparingly, lest they deceive[18] the trees.

[17] Planted. [18] Rob.

At the end of both the side grounds, I would have a mount of some pretty height, leaving the wall of the enclosure breast high, to look abroad into the fields.

For the main garden, I do not deny but there should be some fair alleys ranged on both sides, with fruit-trees; and some pretty tufts of fruit-trees, and arbors with seats, set in some decent order; but these to be by no means set too thick; but to leave the main garden so as it be not close, but the air open and free. For as for shade, I would have you rest upon the alleys of the side grounds, there to walk, if you be disposed, in the heat of the year or day; but to make account that the main garden is for the more temperate parts of the year; and in the heat of summer, for the morning and the evening, or overcast days.

For aviaries, I like them not, except they be of that largeness as they may be turfed, and have living plants and bushes set in them; that the birds may have more scope, and natural nestling, and that no foulness appear in the floor of the aviary. So I have made a platform[19] of a princely garden, partly by precept, partly by drawing, not a model, but some general lines of it; and in this I have spared for no cost. But it is nothing for great princes, that for the most part taking advice with workmen, with no less cost set their things together; and sometimes add statuas and such things for state and magnificence, but nothing to the true pleasure of a garden.

XLVII

OF NEGOTIATING

It is generally better to deal by speech than by letter; and by the mediation of a third than by a man's self. Letters are good, when a man would draw an answer by letter back again; or when it may serve for a man's justification afterwards to produce his own letter; or where it may be danger to be interrupted, or heard by pieces. To deal in person is good, when a man's face breedeth regard, as commonly with inferiors; or in tender cases, where a man's eye upon the countenance of him with whom he speaketh may give him a

[19] Plan.

direction how far to go; and generally, where a man will reserve to himself liberty either to disavow or to expound. In choice of instruments, it is better to choose men of a plainer sort, that are like to do that that is committed to them, and to report back again faithfully the success, than those that are cunning to contrive out of other men's business somewhat to grace themselves, and will help the matter in report for satisfaction' sake. Use also such persons as affect[1] the business wherein they are employed; for that quickeneth much; and such as are fit for the matter; as bold men for expostulation, fair-spoken men for persuasion, crafty men for inquiry and observation, froward[2] and absurd[3] men for business that doth not well bear out[4] itself. Use also such as have been lucky, and prevailed before in things wherein you have employed them; for that breeds confidence, and they will strive to maintain their prescription. It is better to sound a person with whom one deals afar off, than to fall upon the point at first; except you mean to surprise him by some short question. It is better dealing with men in appetite, than with those that are where they would be. If a man deal with another upon conditions, the start or first performance is all; which a man cannot reasonably demand, except either the nature of the thing be such, which must go before; or else a man can persuade the other party that he shall still need him in some other thing; or else that he be counted the honester man. All practice[5] is to discover,[6] or to work.[7] Men discover themselves in trust, in passion, at unawares, and of necessity, when they would have somewhat done and cannot find an apt pretext. If you would work any man, you must either know his nature and fashions, and so lead him; or his ends, and so persuade him; or his weakness and disadvantages, and so awe him; or those that have interest in him, and so govern him. In dealing with cunning persons, we must ever consider their ends, to interpret their speeches; and it is good to say little to them, and that which they least look for. In all negotiations of difficulty, a man may not look to sow and reap at once; but must prepare business, and so ripen it by degrees.

[1] Like. [2] Stubborn. [3] Stupid. [4] Justify. [5] Scheming. [6] Reveal.
[7] Manage, make use of.

XLVIII

OF FOLLOWERS AND FRIENDS

Costly followers are not to be liked; lest while a man maketh his train longer, he make his wings shorter. I reckon to be costly, not them alone which charge the purse, but which are wearisome and importune in suits. Ordinary followers ought to challenge no higher conditions than countenance, recommendation, and protection from wrongs. Factious followers are worse to be liked, which follow not upon affection to him with whom they range themselves, but upon discontentment conceived against some other; whereupon commonly ensueth that ill intelligence[1] that we many times see between great personages. Likewise glorious[2] followers, who make themselves as trumpets of the commendation of those they follow, are full of inconvenience; for they taint business through want of secrecy; and they export honor from a man, and make him a return in envy. There is a kind of followers likewise which are dangerous, being indeed espials;[3] which inquire the secrets of the house, and bear tales of them to others. Yet such men, many times, are in great favor; for they are officious, and commonly exchange tales. The following by certain estates of men, answerable to that which a great person himself professeth (as of soldiers to him that hath been employed in the wars, and the like), hath ever been a thing civil,[4] and well taken even in monarchies; so it be without too much pomp or popularity. But the most honorable kind of following is to be followed as one that apprehendeth to advance virtue and desert in all sorts of persons. And yet, where there is no eminent odds in sufficiency, it is better to take with the more passable,[5] than with the more able. And besides, to speak truth, in base times active men are of more use than virtuous. It is true that in government it is good to use men of one rank equally: for to countenance some extraordinarily is to make them insolent, and the rest discontent; because they may claim a due. But contrariwise, in favor, to use men with much difference and election is good; for it maketh the persons preferred more thankful, and the rest more officious: because all is of favor. It is good discretion not to make too much of any man at the first; because

[1] Understanding.   [2] Boastful.   [3] Spies.   [4] Proper.   [5] Mediocre.

one cannot hold out that proportion. To be governed (as we call it) by one is not safe; for it shows softness, and gives a freedom to scandal and disreputation; for those that would not censure or speak ill of a man immediately will talk more boldly of those that are so great with them, and thereby wound their honor. Yet to be distracted with many is worse; for it makes men to be of the last impression, and full of change. To take advice of some few friends is ever honorable; *for lookers-on many times see more than gamesters; and the vale best discovereth the hill.* There is little friendship in the world, and least of all between equals, which was wont to be magnified. That that is, is between superior and inferior, whose fortunes may comprehend the one the other.

XLIX

OF SUITORS

Many ill matters and projects are undertaken; and private suits do putrefy the public good. Many good matters are undertaken with bad minds; I mean not only corrupt minds, but crafty minds, that intend not performance. Some embrace suits, which never mean to deal effectually in them; but if they see there may be life in the matter by some other mean, they will be content to win a thank, or take a second reward, or at least to make use in the meantime of the suitor's hopes. Some take hold of suits only for an occasion to cross some other; or to make[1] an information whereof they could not otherwise have apt pretext; without care what become of the suit when that turn is served; or, generally, to make other men's business a kind of entertainment to bring in their own. Nay, some undertake suits, with a full purpose to let them fall; to the end to gratify the adverse party or competitor. Surely there is in some sort a right in every suit; either a right in equity, if it be a suit of controversy;[2] or a right of desert, if it be a suit of petition.[3] If affection lead a man to favor the wrong side in justice, let him rather use his countenance to compound[4] the matter than to carry it.[5] If affec-

---

[1] Get.   [2] Law-suit.   [3] For some favor or office.   [4] Compromise.
[5] Get an unjust decision.

tion lead a man to favor the less worthy in desert, let him do it without depraving or disabling[6] the better deserver. In suits which a man doth not well understand, it is good to refer them to some friend of trust and judgment, that may report whether he may deal in them with honor: but let him choose well his referendaries, for else he may be led by the nose. Suitors are so distasted with delays and abuses,[7] that plain dealing in denying to deal in suits at first, and reporting the success[8] barely, and in challenging no more thanks than one hath deserved, is grown not only honorable but also gracious. In suits of favor, the first coming ought to take little place: so far forth consideration may be had of his trust, that if intelligence of the matter could not otherwise have been had but by him, advantage be not taken of the note, but the party left to his other means; and in some sort recompensed for his discovery. To be ignorant of the value of a suit is simplicity; as well as to be ignorant of the right thereof is want of conscience. Secrecy in suits is a great mean of obtaining; for voicing them to be in forwardness may discourage some kind of suitors, but doth quicken and awake others. But timing of the suit is the principal. Timing, I say, not only in respect of the person that should grant it, but in respect of those which are like to cross it. Let a man, in the choice of his mean, rather choose the fittest mean than the greatest mean; and rather them that deal in certain things, than those that are general. The reparation of a denial is sometimes equal to the first grant; if a man show himself neither dejected nor discontented. *Iniquum petas ut æquum feras* [Ask more than is reasonable, that you may get no less] is a good rule, where a man hath strength of favor: but otherwise a man were better rise in his suit; for he that would have ventured at first to have lost the suitor will not in the conclusion lose both the suitor and his own former favor. Nothing is thought so easy a request to a great person, as his letter; and yet, if it be not in a good cause, it is so much out of his reputation. There are no worse instruments than these general contrivers of suits; for they are but a kind of poison and infection to public proceedings.

[6] Decrying or disparaging. [7] Deceits.
[8] Outcome.

L

OF STUDIES

Studies serve for delight, for ornament, and for ability. Their chief use for delight is in privateness and retiring; for ornament, is in discourse; and for ability, is in the judgment and disposition of business. For expert men can execute, and perhaps judge of particulars, one by one; but the general counsels, and the plots and marshalling of affairs, come best from those that are learned. To spend too much time in studies is sloth; to use them too much for ornament, is affectation; to make judgment wholly by their rules, is the humor of a scholar. They perfect nature, and are perfected by experience: for natural abilities are like natural plants, that need proyning,[1] by study; and studies themselves do give forth directions too much at large, except they be bounded in by experience. Crafty men contemn studies, simple men admire them, and wise men use them; for they teach not their own use; but that is a wisdom without them, and above them, won by observation. Read not to contradict and confute; nor to believe and take for granted; nor to find talk and discourse; but to weigh and consider. Some books are to be tasted, others to be swallowed, and some few to be chewed and digested; that is, some books are to be read only in parts; others to be read, but not curiously; and some few to be read wholly, and with diligence and attention. Some books also may be read by deputy, and extracts made of them by others; but that would be only in the less important arguments, and the meaner sort of books, else distilled books are like common distilled waters, flashy[2] things. Reading maketh a full man; conference a ready man; and writing an exact man. And therefore, if a man write little, he had need have a great memory; if he confer little, he had need have a present wit: and if he read little, he had need have much cunning, to seem to know that he doth not. Histories make men wise; poets witty; the mathematics subtile; natural philosophy deep; moral grave; logic and rhetoric able to contend. *Abeunt studia in mores* [Studies pass into and influence manners]. Nay, there is no stond or impediment

[1] Pruning, cultivating.   [2] Insipid.

in the wit but may be wrought out by fit studies; like as diseases of the body may have appropriate exercises. Bowling is good for the stone and reins;[3] shooting for the lungs and breast; gentle walking for the stomach; riding for the head; and the like. So if a man's wit be wandering, let him study the mathematics; for in demonstrations, if his wit be called away never so little, he must begin again. If his wit be not apt to distinguish or find differences, let him study the Schoolmen; for they are *cymini sectores* [splitters of hairs]. If he be not apt to beat over matters, and to call up one thing to prove and illustrate another, let him study the lawyers' cases. So every defect of the mind may have a special receipt.

LI

OF FACTION

MANY have an opinion not wise, that for a prince to govern his estate, or for a great person to govern his proceedings, according to the respect of factions, is a principal part of policy; whereas contrariwise, the chiefest wisdom is either in ordering those things which are general, and wherein men of several factions do nevertheless agree; or in dealing with correspondence to particular persons, one by one. But I say not that the considerations of factions is to be neglected. Mean men, in their rising, must adhere; but great men, that have strength in themselves, were better to maintain themselves indifferent and neutral. Yet even in beginners, to adhere so moderately, as he be a man of the one faction which is most passable with the other, commonly giveth best way. The lower and weaker faction is the firmer in conjunction; and it is often seen that a few that are stiff do tire out a greater number that are more moderate. When one of the factions is extinguished, the remaining subdivideth; as the faction between Lucullus and the rest of the nobles of the senate (which they called *Optimates* [Aristocrats]) held out awhile against the faction of Pompey and Cæsar; but when the senate's authority was pulled down, Cæsar and Pompey soon after brake. The faction or party of Antonius and Octavianus Cæsar against Brutus and

[3] Kidneys.

Cassius held out likewise for a time; but when Brutus and Cassius were overthrown, then soon after Antonius and Octavianus brake and subdivided. These examples are of wars, but the same holdeth in private factions. And therefore those that are seconds in factions do many times, when the faction subdivideth, prove principals; but many times also they prove ciphers and cashiered; for many a man's strength is in opposition; and when that faileth he groweth out of use. It is commonly seen that men once placed take in with the contrary faction to that by which they enter: thinking belike that they have the first sure, and now are ready for a new purchase. The traitor in faction lightly goeth away with it;[1] for when matters have stuck long in balancing, the winning of some one man casteth them, and he getteth all the thanks. The even carriage between two factions proceedeth not always of moderation, but of a trueness to a man's self, with end to make use of both. Certainly in Italy they hold it a little suspect in popes, when they have often in their mouth *Padre commune* [common father]: and take it to be a sign of one that meaneth to refer all to the greatness of his own house. Kings had need beware how they side themselves, and make themselves as of a faction or party; for leagues within the state are ever pernicious to monarchies: for they raise an obligation paramount to obligation of sovereignty, and make the king *tanquam unus ex nobis* [like one of ourselves]; as was to be seen in the League of France. When factions are carried too high and too violently, it is a sign of weakness in princes; and much to the prejudice both of their authority and business. The motions of factions under kings ought to be like the motions (as the astronomers speak) of the inferior orbs, which may have their proper motions, but yet still are quietly carried by the higher motion of *primum mobile*.[2]

LII

OF CEREMONIES AND RESPECTS

HE THAT is only real had need have exceeding great parts of virtue; as the stone had need to be rich that is set without foil.[1] But if

---

[1] Gets an advantage.   [2] See Essay xv. n. 3.
[1] Gold or silver leaf behind a precious stone to add luster.

a man mark it well, it is in praise and commendation of men as it is in gettings and gains: for the proverb is true, *That light gains make heavy purses;* for light gains come thick, whereas great come but now and then. So it is true that small matters win great commendation, because they are continually in use and in note: whereas the occasion of any great virtue cometh but on festivals. Therefore it doth much add to a man's reputation, and is (as Queen Isabella said) *like perpetual letters commendatory,* to have good forms. To attain them it almost sufficeth not to despise them; for so shall a man observe them in others; and let him trust himself with the rest. For if he labor too much to express them, he shall lose their grace; which is to be natural and unaffected. Some men's behavior is like a verse, wherein every syllable is measured; how can a man comprehend great matters, that breaketh his mind too much to small observations? Not to use ceremonies at all is to teach others not to use them again; and so diminisheth respect to himself; especially they be not to be omitted to strangers and formal natures; but the dwelling upon them, and exalting them above the moon, is not only tedious but doth diminish the faith and credit of him that speaks. And certainly there is a kind of conveying of effectual and imprinting[2] passages amongst compliments, which is of singular use, if a man can hit upon it. Amongst a man's peers a man shall be sure of familiarity; and therefore it is good a little to keep state. Amongst a man's inferiors one shall be sure of reverence; and therefore it is good a little to be familiar. He that is too much in anything, so that he giveth another occasion of satiety, maketh himself cheap. To apply one's self to others is good; so it be with demonstration that a man doth it upon regard, and not upon facility. It is a good precept generally in seconding another, yet to add somewhat of one's own: as if you will grant his opinion, let it be with some distinction; if you will follow his motion, let it be with condition; if you allow his counsel, let it be with alleging further reason. Men had need beware how they be too perfect in compliments; for be they never so sufficient otherwise, their enviers will be sure to give them that attribute, to the disadvantage of their greater virtues. It is loss also in business to be too full of respects, or to be curious in observing times and

[2] Impressive.

opportunities. Solomon saith, *He that considereth the wind shall not sow, and he that looketh to the clouds shall not reap.* A wise man will make more opportunities than he finds. Men's behavior should be like their apparel, not too strait or point device,[3] but free for exercise or motion.

LIII

OF PRAISE

PRAISE is the reflection of virtue; but it is as the glass or body which giveth the reflection. If it be from the common people, it is commonly false and naught; and rather followeth vain persons than virtuous. For the common people understand not many excellent virtues. The lowest virtues draw praise from them; the middle virtues work in them astonishment or admiration; but of the highest virtues they have no sense of perceiving at all. But shows, and *species virtutibus similes* [qualities resembling virtues], serve best with them. Certainly fame is like a river, that beareth up things light and swoln, and drowns things weighty and solid. But if persons of quality and judgment concur,[1] then it is (as the Scripture saith) *nomen bonum instar unguenti fragrantis* [a good name like unto a sweet ointment]. It filleth all round about, and will not easily away. For the odors of ointments are more durable than those of flowers. There be so many false points of praise, that a man may justly hold it a suspect. Some praises proceed merely of flattery; and if he be an ordinary flatterer, he will have certain common attributes, which may serve every man; if he be a cunning flatterer, he will follow the arch-flatterer, which is a man's self; and wherein a man thinketh best of himself, therein the flatterer will uphold him most: but if he be an impudent flatterer, look wherein a man is conscious to himself that he is most defective, and is most out of countenance in himself, that will the flatterer entitle him to perforce, *spreta conscientia* [in disdain of conscience]. Some praises come of good wishes and respects, which is a form due in civility to kings and great persons, *laudando præcipere* [to teach in praising], when by telling men what they are, they represent to them what they should

---

[3] Excessively precise.   [1] Agree (in praising).

be. Some men are praised maliciously to their hurt, thereby to stir envy and jealousy towards them: *pessimum genus inimicorum laudantium* [the worst kind of enemies are they that praise]; insomuch as it was a proverb amongst the Grecians, that *he that was praised to his hurt should have a push[2] rise upon his nose;* as we say, *that a blister will rise upon one's tongue that tells a lie.* Certainly moderate praise, used with opportunity, and not vulgar, is that which doth the good. Solomon saith, *He that praiseth his friend aloud, rising early, it shall be to him no better than a curse.* Too much magnifying of man or matter doth irritate contradiction, and procure envy and scorn. To praise a man's self cannot be decent, except it be in rare cases; but to praise a man's office or profession, he may do it with good grace, and with a kind of magnanimity. The cardinals of Rome, which are theologues, and friars, and Schoolmen, have a phrase of notable contempt and scorn towards civil business: for they call all temporal business of wars, embassages, judicature, and other employments, *sbirrerie,* which is *under-sheriffries;* as if they were but matters for under-sheriffs and catchpoles: though many times those under-sheriffries do more good than their high speculations. St. Paul, when he boasts of himself, he doth oft interlace, *I speak like a fool;* but speaking of his calling, he saith, *magnificabo apostolatum meum* [I will magnify my mission].

LIV

OF VAIN-GLORY

It was prettily devised of Æsop, *The fly sat upon the axle-tree of the chariot wheel, and said, What a dust do I raise!* So are there some vain persons, that whatsoever goeth alone or moveth upon greater means, if they have never so little hand in it, they think it is they that carry it. They that are glorious must needs be factious; for all bravery stands upon comparisons. They must needs be violent, to make good their own vaunts. Neither can they be secret, and therefore not effectual; but according to the French proverb, *Beaucoup de bruit, peu de fruit; Much bruit, little fruit.* Yet

[2] Pimple.

certainly there is use of this quality in civil affairs. Where there is an opinion and fame to be created either of virtue or greatness, these men are good trumpeters. Again, as Titus Livius noteth in the case of Antiochus and the Ætolians, *There are sometimes great effects of cross lies;* as if a man that negotiates between two princes, to draw them to join in a war against the third, doth extol the forces of either of them above measure, the one to the other: and sometimes he that deals between man and man raiseth his own credit with both, by pretending greater interest than he hath in either. And in these and the like kinds, it often falls out that somewhat is produced of nothing; for lies are sufficient to breed opinion, and opinion brings on substance. In militar commanders and soldiers, vain-glory is an essential point; for as iron sharpens iron, so by glory[1] one courage sharpeneth another. In cases of great enterprise upon charge and adventure,[2] a composition of glorious natures doth put life into business; and those that are of solid and sober natures have more of the ballast than of the sail. In fame of learning, the flight will be slow without some feathers of ostentation. *Qui de contemnenda gloria libros scribunt, nomen, suum inscribunt* [They that write books on the worthlessness of glory, take care to put their names on the title page]. Socrates, Aristotle, Galen, were men full of ostentation. Certainly vain-glory helpeth to perpetuate a man's memory; and virtue was never so beholding to human nature, as it received his due at the second hand. Neither had the fame of Cicero, Seneca, Plinius Secundus, borne her age so well, if it had not been joined with some vanity in themselves; like unto varnish, that makes ceilings not only shine but last. But all this while, when I speak of vain-glory, I mean not of that property that Tacitus doth attribute to Mucianus; *Omnium quæ dixerat feceratque arte quadam ostentator* [A man that had a kind of art of setting forth to advantage all that he had said or done]: for that proceeds not of vanity, but of natural magnanimity and discretion; and in some persons is not only comely, but gracious. For excusations, cessions, modesty itself well governed, are but arts of ostentation. And amongst those arts there is none better than that which Plinius Secundus speaketh of, which is to be liberal of praise and commendation to others, in

---

[1] Boasting. [2] Cost and risk.

that wherein a man's self hath any perfection. For saith Pliny very wittily, *In commending another you do yourself right; for he that you commend is either superior to you in that you commend, or inferior. If he be inferior, if he be to be commended, you much more; if he be superior, if he be not to be commended, you much less.* Glorious men are the scorn of wise men, the admiration of fools, the idols of parasites, and the slaves of their own vaunts.

LV

OF HONOR AND REPUTATION

The winning of honor is but the revealing of a man's virtue and worth without disadvantage. For some in their actions do woo and effect honor and reputation; which sort of men are commonly much talked of, but inwardly little admired. And some, contrariwise, darken their virtue in the show of it; so as they be undervalued in opinion. If a man perform that which hath not been attempted before; or attempted and given over; or hath been achieved, but not with so good circumstance; he shall purchase more honor, than by effecting a matter of greater difficulty or virtue, wherein he is but a follower. If a man so temper his actions, as in some one of them he doth content every faction or combination of people, the music will be the fuller. A man is an ill husband[1] of his honor, that entereth into any action, the failing wherein may disgrace him more than the carrying of it through can honor him. Honor that is gained and broken[2] upon another hath the quickest reflection, like diamonds cut with facets. And therefore let a man contend to excel any competitors of his in honor, in outshooting them, if he can, in their own bow. Discreet followers and servants help much to reputation. *Omnis fama a domesticis emanat* [All fame proceeds from servants]. Envy, which is the canker of honor, is best extinguished by declaring a man's self in his ends rather to seek merit than fame; and by attributing a man's successes rather to divine Providence and felicity, than to his own virtue or policy. The true marshalling of the degrees of sovereign honor are these: In the first place are *conditores imperiorum,* founders of states and commonwealths; such

---
[1] Manager. [2] Made to shine by competition.

as were Romulus, Cyrus, Cæsar, Ottoman, Ismael. In the second place are *legislatores,* lawgivers; which are also called *second founders* or *perpetui principes* [perpetual rulers], because they govern by their ordinances after they are gone; such were Lycurgus, Solon, Justinian, Eadgar, Alphonsus of Castile, the Wise, that made the *Siete Partidas*[3] [Seven Parts]. In the third place are *liberatores,* or *salvatores* [saviors], such as compound the long miseries of civil wars, or deliver their countries from servitude of strangers or tyrants; as Augustus Cæsar, Vespasianus, Aurelianus, Theodoricus, King Henry the Seventh of England, King Henry the Fourth of France. In the fourth place are *propagatores* or *propugnatores imperii* [champions of the empire]; such as in honorable wars enlarge their territories, or make noble defence against invaders. And in the last place are *patres patriæ* [fathers of their country]; which reign justly, and make the times good wherein they live. Both which last kinds need no examples, they are in such number. Degrees of honor in subjects are, first *participes curarum* [participants in cares], those upon whom princes do discharge the greatest weight of their affairs; their *right hands,* as we call them. The next are *duces belli,* great leaders [in war]; such as are princes' lieutenants, and do them notable services in the wars. The third are *gratiosi,* favorites; such as exceed not this scantling,[4] to be solace to the sovereign, and harmless to the people. And the fourth, *negotiis pares* [equals in business]; such as have great places under princes, and execute their places with sufficiency. There is an honor, likewise, which may be ranked amongst the greatest which happeneth rarely; that is, of such as sacrifice themselves to death or danger for the good of their country; as was M. Regulus, and the two Decii.

LVI

OF JUDICATURE

JUDGES ought to remember that their office is *jus dicere,* and not *jus dare;* to interpret law, and not to make law, or give law. Else will it be like the authority claimed by the Church of Rome, which under pretext of exposition of Scripture doth not stick to add and alter;

[3] The Spanish code of laws. [4] Measure.

and to pronounce that which they do not find; and by show of antiquity to introduce novelty. Judges ought to be more learned than witty, more reverend than plausible, and more advised than confident. Above all things, integrity is their portion and proper virtue. *Cursed* (saith the law) *is he that removeth the landmark.* The mislayer of a mere-stone[1] is to blame. But it is the unjust judge that is the capital remover of landmarks, when he defineth amiss of lands and property. One foul sentence doth more hurt than many foul examples. For these do but corrupt the stream, the other corrupteth the fountain. So saith Solomon, *Fons turbatus, et vena corrupta, est justus cadens in causa sua coram adversario* [A righteous man falling down before the wicked is as a troubled fountain or a corrupt spring]. The office of judges may have reference unto the parties that sue, unto the advocates that plead, unto the clerks and ministers of justice underneath them, and to the sovereign or state above them.

First, for the causes or parties that sue. *There be* (saith the Scripture) *that turn judgment into wormwood;* and surely there be also that turn it into vinegar; for injustice maketh it bitter, and delays make it sour. The principal duty of a judge is to suppress force and fraud; whereof force is the more pernicious when it is open, and fraud when it is close and disguised. Add thereto contentious suits, which ought to be spewed out, as the surfeit of courts. A judge ought to prepare his way to a just sentence, as God useth to prepare his way, by raising valleys and taking down hills: so when there appeareth on either side an high hand, violent prosecution, cunning advantages taken, combination, power, great counsel, then is the virtue of a judge seen, to make inequality equal; that he may plant his judgment as upon an even ground. *Qui fortiter emungit, elicit sanguinem* [Violent wringing makes the nose bleed]; and where the wine-press is hard wrought, it yields a harsh wine, that tastes of the grape-stone. Judges must beware of hard constructions and strained inferences; for there is no worse torture than the torture of laws. Specially in case of laws penal, they ought to have care that that which was meant for terror be not turned into rigor; and that they bring not upon the people that shower whereof the Scrip-

[1] Boundary stone.

ture speaketh, *Pluet super eos laqueos* [He will rain snares upon them]; for penal laws pressed are a *shower of snares* upon the people. Therefore let penal laws, if they have been sleepers of long, or if they be grown unfit for the present time, be by wise judges confined in the execution: *Judicis officium est, ut res, ita tempora rerum, etc.* [A judge must have regard to the time as well as to the matter]. In causes of life and death, judges ought (as far as the law permitteth) in justice to remember mercy; and to cast a severe eye upon the example, but a merciful eye upon the person.

Secondly, for the advocates and counsel that plead. Patience and gravity of hearing is an essential part of justice; and an overspeaking judge is no well-tuned cymbal. It is no grace to a judge first to find that which he might have heard in due time from the bar; or to show quickness of conceit in cutting off evidence or counsel too short; or to prevent information by questions, though pertinent. The parts of a judge in hearing are four: to direct the evidence; to moderate length, repetition, or impertinency of speech; to recapitulate, select, and collate the material points of that which hath been said; and to give the rule or sentence. Whatsoever is above these is too much; and proceedeth either of glory and willingness to speak, or of impatience to hear, or of shortness of memory, or of want of a staid and equal attention. It is a strange thing to see that the boldness of advocates should prevail with judges; whereas they should imitate God, in whose seat they sit; who *represseth the presumptuous,* and *giveth grace to the modest.* But it is more strange, that judges should have noted favorites; which cannot but cause multiplication of fees, and suspicion of by-ways. There is due from the judge to the advocate some commendation and gracing, where causes are well handled and fair pleaded; especially towards the side which obtaineth not; for that upholds in the client the reputation of his counsel, and beats down in him the conceit of his cause. There is likewise due to the public a civil reprehension of advocates, where there appeareth cunning counsel, gross neglect, slight information, indiscreet pressing, or an over-bold defence. And let not the counsel at the bar chop[2] with the judge, nor wind himself into the handling of the cause anew after the judge hath declared his sentence; but,

[2] Bandy words.

on the other side, let not the judge meet the cause half way, nor give occasion for the party to say his counsel or proofs were not heard.

Thirdly, for that that concerns clerks and ministers. The place of justice is an hallowed place; and therefore not only the bench, but the foot-pace[3] and precincts and purprise[4] thereof, ought to be preserved without scandal and corruption. For certainly *grapes* (as the Scripture saith) *will not be gathered of thorns or thistles;* neither can justice yield her fruit with sweetness amongst the briars and brambles of catching and polling[5] clerks and ministers. The attendance of courts is subject to four bad instruments. First, certain persons that are sowers of suits; which make the court swell, and the country pine. The second sort is of those that engage courts in quarrels of jurisdiction, and are not truly *amici curiæ,* but *parasiti curiæ* [not friends but parasites of the court], in puffing a court up beyond her bounds, for their own scraps and advantage. The third sort is of those that may be accounted the left hands of courts; persons that are full of nimble and sinister tricks and shifts, whereby they pervert the plain and direct courses of courts, and bring justice into oblique lines and labyrinths. And the fourth is the poller and exacter of fees; which justifies the common resemblance of the courts of justice to the bush whereunto while the sheep flies for defence in weather, he is sure to lose part of his fleece. On the other side, an ancient clerk, skilful in precedents, wary in proceeding, and understanding in the business of the court, is an excellent finger of a court; and doth many times point the way to the judge himself.

Fourthly, for that which may concern the sovereign and estate. Judges ought above all to remember the conclusion of the Roman Twelve Tables; *Salus populi suprema lex* [The supreme law of all is the weal of the people]; and to know that laws, except they be in order to that end, are but things captious, and oracles not well inspired. Therefore it is an happy thing in a state when kings and states do often consult with judges; and again when judges do often consult with the king and state: the one, when there is matter of law intervenient in business of state; the other, when there is some consideration of state intervenient in matter of law. For many times the things deduced[6] to judgment may be *meum and tuum* [mine

[3] Lobby. [4] Enclosure. [5] Extorting fees. [6] Brought into court.

and thine], when the reason[7] and consequence thereof may trench to[8] point of estate: I call matter of estate, not only the parts of sovereignty, but whatsoever introduceth any great alteration or dangerous precedent; or concerneth manifestly any great portion of people. And let no man weakly conceive that just laws and true policy have any antipathy; for they are like the spirits and sinews, that one moves with the other. Let judges also remember, that Solomon's throne was supported by lions on both sides: let them be lions, but yet lions under the throne; being circumspect that they do not check or oppose any points of sovereignty. Let not judges also be ignorant of their own right, as to think there is not left to them, as a principal part of their office, a wise use and application of laws. For they may remember what the apostle saith of a greater law than theirs; *Nos scimus quia lex bona est, modo quis ea utatur legitime* [We know that the law is good, if a man use it lawfully].

LVII

OF ANGER

To SEEK to extinguish anger utterly is but a bravery[1] of the Stoics. We have better oracles: *Be angry, but sin not. Let not the sun go down upon your anger.* Anger must be limited and confined both in race and in time. We will first speak how the natural inclination and habit to be angry may be attempered and calmed. Secondly, how the particular motions of anger may be repressed, or at least refrained from doing mischief. Thirdly, how to raise anger or appease anger in another.

For the first; there is no other way but to meditate and ruminate well upon the effects of anger, how it troubles man's life. And the best time to do this is to look back upon anger when the fit is thoroughly over. Seneca saith well, *That anger is like ruin, which breaks itself upon that it falls.* The Scripture exhorteth us *to possess our souls in patience.* Whosoever is out of patience, is out of possession of his soul. Men must not turn bees;

        . . . animasque in vulnere ponunt

[that put their lives in the sting].

[7] Principle.   [8] Touch.   [1] Boast.

Anger is certainly a kind of baseness; as it appears well in the weakness of those subjects in whom it reigns; children, women, old folks, sick folks. Only men must beware that they carry their anger rather with scorn than with fear; so that they may seem rather to be above the injury than below it; which is a thing easily done, if a man will give law to himself in it.

For the second point; the causes and motives of anger are chiefly three. First, to be too sensible of hurt; for no man is angry that feels not himself hurt; and therefore tender and delicate persons must needs be oft angry; they have so many things to trouble them, which more robust natures have little sense of. The next is, the apprehension and construction of the injury offered to be, in the circumstances thereof, full of contempt: for contempt is that which putteth an edge upon anger, as much or more than the hurt itself. And therefore when men are ingenious in picking out circumstances of contempt, they do kindle their anger much. Lastly, opinion of the touch of a man's reputation doth multiply and sharpen anger. Wherein the remedy is, that a man should have, as Consalvo was wont to say, *telam honoris crassiorem* [an honor of a stouter web]. But in all refrainings of anger, it is the best remedy to win time; and to make a man's self believe, that the opportunity of his revenge is not yet come, but that he foresees a time for it; and so to still himself in the meantime, and reserve it.

To contain anger from mischief, though it take hold of a man, there be two things whereof you must have special caution. The one, of extreme bitterness of words, especially if they be aculeate[2] and proper;[3] for *cummunia maledicta* [common revilings] are nothing so much; and again, that in anger a man reveal no secrets; for that makes him not fit for society. The other, that you do not peremptorily break off, in any business, in a fit of anger; but howsoever you show bitterness, do not act anything that is not revocable.

For raising and appeasing anger in another; it is done chiefly by choosing of times, when men are frowardest and worst disposed, to incense them. Again, by gathering (as was touched before) all that you can find out to aggravate the contempt. And the two remedies are by the contraries. The former to take good times, when first

---

[2] Stinging.   [3] Personal.

to relate to a man an angry business; for the first impression is much; and the other is, to sever, as much as may be, the construction of the injury from the point of contempt; imputing it to misunderstanding, fear, passion, or what you will.

LVIII

OF VICISSITUDE OF THINGS

SOLOMON saith, *There is no new thing upon the earth*. So that as Plato had an imagination, *That all knowledge was but remembrance;* so Solomon giveth his sentence, *That all novelty is but oblivion*. Whereby you may see that the river of Lethe runneth as well above ground as below. There is an abstruse astrologer that saith, *If it were not for two things that are constant (the one is, that the fixed stars ever stand a like distance one from another, and never come nearer, together, nor go further asunder; the other, that the diurnal motion perpetually keepeth time), no individual would last one moment*. Certain it is, that the matter is in a perpetual flux, and never at a stay. The great winding-sheets, that bury all things in oblivion, are two; deluges and earthquakes. As for conflagrations and great droughts, they do not merely dispeople and destroy. Phaëton's car went but a day. And the three years' drought in the time of Elias was but particular, and left people alive. As for the great burnings by lightnings, which are often in the West Indies, they are but narrow. But in the other two destructions, by deluge and earthquake, it is further to be noted, that the remnant of people which hap to be reserved, are commonly ignorant and mountainous people, that can give no account of the time past; so that the oblivion is all one as if none had been left. If you consider well of the people of the West Indies, it is very probable that they are a newer or a younger people than the people of the Old World. And it is much more likely that the destruction that hath heretofore been there was not by earthquakes (as the Egyptian priest told Solon concerning the island of Atlantis, *that it was swallowed by an earthquake*), but rather that it was desolated by a particular deluge. For earthquakes are seldom in those parts. But on the other side, they have such pouring rivers, as the rivers of Asia and Africk and Europe are but brooks to them. Their Andes, likewise, or mountains, are far higher than those with us; whereby it seems that the remnants of generation of men were in such a particular deluge saved. As for the observation that Machiavel hath, that the jealousy of sects doth much extinguish the memory of things; traducing Gregory the Great, that he did what in him lay to extinguish all heathen antiquities; I do not find that those zeals do any great effects, nor last long; as it appeared in the succession of Sabinian,[1] who did revive the former antiquities.

The vicissitude of mutations in the superior globe[2] are no fit matter for this present argument. It may be, Plato's great year,[3] if the world should last so long, would have some effect; not in renewing the state of like individuals (for that is the fume of those that conceive the celestial bodies have more accurate influences upon these things below than indeed they have), but in gross. Comets, out of question, have likewise power and effect over the gross and mass of things; but they are rather gazed upon, and waited upon in their journey, than wisely observed in their effects; specially in their respective effects; that is, what kind of comet, for magnitude, color, version of the beams, placing in the reign of heaven, or lasting, produceth what kind of effects.

There is a toy which I have heard, and I would not have it given over, but waited upon a little. They say it is observed in the Low Countries (I know not in what part) that every five and thirty years the same kind and suit of years and weathers comes about again; as great frosts, great wet, great droughts, warm winters, summers with little heat, and the like; and they call it the *Prime*. It is a thing I do the rather mention, because, computing backwards, I have found some concurrence.

But to leave these points of nature, and to come to men. The greatest vicissitude of things amongst men, is the vicissitude of sects and religions. For those orbs rule in men's minds most. The true religion is *built upon the rock;* the rest are tossed upon the waves of time. To speak, therefore, of the causes of new sects; and to give

[1] The Pope who succeeded Gregory the Great.   [2] The heavens.
[3] When the great cycle of all the heavenly motions shall be completed.

some counsel concerning them, as far as the weakness of human judgment can give stay to so great revolutions.

When the religion formerly received is rent by discords; and when the holiness of the professors of religion is decayed and full of scandal; and withal the times be stupid, ignorant, and barbarous; you may doubt[4] the springing up of a new sect; if then also there should arise any extravagant and strange spirit to make himself author thereof. All which points held when Mahomet published his law. If a new sect have not two properties, fear it not; for it will not spread. The one is the supplanting or the opposing of authority established; for nothing is more popular than that. The other is the giving licence to pleasures and a voluptuous life. For as for speculative heresies (such as were in ancient times the Arians, and now the Arminians), though they work mightily upon men's wits, yet they do not produce any great alterations in states; except it be by the help of civil occasions. There be three manner of plantations of new sects. By the power of signs and miracles; by the eloquence and wisdom of speech and persuasion; and by the sword. For martyrdoms, I reckon them amongst miracles; because they seem to exceed the strength of human nature: and I may do the like of superlative and admirable holiness of life. Surely there is no better way to stop the rising of new sects and schisms than to reform abuses; to compound the smaller differences; to proceed mildly, and not with sanguinary persecutions; and rather to take off the principal authors by winning and advancing them, than to enrage them by violence and bitterness.

The changes and vicissitude in wars are many; but chiefly in three things; in the seats or stages of the war; in the weapons; and in the manner of the conduct. Wars, in ancient time, seemed more to move from east to west; for the Persians, Assyrians, Arabians, Tartars (which were the invaders) were all eastern people. It is true, the Gauls were western; but we read but of two incursions of theirs: the one to Gallo-Grecia, the other to Rome. But east and west have no certain points of heaven; and no more have the wars, either from the east or west, any certainty of observation. But north and south are fixed; and it hath seldom or never been seen that the

[4] Fear.

far southern people have invaded the northern, but contrariwise. Whereby it is manifest that the northern tract of the world is in nature the more martial region: be it in respect of the stars of that hemisphere; or of the great continents that are upon the north, whereas the south part, for aught that is known, is almost all sea; or (which is most apparent) of the cold of the northern parts, which is that which, without aid of discipline, doth make the bodies hardest, and the courages warmest.

Upon the breaking and shivering of a great state and empire, you may be sure to have wars. For great empires, while they stand, do enervate and destroy the forces of the natives which they have subdued, resting upon their own protecting forces; and then when they fail also, all goes to ruin, and they become a prey. So was it in the decay of the Roman empire; and likewise in the empire of Almaigne, after Charles the Great, every bird taking a feather; and were not unlike to befall to Spain, if it should break. The great accessions and unions of kingdoms do likewise stir up wars; for when a state grows to an over-power, it is like a great flood, that will be sure to overflow. As it hath been seen in the states of Rome, Turkey, Spain, and others. Look when the world hath fewest barbarous peoples, but such as commonly will not marry or generate, except they know means to live (as it is almost everywhere at this day, except Tartary), there is no danger of inundations of people; but when there be great shoals of people, which go on to populate, without foreseeing means of life and sustentation, it is of necessity that once in an age or two they discharge a portion of their people upon other nations; which the ancient northern people were wont to do by lot; casting lots what part should stay at home, and what should seek their fortunes. When a warlike state grows soft and effeminate, they may be sure of a war. For commonly such states are grown rich in the time of their degenerating; and so the prey inviteth, and their decay in valor encourageth a war.

As for the weapons, it hardly falleth under rule and observation: yet we see even they have returns and vicissitudes. For certain it is, that ordnance was known in the city of the Oxidrakes in India; and was that which the Macedonians called thunder and lightning, and magic. And it is well known that the use of ordnance hath been in China above two thousand years. The conditions of weapons, and their improvement, are; First, the fetching afar off; for that outruns the danger; as it is seen in ordnance and muskets. Secondly, the strength of the percussion; wherein likewise ordnance do exceed all arietations[5] and ancient inventions. The third is, the commodious use of them; as that they may serve in all weathers; that the carriage may be light and manageable; and the like.

For the conduct of the war: at the first, men rested extremely upon number: they did put the wars likewise upon main force and valor; pointing days for pitched fields, and so trying it out upon an even match: and they were more ignorant in ranging and arraying their battles.[6] After they grew to rest upon number rather competent than vast; they grew to advantages of place, cunning diversions, and the like: and they grew more skilful in the ordering of their battles.

In the youth of a state, arms do flourish; in the middle age of a state, learning; and then both of them together for a time; in the declining age of a state, mechanical arts and merchandize. Learning hath his infancy, when it is but beginning and almost childish; then his youth, when it is luxuriant and juvenile; then his strength of years, when it is solid and reduced;[7] and lastly, his old age, when it waxeth dry and exhaust. But it is not good to look too long upon these turning wheels of vicissitude, lest we become giddy. As for the philology[8] of them, that is but a circle of tales, and therefore not fit for this writing.

LIX

OF FAME[1]

A Fragment

THE poets make Fame a monster. They describe her in part finely and elegantly, and in part gravely and sententiously. They say, look how many feathers she hath, so many eyes she hath underneath; so many tongues; so many voices; she pricks up so many ears.

---

[5] Battering-rams.   [6] Battalions.   [7] Brought within bounds.   [8] History.
[1] Fame is used here in the two senses of reputation and rumor.

OF FAME

This is a flourish. There follow excellent parables; as that she gathereth strength in going; that she goeth upon the ground and yet hideth her head in the clouds; that in the daytime she sitteth in a watch tower and flieth most by night; that she mingleth things done with things not done; and that she is a terror to great cities. But that which passeth all the rest is: They do recount that the Earth, mother of the giants that made war against Jupiter and were by him destroyed, thereupon in an anger brought forth Fame. For certain it is that rebels, figured by the giants, and seditious fames and libels are but brothers and sisters, masculine and feminine. But now, if a man can tame this monster, and bring her to feed at the hand, and govern her, and with her fly other ravening fowl and kill them, it is somewhat worth. But we are infected with the style of the poets. To speak now in a sad and serious manner: There is not in all the politics a place less handled and more worthy to be handled than this of fame. We will therefore speak of these points: What are false fames; and what are true fames; and how they may be best discerned; how fames may be sown and raised; how they may be spread and multiplied; and how they may be checked and laid dead. And other things concerning the nature of fame. Fame is of that force, as there is scarcely any great action wherein it hath not a great part; especially in the war. Mucianus undid Vitellius by a fame that he scattered: that Vitellius had in purpose to remove the legions of Syria into Germany and the legions of Germany into Syria; whereupon the legions of Syria were infinitely inflamed. Julius Cæsar took Pompey unprovided and laid asleep his industry and preparations by a fame that he cunningly gave out: Cæsar's own soldiers loved him not, and being wearied with the wars and laden with the spoils of Gaul, would forsake him as soon as he came into Italy. Livia settled all things for the succession of her son Tiberius by continual giving out that her husband Augustus was upon recovery and amendment. And it is an usual thing with the pashas to conceal the death of the Great Turk from the janizaries[2] and men of war, to save the sacking of Constantinople and other towns, as their manner is. Themistocles made Xerxes, king of Persia, post apace out of Grecia by giving out that the Grecians had a purpose to

---

[2] The Sultan's bodyguard.

break his bridge of ships which he had made athwart Hellespont. There be a thousand such like examples; and the more they are, the less they need to be repeated; because a man meeteth with them everywhere. Therefore let all wise governors have as great a watch and care over fames as they have of the actions and designs themselves.

[*The essay was not finished.*]

THE NEW ATLANTIS
BY
SIR FRANCIS BACON

INTRODUCTORY NOTE

BACON's literary executor, Dr. Rawley, published "The New Atlantis" in 1627, the year after the author's death. It seems to have been written about 1623, during that period of literary activity which followed Bacon's political fall. None of Bacon's writings gives in short space so vivid a picture of his tastes and aspirations as this fragment of the plan of an ideal commonwealth. The generosity and enlightenment, the dignity and splendor, the piety and public spirit, of the inhabitants of Bensalem represent the ideal qualities which Bacon the statesman desired rather than hoped to see characteristic of his own country; and in Solomon's House we have Bacon the scientist indulging without restriction his prophetic vision of the future of human knowledge. No reader acquainted in any degree with the processes and results of modern scientific inquiry can fail to be struck by the numerous approximations made by Bacon's imagination to the actual achievements of modern times. The plan and organization of his great college lay down the main lines of the modern research university; and both in pure and applied science he anticipates a strikingly large number of recent inventions and discoveries. In still another way is "The New Atlantis" typical of Bacon's attitude. In spite of the enthusiastic and broad-minded schemes he laid down for the pursuit of truth, Bacon always had an eye to utility. The advancement of science which he sought was conceived by him as a means to a practical end—the increase of man's control over nature, and the comfort and convenience of humanity. For pure metaphysics, or any form of abstract thinking that yielded no "fruit," he had little interest; and this leaning to the useful is shown in the practical applications of the discoveries made by the scholars of Solomon's House. Nor does the interest of the work stop here. It contains much, both in its political and in its scientific ideals, that we have as yet by no means achieved, but which contain valuable elements of suggestion and stimulus for the future.

THE NEW ATLANTIS

WE SAILED from Peru, (where we had continued by the space of one whole year,) for China and Japan, by the South Sea; taking with us victuals for twelve months; and had good winds from the east, though soft and weak, for five months space, and more. But then the wind came about, and settled in the west for many days, so as we could make little or no way, and were sometimes in purpose to turn back. But then again there arose strong and great winds from the south, with a point east, which carried us up (for all that we could do), towards the north; by which time our victuals failed us, though we had made good spare of them. So that finding ourselves, in the midst of the greatest wilderness of waters in the world, without victuals, we gave ourselves for lost men and prepared for death. Yet we did lift up our hearts and voices to God above, who *showeth his wonders in the deep,* beseeching him of his mercy, that as in the beginning he discovered the face of the deep, and brought forth dry land, so he would now discover land to us, that we might not perish.

And it came to pass that the next day about evening, we saw within a kenning[1] before us, towards the north, as it were thick clouds, which did put us in some hope of land; knowing how that part of the South Sea was utterly unknown; and might have islands, or continents, that hitherto were not come to light. Wherefore we bent our course thither, where we saw the appearance of land, all that night; and in the dawning of the next day, we might plainly discern that it was a land; flat to our sight, and full of boscage;[2] which made it show the more dark. And after an hour and a half's sailing, we entered into a good haven, being the port of a fair city; not great indeed, but well built, and that gave a pleasant view from the sea: and we thinking every minute long, till we were on land, came close to the shore, and offered to land. But straightways we saw divers of the people, with bastons[3] in their hands (as it were)

[1] Within sight.   [2] Woods.   [3] Staves.

forbidding us to land; yet without any cries of fierceness, but only as warning us off, by signs that they made. Whereupon being not a little discomforted,[4] we were advising with ourselves, what we should do.

During which time, there made forth to us a small boat, with about eight persons in it; whereof one of them had in his hand a tipstaff of a yellow cane, tipped at both ends with blue, who came aboard our ship, without any show of distrust at all. And when he saw one of our number, present himself somewhat before the rest, he drew forth a little scroll of parchment (somewhat yellower than our parchment, and shining like the leaves of writing tables, but otherwise soft and flexible,) and delivered it to our foremost man. In which scroll were written in ancient Hebrew, and in ancient Greek, and in good Latin of the school,[5] and in Spanish, these words: *Land ye not, none of you; and provide to be gone, from this coast, within sixteen days, except you have further time given you. Meanwhile, if you want fresh water or victuals, or help for your sick, or that your ship needeth repairs, write down your wants, and you shall have that, which belongeth to mercy.* This scroll was signed with a stamp of cherubim's wings, not spread, but hanging downwards; and by them a cross. This being delivered, the officer returned, and left only a servant with us to receive our answer.

Consulting hereupon amongst ourselves, we were much perplexed. The denial of landing and hasty warning us away troubled us much; on the other side, to find that the people had languages, and were so full of humanity, did comfort us not a little. And above all, the sign of the cross to that instrument was to us a great rejoicing, and as it were a certain presage of good. Our answer was in the Spanish tongue; *That for our ship, it was well; for we had rather met with calms and contrary winds than any tempests. For our sick, they were many, and in very ill case; so that if they were not permitted to land, they ran danger of their lives.* Our other wants we set down in particular; adding, *That we had some little store of merchandise, which if it pleased them to deal for, it might supply our wants, without being chargeable unto them.* We offered some re-

---

[4] Discouraged.   [5] Academic, as opposed to popular, Latin.

ward in pistolets[6] unto the servant, and a piece of crimson velvet to be presented to the officer; but the servant took them not, nor would scarce look upon them; and so left us, and went back in another little boat, which was sent for him.

About three hours after we had dispatched our answer, there came towards us a person (as it seemed) of place. He had on him a gown with wide sleeves, of a kind of water chamolet,[7] of an excellent azure colour, far more glossy than ours; his under apparel was green; and so was his hat, being in the form of a turban, daintily made, and not so huge as the Turkish turbans; and the locks of his hair came down below the brims of it. A reverend man was he to behold. He came in a boat, gilt in some part of it, with four persons more only in that boat; and was followed by another boat, wherein were some twenty. When he was come within a flightshot[8] of our ship, signs were made to us, that we should send forth some to meet him upon the water; which we presently did in our ship-boat, sending the principal man amongst us save one, and four of our number with him.

When we were come within six yards of their boat, they called to us to stay, and not to approach farther; which we did. And thereupon the man, whom I before described, stood up, and with a loud voice, in Spanish, asked, "Are ye Christians?" We answered, "We were;" fearing the less, because of the cross we had seen in the subscription. At which answer the said person lifted up his right hand towards Heaven, and drew it softly to his mouth (which is the gesture they use, when they thank God;) and then said: "If ye will swear (all of you) by the merits of the Saviour, that ye are no pirates, nor have shed blood, lawfully, nor unlawfully within forty days past, you may have licence to come on land." We said, "We were all ready to take that oath." Whereupon one of those that were with him, being (as it seemed) a notary, made an entry of this act. Which done, another of the attendants of the great person which was with him in the same boat, after his Lord had spoken a little to him, said aloud: "My Lord would have you know, that it is not of pride, or greatness, that he cometh not aboard your ship; but for

---

[6] Pistoles, Spanish gold coins.   [7] Camlet with a wavy surface.
[8] A flight was a light arrow.

that in your answer you declare that you have many sick amongst you, he was warned by the Conservator of Health of the city that he should keep a distance." We bowed ourselves towards him, and answered, "We were his humble servants; and accounted for great honour, and singular humanity towards us, that which was already done; but hoped well, that the nature of the sickness of our men was not infectious." So he returned; and a while after came the Notary to us aboard our ship; holding in his hand a fruit of that country, like an orange, but of color between orange-tawney and scarlet; which cast a most excellent odour. He used it (as it seemeth) for a preservative against infection. He gave us our oath; "By the name of Jesus, and his merits:" and after told us, that the next day, by six of the Clock, in the Morning, we should be sent to, and brought to the Strangers' House, (so he called it,) where we should be accommodated of things, both for our whole, and for our sick. So he left us; and when we offered him some pistolets, he smiling said, "He must not be twice paid for one labour:" meaning (as I take it) that he had salary sufficient of the State for his service. For (as I after learned) they call an officer that taketh rewards, *twice paid*.

The next morning early, there came to us the same officer that came to us at first with his cane, and told us, "He came to conduct us to the Strangers' House; and that he had prevented[9] the hour, because[10] we might have the whole day before us, for our business. For," he said, "if you will follow my advice, there shall first go with me some few of you, and see the place, and how it may be made convenient for you; and then you may send for your sick, and the rest of your number, which ye will bring on land." We thanked him, and said, "That this care, which he took of desolate strangers, God would reward." And so six of us went on land with him: and when we were on land, he went before us, and turned to us, and said, "He was but our servant, and our guide." He led us through three fair streets; and all the way we went, there were gathered some people on both sides, standing in a row; but in so civil a fashion, as if it had been, not to wonder at us, but to welcome us: and divers of them, as we passed by them, put their arms a little abroad;[11] which is their gesture, when they did bid any welcome.

[9] Come before.   [10] In order that.   [11] Stretched out.

The Strangers' House is a fair and spacious house, built of brick, of somewhat a bluer colour than our brick; and with handsome windows, some of glass, some of a kind of cambric oiled. He brought us first into a fair parlour above stairs, and then asked us, "What number of persons we were? And how many sick?" We answered, "We were in all, (sick and whole,) one and fifty persons, whereof our sick were seventeen." He desired us to have patience a little, and to stay till he came back to us; which was about an hour after; and then he led us to see the chambers which were provided for us, being in number nineteen: they having cast[12] it (as it seemeth) that four of those chambers, which were better than the rest, might receive four of the principal men of our company; and lodge them alone by themselves; and the other fifteen chambers were to lodge us two and two together. The chambers were handsome and cheerful chambers, and furnished civilly.[13] Then he led us to a long gallery, like a dorture,[14] where he showed us all along the one side (for the other side was but wall and window), seventeen cells, very neat ones, having partitions of cedar wood. Which gallery and cells, being in all forty, (many more than we needed,) were instituted as an infirmary for sick persons. And he told us withal, that as any of our sick waxed well, he might be removed from his cell, to a chamber; for which purpose there were set forth ten spare chambers, besides the number we spake of before. This done, he brought us back to the parlour, and lifting up his cane a little, (as they do when they give any charge or command) said to us, "Ye are to know, that the custom of the land requireth, that after this day and to-morrow, (which we give you for removing of your people from your ship,) you are to keep within doors for three days. But let it not trouble you, nor do not think yourselves restrained, but rather left to your rest and ease. You shall want nothing, and there are six of our people appointed to attend you, for any business you may have abroad." We gave him thanks, with all affection and respect, and said, "God surely is manifested in this land." We offered him also twenty pistolets; but he smiled, and only said; "What? twice paid!" And so he left us.

Soon after our dinner was served in; which was right good

[12] Planned.   [13] Respectably.   [14] Dormitory.

viands, both for bread and meat; better than any collegiate diet, that I have known in Europe. We had also drink of three sorts, all wholesome and good; wine of the grape; a drink of grain, such as is with us our ale, but more clear: And a kind of cider made of a fruit of that country; a wonderful pleasing and refreshing drink. Besides, there were brought in to us, great store of those scarlet oranges, for our sick; which (they said) were an assured remedy for sickness taken at sea. There was given us also, a box of small gray, or whitish pills, which they wished our sick should take, one of the pills, every night before sleep; which (they said) would hasten their recovery.

The next day, after that our trouble of carriage and removing of our men and goods out of our ship, was somewhat settled and quiet, I thought good to call our company together; and when they were assembled, said unto them; "My dear friends, let us know ourselves, and how it standeth with us. We are men cast on land, as Jonas was, out of the whale's belly, when we were as buried in the deep: and now we are on land, we are but between death and life; for we are beyond, both the old world, and the new; and whether ever we shall see Europe, God only knoweth. It is a kind of miracle hath brought us hither: and it must be little less, that shall bring us hence. Therefore in regard of our deliverance past, and our danger present, and to come, let us look up to God, and every man reform his own ways. Besides we are come here amongst a Christian people, full of piety and humanity: let us not bring that confusion of face upon ourselves, as to show our vices, or unworthiness before them. Yet there is more. For they have by commandment, (though in form of courtesy) cloistered us within these walls, for three days: who knoweth, whether it be not, to take some taste of our manners and conditions?[15] and if they find them bad, to banish us straightways; if good, to give us further time. For these men that they have given us for attendance, may withal have an eye upon us. Therefore for God's love, and as we love the weal of our souls and bodies, let us so behave ourselves, as we may be at peace with God, and may find grace in the eyes of this people." Our company with one voice thanked me for my good admonition, and promised me

[15] Dispositions.

to live soberly and civilly, and without giving any the least occasion of offence. So we spent our three days joyfully, and without care, in expectation what would be done with us, when they were expired. During which time, we had every hour joy of the amendment of our sick; who thought themselves cast into some divine pool of healing; they mended so kindly,[16] and so fast.

The morrow after our three days were past, there came to us a new man, that we had not seen before, clothed in blue as the former was, save that his turban was white, with a small red cross on the top. He had also a tippet of fine linen. At his coming in, he did bend to us a little, and put his arms abroad. We of our parts saluted him in a very lowly and submissive manner; as looking that from him, we should receive sentence of life, or death: he desired to speak with some few of us: whereupon six of us only staid, and the rest avoided[17] the room. He said, "I am by office governor of this House of Strangers, and by vocation I am a Christian priest: and therefore am come to you to offer you my service, both as strangers and chiefly as Christians. Some things I may tell you, which I think you will not be unwilling to hear. The State hath given you license to stay on land, for the space of six weeks; and let it not trouble you, if your occasions ask further time, for the law in this point is not precise; and I do not doubt, but my self shall be able, to obtain for you such further time, as may be convenient. Ye shall also understand, that the Strangers' House is at this time rich, and much aforehand; for it hath laid up revenue these thirty-seven years; for so long it is since any stranger arrived in this part: and therefore take ye no care; the State will defray[18] you all the time you stay; neither shall you stay one day the less for that. As for any merchandise ye have brought, ye shall be well used, and have your return, either in merchandise, or in gold and silver: for to us it is all one. And if you have any other request to make, hide it not. For ye shall find we will not make your countenance to fall by the answer ye shall receive. Only this I must tell you, that none of you must go above a *karan*," (that is with them a mile and an half) "from the walls of the city, without especial leave."

We answered, after we had looked awhile one upon another,

[16] Naturally.   [17] Left.   [18] Pay expenses.

admiring[19] this gracious and parent-like usage; "That we could not tell what to say: for we wanted words to express our thanks; and his noble free offers left us nothing to ask. It seemed to us, that we had before us a picture of our salvation in Heaven; for we that were a while since in the jaws of death, were now brought into a place, where we found nothing but consolations. For the commandment laid upon us, we would not fail to obey it, though it was impossible but our hearts should be enflamed to tread further upon this happy and holy ground." We added; "That our tongues should first cleave to the roofs of our mouths, ere we should forget, either his reverend person, or this whole nation, in our prayers." We also most humbly besought him, to accept of us as his true servants, by as just a right as ever men on earth were bounden; laying and presenting, both our persons, and all we had, at his feet. He said; "He was a priest, and looked for a priest's reward; which was our brotherly love, and the good of our souls and bodies." So he went from us, not without tears of tenderness in his eyes; and left us also confused with joy and kindness, saying amongst ourselves; "That we were come into a land of angels, which did appear to us daily, and present us with comforts, which we thought not of, much less expected."

The next day about ten of the clock, the Governor came to us again, and after salutations, said familiarly; "That he was come to visit us;" and called for a chair, and sat him down: and we, being some ten of us, (the rest were of the meaner sort, or else gone abroad,) sat down with him. And when we were set, he began thus: "We of this island of Bensalem," (for so they call it in their language,) "have this; that by means of our solitary situation; and of the laws of secrecy, which we have for our travellers, and our rare admission of strangers; we know well most part of the habitable world, and are ourselves unknown. Therefore because he that knoweth least is fittest to ask questions, it is more reason, for the entertainment of the time, that ye ask me questions, than that I ask you."

We answered; "That we humbly thanked him that he would give us leave so to do: and that we conceived by the taste we had already, that there was no worldly thing on earth, more worthy to

[19] Wondering at.

be known than the state of that happy land. But above all," (we said,) "since that we were met from the several ends of the world, and hoped assuredly that we should meet one day in the kingdom of Heaven, (for that we were both parts Christians,) we desired to know, (in respect that land was so remote, and so divided by vast and unknown seas, from the land where our Saviour walked on earth,) who was the apostle of that nation, and how it was converted to the faith?" It appeared in his face that he took great contentment in this our question: he said; "Ye knit my heart to you, by asking this question in the first place; for it sheweth that you *first seek the kingdom of heaven;* and I shall gladly, and briefly, satisfy your demand.

"About twenty years after the ascension of our Saviour, it came to pass, that there was seen by the people of Renfusa, (a city upon the eastern coast of our island,) within night, (the night was cloudy, and calm,) as it might be some mile into the sea, a great pillar of light; not sharp, but in form of a column, or cylinder, rising from the sea a great way up towards heaven; and on the top of it was seen a large cross of light, more bright and resplendent than the body of the pillar. Upon which so strange a spectacle, the people of the city gathered apace together upon the sands, to wonder; and so after put themselves into a number of small boats, to go nearer to this marvellous sight. But when the boats were come within (about) sixty yards of the pillar, they found themselves all bound, and could go no further; yet so as they might move to go about, but might not approach nearer: so as the boats stood all as in a theatre, beholding this light as an heavenly sign. It so fell out, that there was in one of the boats one of the wise men, of the society of Salomon's House; which house, or college (my good brethren) is the very eye of this kingdom; who having awhile attentively and devoutly viewed and contemplated this pillar and cross, fell down upon his face; and then raised himself upon his knees, and lifting up his hands to heaven, made his prayers in this manner.

" 'LORD God of heaven and earth, thou hast vouchsafed of thy grace to those of our order, to know thy works of Creation, and the secrets of them: and to discern (as far as appertaineth to the generations of men) between divine miracles, works of nature, works of art, and impostures and illusions of all sorts. I do here acknowledge and testify before this people, that the thing which we now see before our eyes is thy Finger and a true Miracle. And forasmuch as we learn in our books that thou never workest miracles, but to a divine and excellent end, (for the laws of nature are thine own laws, and thou exceedest them not but upon great cause,) we most humbly beseech thee to prosper this great sign, and to give us the interpretation and use of it in mercy; which thou dost in some part secretly promise by sending it unto us.'

"When he had made his prayer, he presently found the boat he was in, moveable and unbound; whereas all the rest remained still fast; and taking that for an assurance of leave to approach, he caused the boat to be softly and with silence rowed towards the pillar. But ere he came near it, the pillar and cross of light brake up, and cast itself abroad, as it were, into a firmament of many stars; which also vanished soon after, and there was nothing left to be seen, but a small ark, or chest of cedar, dry, and not wet at all with water, though it swam. And in the fore-end of it, which was towards him, grew a small green branch of palm; and when the wise man had taken it, with all reverence, into his boat, it opened of itself, and there were found in it a Book and a Letter; both written in fine parchment, and wrapped in sindons[20] of linen. The Book contained all the canonical books of the Old and New Testament, according as you have them; (for we know well what the churches with you receive); and the Apocalypse itself, and some other books of the New Testament, which were not at that time written, were nevertheless in the Book. And for the Letter, it was in these words:

" 'I Bartholomew, a servant of the Highest, and Apostle of Jesus Christ, was warned by an angel that appeareth to me, in a vision of glory, that I should commit this ark to the floods of the sea. Therefore I do testify and declare unto that people where God shall ordain this ark to come to land, that in the same day is come unto them salvation and peace and good-will, from the Father, and from the Lord Jesus.'

"There was also in both these writings, as well the Book, as the Letter, wrought a great miracle, conform[21] to that of the Apostles, in the original Gift of Tongues. For there being at that time in this land Hebrews, Persians, and Indians, besides the natives, every

[20] Pieces.   [21] Similar.

one read upon the Book, and Letter, as if they had been written in his own language. And thus was this land saved from infidelity (as the remainder of the old world was from water) by an ark, through the apostolical and miraculous evangelism of Saint Bartholomew." And here he paused, and a messenger came, and called him from us. So this was all that passed in that conference.

The next day, the same governor came again to us, immediately after dinner, and excused himself, saying: "That the day before he was called from us, somewhat abruptly, but now he would make us amends, and spend time with us if we held his company and conference agreeable." We answered, "That we held it so agreeable and pleasing to us, as we forgot both dangers past and fears to come, for the time we hear him speak; and that we thought an hour spent with him, was worth years of our former life." He bowed himself a little to us, and after we were set again, he said; "Well, the questions are on your part."

One of our number said, after a little pause; that there was a matter, we were no less desirous to know, than fearful to ask, lest we might presume too far. But encouraged by his rare humanity towards us, (that could scarce think ourselves strangers, being his vowed and professed servants,) we would take the hardiness to propound it: humbly beseeching him, if he thought it not fit to be answered, that he would pardon it, though he rejected it. We said; "We well observed those his words, which he formerly spake, that this happy island, where we now stood, was known to few, and yet knew most of the nations of the world; which we found to be true, considering they had the languages of Europe, and knew much of our state and business; and yet we in Europe, (notwithstanding all the remote discoveries and navigations of this last age), never heard of the least inkling or glimpse of this island. This we found wonderful strange; for that all nations have inter-knowledge one of another, either by voyage into foreign parts, or by strangers that come to them: and though the traveller into a foreign country, doth commonly know more by the eye, than he that stayeth at home can by relation of the traveller; yet both ways suffice to make a mutual knowledge, in some degree, on both parts. But for this island, we never heard tell of any ship of theirs that had been seen to arrive upon any shore of Europe; nor of either the East or West Indies; nor yet of any ship of any other part of the world, that had made return from them. And yet the marvel rested not in this. For the situation of it (as his lordship said) in the secret conclave[23] of such a vast sea might cause it. But then, that they should have knowledge of the languages, books, affairs, of those that lie such a distance from them, it was a thing we could not tell what to make of; for that it seemed to us a condition[24] and propriety[25] of divine powers and beings, to be hidden and unseen to others, and yet to have others open and as in a light to them."

At this speech the Governor gave a gracious smile, and said; "That we did well to ask pardon for this question we now asked: for that it imported, as if we thought this land, a land of magicians, that sent forth spirits of the air into all parts, to bring them news and intelligence of other countries." It was answered by us all, in all possible humbleness, but yet with a countenance taking knowledge, that we knew that he spake it but merrily, "That we were apt enough to think there was somewhat supernatural in this island; but yet rather as angelical than magical. But to let his lordship know truly what it was that made us tender and doubtful to ask this question, it was not any such conceit,[26] but because we remembered, he had given a touch[27] in his former speech, that this land had laws of secrecy touching strangers." To this he said; "You remember it aright and therefore in that I shall say to you, I must reserve some particulars, which it is not lawful for me to reveal; but there will be enough left, to give you satisfaction.

"You shall understand (that which perhaps you will scarce think credible) that about three thousand years ago, or somewhat more, the navigation of the world, (especially for remote voyages,) was greater than at this day. Do not think with yourselves, that I know not how much it is increased with you, within these six-score years: I know it well: and yet I say greater then than now; whether it was, that the example of the ark, that saved the remnant of men from the universal deluge, gave men confidence to adventure upon the waters; or what it was; but such is the truth. The Phœnicians, and especially the Tyrians, had great fleets. So had the Cartha-

[23] Private room.   [24] Property.   [25] Quality.   [26] Idea.   [27] Hint.

ginians their colony, which is yet further west. Toward the east the shipping of Egypt and of Palestina was likewise great. China also, and the great Atlantis, (that you call America,) which have now but junks and canoes, abounded then in tall ships. This island, (as appeareth by faithful registers of those times,) had then fifteen hundred strong ships, of great content. Of all this, there is with you sparing memory, or none; but we have large knowledge thereof.

"At that time, this land was known and frequented by the ships and vessels of all the nations before named. And (as it cometh to pass) they had many times men of other countries, that were no sailors, that came with them; as Persians, Chaldeans, Arabians; so as almost all nations of might and fame resorted hither; of whom we have some stirps,[28] and little tribes with us at this day. And for our own ships, they went sundry voyages, as well to your straits, which you call the Pillars of Hercules, as to other parts in the Atlantic and Mediterrane Seas; as to Paguin, (which is the same with Cambaline,[29]) and Quinzy, upon the Oriental Seas, as far as to the borders of the East Tartary.

"At the same time, and an age after, or more, the inhabitants of the great Atlantis did flourish. For though the narration and description, which is made by a great man[30] with you; that the descendants of Neptune planted[31] there; and of the magnificent temple, palace, city, and hill; and the manifold streams of goodly navigable rivers, (which as so many chains environed the same site and temple); and the several degrees of ascent, whereby men did climb up to the same, as if it had been a *scala cœli*,[32] be all poetical and fabulous: yet so much is true, that the said country of Atlantis, as well that of Peru, then called Coya, as that of Mexico, then named Tyrambel, were mighty and proud kingdoms in arms, shipping and riches: so mighty, as at one time (or at least within the space of ten years) they both made two great expeditions; they of Tyrambel through the Atlantic to the Mediterrane Sea; and they of Coya through the South Sea upon this our island: and for the former of these, which was into Europe, the same author amongst you (as it

---

[28] Families. [29] Cambalu, Pekin. [30] Plato, in the "Critias." [31] Settled.
[32] Ladder to heaven.

seemeth) had some relation from the Egyptian priest whom he cited. For assuredly such a thing there was. But whether it were the ancient Athenians that had the glory of the repulse and resistance of those forces, I can say nothing: but certain it is, there never came back either ship or man from that voyage. Neither had the other voyage of those of Coya upon us had better fortune, if they had not met with enemies of greater clemency. For the king of this island, (by name Altabin,) a wise man and a great warrior, knowing well both his own strength and that of his enemies, handled the matter so, as he cut off their land-forces from their ships; and entoiled[33] both their navy and their camp with a greater power than theirs, both by sea and land: and compelled them to render themselves without striking stroke: and after they were at his mercy, contenting himself only with their oath that they should no more bear arms against him, dismissed them all in safety.

"But the divine revenge overtook not long after those proud enterprises. For within less than the space of one hundred years, the great Atlantis was utterly lost and destroyed: not by a great earthquake, as your man saith; (for that whole tract is little subject to earthquakes;) but by a particular[34] deluge or inundation; those countries having, at this day, far greater rivers and far higher mountains to pour down waters, than any part of the old world. But it is true that the same inundation was not deep; not past forty foot, in most places, from the ground; so that although it destroyed man and beast generally, yet some few wild inhabitants of the wood escaped. Birds also were saved by flying to the high trees and woods. For as for men, although they had buildings in many places, higher than the depth of the water, yet that inundation, though it were shallow, had a long continuance; whereby they of the vale that were not drowned, perished for want of food and other things necessary.

"So as marvel you not at the thin population of America, nor at the rudeness and ignorance of the people; for you must account your inhabitants of America as a young people; younger a thousand years, at the least, than the rest of the world: for that there was so

[33] Ensnared.   [34] Partial.

much time between the universal flood and their particular inundation. For the poor remnant of human seed, which remained in their mountains, peopled the country again slowly, by little and little; and being simple and savage people, (not like Noah and his sons, which was the chief family of the earth,) they were not able to leave letters, arts, and civility[35] to their posterity; and having likewise in their mountainous habitations been used (in respect of the extreme cold of those regions) to clothe themselves with the skins of tigers, bears, and great hairy goats, that they have in those parts; when after they came down into the valley, and found the intolerable heats which are there, and knew no means of lighter apparel, they were forced to begin the custom of going naked, which continueth at this day. Only they take great pride and delight in the feathers of birds; and this also they took from those their ancestors of the mountains, who were invited unto it by the infinite flights of birds that came up to the high grounds, while the waters stood below. So you see, by this main accident of time, we lost our traffic with the Americans, with whom of all others, in regard they lay nearest to us, we had most commerce.

"As for the other parts of the world, it is most manifest that in the ages following (whether it were in respect of wars, or by a natural revolution of time,) navigation did every where greatly decay; and specially far voyages (the rather by the use of galleys, and such vessels as could hardly brook the ocean,) were altogether left and omitted. So then, that part of intercourse which could be from other nations to sail to us, you see how it hath long since ceased; except it were by some rare accident, as this of yours. But now of the cessation of that other part of intercourse, which might be by our sailing to other nations, I must yield you some other cause. For I cannot say (if I shall say truly,) but our shipping, for number, strength, mariners, pilots, and all things that appertain to navigation, is as great as ever; and therefore why we should sit at home, I shall now give you an account by itself: and it will draw nearer to give you satisfaction to your principal question.

"There reigned in this land, about nineteen hundred years ago, a king, whose memory of all others we most adore; not superstitiously,

---

[35] Civilization.

but as a divine instrument, though a mortal man; his name was Solamona: and we esteem him as the lawgiver of our nation. This king had a *large heart,* inscrutable for good; and was wholly bent to make his kingdom and people happy. He therefore, taking into consideration how sufficient and substantive[36] this land was to maintain itself without any aid (at all) of the foreigner; being five thousand six hundred miles in circuit, and of rare fertility of soil in the greatest part thereof; and finding also the shipping of this country might be plentifully set on work, both by fishing and by transportations from port to port, and likewise by sailing unto some small islands that are not far from us, and are under the crown and laws of this state; and recalling into his memory the happy and flourishing estate wherein this land then was; so as it might be a thousand ways altered to the worse, but scarce any one way to the better; though nothing wanted to his noble and heroical intentions, but only (as far as human foresight might reach) to give perpetuity to that which was in his time so happily established. Therefore amongst his other fundamental laws of this kingdom, he did ordain the interdicts and prohibitions which we have touching entrance of strangers; which at that time (though it was after the calamity of America) was frequent; doubting[37] novelties, and commixture of manners. It is true, the like law against the admission of strangers without licence is an ancient law in the kingdom of China, and yet continued in use. But there it is a poor thing; and hath made them a curious, ignorant, fearful, foolish nation. But our lawgiver made his law of another temper. For first, he hath preserved all points of humanity, in taking order and making provision for the relief of strangers distressed; whereof you have tasted."

At which speech (as reason was) we all rose up and bowed ourselves. He went on.

"That king also, still desiring to join humanity and policy together; and thinking it against humanity, to detain strangers here against their wills, and against policy that they should return and discover their knowledge of this estate, he took this course: he did ordain that of the strangers that should be permitted to land, as many (at all times) might depart as would; but as many as would

[36] Self-sufficing.   [37] Fearing.

stay should have very good conditions and means to live from the state. Wherein he saw so far, that now in so many ages since the prohibition, we have memory not of one ship that ever returned, and but of thirteen persons only, at several times, that chose to return in our bottoms. What those few that returned may have reported abroad I know not. But you must think, whatsoever they have said could be taken where they came but for a dream. Now for our travelling from hence into parts abroad, our Lawgiver thought fit altogether to restrain it. So is it not in China. For the Chinese sail where they will or can; which sheweth that their law of keeping out strangers is a law of pusillanimity and fear. But this restraint of ours hath one only exception, which is admirable; preserving the good which cometh by communicating with strangers, and avoiding the hurt; and I will now open it to you. And here I shall seem a little to digress, but you will by and by find it pertinent.

"Ye shall understand (my dear friends) that amongst the excellent acts of that king, one above all hath the pre-eminence. It was the erection and institution of an Order or Society, which we call *Salomon's House;* the noblest foundation (as we think) that ever was upon the earth; and the lanthorn of this kingdom. It is dedicated to the study of the works and creatures of God. Some think it beareth the founder's name a little corrupted, as if it should be Solamona's House. But the records write it as it is spoken. So as I take it to be denominate of[38] the king of the Hebrews, which is famous with you, and no stranger to us. For we have some parts of his works, which with you are lost; namely, that natural history, which he wrote, of all plants, from the *cedar of Libanus* to the *moss that groweth out of the wall,* and of all *things that have life and motion.* This maketh me think that our king, finding himself to symbolize[39] in many things with that king of the Hebrews (which lived many years before him), honored him with the title of this foundation. And I am rather induced to be of this opinion, for that I find in ancient records this Order or Society is sometimes called Salomon's House, and sometimes the College of the Six Days Works; whereby I am satisfied that our excellent king had learned from the Hebrews that God had created the world and all that therein is within six

[38] Named after.   [39] Agree.

days: and therefore he instituting that House for the finding out of the true nature of all things, (whereby God might have the more glory in the workmanship of them, and men the more fruit in the use of them), did give it also that second name.

"But now to come to our present purpose. When the king had forbidden to all his people navigation into any part that was not under his crown, he made nevertheless this ordinance; that every twelve years there should be set forth, out of this kingdom two ships, appointed to several voyages; That in either of these ships there should be a mission of three of the Fellows or Brethren of Salomon's House; whose errand was only to give us knowledge of the affairs and state of those countries to which they were designed, and especially of the sciences, arts, manufactures, and inventions of all the world; and withal to bring unto us books, instruments, and patterns in every kind: That the ships, after they had landed the brethren, should return; and that the brethren should stay abroad till the new mission. These ships are not otherwise fraught, than with store of victuals, and good quantity of treasure to remain with the brethren, for the buying of such things and rewarding of such persons as they should think fit. Now for me to tell you how the vulgar sort of mariners are contained[40] from being discovered at land; and how they that must be put on shore for any time, color themselves under the names of other nations; and to what places these voyages have been designed; and what places of rendezvous are appointed for the new missions; and the like circumstances of the practique; I may not do it: neither is it much to your desire. But thus you see we maintain a trade not for gold, silver, or jewels; nor for silks; nor for spices; nor any other commodity of matter; but only for God's first creature, which was Light: to have *light* (I say) of the growth of[41] all parts of the world."

And when he had said this, he was silent; and so were we all. For indeed we were all astonished to hear so strange things so probably told. And he, perceiving that we were willing to say somewhat but had it not ready in great courtesy took us off, and descended to ask us questions of our voyage and fortunes and in the end concluded, that we might do well to think with ourselves what

[40] Prevented.   [41] Produced in.

time of stay we would demand of the state; and bade us not to scant ourselves; for he would procure such time as we desired. Whereupon we all rose up, and presented ourselves[42] to kiss the skirt of his tippet; but he would not suffer us; and so took his leave. But when it came once amongst our people that the state used to offer conditions to strangers that would stay, we had work enough to get any of our men to look to our ship; and to keep them from going presently to the governor to crave conditions. But with much ado we refrained them, till we might agree what course to take.

We took ourselves now for free men, seeing there was no danger of our utter perdition; and lived most joyfully, going abroad and seeing what was to be seen in the city and places adjacent within our tedder; and obtaining acquaintance with many of the city, not of the meanest quality; at whose hands we found such humanity, and such a freedom and desire to take strangers as it were into their bosom, as was enough to make us forget all that was dear to us in our own countries: and continually we met with many things right worthy of observation and relation: as indeed, if there be a mirror in the world worthy to hold men's eyes, it is that country.

One day there were two of our company bidden to a Feast of the Family, as they call it. A most natural, pious, and reverend custom it is, shewing that nation to be compounded of all goodness. This is the manner if it. It is granted to any man that shall live to see thirty persons descended of his body alive together, and all above three years old, to make this feast which is done at the cost of the state. The Father of the Family, whom they call the *Tirsan,* two days before the feast, taketh to him three of such friends as he liketh to choose; and is assisted[43] also by the governor of the city or place where the feast is celebrated; and all the persons of the family, of both sexes, are summoned to attend him. These two days the Tirsan sitteth in consultation concerning the good estate of the family. There, if there be any discord or suits between any of the family, they are compounded and appeased. There, if any of the family be distressed or decayed, order is taken for their relief and competent means to live. There, if any be subject to vice,

[42] Offered.   [43] Attended.

or take ill courses, they are reproved and censured. So likewise direction is given touching marriages, and the courses of life, which any of them should take, with divers other the like orders and advices. The governor assisteth, to the end to put in execution by his public authority the decrees and orders of the Tirsan, if they should be disobeyed; though that seldom needeth; such reverence and obedience they give to the order of nature. The Tirsan doth also then ever choose one man from among his sons, to live in house with him; who is called ever after the Son of the Vine. The reason will hereafter appear.

On the feast day, the father or Tirsan cometh forth after divine service into a large room where the feast is celebrated; which room hath an half-pace[44] at the upper end. Against the wall, in the middle of the half-pace, is a chair placed for him, with a table and carpet before it. Over the chair is a state,[45] made round or oval, and it is of ivy; an ivy somewhat whiter than ours, like the leaf of a silver asp,[46] but more shining; for it is green all winter. And the state is curiously wrought with silver and silk of divers colors, broiding[47] or binding in the ivy; and is ever of the work of some of the daughters of the family; and veiled over at the top with a fine net of silk and silver. But the substance of it is true ivy; whereof, after it is taken down, the friends of the family are desirous to have some leaf or sprig to keep.

The Tirsan cometh forth with all his generation or linage, the males before him, and the females following him; and if there be a mother from whose body the whole linage is descended, there is a traverse[48] placed in a loft above on the right hand of the chair, with a privy[49] door, and a carved window of glass, leaded with gold and blue; where she sitteth, but is not seen. When the Tirsan is come forth, he sitteth down in the chair; and all the linage place themselves against the wall, both at his back and upon the return[50] of the half-pace, in order of their years without difference of sex; and stand upon their feet. When he is set; the room being always full of company, but well kept and without disorder; after some pause, there cometh in from the lower end of the room, a *taratan*

---

[44] Dais, platform. [45] Canopy. [46] Aspen. [47] Interlacing. [48] Curtain.
[49] Private. [50] Side.

(which is as much as an herald) and on either side of him two young lads; whereof one carrieth a scroll of their shining yellow parchment; and the other a cluster of grapes of gold, with a long foot or stalk. The herald and children are clothed with mantles of seawater green satin; but the herald's mantle is streamed[51] with gold, and hath a train.

Then the herald with three curtesies, or rather inclinations, cometh up as far as the half-pace; and there first taketh into his hand the scroll. This scroll is the king's charter, containing gifts of revenew, and many privileges, exemptions, and points of honour, granted to the Father of the Family; and is ever styled and directed, *To such an one our well beloved friend and creditor:* which is a title proper only to this case. For they say the king is debtor to no man, but for propagation of his subjects. The seal set to the king's charter is the king's image, imbossed or moulded in gold; and though such charters be expedited[52] of course, and as of right, yet they are varied by discretion, according to the number and dignity of the family. This charter the herald readeth aloud; and while it is read, the father or Tirsan standeth up supported by two of his sons, such as he chooseth. Then the herald mounteth the half-pace and delivereth the charter into his hand: and with that there is an acclamation by all that are present in their language, which is thus much: *Happy are the people of Bensalem.*

Then the herald taketh into his hand from the other child the cluster of grapes, which is of gold, both the stalk and the grapes. But the grapes are daintily enamelled; and if the males of the family be the greater number, the grapes are enamelled purple, with a little sun set on the top; if the females, then they are enamelled into a greenish yellow, with a crescent on the top. The grapes are in number as many as there are descendants of the family. This golden cluster the herald delivereth also to the Tirsan; who presently delivereth it over to that son that he had formerly chosen to be in house with him: who beareth it before his father as an ensign of honour when he goeth in public, ever after; and is thereupon called the Son of the Vine.

After the ceremony endeth the father or Tirsan retireth; and

[51] Watered.   [52] Issued.

after some time cometh forth again to dinner, where he sitteth alone under the state, as before; and none of his descendants sit with him, of what degree or dignity soever, except he hap to be of Salomon's House. He is served only by his own children, such as are male; who perform unto him all service of the table upon the knee; and the women only stand about him, leaning against the wall. The room below the half-pace hath tables on the sides for the guests that are bidden; who are served with great and comely order; and towards the end of dinner (which in the greatest feasts with them lasteth never above an hour and an half) there is an hymn sung, varied according to the invention of him that composeth it (for they have excellent posy) but the subject of it is (always) the praises of Adam and Noah and Abraham; whereof the former two peopled the world, and the last was the Father of the Faithful: concluding ever with a thanksgiving for the nativity of our Saviour, in whose birth the births of all are only blessed.

Dinner being done, the Tirsan retireth again; and having withdrawn himself alone into a place, where he makes some private prayers, he cometh forth the third time, to give the blessing with all his descendants, who stand about him as at the first. Then he calleth them forth by one and by one, by name, as he pleaseth, though seldom the order of age be inverted. The person that is called (the table being before removed) kneeleth down before the chair, and the father layeth his hand upon his head, or her head, and giveth the blessing in these words: *Son of Bensalem,* (or *daughter of Bensalem,*) *thy father saith it: the man by whom thou hast breath and life speaketh the word: the blessing of the everlasting Father, the Prince of Peace, and the Holy Dove, be upon thee, and make the days of thy pilgrimage good and many.* This he saith to every of them; and that done, if there be any of his sons of eminent merit and virtue, (so they be not above two,) he calleth for them again; and saith, laying his arm over their shoulders, they standing; *Sons, it is well ye are born, give God the praise, and persevere to the end.* And withall delivereth to either of them a jewel, made in the figure[53] of an ear of wheat, which they ever after wear in the front of their turban or hat. This done, they fall to music and dances, and other

[53] Shape.

recreations, after their manner, for the rest of the day. This is the full order of that feast.

By that time six or seven days were spent, I was fallen into straight acquaintance with a merchant of that city, whose name was Joabin. He was a Jew and circumcised: for they have some few stirps[54] of Jews yet remaining among them, whom they leave to their own religion. Which they may the better do, because they are of a far differing disposition from the Jews in other parts. For whereas they hate the name of Christ; and have a secret inbred rancour against the people among whom they live: these (contrariwise) give unto our Saviour many high attributes, and love the nation of Bensalem extremely. Surely this man of whom I speak would ever acknowledge that Christ was born of a virgin and that he was more than a man; and he would tell how God made him ruler of the seraphims which guard his throne; and they call him also the *Milken Way,* and the *Eliah* of the *Messiah;* and many other high names; which though they be inferior to his divine majesty, yet they are far from the language of other Jews.

And for the country of Bensalem, this man would make no end of commending it; being desirous, by tradition among the Jews there, to have it believed that the people thereof were of the generations of Abraham, by another son, whom they call Nachoran; and that Moses by a secret Cabala ordained the Laws of Bensalem which they now use; and that when the Messiah should come, and sit in his throne at Hierusalem, the king of Bensalem should sit at his feet, whereas other kings should keep a great distance. But yet setting aside these Jewish dreams, the man was a wise man, and learned, and of great policy, and excellently seen in the laws and customs of that nation.

Amongst other discourses, one day I told him I was much affected with the relation I had, from some of the company, of their custom, in holding the Feast of the Family; for that (methought) I had never heard of a solemnity wherein nature did so much preside. And because propagation of families proceedeth from the nuptial copulation, I desired to know of him what laws and customs they had concerning marriage; and whether they kept marriage well

[54] Families, stocks.

and whether they were tied to one wife; for that where population is so much affected,[55] and such as with them it seemed to be, there is commonly permission of plurality of wives.

To this he said, "You have reason for to commend that excellent institution of the Feast of the Family. And indeed we have experience that those families that are partakers of the blessing of that feast do flourish and prosper ever after in an extraordinary manner. But hear me now, and I will tell you what I know. You shall understand that there is not under the heavens so chaste a nation as this of Bensalem; nor so free from all pollution or foulness. It is the virgin of the world. I remember I have read in one of your European books, of an holy hermit amongst you that desired to see the Spirit of Fornication; and there appeared to him a little foul ugly Æthiop. But if he had desired to see the Spirit of Chastity of Bensalem, it would have appeared to him in the likeness of a fair beautiful Cherubin. For there is nothing amongst mortal men more fair and admirable, than the chaste minds of this people. Know therefore, that with them there are no stews, no dissolute houses, no courtesans, nor anything of that kind. Nay they wonder (with detestation) at you in Europe, which permit such things. They say ye have put marriage out of office: for marriage is ordained a remedy for unlawful concupiscence; and natural concupiscence seemeth as a spur to marriage. But when men have at hand a remedy more agreeable to their corrupt will, marriage is almost expulsed. And therefore there are with you seen infinite men that marry not, but chuse rather a libertine and impure single life, than to be yoked in marriage; and many that do marry, marry late, when the prime and strength of their years is past. And when they do marry, what is marriage to them but a very bargain; wherein is sought alliance, or portion, or reputation, with some desire (almost indifferent) of issue; and not the faithful nuptial union of man and wife, that was first instituted. Neither is it possible that those that have cast away so basely so much of their strength, should greatly esteem children, (being of the same matter,) as chaste men do. So likewise during marriage, is the case much amended, as it ought to be if those things were tolerated only for necessity? No, but they remain still as a

---
[55] Desired.

very affront to marriage. The haunting of those dissolute places, or resort to courtesans, are no more punished in married men than in bachelors. And the depraved custom of change, and the delight in meretricious embracements, (where sin is turned into art,) maketh marriage a dull thing, and a kind of imposition or tax. They hear you defend these things, as done to avoid greater evils; as advoutries,[56] deflowering of virgins, unnatural lust, and the like. But they say this is a preposterous wisdom; and they call it *Lot's offer,* who to save his guests from abusing, offered his daughters: nay they say farther that there is little gained in this; for that the same vices and appetites do still remain and abound; unlawful lust being like a furnace, that if you stop the flames altogether, it will quench; but if you give it any vent, it will rage. As for masculine love, they have no touch of it; and yet there are not so faithful and inviolate friendships in the world again as are there; and to speak generally, (as I said before,) I have not read of any such chastity, in any people as theirs. And their usual saying is, *That whosoever is unchaste cannot reverence himself;* and they say, *That the reverence of a man's self, is, next religion, the chiefest bridle of all vices."*

And when he had said this, the good Jew paused a little; whereupon I, far more willing to hear him speak on than to speak myself, yet thinking it decent that upon his pause of speech I should not be altogether silent, said only this; "That I would say to him, as the widow of Sarepta said to Elias; that he was come to bring to memory our sins; and that I confess the righteousness of Bensalem was greater than the righteousness of Europe." At which speech he bowed his head, and went on in this manner:

"They have also many wise and excellent laws touching marriage. They allow no polygamy. They have ordained that none do intermarry or contract, until a month be past from their first interview. Marriage without consent of parents they do not make void, but they mulct[57] it in the inheritors: for the children of such marriages are not admitted to inherit above a third part of their parents' inheritance. I have read in a book of one of your men,[58] of a Feigned Commonwealth, where the married couple are permitted, before they contract, to see one another naked. This they dislike; for they

---

[56] Adulteries.   [57] Penalize.   [58] More's *Utopia*.

think it a scorn to give a refusal after so familiar knowledge: but because of many hidden defects in men and women's bodies, they have a more civil way; for they have near every town a couple of pools, (which they call *Adam and Eve's pools,*) where it is permitted to one of the friends of the men, and another of the friends of the woman, to see them severally bathe naked."

And as we were thus in conference, there came one that seemed to be a messenger, in a rich huke,[59] that spake with the Jew: whereupon he turned to me and said; "You will pardon me, for I am commanded away in haste." The next morning he came to me again, joyful as it seemed, and said; "There is word come to the Governor of the city, that one of the Fathers of Salomon's House will be here this day seven-night: we have seen none of them this dozen years. His coming is in state; but the cause of his coming is secret. I will provide you and your fellows of a good standing to see his entry." I thanked him, and told him, I was most glad of the news.

The day being come, he made his entry. He was a man of middle stature and age, comely of person, and had an aspect as if he pitied men. He was clothed in a robe of fine black cloth, with wide sleeves and a cape. His under garment was of excellent white linen down to the foot, girt with a girdle of the same; and a sindon or tippet of the same about his neck. He had gloves, that were curious,[60] and set with stone; and shoes of peach-coloured velvet. His neck was bare to the shoulders. His hat was like a helmet, or Spanish montera;[61] and his locks curled below it decently: they were of colour brown. His beard was cut round, and of the same colour with his hair, somewhat lighter. He was carried in a rich chariot, without wheels, litter-wise; with two horses at either end, richly trapped in blue velvet embroidered; and two footmen on each side in the like attire. The chariot was all of cedar, gilt, and adorned with crystal; save that the fore-end had panels of sapphires, set in borders of gold; and the hinder-end the like of emeralds of the Peru colour. There was also a sun of gold, radiant, upon the top, in the midst; and on the top before, a small cherub of gold, with wings dis-

---

[59] A cape with a hood.   [60] Of elaborate design.   [61] A cap with a round crown and flaps.

played.[62] The chariot was covered with cloth of gold tissued upon blue. He had before him fifty attendants, young men all, in white satin loose coats to the mid leg; and stockings of white silk; and shoes of blue velvet; and hats of blue velvet; with fine plumes of diverse colours, set round like hat-bands. Next before the chariot, went two men, bare-headed, in linen garments down the foot, girt, and shoes of blue velvet; who carried, the one a crosier, the other a pastoral staff like a sheep-hook; neither of them of metal, but the crosier of balm-wood,[63] the pastoral staff of cedar. Horsemen he had none, neither before nor behind his chariot: as it seemeth, to avoid all tumult and trouble. Behind his chariot went all the officers and principals of the companies of the city. He sat alone, upon cushions of a kind of excellent plush, blue; and under his foot curious carpets of silk of diverse colours, like the Persian, but far finer. He held up his bare hand as he went, as blessing the people, but in silence. The street was wonderfully well kept: so that there was never any army had their men stand in better battle-array than the people stood. The windows likewise were not crowded, but everyone stood in them as if they had been placed.

When the shew was past, the Jew said to me; "I shall not be able to attend you as I would, in regard of some charge the city hath laid upon me, for the entertaining of this great person." Three days after the Jew came to me again, and said; "Ye are happy men; for the Father of Salomon's House taketh knowledge of your being here, and commanded me to tell you that he will admit all your company to his presence, and have private conference with one of you, that ye shall choose: and for this hath appointed the next day after to-morrow. And because he meaneth to give you his blessing, he hath appointed it in the forenoon.

We came at our day and hour, and I was chosen by my fellows for the private access. We found him in a fair chamber, richly hanged, and carpeted under foot, without any degrees[64] to the state.[65] He was set upon a low Throne richly adorned, and a rich cloth of state[66] over his head, of blue satin embroidered. He was alone, save that he had two pages of honour, on either hand one, finely attired

---

[62] Spread.   [63] Balsam.   [64] Steps.   [65] Throne.   [66] Canopy.

in white. His undergarments were the like that we saw him wear in the chariot; but instead of his gown, he had on him a mantle with a cape, of the same fine black, fastened about him. When we came in, as we were taught, we bowed low at our first entrance; and when we were come near his chair, he stood up, holding forth his hand ungloved, and in posture of blessing; and we every one of us stooped down, and kissed the hem of his tippet. That done, the rest departed, and I remained. Then he warned [67] the pages forth of the room, and caused me to sit down beside him, and spake to me thus in the Spanish tongue.

"God bless thee, my son; I will give thee the greatest jewel I have. For I will impart unto thee, for the love of God and men, a relation of the true state of Salomon's House. Son, to make you know the true state of Salomon's House, I will keep this order. First, I will set forth unto you the end of our foundation. Secondly, the preparations and instruments we have for our works. Thirdly, the several employments and functions whereto our fellows are assigned. And fourthly, the ordinances and rites which we observe.

"The end of our foundation is the knowledge of causes, and secret motions of things; and the enlarging of the bounds of human empire, to the effecting of all things possible.

"The Preparations and Instruments are these. We have large and deep caves of several depths: the deepest are sunk six hundred fathom: and some of them are digged and made under great hills and mountains: so that if you reckon together the depth of the hill and the depth of the cave, they are (some of them) above three miles deep. For we find, that the depth of a hill, and the depth of a cave from the flat, is the same thing; both remote alike, from the sun and heaven's beams, and from the open air. These caves we call the Lower Region; and we use them for all coagulations, indurations, refrigerations, and conservations[68] of bodies. We use them likewise for the imitation of natural mines; and the producing also of new artificial metals, by compositions and materials which we use, and lay there for many years. We use them also sometimes, (which may seem strange,) for curing of some diseases, and for prolongation of life in some hermits that choose to live there, well accommodated

---

[67] Ordered.   [68] Experiments in thickening, hardening, freezing, and preserving.

of all things necessary, and indeed live very long; by whom also we learn many things.

"We have burials in several earths, where we put diverse cements, as the Chineses do their porcellain. But we have them in greater variety, and some of them more fine. We have also great variety of composts,[69] and soils, for the making of the earth fruitful.

"We have high towers; the highest about half a mile in height; and some of them likewise set upon high mountains; so that the vantage of the hill with the tower is in the highest of them three miles at least. And these places we call the Upper Region; accounting the air between the high places and the low, as a Middle Region. We use these towers, according to their several heights, and situations, for insolation,[70] refrigeration, conservation; and for the view of divers meteors; as winds, rain, snow, hail; and some of the fiery meteors also. And upon them, in some places, are dwellings of hermits, whom we visit sometimes, and instruct what to observe.

"We have great lakes, both salt, and fresh; whereof we have use for the fish and fowl. We use them also for burials of some natural bodies: for we find a difference in things buried in earth or in air below the earth, and things buried in water. We have also pools, of which some do strain fresh water out of salt; and others by art do turn fresh water into salt. We have also some rocks in the midst of the sea, and some bays upon the shore for some works, wherein is required the air and vapor of the sea. We have likewise violent streams and cataracts, which serve us for many motions:[71] and likewise engines [71] for multiplying and enforcing of winds, to set also on going diverse motions.

"We have also a number of artificial wells and fountains, made in imitation of the natural sources and baths; as tincted upon [72] vitriol, sulphur, steel, brass, lead, nitre, and other minerals. And again we have little wells for infusions of many things, where the waters take the virtue quicker and better, than in vessels or basins. And amongst them we have a water which we call Water of Paradise, being, by that we do to it made very sovereign for health, and prolongation of life.

[69] Manures.   [70] Exposing to the action of the sun.   [71] Machines.
[72] Tinctured with.

"We have also great and spacious houses where we imitate and demonstrate meteors; as snow, hail, rain, some artificial rains of bodies and not of water, thunders, lightnings; also generations of bodies in air; as frogs, flies, and divers others.

"We have also certain chambers, which we call Chambers of Health, where we qualify the air as we think good and proper for the cure of divers diseases, and preservation of health.

"We have also fair and large baths, of several mixtures, for the cure of diseases, and the restoring of man's body from arefaction:[73] and others for the confirming of it in strength of sinewes, vital parts, and the very juice and substance of the body.

"We have also large and various orchards and gardens; wherein we do not so much respect beauty, as variety of ground and soil, proper for divers trees and herbs: and some very spacious, where trees and berries are set whereof we make divers kinds of drinks, besides the vineyards. In these we practise likewise all conclusions[74] of grafting, and inoculating[75] as well of wild-trees as fruit-trees, which produceth many effects. And we make (by art) in the same orchards and gardens, trees and flowers to come earlier or later than their seasons; and to come up and bear more speedily than by their natural course they do. We make them also by art greater much than their nature; and their fruit greater and sweeter and of differing taste, smell, colour, and figure, from their nature. And many of them we so order, as they become of medicinal use.

"We have also means to make divers plants rise by mixtures of earths without seeds; and likewise to make divers new plants, differing from the vulgar; and to make one tree or plant turn into another.

"We have also parks and enclosures of all sorts of beasts and birds which we use not only for view or rareness, but likewise for dissections and trials; that thereby we may take light what may be wrought upon the body of man. Wherein we find many strange effects; as continuing life in them, though divers parts, which you account vital, be perished and taken forth; resuscitating of some that seem dead in appearance; and the like. We try also all poisons and other medicines upon them, as well of chirurgery,[76] as physic.

[73] Drying up. [74] Experiments. [75] Budding. [76] Surgery.

By art likewise, we make them greater or taller than their kind [77] is; and contrariwise dwarf them, and stay their growth: we make them more fruitful and bearing than their kind is; and contrariwise barren and not generative. Also we make them differ in colour, shape, activity, many ways. We find means to make commixtures and copulations of different kinds; which have produced many new kinds, and them not barren, as the general opinion is. We make a number of kinds of serpents, worms, flies, fishes, of putrefaction; whereof some are advanced (in effect) to be perfect creatures, like beasts or birds; and have sexes, and do propagate. Neither do we this by chance, but we know beforehand, of what matter and commixture what kind of those creatures will arise.

"We have also particular pools, where we make trials upon fishes, as we have said before of beasts and birds.

"We have also places for breed and generation of those kinds of worms and flies which are of special use; such as are with you your silk-worms and bees.

"I will not hold you long with recounting of our brew-houses, bake-houses, and kitchens, where are made divers drinks, breads, and meats, rare and of special effects. Wines we have of grapes; and drinks of other juice of fruits, of grains, and of roots; and of mixtures with honey, sugar, manna, and fruits dried, and decocted; [78] Also of the tears or woundings of trees; and of the pulp of canes. And these drinks are of several ages, some to the age or last of forty years. We have drinks also brewed with several herbs, and roots, and spices; yea with several fleshes, and white-meats; whereof some of the drinks are such, as they are in effect meat and drink both: so that divers, especially in age, do desire to live with them, with little or no meat or bread. And above all, we strive to have drink of extreme thin parts, to insinuate [79] into the body, and yet without all biting, sharpness, or fretting; insomuch as some of them put upon the back of your hand will, with a little stay,[80] pass through to the palm, and yet taste mild to the mouth. We have also waters which we ripen in that fashion, as they become nourishing; so that they are indeed excellent drink; and many will use no other. Breads we have of several grains, roots, and kernels; yea and some of flesh

[77] Species. [78] Boiled down. [79] Creep or wind. [80] Delay.

and fish dried; with divers kinds of leavenings and seasonings: so that some do extremely move appetites; some do nourish so, as divers do live of them, without any other meat; who live very long. So for meats, we have some of them so beaten and made tender and mortified,[81] yet without all corrupting, as a weak heat of the stomach will turn them into good chylus;[82] as well as a strong heat would meat otherwise prepared. We have some meats also and breads and drinks, which taken by men enable them to fast long after; and some other, that used make the very flesh of men's bodies sensibly[83] more hard and tough and their strength far greater than otherwise it would be.

"We have dispensatories, or shops of medicines. Wherein you may easily think, if we have such variety of plants and living creatures more than you have in Europe, (for we know what you have,) the simples, drugs, and ingredients of medicines, must likewise be in so much the greater variety. We have them likewise of divers ages, and long fermentations. And for their preparations, we have not only all manner of exquisite distillations and separations, and especially by gentle heats and percolations through divers strainers, yea and substances; but also exact forms[84] of composition, whereby they incorporate almost, as they were natural simples.

"We have also divers mechanical arts, which you have not; and stuffs made by them; as papers, linen, silks, tissues; dainty works of feathers of wonderful lustre; excellent dies, and many others; and shops likewise, as well for such as are not brought into vulgar use amongst us as for those that are. For you must know that of the things before recited, many of them are grown into use throughout the kingdom; but yet, if they did flow from our invention, we have of them also for patterns and principals.[85]

"We have also furnaces of great diversities, and that keep great diversity of heats; fierce and quick; strong and constant; soft and mild; blown, quiet; dry, moist; and the like. But above all, we have heats, in imitation of the Sun's and heavenly bodies' heats, that pass divers inequalities, and (as it were) orbs,[86] progresses, and returns, whereby we produce admirable effects. Besides, we have

---

[81] Made tender. [82] Chyle. [83] Perceptibly to the touch. [84] Formulas.
[85] Models. [86] Orbits.

heats of dungs; and of bellies and maws of living creatures, and of their bloods and bodies; and of hays and herbs laid up moist; of lime unquenched; and such like. Instruments also which generate heat only by motion. And farther, places for strong insolations;[87] and again, places under the earth, which by nature, or art, yield heat. These divers heats we use, as the nature of the operation, which we intend, requireth.

"We have also perspective-houses,[88] where we make demonstrations of all lights and radiations; and of all colours: and out of things uncoloured and transparent, we can represent unto you all several colours; not in rain-bows, (as it is in gems, and prisms,) but of themselves single. We represent also all multiplications[89] of light, which we carry to great distance, and make so sharp as to discern small points and lines. Also all colourations of light; all delusions and deceits of the sight, in figures, magnitudes, motions, colours: all demonstrations of shadows. We find also divers means, yet unknown to you, of producing of light originally[90] from divers bodies. We procure means of seeing objects afar off; as in the heaven and remote places; and represent things near as afar off; and things afar off as near; making feigned distances. We have also helps for the sight, far above spectacles and glasses in use. We have also glasses and means to see small and minute bodies perfectly and distinctly; as the shapes and colours of small flies and worms, grains and flaws in gems, which cannot otherwise be seen, observations in urine and blood not otherwise to be seen. We make artificial rain-bows, halo's, and circles about light. We represent also all manner of reflexions, refractions, and multiplications[89] of visual beams of objects.

"We have also precious stones of all kinds, many of them of great beauty, and to you unknown; crystals likewise; and glasses of divers kinds: and amongst them some of metals vitrificated,[91] and other materials besides those of which you make glass. Also a number of fossils, and imperfect minerals, which you have not. Likewise loadstones of prodigious virtue; and other rare stones, both natural and artificial.

---

[87] Exposure to the sun. [88] Places for optical experiments. [89] Intensifications. [90] Spontaneously. [91] Turned into glass.

"We have also sound-houses, where we practise and demonstrate all sounds, and their generation. We have harmonies which you have not, of quarter-sounds, and lesser slides[92] of sounds. Divers instruments of music likewise to you unknown, some sweeter than any you have, together with bells and rings that are dainty and sweet. We represent small sounds as great and deep; likewise great sounds extenuate[93] and sharp; we make divers tremblings and warblings of sounds, which in their original[94] are entire. We represent and imitate all articulate sounds and letters, and the voices and notes of beasts and birds. We have certain helps which set to the ear do further the hearing greatly. We have also divers strange and artificial echoes, reflecting the voice many times, and as it were tossing it: and some that give back the voice louder than it came, some shriller, and some deeper; yea, some rendering the voice differing in the letters or articulate sound from that they receive. We have also means to convey sounds in trunks and pipes, in strange lines and distances.

"We have also perfume-houses; wherewith we join also practices of taste. We multiply smells, which may seem strange. We imitate smells, making all smells to breathe out of other mixtures than those that give them. We make divers imitations of taste likewise, so that they will deceive any man's taste. And in this house we contain[95] also a confiture-house; where we make all sweet-meats, dry and moist; and divers pleasant wines, milks, broths, and sallets; in far greater variety than you have.

"We have also engine-houses, where are prepared engines and instruments for all sorts of motions. There we imitate and practise to make swifter motions than any you have, either out of your muskets or any engine that you have: and to make them and multiply them more easily, and with small force, by wheels and other means: and to make them stronger and more violent than yours are; exceeding your greatest cannons and basilisks.[96] We represent also ordnance and instruments of war, and engines of all kinds: and likewise new mixtures and compositions of gun-powder, wild-fires burning in water, and unquenchable. Also fire-works of all variety both for pleasure and use. We imitate also flights of birds; we have some

[92] Fine shades. [93] Thin. [94] Origin. [95] Include. [96] A kind of cannon.

degrees of flying in the air. We have ships and boats for going under water, and brooking[97] of seas; also swimming-girdles and supporters. We have divers curious clocks, and other like motions of return: and some perpetual motions. We imitate also motions of living creatures, by images, of men, beasts, birds, fishes, and serpents. We have also a great number of other various motions, strange for equality, fineness, and subtilty.

"We have also a mathematical house, where are represented all instruments, as well of geometry as astronomy, exquisitely made.

"We have also houses of deceits of the senses; where we represent all manner of feats of juggling, false apparitions, impostures, and illusions; and their fallacies.[98] And surely you will easily believe that we that have so many things truly natural which induce admiration,[99] could in a world of particulars deceive the senses, if we would disguise those things and labour to make them seem more miraculous. But we do hate all impostures, and lies; insomuch as we have severely forbidden it to all our fellows, under pain of ignominy and fines, that they do not shew any natural work or thing, adorned or swelling; but only pure as it is, and without all affectation of strangeness.

"These are (my son) the riches of Salomon's House.

"For the several employments and offices of our fellows; we have twelve that sail into foreign countries, under the names of other nations, (for our own we conceal); who bring us the books, and abstracts, and patterns of experiments of all other parts. These we call Merchants of Light.

"We have three that collect the experiments which are in all books. These we call Depredators.[100]

"We have three that collect the experiments of all mechanical arts; and also of liberal sciences; and also of practices which are not brought into arts. These we call Mystery-men.[101]

"We have three that try new experiments, such as themselves think good. These we call Pioners or Miners.

"We have three that draw the experiments of the former four into

[97] Withstanding.   [98] Exposures.   [99] Wonder.   [100] Pillagers.
[101] Craftsmen.

titles and tables, to give the better light for the drawing of observations and axioms out of them. These we call Compilers.

"We have three that bend themselves, looking into the experiments of their fellows, and cast about how to draw out of them things of use and practise for man's life, and knowledge, as well for works as for plain demonstration of causes, means of natural divinations, and the easy and clear discovery of the virtues and parts of bodies. These we call Dowry-men [102] or Benefactors.

"Then after divers meetings and consults of our whole number, to consider of the former labours and collections, we have three that take care, out of them, to direct new experiments, of a higher light, more penetrating into nature than the former. These we call Lamps.

"We have three others that do execute the experiments so directed, and report them. These we call Inoculators.

"Lastly, we have three that raise the former discoveries by experiments into greater observations, axioms, and aphorisms. These we call Interpreters of Nature.

"We have also, as you must think, novices and apprentices, that the succession of the former employed men do not fail; besides, a great number of servants and attendants, men and women. And this we do also: we have consultations, which of the inventions and experiences which we have discovered shall be published, and which not: and take all an oath of secrecy, for the concealing of those which we think fit to keep secret: though some of those we do reveal sometimes to the state and some not.

"For our ordinances and rites: we have two very long and fair galleries: in one of these we place patterns and samples of all manner of the more rare and excellent inventions: in the other we place the statuas of all principal inventors. There we have the statua of your Columbus, that discovered the West Indies: also the inventor of ships: your monk that was the inventor of ordnance and of gunpowder: the inventor of music: the inventor of letters: the inventor of printing: the inventor of observations of astronomy: the inventor of works in metal: the inventor of glass: the inventor of silk of the worm: the inventor of wine: the inventor of corn and bread:

[102] Endowment men.

the inventor of sugars: and all these, by more certain tradition than you have. Then have we divers inventors of our own, of excellent works; which since you have not seen, it were too long to make descriptions of them; and besides, in the right understanding of those descriptions you might easily err. For upon every invention of value, we erect a statua to the inventor, and give him a liberal and honourable reward. These statuas are some of brass; some of marble and touch-stone;[103] some of cedar and other special woods gilt and adorned; some of iron; some of silver; some of gold.

"We have certain hymns and services, which we say daily, of Lord and thanks to God for his marvellous works: and forms of prayers, imploring his aid and blessing for the illumination of our labours, and the turning of them into good and holy uses.

"Lastly, we have circuits or visits of divers principal cities of the kingdom; where, as it cometh to pass, we do publish such new profitable inventions as we think good. And we do also declare natural divinations of diseases, plagues, swarms of hurtful creatures, scarcity, tempests, earthquakes, great inundations, comets, temperature of the year, and divers other things; and we give counsel thereupon, what the people shall do for the prevention and remedy of them."

And when he had said this, he stood up; and I, as I had been taught, kneeled down, and he laid his right hand upon my head, and said; "God bless thee, my son; and God bless this relation, which I have made. I give thee leave to publish it for the good of other nations; for we here are in God's bosom, a land unknown." And so he left me; having assigned a value of about two thousand ducats, for a bounty to me and my fellows. For they give great largesses where they come upon all occasions.

[*The rest was not perfected.*]

---

[103] A variety of jasper.

AREOPAGITICA

A SPEECH
FOR THE LIBERTY OF UNLICENSED PRINTING TO THE PARLIAMENT OF ENGLAND
BY
JOHN MILTON

Τὐλεύθερον δ'ἐκεῖνο, εἴ τις θέλει πόλει
Χρησόν τι βούλευμ' εἰς μέσον φέρειν, ἔχων.
Καὶ ταῦθ' ὁ χρῄζων, λαμπρὸς ἔσθ', ὁ μὴ θέλων,
Σιγᾷ, τί τούτων ἐσιν ἰσαίτερον πόλει;
Euripid. Hicetid.

This is true Liberty when free born men
Having to advise the public may speak free,
Which he who can, and will, deserv's high praise,
Who neither can nor will, may hold his peace;
What can be juster in a State than this?
Euripid. Hicetid.

INTRODUCTORY NOTE

THE name of Milton's speech on the freedom of the press was imitated from that of the "Logos Areopagiticos" of the Athenian orator Isocrates (436–338 B.C.), which was also a speech meant to be read, not heard. The oration of Isocrates aimed at re-establishing the old democracy of Athens by restoring the Court of the Areopagus, whence the work derived its title.

During the ascendency of Laud in the Church of England, his instrument, the Court of the Star-Chamber, had reenacted, more oppressively than ever, some of the restrictions imposed during the reign of Elizabeth on the printing of books. These restrictions disappeared with the abolition of the Star-Chamber in 1641, but very soon the Presbyterian majority in the Long Parliament began to pass orders framed with a view to enable them to suppress publications voicing the political and religious views of their opponents. Finally the Order of June, 1643, reproduced here, roused Milton to protest, and he issued his famous plea for unlicensed printing in the following year. As will be seen from the speech itself, he did his best to conciliate the Parliament by making cordial acknowledgment of its services to the cause of liberty, and he sought to persuade them to reverse their action by pointing out its inconsistency with these services. But it does not appear that it produced any immediate effect. While the Independents under Cromwell had the upper hand, the licensing laws were, indeed, very slackly enforced; but with the Restoration came the reenactment of most of the provisions of the Star-Chamber Decree. After being renewed several times for terms of years, they finally were allowed to lapse in 1694, and later attempts to renew them were unsuccessful.

But the importance of Milton's pamphlet is not to be measured by its effect on the political situation which was its immediate occasion. In his enthusiasm for liberty, the master passion of his life, he rose far above the politics of the hour; and the "Areopagitica" holds its supremacy among his prose writings by virtue of its appeal to fundamental principles, and its triumphant assertion of the faith that all that truth needs to assure its victory over error is a fair field and no favor.

ORDER
OF THE LONG PARLIAMENT
FOR THE REGULATING OF PRINTING, 14 June, 1643

BEING THE OCCASION OF
MILTON'S *AREOPAGITICA*

WHEREAS divers good Orders have bin lately made by both **Houses of Parliament**, for suppressing the great late abuses and frequent disorders in Printing many, false forged, scandalous, seditious, libellous, and unlicensed Papers, Pamphlets, and Books to the great defamation of Religion and government. Which orders (notwithstanding the diligence of the Company of *Stationers,* to put them in full execution) have taken little or no effect: By reason the bill in preparation, for redresse of the said disorders, hath hitherto bin retarded through the present distractions, and very many, aswell *Stationers* and *Printers,* as others of sundry other professions not free of the *Stationers* Company, have taken upon them to set up sundry private Printing Presses in corners, and to print, vend, publish and disperse Books, pamphlets and papers, in such multitudes, that no industry could be sufficient to discover or bring to punishment, all the severall abounding delinquents; And by reason that divers of the *Stationers* Company and others being Delinquents (contrary to former orders and the constant custome used among the said Company) have taken liberty to Print, Vend, and publish, the most profitable vendible Copies of Books, belonging to the Company and other *Stationers,* especially of such Agents as are imployed in putting the said Orders in Execution, and that by way of revenge for giveing information against them to the Houses for their Delinquences in Printing, to the great prejudice of the said Company of *Stationers* and Agents, and to their discouragement in this publik service.

It is therefore Ordered by the Lords and Commons in *Parliament,* That no Order or Declaration of both, or either House of Parliament shall be printed by any, but by order of one or both the said Houses: Nor other Book, Pamphlet, paper, nor part of any such Book, Pamphlet, or paper, shall from henceforth be printed, bound, stitched or put to sale by any person or persons whatsoever, unlesse the same be first approved of and licensed under the hands of such person or persons as both, or either of the said Houses shall appoint for the licensing of the same, and entred in the Register Book of the Company of *Stationers,* according to Ancient custom, and the Printer thereof to put his name thereto. And that no person or persons shall hereafter print, or cause to be reprinted any Book or Books, or part of Book, or Books heretofore allowed of and granted to the said Company of *Stationers* for their relief and maintenance of their poore, without the licence or consent of the Master, Wardens and Assistants of the said Company; Nor any Book or Books lawfully licenced and entred in the Register of the said Company for any particular member thereof, without the licence and consent of the owner or owners thereof. Nor yet import any such Book or Books, or part of Book or Books formerly Printed here, from beyond the Seas, upon paine of forfeiting the same to the Owner, or Owners of the Copies of the said Books, and such further punishment as shall be thought fit.

And the Master and Wardens of the said Company, the Gentleman Usher of the House of *Peers,* the Sergeant of the Commons House and their deputies, together with the persons formerly appointed by the Committee of the House of Commons for Examinations, are hereby Authorized and required, from time to time, to make diligent search in all places, where they shall think meete, for all unlicensed Printing Presses, and all Presses any way imployed in the printing of scandalous or unlicensed Papers, Pamphlets, Books, or any Copies of Books belonging to the said Company, or any member thereof, without their approbation and consents, and to seize and carry away such Printing Presses Letters, together with the Nut, Spindle, and other materialls of every such irregular Printer, which they find so misimployed, unto the Common Hall of the said Company, there to be defaced and made unserviceable according to Ancient Custom; And likewise to make diligent search in all suspected Printing-houses, Ware-houses, Shops and other places for such scandalous and unlicensed Books, papers, Pamphlets, and all other Books, not entred, nor signed with the Printers name as aforesaid, being printed, or reprinted by such as have no lawfull interest in them, or any way contrary to this Order, and the same to seize and carry away to the said common hall, there to remain till both or either House of *Parliament* shall dispose thereof, And likewise to apprehend all Authors, Printers, and other persons whatsoever imployed in compiling, printing, stitching, binding, publishing and dispersing of the said scandalous, unlicensed, and unwarrantable papers, books and pamphlets as aforesaid, and all those who shall resist the said Parties in searching after them, and to bring them afore either of the Houses or the Committee of Examinations, that so they may receive such further punishments, as their Offences shall demerit, and not to be released untill they have given satisfaction to the Parties imployed in their apprehension for their paines and charges, and given sufficient caution not to offend in like sort for the future. And all Justices of the Peace, Captaines, Constables and other officers, are hereby ordered and required to be aiding, and assisting to the foresaid persons in the due execution of all, and singular the premisses and in the apprehension of all Offenders against the same. And in case of opposition to break open the Doores and Locks.

And it further ordered, that this Order be forthwith Printed and Published, to the end that notice may be taken thereof, and all Contemners of it left inexcusable.

AREOPAGITICA
A SPEECH
FOR THE LIBERTY OF UNLICENSED PRINTING

THEY who to States and Governors of the Commonwealth direct their speech, High Court of Parliament, or wanting such access in a private condition, write that which they foresee may advance the public good; I suppose them as at the beginning of no mean endeavor, not a little altered[1] and moved inwardly in their minds: Some with doubt of what will be the success,[2] others with fear of what will be the censure,[3] some with hope, others with confidence of what they have to speak. And me perhaps each of these dispositions, as the subject was whereon I entered, may have at other times variously affected; and likely might in these foremost expressions now also disclose which of them swayed most, but that the very attempt of this address thus made, and the thought of whom it hath recourse to, hath got the power within me to a passion,[4] far more welcome than incidental[5] to a preface. Which though I stay not to confess ere any ask, I shall be blameless, if it be no other, than the joy and gratulation which it brings to all who wish and promote their country's liberty; whereof this whole discourse proposed will be a certain testimony, if not a trophy. For this is not the liberty which we can hope, that no grievance ever should arise in the commonwealth, that let no man in this world expect; but when complaints are freely heard, deeply considered, and speedily reformed, then is the utmost bound of civil liberty attained, that wise men look for. To which if I now manifest by the very sound of this which I shall utter, that we are already in good part arrived, and yet from such a steep disadvantage of tyranny and superstition grounded into our principles as was beyond the manhood of a *Roman* recovery,[6] it will be attributed first, as is

---

[1] Troubled. [2] Issue. [3] Judgment. [4] Enthusiasm. [5] Appropriate.
[6] *I. e.*, after the decline of the empire.

most due, to the strong assistance of God our deliverer, next to your faithful guidance and undaunted wisdom, Lords and Commons of *England*. Neither is it in God's esteem the diminution of his glory, when honorable things are spoken of good men and worthy magistrates; which if I now first should begin to do, after so fair a progress of your laudable deeds, and such a long obligement upon the whole realm to your indefatigable virtues, I might be justly reckoned among the tardiest, and the unwillingest of them that praise ye. Nevertheless there being three principal things, without which all praising is but courtship[7] and flattery; first, when that only is praised which is solidly worth praise: next, when greatest likelihoods are brought that such things are truly and really in those persons to whom they are ascribed, the other, when he who praises, by showing that such his actual persuasion is of whom he writes, can demonstrate that he flatters not: the former two of these I have heretofore endeavored, rescuing the employment from him who went about to impair your merits with a trivial and malignant *Encomium*,[8] the latter as belonging chiefly to mine own acquittal, that whom I so extolled I did not flatter, hath been reserved opportunely to this occasion. For he who freely magnifies what hath been nobly done, and fears not to declare as freely what might be done better, gives you the best covenant of his fidelity; and that his loyalest affection and his hope waits on your proceedings. His highest praising is not flattery, and his plainest advice is a kind of praising; for though I should affirm and hold by argument, that it would fare better with truth, with learning, and the commonwealth, if one of your published orders which I should name, were called in, yet at the same time it could not but much redound to the luster of your mild and equal government, when as private persons are hereby animated to think ye better pleased with public advice, than other statists[9] have been delighted heretofore with public flattery. And men will then see what difference there is between the magnanimity of a triennial parliament, and that jealous haughtiness of prelates and cabin counselors that usurped of late, when as they shall observe ye in the midst of your victories and successes

---

[7] Courtiership. [8] Bishop Hall had damned the Parliament with faint praise. [9] Statesmen.

more gently brooking written exceptions against a voted order, than other courts, which had produced nothing worth memory but the weak ostentation of wealth, would have endured the least signified dislike at any sudden proclamation. If I should thus far presume upon the meek demeanor of your civil and gentle greatness, Lords and Commons, as what your published order hath directly said, that to gainsay, I might defend myself with ease, if any should accuse me of being new or insolent, did they but know how much better I find you esteem it to imitate the old and elegant humanity of Greece, than the barbaric pride of a *Hunnish* and *Norwegian* stateliness. And out of those ages, to whose polite wisdom and letters we owe that we are not yet *Goths* and *Jutlanders,* I could name him[10] who from his private house wrote that discourse to the parliament of *Athens,* that persuades them to change the form of *Democracy* which was then established. Such honor was done in those days to men who professed the study of wisdom and eloquence, not only in their own country, but in other lands, that cities and seigniories heard them gladly, and with great respect, if they had ought in public to admonish the state. Thus did *Dion Prusæus* a stranger and a private orator counsel the *Rhodians* against a former edict: and I abound with other like examples, which to set here would be superfluous. But if from the industry of a life wholly dedicated to studious labors, and those natural endowments happily not the worst for two and fifty degrees of northern latitude, so much must be derogated,[11] as to count me not equal to any of those who had this privilege, I would obtain to be thought not so inferior, as yourselves are superior to the most of them who received their counsel: and how far you excel them, be assured, Lords and Commons, there can no greater testimony appear, than when your prudent spirit acknowledges and obeys the voice of reason from what quarter soever it be heard speaking; and renders ye as willing to repeal any act of your own setting forth, as any set forth by your predecessors.

If ye be thus resolved, as it were injury to think ye were not, I know not what should withhold me from presenting ye with a fit instance wherein to show both that love of truth which ye emi-

---

[10] Isocrates.   [11] Subtracted.

nently profess, and that uprightness of your judgment which is not wont to be partial to yourselves; by judging over again that order which ye have ordained *to regulate printing. That no book, pamphlet, or paper shall be henceforth printed, unless the same be first approved and licensed by such,* or at least one of such as shall be thereto appointed. For that part which preserves justly every man's copy[12] to himself, or provides for the poor, I touch not, only wish they be not made pretenses to abuse and persecute honest and painful men, who offend not in either of these particulars. But that other clause of licensing books, which we thought had died with his brother *quadragesimal*[13] and *matrimonial*[13] when the prelates expired, I shall now attend with such a homily, as shall lay before you, first the inventors of it to be those whom you will be loath to own; next what is to be thought in general of reading, what ever sort the books be; and that this order avails nothing to the suppressing of scandalous, seditious, and libelous books, which were mainly intended to be suppressed. Last, that it will be primely to the discouragement of all learning, and the stop of truth, not only by the disexercising and blunting our abilities in what we know already, but by hindering and cropping the discovery that might be yet further made both in religious and civil wisdom.

I deny not, but that it is of greatest concernment in the church and commonwealth, to have a vigilant eye how books demean themselves as well as men; and thereafter to confine, imprison, and do sharpest justice on them as malefactors: for books are not absolutely dead things, but do contain a potency of life in them to be as active as that soul was whose progeny they are; nay they do preserve as in a vial the purest efficacy and extraction of that living intellect that bred them. I know they are as lively, and as vigorously productive, as those fabulous dragons teeth; and being sown up and down, may chance to spring up armed men. And yet on the other hand unless wariness be used, as good almost kill a man as kill a good book; who kills a man kills a reasonable creature, God's image; but he who destroys a good book, kills reason itself, kills the image of God, as it were in the eye. Many a man lives a burden

[12] Copyright.   [13] Regulations of the Episcopal Church relating to Lent and Marriage.

to the earth; but a good book is the precious life-blood of a master spirit, imbalmed and treasured up on purpose to a life beyond life. It is true, no age can restore a life, whereof perhaps there is no great loss; and revolutions of ages do not oft recover the loss of a rejected truth, for the want of which whole nations fare the worse. We should be wary therefore what persecution we raise against the living labors of public men, how we spill[14] that seasoned life of man preserved and stored up in books; since we see a kind of homicide may be thus committed, sometimes a martyrdom, and if it extend to the whole impression, a kind of massacre, whereof the execution ends not in the slaying of an elemental[15] life, but strikes at that ethereal and fifth essence,[16] the breath of reason itself, slays an immortality rather than a life. But lest I should be condemned of introducing license, while I oppose licensing, I refuse not the pains to be so much historical, as will serve to show what has been done by ancient and famous commonwealths, against this disorder, till the very time that this project of licensing crept out of the *Inquisition,* was caught up by our prelates, and hath caught some of our presbyters.

In *Athens* where books and wits were ever busier than in any other part of *Greece,* I find but only two sorts of writings which the magistrate cared to take notice of; those either blasphemous and atheistical, or libelous. Thus the books of *Protagoras* were by the judges of *Areopagus* commanded to be burnt, and himself banished the territory for a discourse begun with his confessing not to know *whether there were gods, or whether not:* And against defaming, it was decreed that none should be traduced by name, as was the manner of *Vetus Comœdia,*[17] whereby we may guess how they censured libeling: And this course was quick enough, as *Cicero* writes, to quell both the desperate wits of other atheists, and the open way of defaming, as the event showed. Of other sects and opinions though tending to voluptuousness, and the denying of divine providence they took no heed. Therefore we do not read that either *Epicurus,* or that libertine school of *Cyrene,* or what the *Cynic* impudence uttered, was ever questioned by the laws. Neither is it re-

[14] Destroy.   [15] Material.   [16] Spiritual element.   [17] The old Attic comedy, *e. g.,* of Aristophanes.

corded that the writings of those old comedians were suppressed, though the acting of them were forbidden; and that *Plato* commended the reading of *Aristophanes* the loosest of them all, to his royal scholar *Dionysius,* is commonly known, and may be excused, if holy *Chrysostome,* as is reported, nightly studied so much the same author and had the art to cleanse a scurrilous vehemence into the style of a rousing sermon. That other leading city of *Greece, Lacedæmon,* considering that *Lycurgus* their law-giver was so addicted to elegant learning, as to have been the first that brought out of *Ionia* the scattered works of *Homer,* and sent the poet *Thales* from *Crete* to prepare and mollify the *Spartan* surliness with his smooth songs and odes, the better to plant among them law and civility, it is to be wondered how museless[18] and unboogish they were, minding naught but the feats of war. There needed no licensing of books among them for they disliked all, but their own *Laconic Apothegms,* and took a slight occasion to chase *Archilochus* out of their city, perhaps for composing in a higher strain than their own soldierly ballads and roundelays could reach to: Or if it were for his broad verses, they were not therein so cautious, but they were as dissolute in their promiscuous conversing,[19] whence *Euripides* affirms in *Andromache,* that their women were all unchaste. Thus much may give us light after what sort books were prohibited among the Greeks. The Romans also for many ages trained up only to a military roughness, resembling most of the *Lacedæmonian* guise, knew of learning little but what their twelve tables, and the *Pontific* college with their *Augurs* and *Flamins* taught them in religion and law, so unacquainted with other learning, that when *Carneades* and *Critolaus,* with the *Stoic Diogenes* coming ambassadors to Rome, took thereby occasion to give the city a taste of their philosophy, they were suspected for seducers by no less a man than *Cato* the censor, who moved it in the senate to dismiss them speedily, and to banish all such *Attic* babblers out of *Italy*. But *Scipio* and others of the noblest senators withstood him and his old *Sabine* austerity; honored and admired the men; and the censor himself at last in his old age fell to the study of that whereof before he was so scrupulous. And yet at the same time *Nævius* and *Plautus*

[18] Inartistic.   [19] Intercourse.

the first Latin comedians had filled the city with all the borrowed scenes of *Menander* and *Philemon*. Then began to be considered there also what was to be done to libelous books and authors; for *Nævius* was quickly cast into prison for his unbridled pen, and released by the *Tribunes* upon his recantation: We read also that libels were burned, and the makers punished by *Augustus*. The like severity no doubt was used if aught were impiously written against their esteemed gods. Except in these two points, how the world went in books, the magistrate kept no reckoning. And therefore *Lucretius* without impeachment versifies his epicurism to *Memmius,* and had the honor to be set forth the second time by *Cicero* so great a father of the commonwealth; although himself disputes against that opinion in his own writings. Nor was the satirical sharpness, or naked plainness of *Lucilius,* or *Catullus,* or *Flaccus,* by any order prohibited. And for matters of state, the story of *Titius Livius,* though it extolled that part which *Pompey* held, was not therefore suppressed by *Octavius Cæsar* of the other faction. But that *Naso* was by him banished in his old age, for the wanton poems of his youth, was but a mere covert of state over some secret cause: and besides, the books were neither banished nor called in. From hence we shall meet with little else but tyranny in the Roman empire, that we may not marvel, if not so often bad, as good books were silenced. I shall therefore deem to have been large enough in producing what among the ancients was punishable to write, save only which, all other arguments were free to treat on.

By this time the emperors were become Christians, whose discipline in this point I do not find to have been more severe than what was formerly in practise. The books of those whom they took to be grand heretics were examined, refuted, and condemned in the general counsels; and not till then were prohibited, or burned by authority of the emperor. As for the writings of heathen authors, unless they were plain invectives against Christianity, as those of *Porphyrius* and *Proclus,* they met with no inderdict that can be cited, till about the year 400, in a *Carthaginian* council, wherein bishops themselves were forbidden to read the books of Gentiles, but heresies they might read: while others long before them on the contrary scrupled more the books of heretics, than of Gentiles. And that the primitive councils and bishops were wont only to declare what books were not commendable, passing no further, but leaving it to each one's conscience to read or to lay by, till after the year 800 is observed already by *Padre Paolo* the great unmasker of the *Trentine* Council. After which time the Popes of *Rome* engrossing what they pleased of political rule into their own hands, extended their dominion over men's eyes, as they had before over their judgments, burning and prohibiting to be read, what they fancied not; yet sparing in their censures, and the books not many which they so dealt with: till *Martin V* by his bull not only prohibited, but was the first that excommunicated the reading of heretical books; for about that time *Wyclif* and *Huss* growing terrible, were they who first drove the papal court to a stricter policy of prohibiting. Which course *Leo X,* and his successors followed, until the Council of Trent, and the Spanish inquisition engendering together brought forth, or perfected those catalogues, and expurging indexes that rake through the entrails of many an old good author, with a violation worse than any could be offered to his tomb. Nor did they stay in matters heretical, but any subject that was not to their palate, they either condemned in a prohibition, or had it straight into the new purgatory of an index. To fill up the measure of encroachment, their last invention was to ordain that no book, pamphlet, or paper should be printed (as if *St. Peter* had bequeathed them the keys of the press also out of Paradise) unless it were approved and licensed under the hands of two or three glutton friars. For example:

Let the Chancellor *Cini* be pleased to see if in this present work be contained ought that may withstand[20] the printing.

Vincent Rabatta, Vicar of *Florence.*

I have seen this present work, and find nothing athwart the Catholic faith and good manners: in witness whereof I have given, etc.

Nicolò Cini, Chancellor of *Florence.*

[20] Forbid.

Attending the precedent relation, it is allowed that this present work of *Davanzati* may be printed,

Vincent Rabbatta, etc.

It may be printed, *July* 15.

Friar *Simon Mompei d'Amelia,*
Chancellor of the holy office in *Florence.*

Sure they have a conceit, if he of the bottomless pit had not long since broke prison, that this quadruple exorcism would bar him down. I fear their next design will be to get into their custody the licensing of that which they say *Claudius* intended, but went not through with. Vouchsafe to see another of their forms the Roman stamp:

Imprimatur,[21] if it seem good to the reverend master of the holy palace,

Belcastro, Vicegerent.
Imprimatur, Friar *Nicolò Rodolphi,* Master of the holy palace.

Sometimes five *Imprimaturs* are seen together dialogue-wise in the Piatza of one title-page, complimenting and ducking each to other with their shaven reverences, whether the author, who stands by in perplexity at the foot of his epistle, shall to the press or to the sponge. These are the pretty responsories, these are the dear antiphonies that so bewitched of late our prelates, and their chaplains with the goodly echo they made; and besotted us to the gay imitation of the lordly *Imprimatur,* one from Lambeth house,[22] another from the West end of *Pauls;*[23] so apishly Romanizing, that the word of command still was set down in Latin; as if the learned grammatical pen that wrote it, would cast no ink without Latin; or perhaps, as they thought, because no vulgar tongue was worthy to express the pure conceit of an *Imprimatur;* but rather, as I hope, for that our English, the language of men ever famous, and foremost in the achievements of liberty, will not easily find servile letters enough to spell such a dictatorie[24] presumption English. And thus ye have the inventors and the original of book-licensing ripped up, and drawn as lineally as any pedigree. We have it not, that can

[21] Let it be printed (Latin). [22] Residence of the Archbishop of Canterbury. [23] Where the Bishop of London formerly lived. [24] Dictatorial.

be heard of, from any ancient state, or polity, or church, nor by any statute left us by our ancestors, elder or later; nor from the modern custom of any reformed city, or church abroad; but from the most Antichristian Council[25] and the most tyrannous inquisition that ever inquired. Till then books were ever as freely admitted into the world as any other birth; the issue of the brain was no more stifled than the issue of the womb: no envious *Juno* sat cross-legged[26] over the nativity of any man's intellectual offspring; but if it proved a monster, who denies, but that it was justly burned, or sunk in the sea. But that a book in worse condition than a peccant soul, should be to stand before a jury ere it be borne to the world, and undergo yet in darkness the judgment of *Radamanth* and his colleagues,[27] ere it can pass the ferry backward into light, was never heard before, till that mysterious iniquity[28] provoked and troubled at the first entrance of reformation, sought out new limbos and new hells, wherein they might include our books also within the number of their damned. And this was the rare morsel so officiously snatched up, and so ill-favoredly imitated by our inquisiturient[29] bishops, and the attendant minorites[30] their chaplains. That ye like not now these most certain authors of this licensing order, and that all sinister intention was far distant from your thoughts, when ye were importuned the passing it, all men who know the integrity of your actions, and how ye honor truth, will clear ye readily.

But some will say, what though the inventors were bad, the thing for all that may be good? It may so: yet if that thing be no such deep invention, but obvious, and easy for any man to light on, and yet best and wisest commonwealths through all ages, and occasions have forborne to use it, and falsest seducers, and oppressors of men were the first who took it up, and to no other purpose but to obstruct and hinder the first approach of Reformation; I am of those who believe, it will be a harder alchemy than *Lullius*[31] ever knew, to sublimate[32] any good use out of such an invention. Yet this only is what I request to gain from this reason, that it may be held a dangerous and suspicious fruit, as certainly it deserves for the tree that bore it, until I can dissect one by one the proper-

---

[25] Council of Trent.   [26] As at the birth of Hercules.   [27] The judges in Hades.
[28] The Church of Rome.   [29] Desirous of becoming inquisitors.   [30] Franciscan friars.   [31] Raymond Lully, a scientist of the 13th century.   [32] Extract.

ties it has. But I have first to finish as was propounded, what is to be thought in general of reading books, whatever sort they be, and whether be more the benefit, or the harm that thence proceeds?

Not to insist upon the examples of *Moses, Daniel* and *Paul,* who were skilful in all the learning of the Egyptians, Chaldeans, and Greeks, which could not probably be without reading their books of all sorts in *Paul* especially, who thought it no defilement to insert into holy Scripture, the sentences of three Greek poets, and one of them a tragedian, the question was, notwithstanding sometimes controverted among the primitive doctors, but with great odds on that side which affirmed it both lawful and profitable, as was then evidently perceived, when *Julian* the Apostate, and subtlest enemy of our faith, made a decree forbidding Christians the study of heathen learning: for, said he, they wound us with our own weapons, and with our own arts and sciences they overcome us. And indeed the Christians were put so to their shifts by this crafty means, and so much in danger to decline into all ignorance, that the two *Apollinarii* were fain as a man may say, to coin all the seven liberal sciences out of the Bible, reducing it into divers forms or orations, poems, dialogues, even to the calculating of a new Christian grammar. But saith the historian *Socrates,* the providence of God provided better than the industry of *Apollinarius* and his son, by taking away that illiterate law with the life of him who devised it. So great an injury they then held it to be deprived of *Hellenic* learning; and thought it a persecution more undermining, and secretly decaying the church than the open cruelty of *Decius* or *Dioclesian.* And perhaps it was the same politic drift that the devil whipped *St. Jerome* in a lenten dream, for reading *Cicero;* or else it was a phantasm bred by the fever which had then seis'd[33] him. For had an angel been his discipliner, unless it were for dwelling too much upon Ciceronianisms, and had chastised the reading, not the vanity, it had been plainly partial; first to correct him for grave *Cicero,* and not for scurril *Plautus* whom he confesses to have been reading not long before; next to correct him only, and let so many more ancient Fathers wax old in those pleasant and florid studies without the

[33] Possessed.

lash of such a tutoring apparition; insomuch that *Basil* teaches how some good use may be made of *Margites* a sportful poem, not now extant, written by *Homer;* and why not then of *Morgante* an Italian romance much to the same purpose. But if it be agreed we shall be tried by visions, there is a vision recorded by *Eusebius* far ancienter than this tale of *Jerome* to the nun *Eustochium,* and besides has nothing of a fever in it. *Dionysius Alexandrinus* was about the year 240, a person of great name in the Church for piety and learning, who had wont to avail himself much against heretics by being conversant in their books; until a certain presbyter laid it scrupulously to his conscience how he durst venture himself among those defiling volumes. The worthy man loath to give offense fell into a new debate with himself what was to be thought; when suddenly a vision sent from God, it is his own epistle that so avers it, confirmed him in these words: read any books what ever come to thy hands, for thou art sufficient both to judge aright, and to examine each matter. To this revelation he assented the sooner, as he confesses, because it was answerable to[34] that of the Apostle to the Thessalonians, prove[35] all things, hold fast that which is good. And he might have added another remarkable saying of the same author; to the pure all things are pure, not only meats and drinks, but all kind of knowledge whether of good or evil; the knowledge can not defile, nor consequently the books, if the will and conscience be not defiled. For books are as meats and viands are, some of good, some of evil substance; and yet God in that unapocryphal vision, said without exception rise *Peter,* kill and eat, leaving the choice to each man's discretion. Wholesome meats to a vitiated stomach differ little or nothing from unwholesome; and best books to a naughty mind are not unappliable to occasions of evil. Bad meats will scarce breed good nourishment in the healthiest concoction: but herein the difference is of bad books, that they to a discreet and judicious reader serve in many respects to discover, to confute, to forewarn, and to illustrate. Whereof what better witness can ye expect I should produce, than one of your own now sitting in Parliament, the chief of learned men reputed in this land, Mr. *Selden,* whose volume of natural and national laws proves, not only by great authorities

[34] Consistent with. [35] Test.

brought together, but by exquisite[36] reasons and theorems almost mathematically demonstrative, that all opinions, yea errors, known, read, and collated, are of main service and assistance toward the speedy attainment of what is truest. I conceive therefore, that when God did enlarge the universal diet of man's body, saving ever the rules of temperance, he then also, as before, left arbitrary the dieting and repasting of our minds; as wherein every mature man might have to exercise his own leading capacity. How great a virtue is temperance, how much of moment through the whole life of man? yet God commits the managing so great a trust, without particular law or prescription, wholly to the demeanor of every grown man. And therefore when he himself tabled[37] the Jews from heaven, that omer which was every man's daily portion of manna, is computed to have been more than might have well sufficed the heartiest feeder thrice as many meals. For those actions which enter into a man, rather than issue out of him, and therefore defile not, God uses not to captivate under a perpetual childhood of prescription, but trusts him with the gift of reason to be his own chooser; there were but little work left for preaching, if law and compulsion [should] grow so fast upon those things which heretofore were governed only by exhortation. *Solomon* informs us that much reading is a weariness to the flesh; but neither he, nor other inspired author, tells us that such or such reading is unlawful: yet certainly had God thought good to limit us herein, it had been much more expedient to have told us what was unlawful, than what was wearisome. As for the burning of those Ephesian books by St. *Paul's* converts, it is replied the books were magic, the Syriac so renders them. It was a private act, a voluntary act, and leaves us to a voluntary imitation: the men in remorse burned those books which were their own; the Magistrate by this example is not appointed: these men practised the books, another might perhaps have read them in some sort usefully. Good and evil we know in the field of this world grow up together almost inseparably; and the knowledge of good is so involved and interwoven with the knowledge of evil, and in so many cunning resemblances hardly to be discerned, that those confused seeds which were imposed on *Psyche* as an incessant labor to cull out, and sort

[36] Carefully sought out.   [37] Fed.

asunder, were not more intermixed. It was from out of the rind of one apple tasted, that the knowledge of good and evil as two twins cleaving together leaped forth into the world. And perhaps this is that doom which *Adam* fell into of knowing good and evil, that is to say of knowing good by evil. As therefore the state of man now is; what wisdom can there be to choose, what continence to forbear without the knowledge of evil? He that can apprehend and consider vice with all her baits and seeming pleasures, and yet abstain, and yet distinguish, and yet prefer that which is truly better, he is the true warfaring Christian. I can not praise a fugitive and cloistered virtue, unexercised and unbreathed, that never sallies out and sees her adversary, but slinks out of the race, where that immortal garland is to be run for, not without dust and heat. Assuredly we bring not innocence into the world, we bring impurity much rather: that which purifies us is trial, and trial is by what is contrary. That virtue therefore which is but a youngling in the contemplation of evil, and knows not the utmost that vice promises to her followers, and rejects it, is but a blank virtue, not a pure; her whiteness is but an excremental[38] whiteness; which was the reason why our sage and serious poet *Spenser,* whom I dare be known to think a better teacher than *Scotus* or *Aquinas,* describing true temperance under the person of *Guion,* brings him in with his palmer through the cave of Mammon, and the bower of earthly bliss that he might see and know, and yet abstain. Since therefore the knowledge and survey of vice is in this world so necessary to the constituting of human virtue, and the scanning of error to the confirmation of truth, how can we more safely, and with less danger scout into the regions of sin and falsity than by reading all manner of tracts, and hearing all manner of reason? And this is the benefit which may be had of books promiscuously read. But of the harm that may result hence three kinds are usually reckoned. First, is feared the infection that may spread; but then all human learning and controversy in religious points must remove out of the world, yea the Bible itself; for that ofttimes relates blasphemy not nicely,[39] it describes the carnal sense of wicked men not unelegantly,[40] it brings in holiest men passionately murmuring against Providence through all the arguments of *Epicurus:* in other

[38] External.   [39] Fastidiously.   [40] Not without elaboration.

great disputes it answers dubiously and darkly to the common reader: and ask a Talmudist what ails the modesty of his marginal keri,[41] that *Moses* and all the Prophets can not persuade him to pronounce the textual chetiv.[42] For these causes we all know the Bible itself put by the Papist into the first rank of prohibited books. The ancientest Fathers must be next removed, as *Clement* of *Alexandria,* and that *Eusebian* book of evangelic preparation, transmitting our ears through a hoard of heathenish obscenities to receive the Gospel. Who finds not that *Irenæus, Epiphanius, Jerome,* and others discover more heresies than they well confute, and that oft for heresy which is the truer opinion. Nor boots it to say for these, and all the heathen writers of greatest infection, if it must be thought so, with whom is bound up the life of human learning, that they wrote in an unknown tongue, so long as we are sure those languages are known as well to the worst of men, who are both most able, and most diligent to instil the poison they suck, first into the courts of princes, acquainting them with the choicest delights, and criticisms of sin. As perhaps did that *Petronius* whom *Nero* called his Arbiter, the master of his revels; and that notorious ribald of *Arezzo,*[43] dreaded, and yet dear to the Italian courtiers. I name not him[44] for posterity's sake, whom *Harry* the Eighth, named in merriment his vicar of hell. By which compendious way all the contagion that foreign books can infuse, will find a passage to the people far easier and shorter than an Indian voyage, though it could be sailed either by the north of *Cataio*[45] eastward, or of *Canada* westward, while our Spanish licensing gags the English press never so severely. But on the other side that infection which is from books of controversy in religion, is more doubtful and dangerous to the learned, than to the ignorant; and yet those books must be permitted untouched by the licenser. It will be hard to instance where any ignorant man hath been ever seduced by Papistical book in English, unless it were commended and expounded to him by some of that clergy: and indeed all such tracts whether false or true are as the Prophecy of *Isaiah* was to the *Eunuch,* not to be *understood without a guide.* But of our priests and doctors how many have been corrupted by

---

[41] Comment.   [42] Text.   [43] Aretino.   [44] Probably the poet Skelton.
[45] Cathay, in Tartary.

studying the comments of Jesuits and *Sorbonnists,*[46] and how fast they could transfuse that corruption into the people, our experience is both late and sad. It is not forgot, since the acute and distinct[47] *Arminius* was perverted merely by the perusing of a nameless discourse written at *Delft,* which at first he took in hand to confute. Seeing therefore that those books, and those in great abundance which are likeliest to taint both life and doctrine, can not be suppressed without the fall of learning, and of all ability in disputation, and that these books of either sort are most and soonest catching to the learned, from whom to the common people whatever is heretical or dissolute may quickly be conveyed, and that evil manners are as perfectly learned without books a thousand other ways which can not be stopped, and evil doctrine not with books can propagate, except a teacher guide, which he might also do without writing, and so beyond prohibiting, I am not able to unfold, how this cautelous[48] enterprise of licensing can be exempted from the number of vain and impossible attempts. And he who were pleasantly disposed, could not well avoid to liken it to the exploit of that gallant man who thought to pound up the crows by shutting his park gate. Besides another inconvenience, if learned men be the first receivers out of books and dispreaders both of vice and error, how shall the licensers themselves be confided in, unless we can confer upon them, or they assume to themselves above all others in the land, the grace of infallibility, and uncorruptedness? And again if it be true, that a wise man like a good refiner can gather gold out of the drossiest volume, and that a fool will be a fool with the best book, yea or without book, there is no reason that we should deprive a wise man of any advantage to his wisdom, while we seek to restrain from a fool that which being restrained will be no hindrance to his folly. For if there should be so much exactness always used to keep that from him which is unfit for his reading, we should in judgment of *Aristotle* not only, but of *Solomon,* and of our Saviour, not vouchsafe him good precepts, and by consequence not willingly admit him to good books, as being certain that a wise man will make better use of an idle pamphlet, than a fool will do of sacred Scripture. It is next

---

[46] From the theological college of the Sorbonne, in Paris.   [47] Clear-thinking.
[48] Tricky, deceptive.

alleged we must not expose ourselves to temptations without necessity, and next to that, not employ our time in vain things. To both these objections one answer will serve, out of the grounds already laid, that to all men such books are not temptations, nor vanities; but useful drugs and materials wherewith to temper and compose effective and strong medicines, which man's life can not want.[49] The rest, as children and childish men, who have not the art to qualify and prepare these working minerals, well may be exhorted to forbear, but hindered forcibly they can not be by all the licensing that sainted inquisition could ever yet contrive; which is what I promised to deliver next, that this order of licensing conduces nothing to the end for which it was framed: and hath almost prevented[50] me by being clear already while thus much hath been explaining. See the ingenuity[51] of truth, who when she gets a free and willing hand, opens herself faster, than the pace of method and discourse can overtake her. It was the task which I began with, to show that no nation, or well instituted state, if they valued books at all, did ever use this way of licensing; and it might be answered, that this is a piece of prudence lately discovered, to which I return, that as it was a thing slight and obvious to think on, for if it had been difficult to find out, there wanted not among them long since, who suggested such a course; which they not following, leave us a pattern of their judgment, that it was not the not knowing, but the not approving, which was the cause of their not using it. *Plato,* a man of high authority indeed, but least of all for his Commonwealth, in the book of his laws, which no city ever received, fed his fancy with making many edicts to his airy[52] burgomasters, which they who otherwise admire him, wish had been rather buried and excused in the *genial* cups of an *academic* night-sitting. By which laws he seems to tolerate no kind of learning, but by unalterable decree, consisting most of practical traditions, to the attainment whereof a library of smaller bulk than his own dialogues would be abundant. And there also enacts that no poet should so much as read to any private man, what he had written, until the judges and lawkeepers had seen it, and allowed it: but that *Plato* meant this law peculiarly to that Commonwealth which he had imagined, and to no other, is evident.

[49] Do without. [50] Anticipated. [51] Ingenuousness, frankness. [52] Imaginary.

Why was he not else a law-giver to himself, but a transgressor, and to be expelled by his own magistrates, both for the wanton epigrams and dialogues which he made, and his perpetual reading of *Sophron Mimus,* and *Aristophanes,* books of grossest infamy, and also for commending the latter of them though he were the malicious libeller of his chief friends,[53] to be read by the tyrant *Dionysius,* who had little need of such trash to spend his time on? But that he knew this licensing of poems had reference and dependence to many other provisos there set down in his fancied republic, which in this world could have no place: and so neither he himself, nor any magistrate, or city ever imitated that course, which taken apart from those other collateral injunctions must needs be vain and fruitless. For if they fell upon[54] one kind of strictness, unless their care were equal to regulate all other things of like aptness to corrupt the mind, that single endeavor they knew would be but a fond labor; to shut and fortify one gate against corruption, and be necessitated to leave others round about wide open. If we think to regulate printing, thereby to rectify manners, we must regulate all recreations and pastimes, all that is delightful to man. No music must be heard, no song be set or sung, but what is grave and *Doric.* There must be licensing dancers, that no gesture, motion, or deportment be taught our youth but what by their allowance shall be thought honest; for such *Plato* was provided of; it will ask more than the work of twenty licensers to examine all the lutes, the violins, and the guitars in every house; they must not be suffered to prattle as they do, but must be licensed what they may say. And who shall silence all the airs and madrigals, that whisper softness in chambers? The windows also, and the balconies must be thought on, there are shrewd[55] books, with dangerous frontispieces set to sale; who shall prohibit them, shall twenty licensers? The villages also must have their visitors to inquire what lectures the bagpipe and the rebbeck[56] reads even to the balladry, and the gamut of every *municipal* fiddler, for these are the countryman's *Arcadias*[57] and his *Monte Mayors.*[57] Next, what more national corruption, for which England hears ill[58] abroad, then household gluttony; who shall be the rectors[59] of our

[53] *E. g.,* of Socrates.   [54] Adopted vigorously.   [55] Wicked.   [56] Fiddle.   [57] Popular novels of the 15th century.   [58] Is ill-spoken of.   [59] Governors.

daily rioting? and what shall be done to inhibit the multitudes that frequent those houses where drunkenness is sold and harbored? Our garments also should be referred to the licensing of some more sober work-masters to see them cut into a less wanton garb. Who shall regulate all the mixed conversation[60] of our youth, male and female together, as is the fashion of this country, who shall still appoint what shall be discoursed, what presumed, and no further? Lastly, who shall forbid and separate all idle resort, all evil company? These things will be, and must be; but how they shall be less hurtful, how less enticing, herein consists the grave and governing wisdom of a State. To sequester out of the world into *Atlantic* and *Utopian* polities,[61] which never can be drawn into use, will not mend our condition; but to ordain wisely as in this world of evil, in the midst whereof God hath placed us unavoidably. Nor is it *Plato's* licensing of books will do this, which necessarily pulls along with it so many other kinds of licensing, as will make us all both ridiculous and weary, and yet frustrate; but those unwritten, or at least unconstraining laws of virtuous education, religious and civil nurture, which *Plato* there mentions, as the bonds and ligaments of the Commonwealth, the pillars and the sustainers of every written statute; these they be which will bear chief sway in such matters as these, when all licensing will be easily eluded. Impunity and remissness, for certain are the bane of a Commonwealth, but here the great art lies to discern in what the law is to bid restraint and punishment, and in what things persuasion only is to work. If every action which is good, or evil in man at ripe years, were to be under pittance, and prescription, and compulsion, what were virtue but a name, what praise could be then due to well-doing, what grammercy[62] to be sober, just, or continent? many there be that complain of divine providence for suffering *Adam* to transgress, foolish tongues! when God gave him reason, he gave him freedom to choose, for reason is but choosing; he had been else a mere artificial *Adam,* such an *Adam* as he is in the motions.[63] We ourselves esteem not of that obedience, or love, or gift, which is of force; God therefore left him free, set before him a provoking object, ever almost in his eyes herein con-

[60] Intercourse. [61] *I. e.,* into imaginary commonwealths, like Bacon's "New Atlantis" and More's "Utopia." [62] Great thanks. [63] Puppet shows.

sisted his merit, herein the right of his reward, the praise of his abstinence. Wherefore did he create passions within us, pleasures round about us, but that these rightly tempered are the very ingredients of virtue? They are not skilful considerers of human things, who imagine to remove sin by removing the matter of sin; for, besides that it is a huge heap increasing under the very act of diminishing though some part of it may for a time be withdrawn from some persons, it can not from all, in such a universal thing as books are; and when this is done, yet the sin remains entire. Though ye take from a covetous man all his treasure he has yet one jewel left, ye can not bereave him of his covetousness. Banish all objects of lust, shut up all youth into the severest discipline that can be exercised in any hermitage, ye can not make them chaste, that came not thither so; such great care and wisdom is required to the right managing of this point. Suppose we could expel sin by this means; look how much we thus expel of sin, so much we expel of virtue: for the matter of them both is the same; remove that, and ye remove them both alike. This justifies the high providence of God, who though he command us temperance, justice, continence, yet pours out before us even to a profuseness all desirable things, and gives us minds that can wander beyond all limit and satiety. Why should we then effect a rigor contrary to the manner of God and of nature, by abridging or scanting those means, which books freely permitted are, both to the trial of virtue, and the exercise of truth. It would be better done to learn that the law must needs be frivolous which goes to restrain things, uncertainly and yet equally working to good, and to evil. And were I the chooser, a dram of well-doing should be preferred before many times as much the forcible hindrance of evil-doing. For God sure esteems the growth and completing of one virtuous person, more than the restraint of ten vicious. And albeit whatever thing we hear or see, sitting, walking, traveling, or conversing may be fitly called our book, and is of the same effect that writings are, yet grant the thing to be prohibited were only books, it appears that this order hitherto is far insufficient to the end which it intends. Do we not see, not once or oftener, but weekly that continued court-libel[64] against the Parliament and city, printed, as the wet sheets can wit-

---

[64] "Mercurius Aulicus," a royalist journal.

ness, and dispersed among us for all that licensing can do? yet this is the prime service a man would think, wherein this order should give proof of itself. If it were executed, you'll say. But certain, if execution be remiss or blindfold now, and in this particular, what will it be hereafter, and in other books. If then the order shall not be vain and frustrate, behold a new labor, Lords and Commons, ye must repeal and proscribe all scandalous and unlicensed books already printed and divulged[65]: after ye have drawn them up into a list, that all may know which are condemned, and which not; and ordain that no foreign books be delivered out of custody, till they have been read over. This office will require the whole time of not a few overseers, and those no vulgar[66] men. There be also books which are partly useful and excellent, partly culpable and pernicious; this work will ask as many more officials to make expurgations and expunctions,[67] that the commonwealth of learning be not damnified.[68] In fine, when the multitude of books increase upon their hands, ye must be fain to catalogue all those printers who are found frequently offending, and forbid the importation of their whole suspected *typography*. In a word, that this order may be exact, and not deficient, ye must reform it perfectly according to the model of *Trent*[69] and *Seville*,[70] which I know ye abhor to do. Yet though ye should condescend to this, which God forbid, the order still would be but fruitless and defective to that end whereto ye meant it. If to prevent sects and schisms, who is so unread or so uncatechised in story, that hath not heard of many sects refusing books as a hindrance, and preserving their doctrine unmixed for many ages, only by unwritten traditions. The Christian faith, for that was once a schism, is not unknown to have spread all over *Asia,* ere any Gospel or Epistle was seen in writing. If the amendment of manners be aimed at, look into Italy and Spain, whether those places be one scruple the better, the more honest, the wiser, the chaster, since all the inquisitional rigor that hath been executed upon books.

Another reason, whereby to make it plain that this order will miss the end it seeks, consider by the quality which ought to be in every licenser. It can not be denied but that he who is made judge to sit

---

[65] Published. [66] Ordinary. [67] Omissions. [68] Injured. [69] Council of Trent.
[70] Headquarters of the Spanish Inquisition.

upon the birth, or death of books whether they may be wafted into this world, or not, had need to be a man above the common measure, both studious, learned, and judicious; there may be else no mean mistakes in the censure of what is passable or not; which is also no mean injury. If he be of such worth as behooves him, there can not be a more tedious and unpleasing journey-work, a greater loss of times levied upon his head, than to be made the perpetual reader of unchosen books and pamphlets, ofttimes huge volumes. There is no book that is acceptable unless at certain seasons; but to be enjoined the reading of that at all times, and in a hand scarce legible, whereof three pages would not down at any time in the fairest print, is an imposition which I can not believe how he that values time, and his own studies, or is but of a sensible nostril should be able to endure. In this one thing I crave leave of the present licensers to be pardoned for so thinking: who doubtless took this office up, looking on it through their obedience to the Parliament, whose command perhaps made all things seem easy and unlaborious to them; but that this short trial hath wearied them out already, their own expressions and excuses to them who make so many journeys to solicit their license, are testimony enough. Seeing therefore those who now possess the employment, by all evident signs with themselves well rid of it, and that no man of worth, none that is not a plain unthrift of his own hours is ever likely to succeed them, except he mean to put himself to the salary of a press-corrector, we may easily foresee what kind of licensers we are to expect hereafter, either ignorant, imperious, and remiss, or basely pecuniary. This is what I had to show wherein this order can not conduce to that end, whereof it bears the intention.

I lastly proceeded from the no good it can do, to the manifest hurt it causes, in being first the greatest discouragement and affront that can be offered to learning and to learned men. It was the complaint and lamentation of prelates, upon every least breath of a motion to remove pluralities,[71] and distribute more equally church revenues, that then all learning would be forever dashed and discouraged. But as for that opinion, I never found cause to think that the tenth part

---

[71] The holding of several livings by one clergyman had been a chief cause of complaint against the Episcopal Church.

of learning stood or fell with the clergy: nor could I ever but hold it for a sordid and unworthy speech of any churchman who had a competency left him. If therefore ye be loath to dishearten utterly and discontent, not the mercenary crew of false pretenders to learning, but the free and ingenuous sort of such as evidently were born to study, and love learning for itself, not for lucre, or any other end, but the service of God and of truth, and perhaps that lasting fame and perpetuity of praise which God and good men have consented shall be the reward of those whose published labors advance the good of mankind, then know, that so far to distrust the judgment and the honesty of one who hath but a common repute in learning, and never yet offended, as not to count him fit to print his mind without a tutor and examiner, lest he should drop a schism, or something of corruption, is the greatest displeasure and indignity to a free and knowing spirit that can be put upon him. What advantage is it to be a man over it is to be a boy at school, if we have only escaped the ferular,[72] to come under the fescu[72] of an *Imprimatur?* if serious and elaborate writings, as if they were no more than the theme of a grammar lad under his pedagogue must not be uttered[73] without the cursory eyes of a temporizing and extemporizing licenser. He who is not trusted with his own actions, his drift not being known to be evil, and standing to the hazard of law and penalty, has no great argument to think himself reputed in the commonwealth wherein he was born, for other than a fool or a foreigner. When a man writes to the world, he summons up all his reason, and deliberation to assist him; he searches, meditates, is industrious, and likely consults and confers with his judicious friends; after all which done he takes himself to be informed in what he writes, as well as any that wrote before him; if in this the most consummate act of his fidelity and ripeness, no years, no industry, no former proof of his abilities can bring him to that state of maturity, as not to be still mistrusted and suspected, unless he carry all his considerate diligence, all his midnight watchings, and expense of *Palladian*[74] oil, to the hasty view of an unleisured licenser, perhaps much his younger, perhaps far his inferior in judgment, perhaps one who never knew the labor of book-writing, and if he be not repulsed, or slighted, must appear in

[72] Rod. [73] Published. [74] From Pallas, goddess of learning.

print like a puny[75] with his guardian, and his censor's hand on the back of his title to be his bail and surety, that he is no idiot, or seducer, it can not be but a dishonor and derogation to the author, to the book, to the privilege and dignity of learning. And what if the author shall be one so copious of fancy, as to have many things well worth the adding, come into his mind after licensing, while the book is yet under the press, which not seldom happens to the best and most diligent writers; and that perhaps a dozen times in one book. The printer dares not go beyond his licensed copy; so often then must the author trudge to his leave-giver, that those his new insertions may be viewed; and many a jaunt will be made, ere that licenser, for it must be the same man, can either be found, or found at leisure; meanwhile either the press must stand still, which is no small damage, or the author lose his most accurate thoughts, and send the book forth worse than he had made it, which to a diligent writer is the greatest melancholy and vexation that can befall. And how can a man teach with authority, which is the life of teaching, how can he be a doctor in his book as he ought to be, or else had better be silent, whenas all he teaches, all he delivers, is but under the tuition, under the correction of his patriarchal licenser to blot or alter what precisely accords not with the hidebound humor which he calls his judgment? When every acute reader upon the first sight of a pedantic license, will be ready with these like words to ding[76] the book a quoit's distance from him: "I hate a pupil teacher, I endure not an instructor that comes to me under the wardship of an overseeing fist. I know nothing of the licenser, but that I have his own hand here for his arrogance; who shall warrant me his judgment?" "The State, sir," replies the Stationer, but has a quick return: "The State shall be my governors, but not my critics; they may be mistaken in the choice of a licenser, as easily as this licenser may be mistaken in an author: this is some common stuff;" and he might add from Sir *Francis Bacon,* That *such authorized books are but the language of the times.* For though a licenser should happen to be judicious more than ordinarily, which will be a great jeopardy of the next succession, yet his very office, and his commission enjoins him to let pass nothing but what is vulgarly received already. Nay, which is

[75] Minor.   [76] Throw violently.

more lamentable, if the work of any deceased author, though never so famous in his lifetime, and even to this day, come to other hands for license to be printed, or reprinted, if there be found in his book one sentence of a venturous edge, uttered in the height of zeal, and who knows whether it might not be the dictate of a divine spirit, yet not suiting with every low decrepit humor of their own, though it were *Knox* himself, the reformer of a kingdom that spake it, they will not pardon him their dash:[77] the sense of that great man shall to all posterity be lost, for the fearfulness, or the presumptuous rashness of a perfunctory licenser. And to what an author this violence hath been lately done, and in what book of greatest consequence to be faithfully published, I could now instance, but shall forbear till a more convenient season. Yet if these things be not resented seriously and timely by them who have the remedy in their power, but that such iron molds[78] as these shall have authority to gnaw out the choicest periods of the most exquisite books, and to commit such a treacherous fraud against the orphan remainders of worthiest men after death, the more sorrow will belong to that hapless race of men, whose misfortune it is to have understanding. Henceforth let no man care to learn, or care to be more than worldly wise; for certainly in higher matters to be ignorant and slothful, to be a common steadfast dunce will be the only pleasant life, and only in request.

And as it is a particular disesteem of every knowing person alive, and most injurious to the written labors and monuments of the dead, so to me it seems an undervaluing and vilifying[79] of the whole nation. I can not set so light by all the invention, the art, the wit, the grave and solid judgment which is in England, as that it can be comprehended in any twenty capacities how good soever, much less that it should not pass except their superintendence be over it, except it be sifted and strained with their strainers, that it should be uncurrent without their manual stamp. Truth and understanding are not such wares as to be monopolized and traded in by tickets[80] and statutes, and standards. We must not think to make a staple commodity of all the knowledge in the land, to mark and license it like our broadcloth, and our wool packs. What is it but a servitude like that imposed by the Philistines, not to be allowed the sharpen-

[77] Dare to blot it out. [78] Rust. [79] Cheapening. [80] Receipts.

ing of our own axes and coulters, but we must repair from all quarters to twenty licensing forges. Had any one written and divulged erroneous things and scandalous to honest life, misusing and forfeiting the esteem had of his reason among men, if after conviction this only censure were adjudged him, that he should never henceforth write, but what were first examined by an appointed officer, whose hand should be annexed to pass his credit for him, that now he might be safely read, it could not be apprehended less than a disgraceful punishment. Whence to include the whole nation, and those that never yet thus offended, under such a diffident[81] and suspectful prohibition, may plainly be understood what a disparagement it is. So much the more, when as debtors and delinquents may walk abroad without a keeper, but unoffensive books must not stir forth without a visible jailer in their title. Nor is it to the common people less than a reproach; for if we be so jealous over[82] them, as that we dare not trust them with an English pamphlet, what do we but censure them for a giddy, vicious, and ungrounded people; in such a sick and weak estate of faith and discretion, as to be able to take nothing down but through the pipe of a licenser. That this is care or love of them, we can not pretend, whenas in those popish places where the laity are most hated and despised the same strictness is used over them. Wisdom we can not call it, because it stops but one breach of license, nor that neither; whenas those corruptions which it seeks to prevent, break in faster at other doors which can not be shut.

And in conclusion it reflects to the disrepute of our ministers also, of whose labors we should hope better, and of the proficiency which their flock reaps by them, than that after all this light of the Gospel which is, and is to be, and all this continual preaching, they should be still frequented with such an unprincipled, unedified, and laick[83] rabble, as that the whiff of every new pamphlet should stagger them out of their catechism, and Christian walking. This may have much reason to discourage the ministers when such a low conceit is had of all their exhortations, and the benefiting of their hearers, as that they are not thought fit to be turned loose to three sheets of paper without a licenser, that all the sermons, all the lectures preached,

[81] Distrusting.   [82] Suspect.   [83] Ignorant.

printed, vented in such numbers, and such volumes, as have now well-nigh made all other books unsalable, should not be armor enough against one single *enchiridion*,[84] without the castle St. *Angelo*[85] of an *Imprimatur*.

And lest some should persuade ye, Lord and Commons, that these arguments of learned men's discouragement at this your order, are mere flourishes, and not real, I could recount what I have seen and heard in other countries, where this kind of inquisition tyrannizes; when I have sat among their learned men, for that honor I had, and been counted happy to be born in such a place of *Philosophic* freedom, as they supposed England was, while themselves did nothing but bemoan the servile condition into which learning amongst them was brought; that this was it which had damped the glory of Italian wits; that nothing had been there written now these many years but flattery and fustian. There it was that I found and visited the famous *Galileo* grown old, a prisoner to the Inquisition, for thinking in astronomy, otherwise than the Franciscan and Dominican licensers thought. And though I knew that England then was groaning loudest under the prelatical yoke, nevertheless I took it as a pledge of future happiness, that other nations were so persuaded of her liberty. Yet was it beyond my hope that those worthies were then breathing in her air, who should be her leaders to such a deliverance, as shall never be forgotten by any revolution of time that this world hath to finish. When that was once begun, it was as little in my fear, that what words of complaint I heard among learned men of other parts uttered against the Inquisition, the same I should hear by as learned men at home uttered in time of Parliament against an order of licensing; and that so generally, that when I disclosed myself a companion of their discontent, I might say, if without envy, that he[86] whom an honest *quæstorship* had endeared to the *Sicilians,* was not more by them importuned against *Verres,* than the favorable opinion which I had among many who honor ye, and are known and respected by ye, loaded me with entreaties and persuasions, that I would not despair to lay together that which just reason should bring into my mind, toward the removal of an undeserved

[84] A pun on the two meanings of dagger and hand-book.
[85] The Pope's fortress.   [86] Cicero.

thraldom upon learning. That this is not therefore the disburdening of a particular fancy, but the common grievance of all those who had prepared their minds and studies above the vulgar pitch to advance truth in others, and from others to entertain it, thus much may satisfy. And in their name I shall for neither friend nor foe conceal what the general murmur is; that if it come to inquisitioning again, and licensing, and that we are so timorous of ourselves, and so suspicious of all men, as to fear each book, and the shaking of every leaf, before we know what the contents are, if some who but of late were little better than silenced from preaching, shall come now to silence us from reading, except what they please, it can not be guessed what is intended by some but a second tyranny over learning: and will soon put it out of controversy that bishops and presbyters are the same to us both name and thing. That those evils of prelacy which before from five or six and twenty sees were distributively charged upon the whole people, will now light wholly upon learning, is not obscure to us: whereas now the pastor of a small unlearned parish, on the sudden shall be exalted archbishop over a large diocese of books, and yet not remove, but keep his other cure too, a mystical pluralist. He who but of late cried down the sole ordination of every novice bachelor of art, and denied sole jurisdiction over the simplest parishioner, shall now at home in his private chair assume both these over worthiest and most excellent books and ablest authors that write them. This is not, ye covenants and protestations that we have made, this is not to put down prelacy, this is but to chop[87] an episcopacy, this is but to translate the palace *Metropolitan* from one kind of dominion into another, this is but an old canonical sleight[88] of *commuting* our penance.[89] To startle thus betimes at a mere unlicensed pamphlet will after a while be afraid of every conventicle,[90] and a while after will make a conventicle of every Christian meeting. But I am certain that a state governed by the rules of justice and fortitude, or a church built and founded upon the rock of faith and true knowledge, can not be so pusillanimous. While things are yet not constituted in religion, that freedom of writing should be re-

---

[87] Exchange. [88] Trick allowed by the canon law.
[89] Exchanging one kind of penance for another. [90] Non-conformist assembly.

strained by a discipline imitated from the prelates, and learned by them from the Inquisition to shut us up all again into the breast of a licenser, must needs give cause of doubt and discouragement to all learned and religious men.

Who can not but discern the fineness of this politic drift, and who are the contrivers; that while bishops were to be baited[91] down, then all presses might be open; it was the people's birthright and privilege in time of Parliament, it was the breaking forth of light. But now the bishops abrogated and voided out[92] of the church, as if our Reformation sought no more, but to make room for others into their seats under another name, the episcopal arts begin to bud again, the cruse of truth must run no more oil, liberty of printing must be enthralled again under a prelatical commission of twenty, the privilege of the people nullified, and which is worse, the freedom of learning must groan again and to her old fetters; all this the Parliament yet sitting. Although their own late arguments and defenses against the prelates might remember them that this obstructing violence meets for the most part with an event utterly opposite to the end which it drives at: instead of suppressing sects and schisms, it raises them and invests them with a reputation: *"The punishing of wits enhances their authority,"* saith the Viscount St. *Albans, "and a forbidden writing is thought to be a certain spark of truth that flies up in the faces of them who seek to tread it out."* This order therefore may prove a nursing mother to sects, but I shall easily show how it will be a step-dame to truth: and first by disenabling us to the maintenance of what is known already.

Well knows he who uses to consider, that our faith and knowledge thrives by exercise, as well as our limbs and complexion.[93] Truth is compared in Scripture to a streaming fountain; if her waters flow not in a perpetual progression, they sicken into a muddy pool of conformity and tradition. A man may be a heretic in the truth; and if he believe things only because his pastor says so, or the Assembly so determines, without knowing other reason, though his belief be true, yet the very truth he holds, becomes his heresy. There is not any burden that some would gladder post off to another,

[91] Worried (as by dogs).   [92] Abolished.   [93] Constitution.

than the charge and care of their religion. There be, who knows not that there be of Protestants and professors[94] who live and die in as errant and implicit[95] faith, as any lay Papist or Loretto.[96] A wealthy man addicted to his pleasure and to his profits, finds religion to be a traffic so entangled, and of so many piddling[97] accounts, that of all mysteries[98] he can not skill[99] to keep a stock going upon that trade. What should he do? fain he would have the name to be religious, fain he would bear up with his neighbors in that. What does he therefore, but resolves to give over toiling, and to find himself out some factor,[100] to whose care and credit he may commit the whole managing of his religious affairs; some divine of note and estimation that must be. To him he adheres, resigns the whole warehouse of his religion, with all the locks and keys into his custody; and indeed makes the very person of that man his religion; esteems his associating with him a sufficient evidence and commendatory of his own piety. So that a man may say his religion is now no more within himself, but is become an individual[101] movable, and goes and comes near him, according as that good man frequents the house. He entertains him, gives him gifts, feasts him, lodges him; his religion comes home at night, prays, is liberally supped, and sumptuously laid to sleep, rises, is saluted, and after the malmsey,[102] or some well spiced bruage,[103] and better breakfasted than he whose morning appetite would have gladly fed on green figs between *Bethany* and *Jerusalem,* his religion walks abroad at eight, and leaves his kind entertainer in the shop trading all day without his religion.

Another sort there be who when they hear that all things shall be ordered, all things regulated and settled; nothing written but what passes through the custom-house of certain publicans[104] that have the tunaging and the poundaging[105] of all free spoken truth, will straight give themselves up into your hands, make them and cut them out what religion ye please; there be delights, there be recreations and jolly pastimes that will fetch the day about from sun to sun, and rock the tedious year as in a delightful dream. What[106]

[94] Puritans. [95] Taken on trust. [96] A famous place of pilgrimage in central Italy. [97] Petty. [98] Trades. [99] Manage. [100] Agent. [101] Separable. [102] The morning draft of wine. [103] Ale, or other drink. [104] Tax-collectors. [105] A reference to the illegal tax levied by Charles I. [106] Why.

need they torture their heads with that which others have taken so strictly, and so unalterably into their own purveying? These are the fruits which a dull ease and cessation of our knowledge will bring forth among the people. How goodly, and how to be wished were such an obedient unanimity as this, what a fine conformity would it starch us all into? Doubtless a staunch and solid piece of framework, as any January could freeze together.

Nor much better will be the consequence even among the clergy themselves; it is no new thing never heard of before, for a *parochial* minister, who has his reward, and is at his *Hercules* pillars[107] in a warm benefice, to be easily inclinable, if he have nothing else that may rouse up his studies, to finish his circuit[108] in an English concordance and a *topic folio,*[109] the gatherings and savings of a sober graduateship, a *Harmony*[110] and a *Catena,*[111] treading the constant round of certain common doctrinal heads, attended with their uses, motives, marks and means, out of which as out of an alphabet or sol fa by forming and transforming, joining and disjoining variously a little book-craft, and two hours meditation might furnish him unspeakably to the performance of more than a weekly charge of sermoning: not to reckon up the infinite helps of interlinearies,[112] breviaries,[113] *synopses,*[114] and other loitering gear.[114] But as for the multitude of sermons ready printed and piled up, on every text that is not difficult, our London trading St. *Thomas* in his vestry, and add to boot St. *Martin* and St. *Hugh,* have not within their hallowed limits more vendible ware of all sorts ready made:[115] so that penury he never need fear of pulpit provision, having where so plenteously to refresh his magazine. But if his rear and flanks be not impaled,[116] if his back door be not secured by the rigid licenser, but that a bold book may now and then issue forth, and give the assault to some of his old collections in their trenches, it will concern him then to keep waking, to stand in watch, to set good guards and sentinels about his received opinions, to walk the round and counter-round

---

[107] Limit of his ambition, as the Straits of Gibraltar were the limits of the ancient world. [108] *I. e.,* of studies. [109] Commonplace book. [110] *E. g.,* of the Gospels. [111] Chain or list of authorities. [112] Translations. [113] Abridgments. [114] Lazy man's apparatus. [115] "*I. e.,* our largest and busiest marts are as well stocked with sermons as with any other ware whatever."—*Hales.* [116] Palisaded.

with his fellow inspectors, fearing lest any of his flock be seduced, who also then would be better instructed, better exercised and disciplined. And God send that the fear of this diligence which must then be used, do not make us affect the laziness of a licensing church.

For if we be sure we are in the right, and do not hold the truth guiltily, which becomes not, if we ourselves condemn not our own weak and frivolous teaching, and the people for an untaught and irreligious gadding rout, what can be more fair, than when a man judicious, learned, and of a conscience, for aught we know, as good as theirs that taught us what we know, shall not privily from house to house, which is more dangerous, but openly by writing publish to the world what his opinion is, what his reasons, and wherefore that which is now thought can not be sound. Christ urged it as wherewith to justify himself, that he preached in public; yet writing is more public than preaching; and more easy to refutation, if need be, there being so many whose business and profession merely it is, to be the champions of truth; which if they neglect, what can be imputed but their sloth, or inability?

Thus much we are hindered and disinured[117] by this course of licensing toward the true knowledge of what we seem to know. For how much it hurts and hinders the licensers themselves in the calling of their ministry, more than any secular employment, if they will discharge that office as they ought, so that of necessity they must neglect either the one duty or the other, I insist not, because it is a particular, but leave it to their own conscience, how they will decide it there.

There is yet behind of what I purposed to lay open, the incredible loss, and detriment that this plot of licensing puts us to, more than if some enemy at sea should stop up all our havens and ports, and creeks, it hinders and retards the importation of our richest merchandise, truth; nay it was first established and put into practise by antichristian malice and mystery[118] on set purpose to extinguish, if it were possible, the light of Reformation, and to settle falsehood; little differing from that policy wherewith the Turk upholds his *Alcoran,* by the prohibition of printing. 'Tis not denied, but gladly confessed, we are to send our thanks and vows to heaven, louder

[117] Put out of practise.   [118] Trickery.

than most of nations, for that great measure of truth which we enjoy, especially in those main points between us and the pope, with his appurtenances the prelates: but he who thinks we are to pitch our tent here, and have attained the utmost prospect of reformation, that the mortal glass wherein we contemplate, can show us, till we come to *beatific* vision, that man by this very opinion declares, that he is yet far short of truth.

Truth indeed came once into the world with her divine master, and was a perfect shape most glorious to look on: but when he ascended, and his apostles after him were laid asleep, then straight arose a wicked race of deceivers, who as that story goes of the *Egyptian Typhon* with his conspirators, how they dealt with the good *Osiris*, took the virgin Truth, hewed her lovely form into a thousand pieces, and scattered them to the four winds. From that time ever since, the sad friends of Truth, such as dare appear, imitating the careful search that *Isis* made for the mangled body of *Osiris*, went up and down gathering up limb by limb still as they could find them. We have not yet found them all, Lords and Commons, nor ever shall do, till her Master's second coming; he shall bring together every joint and member, and shall mold them into an immortal feature of loveliness and perfection. Suffer not these licensing prohibitions to stand at every place of opportunity forbidding and disturbing them that continue seeking, that continue to do our obsequies to the torn body of our martyred saint. We boast our light; but if we look not wisely on the sun itself, it smites us into darkness. Who can discern those planets that are oft *Combust*,[119] and those stars of brightest magnitude that rise and set with the sun, until the opposite motion of their orbs bring them to such a place in the firmament, where they may be seen evening or morning. The light which we have gained, was given us, not to be ever staring on, but by it to discover onward things more remote from our knowledge. It is not the unfrocking of a priest, the unmitering of a bishop, and the removing him from off the *Presbyterian* shoulders that will make us a happy nation, no, if other things as great in the church, and in the rule of life both economical and political be not looked into and reformed, we have looked so long upon the blaze that *Zuinglius* and

---

[119] Within 8½° of the sun.

Calvin hath beaconed up to us, that we are stark blind. There be who perpetually complain of schisms and sects, and make it such a calamity that any man dissents from their maxims. 'Tis their own pride and ignorance which causes the disturbing, who neither will hear with meekness, nor can convince, yet all must be suppressed which is not found in their *Syntagma*.[120] They are the troublers, they are the dividers of unity, who neglect and permit not others to unite those dissevered pieces which are yet wanting to the body of Truth. To be still searching what we know not, by what we know, still closing up truth to truth as we find it (for all her body is *homogeneal*,[121] and proportional) this is the golden rule in *theology* as well as in arithmetic, and makes up the best harmony in a church; not the forced and outward union of cold, and neutral, and inwardly divided minds.

Lords and Commons of England, consider what nation it is whereof ye are, and whereof ye are the governors: a nation not slow and dull, but of a quick, ingenious, and piercing spirit, acute to invent, subtle and sinewy to discourse, not beneath the reach of any point the highest that human capacity can soar to. Therefore the studies of learning in her deepest sciences have been so ancient, and so eminent among us, that writers of good antiquity, and ablest judgment have been persuaded that even the school of *Pythagoras,* and the *Persian* wisdom took beginning from the old philosophy of this island. And that wise and civil[122] Roman, *Julius Agricola,* who governed once here for *Cæsar,* preferred the natural wits of Britain, before the labored studies of the French. Nor is it for nothing that the grave and frugal *Transilvanian* sends out yearly from as far as the mountainous borders of *Russia,* and beyond the *Hercynian*[123] wilderness, not their youth, but their staid men, to learn our language, and our *theologic* arts. Yet that which is above all this, the favor and the love of heaven we have great argument to think in a peculiar manner propitious and propending[124] toward us. Why else was this nation chosen before any other, that out of her as out of *Sion* should be proclaimed and sounded forth the first tidings and trumpet of Reformation to all *Europe.* And had it not been the

[120] Summary of doctrine.   [121] All made up of truth.   [122] Cultivated.
[123] Used of the German forests.   [124] Inclining.

obstinate perverseness of our prelates against the divine and admirable spirit of *Wyclif,* to suppress him as a schismatic and innovator, perhaps neither the *Bohemian Huss* and *Jerome,* no nor the name of *Luther,* or of *Calvin* had been ever known: the glory of reforming all our neighbors had been completely ours. But now, as our obdurate clergy have with violence demeaned[125] the matter, we are become hitherto the latest and the backwardest scholars, of whom God offered to have made us the teachers. Now once again by all concurrence of signs, and by the general instinct of holy and devout men, as they daily and solemnly express their thoughts, God is decreeing to begin some new and great period in his Church, even to the reforming of Reformation itself: what does he then but reveal Himself to his servants, and as his manner is, first to his Englishmen; I say as his manner is, first to us, though we mark not the method of his counsels, and are unworthy. Behold now this vast city; a city of refuge, the mansion house of liberty, encompassed and surrounded with his protection; the shop of war hath not there more anvils and hammers waking, to fashion out the plates and instruments of armed justice in defense of beleaguered truth, than there be pens and heads there, sitting by their studious lamps, musing, searching, revolving new notions and ideas wherewith to present, as with their homage and their fealty the approaching Reformation: others as fast reading, trying all things, assenting to the force of reason and convincement. What could a man require more from a nation so pliant and so prone to seek after knowledge. What wants there to such a towardly and pregnant soil, but wise and faithful laborers, to make a knowing people, a nation of prophets, of sages, and of worthies. We reckon more than five months yet to harvest; there need not be five weeks, had we but eyes to lift up, the fields are white already. Where there is much desire to learn, there of necessity will be much arguing, much writing, many opinions; for opinion in good men is but knowledge in the making. Under these fantastic[126] terrors of sect and schism, we wrong the earnest and zealous thirst after knowledge and understanding which God hath stirred up in this city. What some lament of, we rather should rejoice at, should rather praise this pious forwardness among

[125] Conducted.   [126] Imaginary.

men, to reassume the ill deputed care of their religion into their own hands again. A little generous prudence, a little forbearance of one another, and some grain of charity might win all these diligences to join, and unite in one general and brotherly search after truth; could we but forego this prelatical tradition of crowding free consciences and Christian liberties into canons and precepts of men. I doubt not, if some great and worthy stranger should come among us, wise to discern the mold and temper of a people, and how to govern it, observing the high hopes and aims, the diligent alacrity of our extended[127] thoughts and reasonings in the persuance of truth and freedom, but that he would cry out as *Pyrrhus* did, admiring the Roman docility and courage, if such were my *Epirots,* I would not despair the greatest design that could be attempted to make a church or kingdom happy. Yet these are the men cried out against for schismatics and sectarians; as if, while the temple of the Lord was building, some cutting, some squaring the marble, others hewing the cedars, there should be a sort of irrational men who could not consider there must be many schisms and many dissections made in the quarry and in the timber, ere the house of God can be built. And when every stone is laid artfully together, it can not be united into a continuity, it can but be contiguous in this world; neither can every piece of the building be of one form; nay rather the perfection consists in this, that out of many moderate varieties and brotherly dissimilitudes that are not vastly disproportional arises the goodly and the graceful symmetry that commends the whole pile and structure. Let us therefore be more considerate builders, more wise in spiritual architecture, when great reformation is expected. For now the time seems come, wherein *Moses* the great prophet may sit in heaven rejoicing to see that memorable and glorious wish of his fulfilled, when not only our seventy elders, but all the Lord's people are become prophets. No marvel then though some men, and some good men too perhaps, but young in goodness, as *Joshua* then was, envy them. They fret, and out of their own weakness are in agony, lest those divisions and subdivisions will undo us. The adversary again applauds, and waits the hour, when they have branched themselves out, saith he, small enough into parties and partitions, than will be

[127] Advanced.

our time. Fool! he sees not the firm root, out of which we all grow, though into branches: nor will beware until he sees our small divided maniples[128] cutting through at every angle of his ill united and unwieldy brigade. And that we are to hope better of all these supposed sects and schisms, and that we shall not need that solicitude honest perhaps though over timorous of them that vex in his behalf, but shall laugh in the end, at those malicious applauders of our differences, I have these reasons to persuade me.

First when a city shall be as it were besieged and blocked about, her navigable river infested, inroads and incursions round, defiance and battle oft rumored to be marching up even to her walls, and suburb trenches, that then the people, or the greater part, more than at other times, wholly taken up with the study of highest and most important matters to be reformed, should be disputing, reasoning, reading, inventing, discoursing, even to a rarity,[129] and admiration, things not before discoursed or written of, argues first a singular good will, contentedness and confidence in your prudent foresight, and safe government, Lords and Commons; and from thence derives itself[130] to a gallant bravery and well grounded contempt of their enemies, as if there were no small number of as great spirits among us, as his was, who when Rome was nigh besieged by *Hannibal* being in the city, bought that piece of ground at no cheap rate, whereon *Hannibal* himself encamped his own regiment. Next it is a lively and cheerful presage of our happy success and victory. For as in a body, when the blood is fresh, the spirits pure and vigorous, not only to vital, but to rational faculties, and those in the acutest, and the pertest[131] operations of wit and subtlety, it argues in what good plight and constitution the body is, so when the cheerfulness of the people is so sprightly up, as that it has, not only wherewith to guard well its own freedom and safety, but to spare, and to bestow upon the solidest and sublimest points of controversy, and new invention, it betoken us not degenerated, nor drooping to a fatal decay, but casting off the old and wrinkled skin of corruption to outlive these pangs and wax young again, entering the glorious ways of truth and prosperous virtue destined to become great and honorable in these latter ages. Methinks I see in my mind a noble and

[128] Companies.   [129] Rare degree.   [130] Flows on.   [131] Sprightliest.

puissant nation rousing herself like a strong man after sleep, and shaking her invincible locks: Methinks I see her as an eagle muing[132] her mighty youth, and kindling her undazzled eyes at the full midday beam; purging and unscaling her long abused sight at the fountain itself of heavenly radiance, while the whole noise[133] of timorous and flocking birds, with those also that love the twilight, flutter about, amazed at what she means, and in their envious gabble would prognosticate a year of sects and schisms.

What should ye do then, should ye suppress all this flowery crop of knowledge and new light sprung up and yet springing daily in this city, should ye set an oligarchy of twenty ingrossers[134] over it, to bring a famine upon our minds again, when we shall know nothing but what is measured to us by their bushel? Believe it, Lords and Commons, they who counsel ye to such a suppressing, do as good as bid ye suppress yourselves; and I will soon show how. If it be desired to know the immediate cause of all this free writing and free speaking, there can not be assigned a truer than your own mild, and free, and human government: it is the liberty, Lords and Commons, which your own valorous and happy counsels have purchased us, liberty which is the nurse of all great wits; this is that which hath rarified and enlightened our spirits like the influence of heaven; this is that which hath enfranchised, enlarged and lifted up our apprehensions degrees above themselves. Ye can not make us now less capable, less knowing, less eagerly pursuing of the truth, unless ye first make yourselves, that made us so, less the lovers, less the founders of our true liberty. We can grow ignorant again, brutish, formal, and slavish, as ye found us; but ye then must first become that which ye can not be, oppressive, arbitrary, and tyrannous, as they were from whom ye have freed us. That our hearts are now more capacious, our thoughts more erected to the search and expectation of great and exact things, is the issue of your own virtue propagated in us; ye can not suppress that unless ye reinforce an abrogated and merciless law, that fathers may despatch at will their own children. And who shall then stick closest to ye, and excite others? not he who takes up arms for cote and conduct,[135] and his

---

[132] Renewing (by moulting). [133] Noisy band. [134] Monopolists.
[135] *I. e.*, to resist illegal taxation for clothing and conveying troops.

four nobles of Danegelt.[136] Although I dispraise not the defense of just immunities, yet love my peace better, if that were all. Give me the liberty to know, to utter, and to argue freely according to conscience, above all liberties.

What would be best advised then, if it be found so hurtful and so unequal to suppress opinions for the newness, or the unsuitableness to a customary acceptance, will not be my task to say; I only shall repeat what I have learned from one of your own honorable number, a right noble and pious lord, who had he not sacrificed his life and fortunes to the church and commonwealth, we had not now missed and bewailed a worthy and undoubted patron of this argument. Ye know him I am sure; yet I for honor's sake, and may it be eternal to him, shall name him, the Lord *Brook*. He writing of episcopacy, and by the way treating of sects and schisms, left ye his vote, or rather now the last words of his dying charge, which I know will ever be of dear and honored regard with ye, so full of meekness and breathing charity, that next to his last testament, who bequeathed love and peace to his disciples, I can not call to mind where I have read or heard words more mild and peaceful. He there exhorts us to hear with patience and humility those, however they be miscalled, that desire to live purely, in such a use of God's ordinances, as the best guidance of their conscience gives them, and to tolerate them, though in some disconformity to ourselves. The book itself will tell us more at large being published to the world, and dedicated to the Parliament by him who both for his life and for his death deserves, that what advice he left be not laid by without perusal.

And now the time in special is, by privilege to write and speak what may help to the further discussion of matters in agitation. The temple of Janus with his two controversial faces might now not unsignificantly be set open.[137] And though all the winds of doctrine were let loose to play upon the earth, so truth be in the field, we do injuriously by licensing and prohibiting to misdoubt her strength. Let her and falsehood grapple; who ever knew truth put to the worse, in a free and open encounter. Her confuting is the

[136] *I. e.,* ship-money. The references here are to those who took up arms in the civil war rather than submit to the illegal taxes of Charles I.
[137] Indicating a time of war.

best and surest suppressing. He who hears what praying there is for light and clearer knowledge to be sent down among us, would think of other matters to be constituted beyond the discipline of Geneva,[138] framed and fabricated already to our hands. Yet when the new light which we beg for shines in upon us, there be who envy, and oppose, if it come not first in at their casements. What a collusion is this, whenas we are exhorted by the wise man to use diligence, *to seek for wisdom as for hidden treasures* early and late, that another order shall enjoin us to know nothing but by statute. When a man hath been laboring the hardest labor in the deep mines of knowledge, hath furnished out his findings in all their equipage, drawn forth his reasons as it were a battle ranged, scattered and defeated all objections in his way, calls out his adversary into the plain, offers him the advantage of wind and sun, if he please; only that he may try the matter by dint of argument, for his opponents then to skulk, to lay ambushments, to keep a narrow bridge of licensing where the challenger should pass, though it be valor enough in soldiership, is but weakness and cowardice in the wars of truth. For who knows not that truth is strong next to the Almighty; she needs no policies, no stratagems, no licensings to make her victorious, those are the shifts and the defenses that error uses against her power: give her but room, and do not bind her when she sleeps, for then she speaks not true, as the old Proteus did, who spake oracles only when he was caught and bound, but then rather she turns herself into all shapes, except her own, and perhaps tunes her voice according to the time, as *Micaiah* did before Ahab, until she be adjured into her own likeness. Yet is it not impossible that she may have more shapes than one. What else is all that rank of things indifferent, wherein truth may be on this side, or on the other, without being unlike herself. What but a vain shadow else is the abolition of those *ordinances, that handwriting nailed to the cross,* what great purchase is this Christian liberty which *Paul* so often boasts of. His doctrine is, that he who eats or eats not, regards a day, or regards it not, may do either to the Lord. How many other things might be tolerated in peace, and left to conscience, had we but charity, and were it not the chief stronghold of our hypocrisy

[138] The Presbyterian system.

to be ever judging one another. I fear yet this iron yoke of outward conformity hath left a slavish print upon our necks; the ghost of a linen decency[139] yet haunts us. We stumble and are impatient at the least dividing of one visible congregation from another, though it be not in fundamentals; and through our forwardness to suppress, and our backwardness to recover any enthralled piece of truth out of the grip of custom, we care not to keep truth separated from truth, which is the fiercest rent and disunion of all. We do not see that while we still affect by all means a rigid external formality, we may as soon fall again into a gross conforming stupidity, a stark and dead congealment of *wood and hay and stubble* forced and frozen together, which is more to the sudden degenerating of a church than many *subdichotomies*[140] of petty schisms. Not that I can think well of every light separation, or that all in a church is to be expected *gold and silver and precious stones:* it is not possible for man to sever the wheat from the tares, the good fish from the other fry; that must be the angels' ministry at the end of mortal things. Yet if all can not be of one mind, as who looks they should be? this doubtless is more wholesome, more prudent, and more Christian that many be tolerated, rather than all compelled. I mean not tolerated popery, and open superstition, which as it extirpates all religions and civil supremacies, so itself should be extirpated, provided first that all charitable and compassionate means be used to win and regain the weak and misled: that also which is impious or evil absolutely either against faith or manners no law can possibly permit, that intends not to unlaw itself: but those neighboring differences, or rather indifferences, are what I speak of, whether in some point of doctrine or of discipline, which though they may be many, yet need not interrupt *the unity of spirit,* if we could but find among us *the bond of peace.* In the meanwhile if any one would write, and bring his helpful hand to the slow-moving reformation we labor under, if truth have spoken to him before others, or but seemed at least to speak, who hath so be-Jesuited[141] us that we should trouble that man with asking license to do so worthy a deed? and not consider this, that if it come to prohibiting, there is not aught more likely to be prohibited than truth itself; whose first appearance to our eyes

[139] Priestly vestments.   [140] Subdivisions.   [141] Made Jesuits of.

bleared and dimmed with prejudice and custom, is more unsightly and unplausible than many errors, even as the person is of many a great man slight and contemptible to see to. And what do they tell us vainly of new opinions, when this very opinion of theirs, that none must be heard, but whom they like, is the worst and newest opinion of all others; and is the chief cause why sects and schisms do so much abound, and true knowledge is kept at distance from us; besides yet a greater danger which is in it. For when God shakes a kingdom with strong and healthful commotions to a general reforming, 'tis not untrue that many sectarians and false teachers are then busiest in seducing; but yet more true it is, that God then raises to his own work men of rare abilities, and more than common industry, not only to look back and revise what hath been taught heretofore, but to gain further and go on, some new enlightened steps in the discovery of truth. For such is the order of God's enlightening his church, to dispense and deal out by degrees his beam, so as our earthly eyes may best sustain it. Neither is God appointed and confined, where and out of what place these his chosen shall be first heard to speak; for he sees not as man sees, chooses not as man chooses, lest we should devote ourselves again to set places, and assemblies, and outward callings of men; planting our faith one while in the old convocation house,[142] and another while in the chapel at Westminster;[143] when all the faith and religion that shall be there canonized,[144] is not sufficient without plain convincement, and the charity of patient instruction to supple the least bruise of conscience, to edify the meanest Christian, who desires to walk in the spirit, and not in the letter of human trust, for all the number of voices that can be there made, no though *Harry* the Seventh himself there, with all his liege tombs[145] about him, should lend them voices from the dead, to swell their number. And if the men be erroneous who appear to be the leading schismatics, what withholds us but our sloth, our self-will, and distrust in the right cause, that we do not give them gentle meetings and gentle dismissions, that we debate not and examine the matter thoroughly with liberal and frequent audience; if not for their sakes, yet for our own? seeing no man who hath tasted learning, but will confess the many ways

---

[142] Where the Episcopal clergy met to legislate.   [143] Where the Presbyterian divines drew up their Confession.   [144] Put into canons or rules.
[145] In Westminster Abbey.

of profiting by those who not contented with stale receipts are able to manage, and set forth new positions to the world. And were they but as the dust and cinders of our feet, so long as in that notion they may serve to polish and brighten the armor of truth, even for that respect they were not utterly to be cast away. But if they be of those whom God hath fitted for the special use of these times with eminent and ample gifts, and those perhaps neither among the priests, nor among the Pharisees, and we in the haste of a precipitant zeal shall make no distinction, but resolve to stop their mouths, because we fear they come with new and dangerous opinions, as we commonly forejudge them ere we understand them, no less than woe to us, while thinking thus to defend the gospel, we are found the persecutors.

There have been not a few since the beginning of this Parliament, both of the presbytery and others who by their unlicensed books to the contempt of an *Imprimatur* first broke that triple ice clung about our hearts, and taught the people to see day: I hope that none of those were the persuaders to renew upon us this bondage which they themselves have wrought so much good by condemning. But if neither the check that *Moses* gave to young *Joshua,* nor the countermand which our Saviour gave to young *John,* who was so ready to prohibit those whom he thought unlicensed, be not enough to admonish our elders how unacceptable to God their testy mood of prohibiting is, if neither their own remembrance what evil hath abounded in the church by this let[146] of licensing, and what good they themselves have begun by transgressing it, be not enough, but that they will persuade, and execute the most *Dominican* part of the Inquisition over us, and are already with one foot in the stirrup so active at suppressing, it would be no unequal distribution in the first place, to suppress the suppressors themselves; whom the change of their condition hath puffed up, more than their late experience of harder times hath made wise.

And as for regulating the press, let no man think to have the honor of advising ye better than yourselves have done in that order published next before this, that no book be printed, unless the printer's and the author's name, or at least the printer's be registered. Those which otherwise come forth, if they be found mis-

[146] Hindrance.

chievous and libelous, the fire and the executioner will be the timeliest and the most effectual remedy, that man's prevention can use. For this *authentic* Spanish policy of licensing books, if I have said aught will prove the most unlicensed book itself within a short while; and was the immediate image of a star-chamber decree to that purpose made in those very times when that court did the rest of those her pious works, for which she is now fallen from the stars with *Lucifer*. Whereby you may guess what kind of state prudence, what love of the people, what care of religion, or good manners there was at the contriving although with singular hypocrisy it pretended to bind books to their good behavior. And how it got the upper hand of your precedent order so well constituted before, if we may believe those men whose profession gives them cause to inquire most, it may be doubted there was in it the fraud of some old *patentees* and *monopolizers* in the trade of book-selling; who under pretence of the poor in their company not to be defrauded, and the just retaining of each man his several copy, which God forbid should be gainsaid, brought divers glozing colors[147] to the house, which were indeed but colors, and serving to no end except it be to exercise a superiority over their neighbors, men who do not therefore labor in an honest profession to which learning is indebted, that they should be made other men's vassals. Another end is thought was aimed at by some of them in procuring by petition this order, that having power in their hands, malignant[148] books might the easier escape abroad, as the event shows. But of these *sophisms* and *elenchs* of merchandise I skill not:[149] This I know, that errors in a good government and in a bad are equally almost incident;[150] for what magistrate may not be misinformed, and much the sooner, if liberty of printing be reduced into the power of a few, but to redress willingly and speedily what hath been erred, and in highest authority to esteem a plain advertisement more than others have done a sumptuous bribe, is a virtue (honored Lords and Commons), answerable to[151] your highest actions, and whereof none can participate but greatest and wisest men.

[147] Plausible pretexts.   [148] Royalist.   [149] I have no knowledge of these tricks of trade and the exposure of them.   [150] Liable to occur.   [151] Consistent with.

MILTON'S
TRACTATE ON EDUCATION

FROM THE EDITION OF 1673

INTRODUCTORY NOTE

Mr. Samuel Hartlib, to whom the following letter was addressed, was the son of a Polish merchant of German descent and an English mother. He lived in London during a large part of his life, and was actively interested in a vast number of educational and philanthropic schemes. It appears from the "Tractate" itself that he had requested Milton to put into writing some of the ideas on the education of a gentleman which they had from time to time touched on in conversation; and the present treatise is the result.

Beginning with the definition of a "complete and generous education" as one "which fits a man to perform justly, skilfully, and magnanimously all the offices, both public and private, of peace and war," Milton proceeds to lay down a program which is likely to startle the modern reader. The stress on Latin and Greek at the beginning is easily accounted for by the fact that in Milton's day these tongues were the only keys to the storehouse of learning; but the casual way in which Chaldean and Syrian are added to Hebrew seems to indicate that the author tended to overestimate the ease with which the ordinary youth acquires languages. But the mark of the system here expounded is that language is to be merely a means, not an end; that things and not words constitute the elements of education. Thus the Greek and Latin authors prescribed are chosen for the value of their subject matter, and provision is made for a comprehensive knowledge of the science of the time, as well as for training in religion and morals. The suggestions made for exercise have the same practical and utilitarian tendency, fencing, wrestling, and horsemanship being prescribed with a view to soldiership. Nor are the arts neglected, for poetry and music are given their place both as recreation and as influences on character.

This is indeed, as Milton confesses, "not a bow for every man to shoot in"; but as an ideal it is rich in both stimulus and practical suggestion.

OF EDUCATION

To Master *Samuel Hartlib.*

Mr. *Hartlib,*

I AM long since persuaded, that to say, or do aught worth memory and imitation, no purpose or respect[1] should sooner move us, than simply the love of God, and of mankind. Nevertheless to write now the reforming of education, though it be one of the greatest and noblest designs that can be thought on, and for the want whereof this nation perishes, I had not yet at this time been induced, but by your earnest entreaties, and serious conjurements;[2] as having my mind for the present half diverted in the pursuance of some other assertions,[3] the knowledge and the use of which, can not but be a great furtherance both to the enlargement of truth, and honest living, with much more peace. Nor should the laws of any private friendship have prevailed with me to divide thus, or transpose[4] my former thoughts, but that I see those aims, those actions which have won you with me the esteem[5] of a person sent hither by some good providence from a far country to be the occasion and the incitement of great good to this island. And, as I hear, you have obtained the same repute with men of most approved wisdom, and some of highest authority among us. Not to mention the learned correspondence which you hold in foreign parts, and the extraordinary pains and diligence which you have used in this matter both here, and beyond the seas; either by the definite will of God so ruling, or the peculiar sway of nature, which also is God's working. Neither can I think that so reputed, and so valued as you are, you would to the forfeit of your own discerning ability, impose upon me an unfit and over-ponderous argument, but that the satisfaction which you profess to have received from those incidental discourses

---

[1] Consideration. [2] Appeals. [3] As, *e. g.,* unlicensed printing and divorce.
[4] Change. [5] Reputation.

which we have wandered into, hath pressed and almost constrained you into a persuasion, that what you require from me in this point, I neither ought, nor can in conscience defer beyond this time both of so much need at once, and so much opportunity to try what God hath determined. I will not resist therefore, whatever it is either of divine, or human obligement that you lay upon me; but will forthwith set down in writing, as you request me, that voluntary *Idea,* which hath long in silence presented itself to me, of a better education, in extent and comprehension far more large, and yet of time far shorter, and of attainment far more certain, than hath been yet in practise.

Brief I shall endeavor to be; for that which I have to say, assuredly this nation hath extreme need should be done sooner than spoken. To tell you therefore what I have benefited herein among old renowned authors, I shall spare; and to search what many modern *Januas*[6] and *Didactics*[6] more than ever I shall read, have projected, my inclination leads me not. But if you can accept of these few observations which have flowered off, and are, as it were, the burnishing[7] of many studious and contemplative years altogether spent in the search of religious and civil knowledge, and such as pleased you so well in the relating, I here give you them to dispose of.

The end then of learning is to repair the ruins of our first parents by regaining to know God aright, and out of that knowledge to love him, to imitate him, to be like him, as we may the nearest by possessing our souls of true virtue, which being united to the heavenly grace of faith makes up the highest perfection. But because our understanding can not in this body found itself but on sensible[8] things, nor arrive so clearly to the knowledge of God and things invisible, as by orderly conning over the visible and inferior creature, the same method is necessarily to be followed in all discreet teaching. And seeing every nation affords not experience and tradition enough for all kind of learning, therefore we are chiefly taught the languages of those people who have at any time been most industrious after wisdom; so that language is but the instrument conveying to us things useful to be known. And though a linguist should

---

[6] Works on education by John Amos Comenius, a great educational reformer and a friend of Hartlib's.
[7] Fragments rubbed off in polishing. [8] Perceived by the senses.

pride himself to have all the tongues that *Babel* cleft the world into, yet if he have not studied the solid things in them as well as the words and lexicons, he were nothing so much to be esteemed a learned man, as any yoeman or tradesman competently wise in his mother dialect only. Hence appear the many mistakes which have made learning generally so unpleasing and so unsuccessful; first we do amiss to spend seven or eight years merely in scraping together so much miserable Latin and Greek, as might be learned other wise easily and delightfully in one year. And that which casts our proficiency therein so much behind, is our time lost partly in too oft idle vacancies[9] given both to schools and universities, partly in a preposterous[10] exaction, forcing the empty wits of children to compose themes, verses and orations, which are the acts of ripest judgment and the final work of a head filled by long reading and observing, with elegant maxims, and copious invention. These are not matters to be wrung from poor striplings, like blood out of the nose, or the plucking of untimely fruit: besides the ill habit which they get of wretched barbarizing against the Latin and Greek *idiom,* with their untutored *Anglicisms,* odious to be read, yet not to be avoided without a well continued and judicious conversing[11] among pure authors digested, which they scarce taste, whereas, if after some preparatory grounds of speech by their certain forms got into memory, they were led to the praxis[12] thereof in some chosen short books lessoned throughly to them, they might then forthwith proceed to learn the substance of good things, and arts in due order, which would bring the whole language quickly into their power. This I take to be the most rational and most profitable way of learning languages, and whereby we may best hope to give account to God of our youth spent herein: and for the usual method of teaching arts, I deem it to be an old error of universities not yet well recovered from the scholastic grossness of barbarous ages, that instead of beginning with arts most easy, and those be such as are most obvious to the sense, they present their young unmatriculated novices at first coming with the most intellective[13] abstractions of logic and metaphysics; so that they having but newly left those grammatic flats

---

[9] Holidays. [10] Lit., in inverted order. [11] Familiar intercourse.
[12] Practical application. [13] Intellectual.

and shallows where they stuck unreasonably to learn a few words with lamentable construction, and now on the sudden transported under another climate to be tossed and turmoiled with their unballasted wits in fathomless and unquiet deeps of controversy, do for the most part grow into hatred and contempt of learning, mocked and deluded all this while with ragged notions and babblements, while they expected worthy and delightful knowledge; till poverty or youthful years call them importunately their several ways, and hasten them with the sway[14] of friends either to an ambitious and mercenary, or ignorantly zealous divinity; some allured to the trade of law, grounding their purposes not on the prudent and heavenly contemplation of justice and equity which was never taught them, but on the promising and pleasing thoughts of litigious terms, fat contentions and flowing fees; others betake them to State affairs, with souls so unprincipled in virtue and true generous breeding, that flattery, and court shifts[15] and tyrannous aphorisms appear to them the highest points of wisdom; instilling their barren hearts with a conscientious slavery,[16] if, as I rather think, it be not feigned. Others lastly of a more delicious and airy spirit,[17] retire themselves knowing no better, to the enjoyments of ease and luxury, living out their days in feast and jollity; which indeed is the wisest and the safest course of all these, unless they were with more integrity undertaken. And these are the fruits of misspending our prime youth at the schools and universities as we do, either in learning mere words or such things chiefly, as were better unlearned.

I shall detain you no longer in the demonstration of what we should not do, but straight conduct ye to a hill side where I will point ye out the right path of a virtuous and noble education; laborious indeed at the first ascent, but else so smooth, so green, so full of goodly prospect, and melodious sounds on every side, that the harp of *Orpheus*[18] was not more charming. I doubt not but ye shall have more ado to drive our dullest and laziest youth, our stocks and stubs from the infinite desire of such a happy nurture, than we have not to hale and drag our choicest and hopefulest wits to that asinine feast of sowthistles and brambles which is commonly set before them, as

---

[14] Influence. [15] Tricks. [16] A slavery which they try to believe conscientious.
[17] Delicate and spiritual nature.   [18] Which charmed even trees and stones.

all the food and entertainment of their tenderest and most docible[19] age. I call therefore a complete and generous education that which fits a man to perform justly, skilfully and magnanimously all the offices both private and public, of peace and war. And how all this may be done between twelve, and one and twenty, less time than is now bestowed in pure trifling at grammar and *sophistry,* is to be thus ordered.

First to find out a spacious house and ground about it fit for an academy, and big enough to lodge a hundred and fifty persons, whereof twenty or thereabout may be attendants, all under the government of one, who shall be thought of desert sufficient, and ability either to do all, or wisely to direct, and oversee it done. This place should be at once both school and university, not heeding a remove to any other house of scholarship, except it be some peculiar College of Law, or Physic, where they mean to be practitioners; but as for those general studies which take up all our time from *Lilly*[20] to the commencing,[21] as they term it, Master of Art, it should be absolute. After this pattern, as many Edifices may be converted to this use, as shall be needful in every city throughout this land, which would tend much to the increase of learning and civility everywhere. This number, less or more thus collected, to the convenience of a foot company, or interchangeably two troops of cavalry, should divide their day's work into three parts, as it lies orderly. Their studies, their exercise, and their diet.

For the studies, first they should begin with the chief and necessary rules of some good grammar, either that now used, or any better: and while this is doing, their speech is to be fashioned to a distinct and clear pronunciation, as near as may be to the *Italian,* especially in the vowels. For we *Englishmen* being far northerly, do not open our mouths in the cold air, wide enough to grace a southern tongue; but are observed by all other nations to speak exceeding close and inward: So that to smatter Latin with an English mouth, is as ill a hearing as Law-French. Next to make them expert in the usefulest points of grammar, and withal to season[22] them, and win them early to the love of virtue and true labor, ere any flattering seducement, or vain principle seize them wandering, some easy and delight-

---

[19] Docile.   [20] Lilly's "Latin Primer."   [21] Graduation.   [22] Imbue.

ful book of education would be read to them; whereof the Greeks have store, as *Cebes*,[23] *Plutarch*,[24] and other Socratic discourses. But in Latin we have none of classic authority extant, except the two or three first books of *Quintilian*,[25] and some select pieces elsewhere. But here the main skill and groundwork will be, to temper[26] them such lectures and explanations upon every opportunity as may lead and draw them in willing obedience, inflamed with the study of learning, and the admiration of virtue; stirred up with high hopes of living to be brave men, and worthy patriots, dear to God, and famous to all ages. That they may despise and scorn all their childish, and ill-taught qualities, to delight in manly, and liberal exercises: which he who hath the art, and proper eloquence to catch them with, what with mild and effectual persuasions, and what with the intimation of some fear, if need be, but chiefly by his own example, might in a short space gain them to an incredible diligence and courage: infusing into their young breasts such an ingenuous and noble ardor, as would not fail to make many of them renowned and matchless men. At the same time, some other hour of the day, might be taught them the rules of arithmetic, and soon after the elements of geometry even playing, as the old manner was. After evening repast, till bed-time their thoughts will be best taken up in the easy grounds of religion, and the story of Scripture. The next step would be to the authors on *agriculture, Cato, Varro, and Columella,* for the matter is most easy, and if the language be difficult, so much the better, it is not a difficulty above their years. And here will be an occasion of inciting and enabling them hereafter to improve the tillage of their country, to recover the bad soil, and to remedy the waste that is made of good; for this was one of *Hercules'* praises. Ere half these authors be read (which will soon be with plying[27] hard, and daily) they can not choose but be masters of any ordinary prose.[28] So that it will be then seasonable for them to learn in any modern author, the use of the globes, and all the maps; first with the old names, and then with the new: or they might be then capable to read any compendious method of natural philosophy.

[23] A disciple of Socrates, to whom was ascribed a book on the cultivation of virtue. [24] Author of the famous "Lives." He lived about 100 A.D. [25] The Latin rhetorician, b. 42 A.D. [26] Adept. [27] Applying themselves. [28] *I. e.*, Latin prose.

OF EDUCATION

And at the same time might be entering into the Greek tongue, after the same manner as was before prescribed in the Latin: whereby the difficulties of grammar being soon overcome, all the historical physiology of *Aristotle* and *Theophrastus*[29] are open before them, and as I may say, under contribution. The like access will be to *Vitruvius*,[30] to *Seneca's* natural questions,[31] to *Mela*,[32] *Celsus*,[33] *Pliny*,[34] or *Solinus*.[35] And having thus passed the principles of *arithmetic, geometry, astronomy,* and *geography* with a general compact of physics, they may descend in *mathematics* to the instrumental science of *trigonometry* and from thence to fortification, architecture, engineering, or navigation. And in natural philosophy they may proceed leisurely from the history of meteors, minerals, plants and living creatures as far as anatomy. Then also in course might be read to them out of some not tedious writer the institution of physic; that they may know the tempers,[36] the humors,[36] the seasons, and how to manage a crudity;[37] which he who can wisely and timely do, is not only a great physician to himself, and to his friends, but also may at some time or other, save an army by this frugal and expenseless means only; and not let the healthy and stout bodies of young men rot away under him for want of this discipline; which is a great pity, and no less a shame to the commander. To set forward all these proceedings in nature and mathematics, what hinders, but that they may procure, as often as shall be needful, the helpful experiences of hunters, fowlers, fishermen, shepherds, gardeners, apothecaries; and in the other sciences, architects, engineers, mariners, anatomists; who doubtless would be ready some for reward, and some to favor such a hopeful seminary. And this will give them such a real tincture of natural knowledge, as they shall never forget, but daily augment with delight. Then also those poets which are now counted most hard, will be both facile and pleasant, *Orpheus, Hesiod, Theocritus, Aratus, Nicander, Oppian, Dionysius,* and in Latin *Lucretius, Manilius,* and the rural part of *Virgil.*

[29] A pupil of Aristotle's. [30] On architecture. [31] On physics. [32] On geography.
[33] On medicine. [34] On natural history. [35] An abridgement of Pliny.
[36] The temperament was supposed to be due to the predominance of one of the four humors in the body. [37] Indigestion.

By this time, years and good general precepts will have furnished them more distinctly with that act of reason which in *ethics* is called *proairesis*[38] that they may with some judgment contemplate upon moral good and evil. Then will be required a special reenforcement of constant and sound indoctrinating to set them right and firm, instructing them more amply in the knowledge of virtue and the hatred of vice: while their young and pliant affections are led through all the moral works of *Plato, Xenophon, Cicero, Plutarch, Laertius*[39] and those *Locrian* remnants;[40] but still to be reduced[41] in their nightward studies wherewith they close the day's work, under the determinate[42] sentence of *David* or *Solomon,* or the evanges[43] and apostolic scriptures. Being perfect in the knowledge of personal duty, they may then begin the study of economics. And either now, or before this, they may have easily learned at any odd hour the *Italian tongue.* And soon after, but with wariness and good antidote, it would be wholesome enough to let them taste some choice comedies, Greek, Latin, or *Italian:* Those tragedies also that treat of household matters, as Trachiniæ,[44] Alcestis[45] and the like. The next remove must be to the study of politics; to know the beginning, end, and reasons of political societies; that they may not in a dangerous fit of the commonwealth be such poor, shaken, uncertain reeds, of such a tottering conscience, as many of our great counselors have lately shown themselves, but steadfast pillars of the state. After this they are to dive into the ground of law and legal justice; delivered first, and with best warrant by *Moses;* and as far as human prudence can be trusted, in those extolled remains of Grecian lawgivers, *Lycurgus, Solon, Zaleucus, Charondas,*[46] and thence to all the Roman *edicts* and tables with their *Justinian;* and so down to the *Saxon* and common laws of *England,* and the statutes. Sundays also and every evening may be now understandingly spent in the highest matters of *theology,* and church history ancient and modern: and ere this time the Hebrew tongue at a set hour might have been gained, that the Scriptures may be now read in their own original; whereto it would be no impossibility to add

[38] The choice between good and evil. [39] Diogenes Laertius, who wrote a history of philosophy. [40] Ascribed to Timæus. [41] Brought back. [42] Authoritative. [43] Gospels. [44] By Sophocles. [45] By Euripides. [46] Lawgivers respectively to Sparta, Athens, the Locrians in southern Italy, and certain cities in Sicily.

the *Chaldey*,[47] and the *Syrian*[48] dialect. When all these employments are well conquered, then will the choice histories, *heroic poems,* and *Attic* tragedies of stateliest and most regal argument, with all the famous political orations offer themselves; which if they were not only read; but some of them got by memory, and solemnly pronounced with right accent, and grace, as might be taught, would endow them even with the spirit and vigor of *Demosthenes,* or *Cicero, Euripides,* or *Sophocles.* And now lastly will be the time to read with them those organic[49] arts which enable men to discourse and write perspicuously, elegantly, and according to the fitted style of lofty, mean or lowly. Logic therefore so much as is useful, is to be referred to this due place with all her well couched[50] heads and topics, until to be time to open her contracted palm into a graceful and ornate rhetoric taught out of the rule of *Plato, Aristotle, Phalereus, Cicero, Hermogenes, Longinus.* To which poetry would be made subsequent, or indeed rather precedent, as being less subtle and fine, but more simple, sensuous and passionate. I mean not here the prosody of a verse, which they could not have hit on before among the rudiments of grammar; but that sublime art which in *Aristotle's Poetics,* in *Horace,* and the *Italian* commentaries of *Castelvetro, Tasso, Mazzoni,* and others, teaches what the laws are of a true *epic* poem, what of a *dramatic,* what of a *lyric,* what decorum is, which is the grand masterpiece to observe. This would make them soon perceive what despicable creatures our common rimers and playwriters be, and show them, what religious, what glorious and magnificent use might be made of poetry both in divine and human things. From hence and not till now will be the right season of forming them to be able writers and composers in every excellent matter, when they shall be thus fraught with an universal insight into things. Or whether they be to speak in Parliament or council, honor and attention would be waiting on their lips. There would then also appear in pulpits other visages, other gestures, and stuff otherwise wrought than what we now sit under, ofttimes to as great a trial of our patience as any other that they preach to us. These are the studies wherein our noble and our gentle

---

[47] Chaldean, a language akin to Hebrew.   [48] Aramaic, the language of Palestine in the time of Christ.   [49] Practical.   [50] Arranged.

youth ought to bestow their time in a disciplinary way from twelve to one and twenty; unless they rely more upon their ancestors dead, than upon themselves living. In which methodical course it is so supposed they must proceed by the steady pace of learning onward, as at convenient times for memories' sake to retire back into the middle ward,[51] and sometimes into the rear of what they have been taught, until they have confirmed, and solidly united the whole body of their perfected knowledge, like the last embattling of a Roman legion. Now will be worth the seeing what exercises and recreations may best agree, and become these studies.

Their Exercise.

The course of study hitherto briefly described, is, what I can guess by reading, likest to those ancient and famous schools of *Pythagoras, Plato, Isocrates, Aristotle* and such others, out of which were bred up such a number of renowned philosophers, orators, historians, poets and princes all over *Greece, Italy,* and *Asia,* besides the flourishing studies of *Cyrene* and *Alexandria.* But herein it shall exceed them, and supply a defect as great as that which *Plato* noted in the commonwealth of *Sparta,* whereas that city trained up their youth most for war, and these in their Academies and *Lycæum,* all for the gown,[52] this institution of breeding which I here delineate, shall be equally good both for peace and war. Therefore about an hour and a half ere they eat at noon should be allowed them for exercise and due rest afterward: but the time for this may be enlarged at pleasure, according as their rising in the morning shall be early. The exercise which I commend first, is the exact use of their weapon, to guard and to strike safely with edge, or point; this will keep them healthy, nimble, strong, and well in breath, is also the likeliest means to make them grow large and tall, and to inspire them with a gallant and fearless courage, which being tempered with seasonable lectures and precepts to them of true fortitude and patience, will turn into a native and heroic valor, and make them hate the cowardice of doing wrong. They must be also practised in all the locks and grips of wrestling, wherein Englishmen were wont to excel, as need may often be in fight to tug or grapple, and to close.

[51] Center. [52] Civil life.

OF EDUCATION

And this perhaps will be enough, wherein to prove and heat their single strength. The interim of unsweating[53] themselves regularly, and convenient rest before meat may both with profit and delight be taken up in recreating and composing their travailed[54] spirits with the solemn and divine harmonies of music heard or learned; either while the skilful *organist plies his grave* and fancied descant, in lofty fugues, or the whole symphony with artful and unimaginable touches adorn and grace the well studied chords of some choice composer, sometimes the lute, or soft organ stop waiting on elegant voices either to religious, martial, or civil ditties; which if wise men and prophets be not extremely out,[55] have a great power over dispositions and manners, to smooth and make them gentle from rustic harshness and distempered passions. The like also would not be unexpedient after meat to assist and cherish Nature in her first concoction,[56] and send their minds back to study in good tune and satisfaction. Where having followed it closer under vigilant eyes till about two hours before supper, they are by a sudden alarum or watchword, to be called out to their military motions, under sky or covert, according to the season, as was the Roman wont: first on foot, then as their age permits, on horseback, to all the art of cavalry; that having in sport, but with much exactness, and daily muster, served out the rudiments of their soldiership in all the skill of embattling, marching, encamping, fortifying, besieging and battering, with all the helps of ancient and modern stratagems, *tactics* and warlike maxims, they may as it were out of a long war come forth renowned and perfect commanders in the service of their country. They would not then, if they were trusted with fair and hopeful armies, suffer them for want of just and wise discipline to shed away from about them like sick feathers, though they never so oft supplied: they would not suffer their empty and unrecruitable[57] colonels of twenty men in a company to quaff out,[58] or convey,[59] into secret hoards, the wages of a delusive list, and a miserable remnant: yet in the meanwhile to be overmastered with a score or two of drunkards, the only soldiery left about them, or else to comply with all rapines and violences. No certainly, if they knew

---

[53] Cooling off. [54] Tired with exercise. [55] Mistaken. [56] Digestion.
[57] Unable to enlist recruits. [58] Spend in drinking. [59] Steal.

aught of that knowledge that belongs to good men or good governors, they would not suffer these things. But to return to our own institute, besides these constant exercises at home, there is another opportunity of gaining experience to be won from pleasure itself abroad; in those vernal seasons of the year, when the air is calm and pleasant, it were an injury and sullenness against nature not to go out, and see her riches, and partake in her rejoicing with heaven and earth. I should not therefore be a persuader to them of studying much then, after two or three years that they have well laid their grounds, but to ride out in companies with prudent and staid guides, to all the quarters of the land: learning and observing all places of strength, all commodities[60] of building and of soil, for towns and tillage, harbors and ports for trade. Sometimes taking sea as far as to our navy, to learn there also what they can in the practical knowledge of sailing and of sea-fight. These ways would try all their peculiar gifts of nature, and if there were any secret excellence among them, would fetch it out, and give it fair opportunities to advance itself by, which could not but mightily redound to the good of this nation, and bring into fashion again those old admired virtues and excellencies, with far more advantage now in this purity of Christian knowledge. Nor shall we then need the monsieurs of *Paris,* to take our hopeful youth into their slight[61] and prodigal custodies and send them over back again transformed into mimics, apes, and kickshaws. But if they desire to see other countries at three or four and twenty years of age, not to learn principles but to enlarge experience, and make wise observation, they will by that time be such as shall deserve the regard and honor of all men where they pass, and the society and friendship of those in all places who are best and most eminent. And perhaps then other nations will be glad to visit us for their breeding, or else to imitate us in their own country.

Now lastly for their diet there can not be much to say, save only that it would be best in the same house; for much time else would be lost abroad, and many ill habits got; and that it should be plain, healthful, and moderate I suppose is out of controversy. Thus Mr. *Hartlib,* you have a general view in writing, as your desire was, of that which at several times I had discoursed with you concerning

---

[60] Advantages.   [61] Evil.

the best and noblest way of education; not beginning as some have done from the cradle, which yet might be worth many considerations, if brevity had not been my scope, many other circumstances also I could have mentioned, but this to such as have the worth in them to make trial, for light and direction may be enough. Only I believe that this is not a bow for every man to shoot in that counts himself a teacher; but will require sinews almost equal to those which *Homer* gave *Ulysses,* yet I am withal persuaded that it may prove much more easy in the assay,[62] than it now seems at distance, and much more illustrious: howbeit not more difficult than I imagine, and that imagination presents me with nothing but very happy and very possible according to best wishes; if God have so decreed, and this age have spirit and capacity enough to apprehend.

[62] Attempt.

RELIGIO MEDICI
BY
SIR THOMAS BROWNE

INTRODUCTORY NOTE

SIR THOMAS BROWNE was born in London on October 19, 1605, educated at Winchester and Oxford, and trained for the practise of medicine. After traveling on the Continent he finally settled as a physician in Norwich, and enjoyed a distinguished professional reputation. Later he became equally famous as a scholar and antiquary, and was knighted by Charles II on the occasion of the King's visit to Norwich in 1671. In 1641 he married, and he was survived by four of his ten children. He died on his seventy-seventh birthday.

His "Religio Medici" seems to have been written about 1635, without being intended for publication. In 1642, however, two surreptitious editions appeared, and he was induced by the inaccuracies of these to issue an authorized edition in 1643. Since that time between thirty and forty editions have appeared, and the work has been translated into Latin, Dutch, French, German, and Italian. Of his other works the most famous are "Pseudodoxia Epidemica, or Enquiries into Vulgar Errors" (1646), a treatise of vast learning and much entertainment; "Hydriotaphia, or Urn Burial," a discourse on burial customs, which closes with a chapter on death and immortality, the majestic eloquence of which places Browne in the first rank of writers of English prose; and "The Garden of Cyrus," a fantastic account of horticulture from the Garden of Eden down to the time of Cyrus, King of Persia, with much discussion on the mystical significations of the number five. His miscellaneous writings cover a great variety of subjects, religious, scientific, and antiquarian.

The "Religio Medici" is an excellent typical example of the author's style. At once obscured and enriched by his individual and sometimes far-fetched vocabulary, his full and sonorous periods remain the delight of readers with an ear for the cadences of English prose. The matter of the book also reveals a personality of great charm and humor, a mind at once surprisingly acute and surprisingly credulous, and a character of an exalted nobility.

TO THE READER

CERTAINLY that man were greedy of Life, who should desire to live when all the world were at an end; and he must needs be very impatient, who would repine at death in the society of all things that suffer under it. Had not almost every man suffered by the Press, or were not the tyranny thereof become universal, I had not wanted reason for complaint: but in times wherein I have lived to behold the highest perversion of that excellent invention, the name of his Majesty defamed, the Honour of Parliament depraved, the Writings of both depravedly, anticipatively, counterfeitly imprinted; complaints may seem ridiculous in private persons; and men of my condition may be as incapable of affronts, as hopeless of their reparations. And truely, had not the duty I owe unto the importunity of friends, and the allegiance I must ever acknowledge unto truth, prevailed with me, the inactivity of my disposition might have made these sufferings continual, and time, that brings other things to light, should have satisfied me in the remedy of its oblivion. But because things evidently false are not onely printed, but many things of truth most falsly set forth, in this latter I could not but think my self engaged: for, though we have no power to redress the former, yet in the other the reparation being within our selves, I have at present represented unto the world a full and intended Copy of that Piece, which was most imperfectly and surreptitiously published before.

This, I confess, about seven years past, with some others of affinity thereto, for my private exercise and satisfaction, I had at leisurable hours composed; which being communicated unto one, it became common unto many, and was by Transcription successively corrupted, untill it arrived in a most depraved Copy at the Press. He that shall peruse that work, and shall take notice of sundry particularities and personal expressions therein, will easily discern the intention was not publick; and, being a private Exercise directed to my self, what is delivered therein, was rather a memorial unto *me,* than an Example or Rule unto any other; and therefore, if there be any singularity therein correspondent unto the private conceptions of any man, it doth not advantage them; or if dissentaneous[1] thereunto, it no way overthrows them. It was penned in such a place, and with such disadvantage, that, (I protest,) from the first setting of pen unto paper, I had not the assistance of any good Book whereby to promote my invention or relieve my memory; and there-

[1] Not in accordance.

fore there might be many real lapses therein, which others might take notice of, and more that I suspected my self. It was set down many years past, and was the sense of my conceptions at that time, not an immutable Law unto my advancing judgement at all times; and therefore there might be many things therein plausible unto my passed apprehension, which are not agreeable unto my present self. There are many things delivered Rhetorically, many expressions therein meerly Tropical, and as they best illustrate my intention; and therefore also there are many things to be taken in a soft and flexible sense, and not to be called unto the rigid test of Reason. Lastly, all that is contained therein is in submission unto maturer discernments; and, as I have declared, shall no further father them than the best and learned judgments shall authorize them: under favour of which considerations I have made its secrecy publick, and committed the truth thereof to every Ingenuous Reader.

THO. BROWNE.

RELIGIO MEDICI

THE FIRST PART

FOR my Religion, though there be several Circumstances that might perswade the World I have none at all, (as the general scandal of my Profession,[2] the natural course of my Studies, the indifferency of my Behaviour and Discourse in matters of Religion, neither violently Defending one, nor with that common ardour and contention Opposing another;) yet, in despight hereof, I dare without usurpation assume the honourable Stile of a Christian. Not that I meerly owe this Title to the Font, my Education, or the clime wherein I was born, (as being bred up either to confirm those Principles my Parents instilled into my unwary Understanding, or by a general consent proceed in the Religion of my Country;) but having in my riper years and confirmed Judgment seen and examined all, I find my self obliged by the Principles of Grace, and the Law of mine own Reason, to embrace no other Name but this. Neither doth herein my zeal so far make me forget the general Charity I owe unto Humanity, as rather to hate than pity Turks, Infidels, and (what is worse,) Jews; rather contenting my self to enjoy that happy Stile, than maligning those who refuse so glorious a Title.

II. But, because the Name of a Christian is become too general to express our Faith, (there being a Geography of Religions as well as Lands, and every Clime distinguished not only by their Laws and Limits, but circumscribed by their Doctrines and Rules of Faith;) to be particular, I am of that Reformed new-cast Religion, wherein I dislike nothing but the Name; of the same belief our Saviour taught, the Apostles disseminated, the Fathers authorized, and the Martyrs confirmed; but by the sinister ends of Princes, the ambition and avarice of Prelates, and the fatal corruption of times, so

[2] *Cf.* the saying, "Among three physicians, two atheists."

decayed, impaired, and fallen from its native Beauty, that it required the careful and charitable hands of these times to restore it to its primitive Integrity. Now the accidental occasion whereupon, the slender means whereby, the low and abject condition of the Person[3] by whom so good a work was set on foot, which in our Adversaries beget contempt and scorn, fills me with wonder, and is the very same Objection the insolent Pagans first cast at CHRIST and His Disciples.

III. Yet have I not so shaken hands with those desperate Resolutions,[4] (who had rather venture at large their decayed bottom, than bring her in to be new trimm'd in the Dock; who had rather promiscuously retain all, than abridge any, and obstinately be what they are, than what they have been,) as to stand in Diameter[5] and Swords point with them. We have reformed from them, not against them; for (omitting those Improperations[6] and Terms of Scurrility betwixt us, which only difference our Affections, and not our Cause,) there is between us one common Name and Appellation, one Faith and necessary body of Principles common to us both; and therefore I am not scrupulous to converse and live with them, to enter their Churches in defect of ours, and either pray with them, or for them. I could never perceive any rational Consequence from those many Texts which prohibit the Children of Israel to pollute themselves with the Temples of the Heathens; we being all Christians, and not divided by such detested impieties as might prophane our Prayers, or the place wherein we make them; or that a resolved Conscience may not adore her Creator any where, especially in places devoted to His Service; where, if *their* Devotions offend Him, mine may please Him; if theirs prophane it, mine may hallow it. Holy-water and Crucifix (dangerous to common people,) deceive not my judgment, nor abuse my devotion at all. I am, I confess, naturally inclined to that which misguided Zeal terms *Superstition*. My common conversation[7] I do acknowledge austere, my behaviour full of rigour, sometimes not without morosity; yet at my Devotion I love to use the civility of my knee, my hat, and hand, with all those outward and sensible motions which may express or promote

---

[3] Probably Luther is meant.   [4] Persons who have resolved.   [5] Direct opposition.
[6] Taunts.   [7] Manner of life.

my invisible Devotion. I should violate my own arm rather than a Church; nor willingly deface the name of Saint or Martyr. At the sight of a Cross or Crucifix I can dispense with my hat, but scarce with the thought or memory of my Saviour. I cannot laugh at, but rather pity, the fruitless journeys of Pilgrims, or contemn the miserable condition of Fryars; for, though misplaced in Circumstances, there is something in it of Devotion. I could never hear the Ave-Mary Bell without an elevation; or think it a sufficient warrant, because *they* erred in one circumstance, for me to err in all, that is, in silence and dumb contempt. Whilst, therefore, they directed their Devotions to *Her,* I offered mine to GOD, and rectified the Errors of their Prayers by rightly ordering mine own. At a solemn Procession I have wept abundantly, while my consorts, blind with opposition and prejudice, have fallen into an excess of scorn and laughter. There are, questionless, both in Greek, Roman, and African Churches, Solemnities and Ceremonies, whereof the wiser Zeals do make a Christian use, and stand condemned by us, not as evil in themselves, but as allurements and baits of superstition to those vulgar heads that look asquint on the face of Truth, and those unstable Judgments that cannot consist in the narrow point and centre of Virtue without a reel or stagger to the Circumference.

IV. As there were many Reformers, so likewise many Reformations; every Country proceeding in a particular way and method, according as their national Interest, together with their Constitution and Clime, inclined them; some angrily, and with extremity; others calmly, and with mediocrity; not rending, but easily dividing the community, and leaving an honest possibility of a reconciliation; which though peaceable Spirits do desire, and may conceive that revolution of time and the mercies of GOD may effect, yet that judgment that shall consider the present antipathies between the two extreams, their contrarieties in condition, affection, and opinion, may with the same hopes expect an union in the Poles of Heaven.

V. But (to difference my self nearer, and draw into a lesser Circle,) there is no Church whose every part so squares unto my Conscience; whose Articles, Constitutions, and Customs seem so consonant unto reason, and as it were framed to my particular Devotion, as this whereof I hold my Belief, the Church of England; to whose Faith I am a sworn Subject, and therefore in a double Obligation subscribe unto her Articles, and endeavour to observe her Constitutions. Whatsoever is beyond, as points indifferent, I observe according to the rules of my private reason, or the humor and fashion of my Devotion; neither believing this, because Luther affirmed it, or disproving that, because Calvin hath disavouched it. I condemn not all things in the Council of Trent, nor approve all in the Synod of Dort. In brief, where the Scripture is silent, the Church is my Text; where that speaks, 'tis but my Comment: where there is a joynt silence of both, I borrow not the rules of my Religion from Rome or Geneva, but the dictates of my own reason. It is an unjust scandal of our adversaries, and a gross errour in our selves, to compute the Nativity of our Religion from Henry the Eighth, who, though he rejected the Pope, refus'd not the faith of Rome, and effected no more than what his own Predecessors desired and assayed in Ages past, and was conceived the State of Venice would have attempted in our days. It is as uncharitable a point in *us* to fall upon those popular scurrilities and opprobrious scoffs of the Bishop of Rome, to whom, as a temporal Prince, we owe the duty of good language. I confess there is cause of passion between us: by his sentence I stand excommunicated; *Heretick* is the best language he affords me; yet can no ear witness I ever returned him the name of *Antichrist, Man of Sin,* or *Whore of Babylon.* It is the method of Charity to suffer without reaction: those usual Satyrs and invectives of the Pulpit may perchance produce a good effect on the vulgar, whose ears are opener to Rhetorick than Logick; yet do they in no wise confirm the faith of wiser Believers, who know that a good cause needs not to be patron'd by passion, but can sustain itself upon a temperate dispute.

VI. I could never divide myself from any man upon the difference of an opinion, or be angry with his judgment for not agreeing with me in that from which perhaps within a few days I should dissent my self. I have no Genius to disputes in Religion, and have often thought it wisdom to decline them, especially upon a disadvantage, or when the cause of Truth might suffer in the weakness of my patronage. Where we desire to be informed, 'tis good to contest with men above our selves; but to confirm and establish our opinions, 'tis best to argue with judgments below our own, that the frequent spoils and Victories over their reasons may settle in ourselves an esteem and confirmed Opinion of our own. Every man is not a proper Champion for Truth, nor fit to take up the Gauntlet in the cause of Verity: many from the ignorance of these Maximes, and an inconsiderate Zeal unto Truth, have too rashly charged the Troops of Error, and remain as Trophies unto the enemies of Truth. A man may be in as just possession of Truth as of a City, and yet be forced to surrender; 'tis therefore far better to enjoy her with peace, than to hazzard her on a battle. If, therefore, there rise any doubts in my way, I do forget them, or at least defer them till my better setled judgement and more manly reason be able to resolve them; for I perceive every man's own reason is his best Œdipus, and will, upon a reasonable truce, find a way to loose those bonds wherewith the subtleties of error have enchained our more flexible and tender judgements. In Philosophy, where Truth seems double-fac'd, there is no man more Paradoxical than my self: but in Divinity I love to keep the Road; and, though not in an implicite, yet an humble faith, follow the great wheel of the Church, by which I move, not reserving any proper Poles or motion from the Epicycle[8] of my own brain. By this means I leave no gap for Heresies, Schisms, or Errors, of which at present I hope I shall not injure Truth to say I have no taint or tincture. I must confess my greener studies have been polluted with two or three; not any begotten in the latter Centuries, but old and obsolete, such as could never have been revived, but by such extravagant and irregular heads as mine: for indeed Heresies perish not with their Authors, but, like the river Arethusa, though they lose their currents in one place, they rise up again in another. One General Council is not able to extirpate one single Heresie: it may be cancell'd for the present; but revolution of time, and the like aspects from Heaven, will restore it, when it will flourish till it be condemned again. For as though there were a Metempsuchosis, and the soul of one man passed into another, Opinions do find, after certain Revolutions, men and minds like those that first begat them. To see our selves again, we need

---

[8] Astronomy, a smaller circle whose center describes a larger.

not look for Plato's year:[9] every man is not only himself; there hath been many Diogenes, and as many Timons, though but few of that name: men are liv'd over again, the world is now as it was in Ages past; there was none then, but there hath been some one since that parallels him, and is, as it were, his revived self.

VII. Now the first of mine was that of the Arabians, That the Souls of men perished with their Bodies, but should yet be raised again at the last day. Not that I did absolutely conceive a mortality of the Soul; but if that were, (which Faith, not Philosophy, hath yet throughly disproved,) and that both entred the grave together, yet I held the same conceit thereof that we all do of the body, that it should rise again. Surely it is but the merits of our unworthy Natures, if we sleep in darkness until the last Alarum. A serious reflex upon my own unworthiness did make me backward from challenging this prerogative of my Soul: so that I might enjoy my Saviour at the last, I could with patience be nothing almost unto Eternity.

The second was that of Origen, That GOD would not persist in His vengeance for ever, but after a definite time of His wrath, He would release the damned Souls from torture. Which error I fell into upon a serious contemplation of the great Attribute of GOD, His Mercy; and did a little cherish it in my self, because I found therein no malice, and a ready weight to sway me from the other extream of despair, whereunto Melancholy and Contemplative Natures are too easily disposed.

A third there is, which I did never positively maintain or practise, but have often wished it had been consonant to Truth, and not offensive to my Religion, and that is, the Prayer for the Dead; whereunto I was inclin'd from some charitable inducements, whereby I could scarce contain my Prayers for a friend at the ringing of a Bell, or behold his Corps without an Orison for his Soul. 'Twas a good way, methought, to be remembered by posterity, and far more noble than an History.

These opinions I never maintained with pertinacy, or endeavoured to eneagle any mans belief unto mine, nor so much as ever

---

[9] A period of thousands of years, at the end of which all things should return to their former state.

revealed or disputed them with my dearest friends; by which means I neither propagated them in others, nor confirmed them in my self; but suffering them to flame upon their own substance, without addition of new fuel, they went out insensibly of themselves. Therefore these Opinions, though condemned by lawful Councels, were not Heresies in me, but bare Errors, and single Lapses of my understanding, without a joynt depravity of my will. Those have not onely depraved understandings, but diseased affections, which cannot enjoy a singularity without an Heresie, or be the Author of an Opinion without they be of a Sect also. This was the villany of the first Schism of Lucifer, who was not content to err alone, but drew into his Faction many Legions of Spirits; and upon this experience he tempted only Eve, as well understanding the Communicable nature of Sin, and that to deceive but one, was tacitely and upon consequence to delude them both.

VIII. That Heresies should arise, we have the Prophesie of CHRIST; but that old ones should be abolished, we hold no prediction. That there must be Heresies, is true, not only in our Church, but also in any other: even in doctrines heretical, there will be super-heresies; and Arians not only divided from their Church, but also among themselves. For heads that are disposed unto Schism and complexionally propense[10] to innovation, are naturally indisposed for a community, nor will be ever confined unto the order or œconomy of one body; and therefore, when they separate from others, they knit but loosely among themselves; nor contented with a general breach or dichotomy with their Church do subdivide and mince themselves almost into Atoms. 'Tis true, that men of singular parts and humours have not been free from singular opinions and conceits in all Ages; retaining something, not only beside the opinion of his own Church or any other, but also any particular Author; which, notwithstanding, a sober Judgment may do without offence or heresie; for there is yet, after all the Decrees of Councils and the niceties of the Schools, many things untouch'd, unimagin'd, wherein the liberty of an honest reason may play and expatiate with security, and far without the circle of an Heresie.

IX. As for those wingy Mysteries in Divinity, and airy subtleties

[10] Inclined by temperament.

in Religion, which have unhing'd the brains of better heads, they never stretched the *Pia Mater*[11] of mine. Methinks there be not impossibilities enough in Religion for an active faith; the deepest Mysteries ours contains have not only been illustrated, but maintained, by Syllogism and the rule of Reason. I love to lose my self in a mystery, to pursue my Reason to an *O altitudo!* 'Tis my solitary recreation to pose my apprehension with those involved Ænigmas and riddles of the Trinity, with Incarnation, and Resurrection. I can answer all the Objections of Satan and my rebellious reason with that odd resolution I learned of Tertullian, *Certum est, quia impossibile est.* I desire to exercise my faith in the difficultest point; for to credit ordinary and visible objects is not faith, but perswasion. Some believe the better for seeing CHRIST's Sepulchre; and, when they have seen the Red Sea, doubt not of the Miracle. Now, contrarily, I bless my self and am thankful that I lived not in the days of Miracles, that I never saw CHRIST nor His Disciples. I would not have been one of those Israelites that pass'd the Red Sea, nor one of CHRIST's patients on whom He wrought His wonders; then had my faith been thrust upon me, nor should I enjoy that greater blessing pronounced to all that believe and saw not. 'Tis an easie and necessary belief, to credit what our eye and sense hath examined. I believe He was dead, and buried, and rose again; and desire to see Him in His glory, rather than to contemplate Him in His Cenotaphe or Sepulchre. Nor is this much to believe; as we have reason, we owe this faith unto History: *they* only had the advantage of a bold and noble Faith, who lived before His coming, who upon obscure prophesies and mystical Types could raise a belief, and expect apparent impossibilities.

X. 'Tis true, there is an edge in all firm belief, and with an easie Metaphor we may say, the *Sword* of Faith; but in these obscurities I rather use it in the adjunct the Apostle gives it, a *Buckler;* under which I conceive a wary combatant may lye invulnerable. Since I was of understanding to know we knew nothing, my reason hath been more pliable to the will of Faith; I am now content to understand a mystery without a rigid definition, in an easier and Pla-

[11] A membrane surrounding the brain.

tonick description. That allegorical description of Hermes[12] pleaseth me beyond all the Metaphysical definitions of Divines. Where I cannot satisfy my reason, I love to humour my fancy: I had as live you tell me that *anima est angelus hominis, est Corpus* DEI, [the soul is man's angel, God's body] as *Entelechia;*[13]—*Lux est umbra* DEI, [Light is God's shadow] as *actus perspicui*.[14] Where there is an obscurity too deep for our Reason, 'tis good to sit down with a description, periphrasis, or adumbration; for by acquainting our Reason how unable it is to display the visible and obvious effects of Nature, it becomes more humble and submissive unto the subtleties of Faith; and thus I teach my haggard[15] and unreclaimed Reason to stoop unto the lure of Faith. I believe there was already a tree whose fruit our unhappy Parents tasted, though, in the same Chapter when GOD forbids it, 'tis positively said, the plants of the field were not yet grown, *for* GOD *had not caus'd it to rain upon the earth*. I believe that the Serpent, (if we shall literally understand it,) from his proper form and figure, made his motion on his belly before the curse. I find the tryal of the Pucellage and virginity of Women, which GOD ordained the Jews, is very fallible. Experience and History informs me, that not onely many particular Women, but likewise whole Nations, have escaped the curse of Childbirth, which GOD seems to pronounce upon the whole Sex. Yet I do believe that all this is true, which indeed my Reason would perswade me to be false; and this I think is no vulgar part of Faith, to believe a thing not only above but contrary to Reason, and against the Arguments of our proper Senses.

XI. In my solitary and retired imagination

(*neque enim cum porticus aut me
Lectulus accepit, desum mihi,*)

[for when porch or bed has received me, I do not lose myself]

I remember I am not alone, and therefore forget not to contemplate Him and His Attributes Who is ever with me, especially those two

---

[12] The description alluded to, "God is a sphere whose center is everywhere and circumference nowhere," is said not to be found in the books which pass under the name of the fabulous Hermes Trismegistus. [13] Aristotle's word for "actual being."
[14] The active force of the clear. [15] Intractable: used of a hawk.

mighty ones, His Wisdom and Eternity. With the one I recreate, with the other I confound, my understanding; for who can speak of Eternity without a solœcism, or think thereof without an Extasie? Time we may comprehend; 'tis but five days elder then our selves, and hath the same Horoscope with the World; but to retire so far back as to apprehend a beginning, to give such an infinite start forwards as to conceive an end, in an essence that we affirm hath neither the one nor the other, it puts my Reason to St. Paul's Sanctuary.[16] My Philosophy dares not say the Angels can do it. God hath not made a Creature that can comprehend Him; 'tis a privilege of His own nature. I AM THAT I AM, was His own definition unto Moses; and 'twas a short one, to confound mortality, that durst question God, or ask Him what He was. Indeed, He onely is; all others have and shall be. But in Eternity there is no distinction of Tenses; and therefore that terrible term *Predestination,* which hath troubled so many weak heads to conceive, and the wisest to explain, is in respect to God no prescious[17] determination of our Estates to come, but a definitive blast of His Will already fulfilled, and at the instant that He first decreed it; for to His Eternity, which is indivisible and all together, the last Trump is already sounded, the reprobates in the flame, and the blessed in Abraham's bosome. St. Peter speaks modestly,[18] when he saith, *a thousand years to* God *are but as one day;* for, to speak like a Philosopher, those continued instances of time which flow into a thousand years, make not to Him one moment: what to us is to come, to His Eternity is present, His whole duration being but one permanent point, without Sucession, Parts, Flux, or Division.

XII. There is no Attribute that adds more difficulty to the mystery of the Trinity, where, though in a relative way of Father and Son, we must deny a priority. I wonder how Aristotle could conceive the World eternal, or how he could make good two Eternities. His similitude of a Triangle comprehended in a square doth somewhat illustrate the Trinity of our Souls, and that the Triple Unity of God; for there is in us not three, but a Trinity of Souls; because there is in us, if not three distinct Souls, yet differing faculties, that

---

[16] This has been taken as a reference to Rom. xi. 33, but the exact meaning is uncertain.   [17] Foreknowing.   [18] Moderately.

can and do subsist apart in different Subjects, and yet in us are so united as to make but one Soul and substance.

If one Soul were so perfect as to inform three distinct Bodies, that were a petty Trinity: conceive the distinct number of three, not divided nor separated by the intellect, but actually comprehended in its Unity, and that is a perfect Trinity. I have often admired the mystical way of Pythagoras, and the secret Magick of numbers. *Beware of Philosophy,* is a precept not to be received in too large a sense; for in this Mass of Nature there is a set of things that carry in their Front (though not in Capital Letters, yet in Stenography and short Characters,) something of Divinity, which to wiser Reasons serve as Luminaries in the Abyss of Knowledge, and to judicious beliefs as Scales[19] and Roundles[20] to mount the Pinacles and highest pieces of Divinity. The severe Schools shall never laugh me out of the Philosophy of Hermes, that this visible World is but a Picture of the invisible, wherein, as in a Pourtraict, things are not truely, but in equivocal shapes, and as they counterfeit some more real substance in that invisible fabrick.

XIII. That other Attribute wherewith I recreate my devotion, is His Wisdom, in which I am happy; and for the contemplation of this only, do not repent me that I was bred in the way of Study: the advantage I have of the vulgar, with the content and happiness I conceive therein, is an ample recompence for all my endeavours, in what part of knowledge soever. Wisdom is His most beauteous Attribute; no man can attain unto it, yet Solomon pleased GOD when he desired it. He is wise, because He knows all things; and He knoweth all things, because He made them all: but His greatest knowledge is in comprehending *that* He made not, that is, Himself. And this is also the greatest knowledge in man. For this do I honour my own profession, and embrace the Counsel even of the Devil himself: had he read such a Lecture in Paradise as he did at Delphos,[21] we had better known our selves, nor had we stood in fear to know *him.* I know He is wise in all, wonderful in what we conceive, but far more in what we comprehend not; for we behold Him but asquint, upon reflex or shadow; our understanding is

---

[19] Ladders.   [20] Steps of a ladder.   [21] "Know thyself." This, like other ancient oracles, Browne ascribes to the Devil.

dimmer than Moses Eye; we are ignorant of the back-parts or lower side of His Divinity; therefore to prie into the maze of His Counsels is not only folly in man, but presumption even in Angels. Like us, they are His Servants, not His Senators; He holds no Counsel, but that mystical one of the Trinity, wherein, though there be three Persons, there is but one mind that decrees without contradiction. Nor needs He any: His actions are not begot with deliberation, His Wisdom naturally knows what's best; His intellect stands ready fraught with the superlative and purest Ideas of goodness; consultation and election, which are two motions in us, make but one in Him, His actions springing from His power at the first touch of His will. These are Contemplations metaphysical: my humble speculations have another Method, and are content to trace and discover those expressions He hath left in His Creatures, and the obvious effects of Nature. There is no danger to profound[22] these mysteries, no *sanctum sanctorum* in Philosophy. The World was made to be inhabited by Beasts, but studied and contemplated by Man: 'tis the Debt of our Reason we owe unto GOD, and the homage we pay for not being Beasts. Without this, the World is still as though it had not been, or as it was before the sixth day, when as yet there was not a Creature that could conceive or say there was a World. The Wisdom of GOD receives small honour from those vulgar Heads that rudely stare about, and with a gross rusticity admire His works: those highly magnifie Him, whose judicious inquiry into His Acts, and deliberate research into His Creatures, return the duty of a devout and learned admiration. Therefore,

> Search while thou wilt, and let thy Reason go,
> To ransome Truth, even to th' Abyss below;
> Rally the scattered Causes; and that line,
> Which Nature twists, be able to untwine.
> It is thy Makers will, for unto none
> But unto Reason can He e're be known.
> The Devils do know Thee, but those damnèd Meteors
> Build not Thy Glory, but confound Thy Creatures.
> Teach my indeavours so Thy works to read,
> That learning them in Thee, I may proceed.
> Give Thou my reason that instructive flight,

[22] Plunge into.

Whose weary wings may on Thy hands still light.
Teach me to soar aloft, yet ever so,
When neer the Sun, to stoop again below.
Thus shall my humble Feathers safely hover,
And, though near Earth, more than the Heavens discover.
And then at last, when homeward I shall drive,
Rich with the Spoils of Nature, to my Hive,
There will I sit like that industrious Flie,
Buzzing Thy praises, which shall never die,
Till Death abrupts them, and succeeding Glory
Bid me go on in a more lasting story.

And this is almost all wherein an humble Creature may endeavour to requite and some way to retribute[23] unto his Creator: for if *not he that saith, "Lord, Lord," but he that doth the will of his Father, shall be saved;* certainly our wills must be our performances, and our intents make out our Actions; otherwise our pious labours shall find anxiety in our Graves, and our best endeavours not hope, but fear, a resurrection.

XIV. There is but one first cause, and four second causes of all things. Some are without efficient, as God; others without matter, as Angels; some without form, as the first matter: but every Essence, created or uncreated, hath its final cause, and some positive end both of its Essence and Operation. This is the cause I grope after in the works of Nature; on this hangs the Providence of God. To raise so beauteous a structure as the World and the Creatures thereof, was but His Art; but their sundry and divided operations, with their predestinated ends, are from the Treasure of His Wisdom. In the causes, nature, and affections[24] of the Eclipses of the Sun and Moon, there is most excellent speculation; but to profound[22] farther, and to contemplate a reason why His Providence hath so disposed and ordered their motions in that vast circle as to conjoyn and obscure each other, is a sweeter piece of Reason, and a diviner point of Philosophy. Therefore sometimes, and in some things, there appears to me as much Divinity in Galen his books *De Usu Partium,* as in Suarez Metaphysicks. Had Aristotle been as curious in the enquiry of this cause as he was of the other, he had not left behind him an imperfect piece of Philosophy, but an absolute tract of Divinity.

[22] Plunge into.   [23] Render back.   [24] Influences.

XV. *Natura nihil agit frustra,* [Nature does nothing in vain] is the only indisputed Axiome in Philosophy. There are no Grotesques in Nature; not anything framed to fill up empty Cantons,[25] and unnecessary spaces. In the most imperfect Creatures, and such as were not preserved in the Ark, but, having their Seeds and Principles in the womb of Nature, are every where, where the power of the Sun is, in these is the Wisdom of His hand discovered. Out of this rank Solomon chose the object of his admiration. Indeed what Reason may not go to School to the Wisdom of Bees, Ants, and Spiders? what wise hand teacheth *them* to do what Reason cannot teach *us?* Ruder heads stand amazed at those prodigious pieces of Nature, Whales, Elephants, Dromidaries and Camels; these, I confess, are the Colossus and majestick pieces of her hand: but in these narrow Engines there is more curious Mathematicks; and the civility of these little Citizens more neatly sets forth Wisdom of their Maker. Who admires not Regio-Montanus[26] his Fly beyond his Eagle, or wonders not more at the operation of two Souls[27] in those little Bodies, than but one in the Trunk of a Cedar? I could never content my contemplations with those general pieces of wonder, the Flux and Reflux of the Sea, the increase of Nile, the conversion of the Needle to the North; and have studied to match and parallel those in the more obvious and neglected pieces of Nature, which without further travel I can do in the Cosmography of myself. We carry with us the wonders we seek without us: there is all Africa and her prodigies in us; we are that bold and adventurous piece of Nature, which he that studies wisely learns in a compendium what others labour at in a divided piece and endless volume.

XVI. Thus there are two Books from whence I collect my Divinity; besides that written one of GOD, another of His servant Nature, that universal and publick Manuscript, that lies expans'd unto the Eyes of all: those that never saw Him in the one, have discovered Him in the other. This was the Scripture and Theology of the Heathens: the natural motion of the Sun made *them* more admire Him than its supernatural station did the Children of Israel; the

---

[25] Corners. [26] John Müller of Königsberg (1636–75), who made an automatic iron fly on a wooden eagle. [27] The sensitive and the vegetative.

ordinary effects of Nature wrought more admiration in *them* than in the other all His Miracles. Surely the Heathens knew better how to joyn and read these mystical Letters than we Christians, who cast a more careless Eye on these common Hieroglyphicks, and disdain to suck Divinity from the flowers of Nature. Nor do I so forget GOD as to adore the name of Nature; which I define not, with the Schools, to be the principle of motion and rest, but that streight and regular line, that settled and constant course the Wisdom of GOD hath ordained the actions of His creatures, according to their several kinds. To make a revolution every day is the Nature of the Sun, because of that necessary course which GOD hath ordained it, from which it cannot swerve but by a faculty from that voice which first did give it motion. Now this course of Nature GOD seldome alters or perverts, but, like an excellent Artist, hath so contrived His work, that with the self same instrument, without a new creation, He may effect His obscurest designs. Thus He sweetneth the Water with a Wood,[28] preserveth the Creatures in the Ark, which the blast of His mouth might have as easily created; for GOD is like a skilful Geometrician, who, when more easily and with one stroak of his Compass he might describe or divide a right line, had yet rather do this in a circle or longer way, according to the constituted and forelaid principles of his Art. Yet this rule of His He doth sometimes pervert, to acquaint the World with His Prerogative, lest the arrogancy of our reason should question His power, and conclude He could not. And thus I call the effects of Nature the works of GOD, Whose hand and instrument she only is; and therefore to ascribe His actions unto her, is to devolve the honour of the principal agent upon the instrument; which if with reason we may do, then let our hammers rise up and boast they have built our houses, and our pens receive the honour of our writings. I hold there is a general beauty in the works of GOD, and therefore no deformity in any kind or species of creature whatsoever. I cannot tell by what Logick we call a Toad, a Bear, or an Elephant ugly; they being created in those outward shapes and figures which best express the actions of their inward forms, and having past that general Visitation[29] of GOD, Who saw that all that He had made was good, that is, conformable

[28] Exod. xv. 25.   [29] Inspection, Gen. i. 31.

to His Will, which abhors deformity, and is the rule of order and beauty. There is no deformity but in Monstrosity; wherein, notwithstanding, there is a kind of Beauty; Nature so ingeniously contriving the irregular parts, as they become sometimes more remarkable than the principal Fabrick. To speak yet more narrowly, there was never any thing ugly or mis-shapen, but the Chaos; wherein, notwithstanding, (to speak strictly,) there was no deformity, because no form; nor was it yet impregnant by the voice of GOD. Now Nature is not at variance with Art, nor Art with Nature, they being both servants of His Providence. Art is the perfection of Nature. Were the World now as it was the sixth day, there were yet a Chaos. Nature hath made one World, and Art another. In brief, all things are artificial; for Nature is the Art of GOD.

XVII. This is the ordinary and open way of His Providence, which Art and Industry have in a good part discovered; whose effects we may foretel without an Oracle: to foreshew these, is not Prophesie, but Prognostication. There is another way, full of Meanders and Labyrinths, whereof the Devil and Spirits have no exact Ephemerides;[30] and that is a more particular and obscure method of His Providence, directing the operations of individuals and single Essences: this we call *Fortune,* that serpentine and crooked line, whereby He draws those actions His Wisdom intends, in a more unknown and secret way. This cryptick and involved method of His Providence have I ever admired; nor can I relate the History of my life, the occurrences of my days, the escapes of dangers, and hits of chance, with a *Bezo las Manos*[31] to Fortune, or a bare *Gramercy* to my good Stars. Abraham might have thought the Ram in the thicket came thither by accident; humane[32] reason would have said that meer chance conveyed Moses in the Ark to the sight of Pharaoh's Daughter: what a Labyrinth is there in the story of Joseph, able to convert a Stoick! Surely there are in every man's Life certain rubs, doublings, and wrenches, which pass a while under the effects of chance, but at the last, well examined, prove the meer hand of GOD. 'Twas not dumb chance, that, to discover the Fougade or Powder-plot, contrived a miscarriage

---

[30] Tables of the daily state of the heavens, used as bases for prognostications.
[31] Spanish, "I kiss hands," an acknowledgment of favor received. [32] Human.

in the Letter.[33] I like the Victory of '88 the better for that one occurrence, which our enemies imputed to our dishonour and the partiality of Fortune, to wit, the tempests and contrariety of Winds. King Philip did not detract from the Nation, when he said, *he sent his Armado to fight with men, and not to combate with the Winds.* Where there is a manifest disproportion between the powers and forces of two several agents, upon a Maxime of reason we may promise the Victory to the Superiour; but when unexpected accidents slip in, and unthought of occurrences intervene, these must proceed from a power that owes no obedience to those Axioms; where, as in the writing upon the wall, we may behold the hand, but see not the spring that moves it. The success of that petty Province of Holland (of which the Grand Seignour[34] proudly said, *if they should trouble him as they did the Spaniard, he would send his men with shovels and pick-axes, and throw it into the Sea,*) I cannot altogether ascribe to the ingenuity and industry of the people, but the mercy of GOD, that hath disposed them to such a thriving Genius; and to the will of His Providence, that disposeth her favour to each Country in their pre-ordinate season. All cannot be happy at once; for, because the glory of one State depends upon the ruine of another, there is a revolution and vicissitude of their greatness, and must obey the swing of that wheel, not moved by Intelligences, but by the hand of GOD, whereby all Estates arise to their *Zenith* and Vertical points according to their predestinated periods. For the lives, not only of men, but of Commonwealths, and the whole World, run not upon an *Helix*,[35] that still enlargeth, but on a Circle, where, arriving to their Meridian, they decline in obscurity, and fall under the Horizon again.

XVIII. These must not therefore be named the effects of Fortune, but in a relative way, and as we term the works of Nature. It was the ignorance of mans reason that begat this very name, and by a careless term miscalled the Providence of GOD; for there is no liberty for causes to operate in a loose and stragling way; nor any effect whatsoever, but hath its warrant from some universal or superiour Cause. 'Tis not a ridiculous devotion to say a prayer before

[33] A miscarriage of the plot by means of the letter to Lord Monteagle, by which the plot was discovered. [34] The Sultan of Turkey. [35] Spiral.

a game at Tables; for even in *sortilegies*[36] and matters of greatest uncertainty there is a setled and preordered course of effects. It is we that are blind, not Fortune: because our Eye is too dim to discover the mystery of her effects, we foolishly paint her blind, and hoodwink the Providence of the Almighty. I cannot justifie that contemptible Proverb, *That fools only are Fortunate,* or that insolent Paradox, *That a wise man is out of the reach of Fortune;* much less those opprobrious epithets of Poets, *Whore, Bawd,* and *Strumpet.* 'Tis, I confess, the common fate of men of singular gifts of mind to be destitute of those of Fortune, which doth not any way deject the Spirit of wiser judgements, who throughly understand the justice of this proceeding; and being inriched with higher donatives,[37] cast a more careless eye on these vulgar parts of felicity. It is a most unjust ambition to desire to engross the mercies of the Almighty, not to be content with the goods of mind, without a possession of those of body or Fortune; and it is an error worse than heresie, to adore these complemental and circumstantial pieces of felicity, and undervalue those perfections and essential points of happiness wherein we resemble our Maker. To wiser desires it is satisfaction enough to deserve, though not to enjoy, the favours of Fortune: let Providence provide for Fools. 'Tis not partiality, but equity in GOD, Who deals with us but as our natural Parents: those that are able of Body and Mind He leaves to their deserts; to those of weaker merits He imparts a larger portion, and pieces out the defect of one by the excess of the other. Thus have we no just quarrel with Nature for leaving us naked; or to envy the Horns, Hoofs, Skins, and Furs of other Creatures, being provided with Reason, that can supply them all. We need not labour with so many Arguments to confute Judicial Astrology; for, if there be a truth therein, it doth not injure Divinity. If to be born under *Mercury* disposeth us to be witty, under *Jupiter* to be wealthy; I do not owe a Knee unto these, but unto that merciful Hand that hath ordered my indifferent and uncertain nativity unto such benevolous Aspects. Those that hold that all things are governed by Fortune, had not erred, had they not persisted[38] there. The Romans, that erected a Temple to Fortune, acknowledged therein, though in a blinder

[36] Drawing lots.   [37] Gifts.   [38] Stood still.

way, somewhat of Divinity; for, in a wise supputation,[39] all things begin and end in the Almighty. There is a nearer way to Heaven than Homer's Chain;[40] an easie Logic may conjoyn Heaven and Earth in one Argument, and with less than a *Sorites*[41] resolve all things into GOD. For though we christen effects by their most sensible[42] and nearest Causes, yet is GOD the true and infallible Cause of all; whose concourse,[43] though it be general, yet doth it subdivide it self into the particular Actions of every thing, and is that Spirit, by which each singular Essence not only subsists, but performs its operation.

XIX. The bad construction and perverse comment on these pair of second Causes, or visible hands of GOD, have perverted the Devotion of many unto Atheism; who, forgetting the honest Advisoes[44] of Faith, have listened unto the conspiracy of Passion and Reason. I have therefore always endeavoured to compose those Feuds and angry Dissentions between Affection, Faith, and Reason; for there is in our Soul a kind of Triumvirate, or triple Government of three Competitors, which distract the Peace of this our Commonwealth, not less than did that other the State of Rome.

As Reason is a Rebel unto Faith, so Passion unto Reason: as the propositions of Faith seem absurd unto Reason, so the Theorems of Reason unto Passion, and both unto Faith. Yet a moderate and peaceable discretion may so state and order the matter, that they may be all Kings, and yet make but one Monarchy, every one exercising his Soveraignty and Prerogative in a due time and place, according to the restraint and limit of circumstance. There is, as in Philosophy, so in Divinity, sturdy doubts and boisterous Objections, wherewith the unhappiness of our knowledge too nearly acquainteth us. More of these no man hath known than myself, which I confess I conquered, not in a martial posture, but on my Knees. For our endeavours are not only to combat with doubts, but always to dispute with the Devil. The villany of that Spirit takes a hint of Infidelity from our Studies, and, by demonstrating a naturality in one way, makes us mistrust a miracle in another. Thus, having perused the *Archidoxis*[45] and read the secret Sympathies of things,

---

[39] Calculation. [40] Iliad viii. 19. [41] A series of syllogisms. [42] Perceptible to sense. [43] Cooperation. [44] Admonitions. [45] A work by Paracelsus.

he would disswade my belief from the miracle of the Brazen Serpent, make me conceit that Image worked by Sympathy, and was but an Ægyptian trick to cure their Diseases without a miracle. Again, having seen some experiments of *Bitumen,* and having read far more of *Naphtha,* he whispered to my curiosity the fire of the Altar might be natural; and bid me mistrust a miracle in Elias, when he entrenched the Altar round with Water; for that inflamable substance yields not easily unto Water, but flames in the Arms of its Antagonist. And thus would he inveagle my belief to think the combustion of Sodom might be natural, and that there was an Asphaltick and Bituminous nature in that Lake before the fire of Gomorrah. I know that *Manna* is now plentifully gathered in Calabria; and Josephus tells me, in his days it was as plentiful in Arabia; the Devil therefore made the *quære, Where was then the miracle in the days of Moses? the Israelites saw but that in his time, the Natives of those Countries behold in ours.* Thus the Devil played at Chess with me, and yielding a Pawn, thought to gain a Queen of me, taking advantage of my honest endeavours; and whilst I laboured to raise the structure of my Reason, he strived to undermine the edifice of my Faith.

XX. Neither had these or any other ever such advantage of me, as to incline me to any point of Infidelity or desperate positions of Atheism; for I have been these many years of opinion there was never any. Those that held Religion was the difference of Man from Beasts, have spoken probably, and proceed upon a principle as inductive as the other. That doctrine of Epicurus, that denied the Providence of GOD, was no Atheism, but a magnificent and high strained conceit of His Majesty, which he deemed too sublime to mind the trivial Actions of those inferior Creatures. That *fatal Necessity* of the Stoicks is nothing but the immutable Law of His Will. Those that heretofore denied the Divinity of the HOLY GHOST, have been condemned but as Hereticks; and those that now deny our Saviour, (though more than Hereticks,) are not so much as Atheists; for, though they deny two persons in the Trinity, they hold, as we do, there is but one GOD.

That Villain and Secretary of Hell,[46] that composed that mis-

---
[46] Name unknown.

creant piece *Of the Three Impostors,* though divided from all Religions, and was neither Jew, Turk, nor Christian, was not a positive Atheist. I confess every Country hath its Machiavel, every age its Lucian, whereof common Heads must not hear, nor more advanced Judgments too rashly venture on: it is the Rhetorick of Satan, and may pervert a loose or prejudicate belief.

XXI. I confess I have perused them all, and can discover nothing that may startle a discreet belief; yet are there heads carried off with the Wind and breath of such motives. I remember a Doctor in Physick, of Italy, who could not perfectly believe the immortality of the Soul, because Galen seemed to make a doubt thereof. With another I was familiarly acquainted in France, a Divine, and a man of singular parts, that on the same point was so plunged and gravelled with three lines of Seneca, that all our Antidotes, drawn from both Scripture and Philosophy, could not expel the poyson of his errour. There are a set of Heads, that can credit the relations of Mariners, yet question the Testimonies of St. Paul; and peremptorily maintain the traditions of Ælian or Pliny, yet in Histories of Scripture raise Queries and Objections, believing no more than they can parallel in humane[47] Authors. I confess there are in Scripture Stories that do exceed the Fables of Poets, and to a captious Reader sound like *Garagantua* or *Bevis.* Search all the Legends of times past, and the fabulous conceits of these present, and 'twill be hard to find one that deserves to carry the Buckler unto Sampson; yet is all this of an easie possibility, if we conceive a Divine concourse,[48] or an influence but from the little Finger of the Almighty. It is impossible that either in the discourse of man, or in the infallible Voice of God, to the weakness of our apprehensions, there should not appear irregularities, contradictions, and antinomies:[49] my self could shew a Catalogue of doubts, never yet imagined nor questioned, as I know, which are not resolved at the first hearing; not fantastick Queries or Objections of Air; for I cannot hear of Atoms in Divinity. I can read the History of the Pigeon that was sent out of the Ark, and returned no more, yet not question how she found out her Mate that was left behind: that Lazarus was raised from the dead, yet not demand where in the interim his Soul awaited; or

[47] Human. [48] Cooperation. [49] Contradictions of natural law.

raise a Lawcase, whether his Heir might lawfully detain his inheritance bequeathed unto him by his death, and he, though restored to life, have no Plea or Title unto his former possessions. Whether Eve was framed out of the left side of Adam, I dispute not; because I stand not yet assured which is the right side of a man, or whether there be any such distinction in Nature: that she was edified out of the Rib of Adam I believe, yet raise no question who shall arise with that Rib at the Resurrection. Whether Adam was an Hermaphrodite, as the Rabbins contend upon the Letter of the Text, because it is contrary to reason, there should be an Hermaphrodite before there was a Woman, or a composition of two Natures before there was a second composed. Likewise, whether the World was created in Autumn, Summer, or the Spring, because it was created in them all; for whatsoever Sign the Sun possesseth, those four Seasons are actually existent. It is the nature of this Luminary to distinguish the several Seasons of the year, all which it makes at one time in the whole Earth, and successive in any part thereof. There are a bundle of curiosities, not only in Philosophy, but in Divinity, proposed and discussed by men of most supposed abilities, which indeed are not worthy our vacant hours, much less our serious Studies: Pieces only fit to be placed in *Pantagruel's* Library, or bound up with Tartaretus *De modo Cacandi*.[50]

XXII. These are niceties that become not those that peruse so serious a Mystery. There are others more generally questioned and called to the Bar, yet methinks of an easie and possible truth.

'Tis ridiculous to put off or drown the general Flood of Noah in that particular inundation of Deucalion. That there was a Deluge once, seems not to me so great a Miracle, as that there is not one always. How all the kinds of Creatures, not only in their own bulks, but with a competency of food and sustenance, might be preserved in one Ark, and within the extent of three hundred Cubits, to a reason that rightly examines it will appear very feasible. There is another secret, not contained in the Scripture, which is more hard to comprehend, and put the honest Father[51] to the refuge of a

---

[50] The title of an imaginary book in the list given by Rabelais in his "Pantagruel."
[51] St. Augustine.

Miracle; and that is, not only how the distinct pieces of the World and divided Islands, should be first planted by men, but inhabited by Tigers, Panthers, and Bears. How America abounded with Beasts of prey and noxious Animals, yet contained not in it that necessary Creature, a Horse, is very strange. By what passage those, not only Birds, but dangerous and unwelcome Beasts, came over; how there be Creatures there, which are not found in this Triple Continent; (all which must needs be strange unto us, that hold but one Ark, and that the Creatures began their progress from the Mountains of Ararat:) they who, to salve this, would make the Deluge particular, proceed upon a principle that I can no way grant; not only upon the negative of Holy Scriptures, but of mine own Reason, whereby I can make it probable, that the World was as well peopled in the time of Noah as in ours; and fifteen hundred years to people the World, as full a time for them, as four thousand years since have been to us.

There are other assertions and common Tenents drawn from Scripture, and generally believed as Scripture, whereunto, notwithstanding, I would never betray the liberty of my Reason. 'Tis a Postulate to me, that Methusalem was the longest liv'd of all the Children of Adam; and no man will be able to prove it, when, from the process of the Text, I can manifest it may be otherwise. That Judas perished by hanging himself, there is no certainty in Scripture: though in one place it seems to affirm it, and by a doubtful word hath given occasion to translate it; yet in another place, in a more punctual description, it makes it improbable, and seems to overthrow it. That our Fathers, after the Flood, erected the Tower of Babel to preserve themselves against a second Deluge, is generally opinioned and believed; yet is there another intention of theirs expressed in Scripture: besides, it is improbable from the circumstances of the place, that is, a plain in the Land of Shinar. These are no points of Faith, and therefore may admit a free dispute.

There are yet others, and those familiarly concluded from the text, wherein (under favour,) I see no consequence. The Church of Rome confidently proves the opinion of Tutelary Angels from that Answer, when Peter knockt at the Door, *'Tis not he, but his Angel;* that is (might some say,) his *Messenger,* or some body from him; for so the Original signifies, and is as likely to be the doubtful Families meaning. This exposition I once suggested to a young Divine, that answered upon this point; to which I remember the Franciscan Opponent replyed no more, but *That it was a new, and no authentick interpretation.*

XXIII. These are but the conclusions and fallible discourses of man upon the Word of GOD, for such I do believe the Holy Scriptures: yet, were it of man, I could not chuse but say, it was the singularest and superlative piece that hath been extant since the Creation. Were I a Pagan, I should not refrain the Lecture[52] of it; and cannot but commend the judgment of Ptolomy,[53] and thought not his Library compleat without it. The Alcoran of the Turks (I speak without prejudice,) is an ill composed Piece, containing in vain and ridiculous Errors in Philosophy, impossibilities, fictions, and vanities beyond laughter, maintained by evident and open Sophisms, the Policy of Ignorance, deposition of Universities, and banishment of Learning, that hath gotten Foot by Arms and violence: this without a blow hath disseminated it self through the whole Earth. It is not unremarkable what Philo first observed, that the Law of Moses continued two thousand years without the least alteration; whereas, we see the Laws of other Common-weals do alter with occasions; and even those that pretended their original from some Divinity, to have vanished without trace or memory. I believe, besides Zoroaster, there were divers that writ before Moses, who, notwithstanding, have suffered the common fate of time. Mens Works have an age like themselves; and though they out-live their Authors, yet have they a stint[54] and period to their duration: this only is a work too hard for the teeth of time, and cannot perish but in the general Flames, when all things shall confess their Ashes.

XXIV. I have heard some with deep sighs lament the lost lines of Cicero; others with as many groans deplore the combustion of the Library of Alexandria: for my own part, I think there be too many in the World, and could with patience behold the urn and ashes of the Vatican, could I, with a few others, recover the perished leaves of Solomon. I would not omit a copy of Enoch's Pillars,[55] had they

[52] Reading. [53] King of Egypt. [54] Limit.
[55] Josephus says that the descendants of Seth erected two pillars on which all human inventions so far made were engraved.

many nearer Authors than Josephus, or did not relish somewhat of the Fable. Some men have written more than others have spoken; Pineda[56] quotes more Authors in one work, than are necessary in a whole World. Of those three great inventions[57] in Germany, there are two which are not without their incommodities, and 'tis disputable whether they exceed not their use and commodities. 'Tis not a melancholy *Utinam*[58] of my own, but the desires of better heads, that there were a general Synod; not to unite the incompatible difference of Religion, but for the benefit of learning, to reduce it as it lay at first, in a few and solid Authors; and to condemn to the fire those swarms and millions of Rhapsodies, begotten only to distract and abuse the weaker judgements of Scholars, and to maintain the trade and mystery of Typographers.

XXV. I cannot but wonder with what exception the Samaritans could confine their belief to the Pentateuch, or five Books of Moses. I am ashamed at the Rabbinical Interpretation of the Jews upon the Old Testament, as much as their defection from the New: and truly it is beyond wonder, how that contemptible and degenerate issue of Jacob, once so devoted to Ethnick[59] Superstition, and so easily seduced to the Idolatry of their Neighbours, should now in such an obstinate and peremptory belief adhere unto their own Doctrine, expect impossibilities, and, in the face and eye of the Church, persist without the least hope of Conversion. This is a vice in *them,* that were a vertue in *us;* for obstinacy in a bad Cause is but constancy in a good. And herein I must accuse those of my own Religion, for there is not any of such a fugitive Faith, such an unstable belief, as a Christian; none that do so oft transform themselves, not unto several shapes of Christianity and of the same Species, but unto more unnatural and contrary Forms of Jew and Mahometan; that, from the name of *Saviour,* can condescend to the bare term of *Prophet;* and, from an old belief that He is come, fall to a new expectation of His coming. It is the promise of Christ to make us all one Flock; but how and when this Union shall be, is as obscure to me as the last day. Of those four Members of Religion[60] we hold a slender proportion. There are, I confess, some

---

[56] Juan de Pineda published his "Monarchia Ecclesiastica" in 1588.
[57] One MS. explains these as guns, printing, and the mariner's compass. [58] Latin, would that! [59] Gentile. [60] Pagans, Mohammedans, Jews, and Christians.

new additions, yet small to those which accrew to our Adversaries, and those only drawn from the revolt of Pagans, men but of negative Impieties, and such as deny CHRIST, but because they never heard of Him. But the Religion of the Jew is expresly against the Christian, and the Mahometan against both. For the Turk, in the bulk he now stands, he is beyond all hope of conversion; if he fall asunder, there may be conceived hopes, but not without strong improbabilities. The Jew is obstinate in all fortunes; the persecution of fifteen hundred years hath but confirmed them in their Errour: they have already endured whatsoever may be inflicted, and have suffered in a bad cause, even to the condemnation of their enemies. Persecution is a bad and indirect way to plant Religion: it hath been the unhappy method of angry Devotions,[61] not only to confirm honest Religion, but wicked Heresies, and extravagant Opinions. It was the first stone and Basis of our Faith; none can more justly boast of Persecutions, and glory in the number and valour of Martyrs. For, to speak properly, those are true and almost only examples of fortitude: those that are fetch'd from the field, or drawn from the actions of the Camp, are not oft-times so truely precedents of valour as audacity, and at the best attain but to some bastard piece of fortitude. If we shall strictly examine the circumstances and requisites which Aristotle requires to true and perfect valour, we shall find the name only in his Master, Alexander, and as little in that Roman Worthy, Julius Cæsar; and if any in that easie and active way have done so nobly as to deserve that name, yet in the passive and more terrible piece these have surpassed, and in a more heroical way may claim the honour of that Title. 'Tis not in the power of every honest Faith to proceed thus far, or pass to Heaven through the flames. Every one hath it not in that full measure, nor in so audacious and resolute a temper, as to endure those terrible tests and trials; who, notwithstanding, in a peaceable way, do truely adore their Saviour, and have (no doubt,) a Faith acceptable in the eyes of GOD.

XXVI. Now, as all that dye in the War are not termed *Souldiers;* so neither can I properly term all those that suffer in matters of Religion, *Martyrs.* The Council of Constance condemns John Huss

[61] Devotees.

for an Heretick; the Stories of his own Party stile him a Martyr: he must needs offend the Divinity of both, that says he was neither the one nor the other. There are many (questionless), canonized on earth, that shall never be Saints in Heaven; and have their names in Histories and Martyrologies, who in the eyes of GOD are not so perfect Martyrs as was that wise Heathen, Socrates, that suffered on a fundamental point of Religion, the unity of GOD. I have often pitied the miserable Bishop[62] that suffered in the cause of Antipodes; yet cannot chuse but accuse *him* of as much madness, for exposing his living on such a trifle, as those of ignorance and folly, that condemned him. I think my conscience will not give me the lye, if I say there are not many extant that in a noble way fear the face of death less than myself; yet, from the moral duty I owe to the Commandment of GOD, and the natural respects that I tender unto the conservation of my essence and being, I would not perish upon a Ceremony, Politick points, or indifferency: nor is my belief of that untractible temper, as not to bow at their obstacles, or connive at matters wherein there are not manifest impieties. The leaven, therefore, and ferment of all, not only civil but Religious actions, is Wisdom; without which, to commit our selves to the flames is Homicide, and (I fear,) but to pass through one fire into another.

XXVII. That Miracles are ceased, I can neither prove, nor absolutely deny, much less define the time and period of their cessation. That they survived CHRIST, is manifest upon the Record of Scripture; that they out-lived the Apostles also, and were revived at the Conversion of Nations many years after, we cannot deny, if we shall not question those Writers whose testimonies we do not controvert in points that make for our own opinions. Therefore that may have some truth in it that is reported by the Jesuites of their Miracles in the Indies; I could wish it were true, or had any other testimony than their own Pens. *They* may easily believe those Miracles abroad, who daily conceive a greater at home, the transmutation of those visible elements into the Body and Blood of our Saviour. For the conversion of Water into Wine, which He wrought in Cana, or, what the Devil would have had Him done in the Wilderness, of

---

[62] Virgilius, Bishop of Salzburg in the 8th century, was said to have asserted the existence of the Antipodes.

Stones into Bread, compared to this, will scarce deserve the name of a Miracle: though indeed, to speak properly, there is not one Miracle greater than another, they being the extraordinary effects of the Hand of God, to which all things are of an equal facility; and to create the World, as easie as one single Creature. For this is also a Miracle, not onely to produce effects against or above Nature, but before Nature; and to create Nature, as great a Miracle as to contradict or transcend her. We do too narrowly define the Power of God, restraining it to our capacities. I hold that God can do all things; how He should work contradictions, I do not understand, yet dare not therefore deny. I cannot see why the Angel of God should question Esdras to recal the time past, if it were beyond His own power; or that God should pose mortality in that which He was not able to perform Himself. I will not say God cannot, but He will not, perform many things, which we plainly affirm He cannot. This, I am sure, is the mannerliest proposition, wherein, notwithstanding, I hold no Paradox; for, strictly, His power is the same with His will, and they both, with all the rest, do make but one God.

XXVIII. Therefore that Miracles have been, I do believe; that they may yet be wrought by the living, I do not deny; but have no confidence in those which are fathered on the dead. And this hath ever made me suspect the efficacy of reliques, to examine the bones, question the habits and appurtenances of Saints, and even of Christ Himself. I cannot conceive why the Cross that Helena found, and whereon Christ Himself dyed, should have power to restore others unto life. I excuse not Constantine from a fall off his Horse, or a mischief from his enemies, upon the wearing those nails on his bridle, which our Saviour bore upon the Cross in His Hands. I compute among your *Piæ fraudes*,[63] nor many degrees before consecrated Swords and Roses, that which Baldwyn, King of Jerusalem, returned the Genovese for their cost and pains in his War, to wit, the ashes of John the Baptist. Those that hold the sanctity of their Souls doth leave behind a tincture and sacred faculty on their bodies, speak naturally of Miracles, and do not salve the doubt. Now one reason I tender so little Devotion unto Reliques, is, I think, the

[63] Pious frauds.

slender and doubtful respect I have always held unto Antiquities. For that indeed which I admire, is far before Antiquity, that is, Eternity; and that is, GOD Himself; Who, though He be styled *the Ancient of Days,* cannot receive the adjunct of Antiquity; Who was before the World, and shall be after it, yet is not older than it; for in His years there is no Climacter;[64] His duration is Eternity, and far more venerable than Antiquity.

XXIX. But above all things I wonder how the curiosity of wiser heads could pass that great and indisputable Miracle, the cessation of Oracles; and in what swoun their Reasons lay, to content themselves and sit down with such a far-fetch'd and ridiculous reason as Plutarch alleadgeth for it. The Jews, that can believe the supernatural Solstice of the Sun in the days of Joshua, have yet the impudence to deny the Eclipse, which every Pagan confessed, at His death: but for this, it is evident beyond all contradiction, the Devil himself confessed it.[65] Certainly it is not a warrantable curiosity, to examine the verity of Scripture by the concordance of humane history, or to seek to confirm the Chronicle of Hester or Daniel, by the authority of Megasthenes or Herodotus. I confess, I have had an unhappy curiosity this way, till I laughed my self out of it with a piece of Justine, where he delivers that the Children of Israel for being scabbed were banished out of Egypt. And truely since I have understood the occurrences of the World, and know in what counterfeit shapes and deceitful vizards times present represent on the stage things past, I do believe them little more then things to come. Some have been of my opinion, and endeavoured to write the History of their own lives; wherein Moses hath outgone them all and left not onely the story of his life, but (as some will have it,) of his death also.

XXX. It is a riddle to me, how this story of Oracles hath not worm'd out of the World that doubtful conceit of Spirits and Witches; how so many learned heads should so far forget their Metaphysicks, and destroy the ladder and scale of creatures, as to question the existence of Spirits. For my part, I have ever believed, and do now know, that there are Witches: they that doubt of these,

[64] The point in a man's life when his powers begin to decay.
[65] "In his oracle to Augustus."—*T. B.*

do not onely deny *them*, but Spirits; and are obliquely and upon consequence a sort not of Infidels, but Atheists. Those that to confute their incredulity desire to see apparitions, shall questionless never behold any, nor have the power to be so much as Witches; the Devil hath them already in a heresie as capital as Witchcraft; and to appear to them, were but to convert them. Of all the delusions wherewith he deceives morality, there is not any that puzzleth me more than the Legerdemain of Changelings. I do not credit those transformations of reasonable creatures into beasts, or that the Devil hath a power to transpeciate[66] a man into a Horse, who tempted CHRIST (as a trial of His Divinity,) to convert but stones into bread. I could believe that Spirits use with man the act of carnality, and that in both sexes; I conceive they may assume, steal, or contrive a body, wherein there may be action enough to content decrepit lust, or passion to satisfie more active veneries;[67] yet, in both, without a possibility of generation: and therefore that opinion that Antichrist should be born of the Tribe of Dan by conjunction with the Divil, is ridiculous, and a conceit fitter for a Rabbin than a Christian. I hold that the Devil doth really possess some men, the spirit of Melancholy others, the spirit of Delusion others; that, as the Devil is concealed and denyed by some, so GOD and good Angels are pretended by others, whereof the late defection[68] of the Maid of Germany hath left a pregnant example.

XXXI. Again, I believe that all that use sorceries, incantations, and spells, are not Witches, or, as we term them, *Magicians*. I conceive there is a traditional Magick, not learned immediately from the Devil, but at second hand from his Scholars, who, having once the secret betrayed, are able, and do emperically practise without his advice, they both proceeding upon the principles of Nature; where actives, aptly conjoyned to disposed passives, will under any Master produce their effects. Thus I think at first a great part of Philosophy was Witchcraft; which, being afterward derived to one another, proved but Philosophy, and was indeed no more but the honest effects of Nature: what, invented by us, is Philosophy, learned from him, is Magick. We do surely owe the discovery of many se-

---

[66] Transform. [67] Sexual desires.
[68] MS. copies read "detection." The allusion has not been explained.

crets to the discovery of good and bad Angels. I could never pass that sentence of Paracelsus without an asterisk or annotation; *Ascendens constellatum multa revelat quærentibus magnalia naturæ,* (i. e. *opera* DEI.)[69] [The ascending constellation reveals to inquirers many of nature's great things.] I do think that many mysteries ascribed to our own inventions have been the courteous revelations of Spirits; (for those noble essences in Heaven bear a friendly regard unto their fellow Natures on Earth;) and therefore believe that those many prodigies and ominous prognosticks, which forerun the ruines of States, Princes, and private persons, are the charitable premonitions of good Angels, which more careless enquiries term but the effects of chance and nature.

XXXII. Now, besides these particular and divided Spirits, there may be (for ought I know,) an universal and common Spirit to the whole World. It was the opinion of Plato, and it is yet of the Hermetical Philosophers. If there be a common nature that unites and tyes the scattered and divided individuals into one species, why may there not be one that unites them all? However, I am sure there is a common Spirit that plays within us, yet makes no part of us; and that is, the Spirit of GOD, the fire and scintillation of that noble and mighty Essence, which is the life and radical heat of Spirits, and those essences that know not the vertue of the Sun; a fire quite contrary to the fire of Hell. This is that gentle heat that brooded on the waters, and in six days hatched the World; this is that irradiation that dispels the mists of Hell, the clouds of horrour, fear, sorrow, despair; and preserves the region of the mind in serenity. Whosoever feels not the warm gale and gentle ventilation of this Spirit, though I feel his pulse, I dare not say he lives: for truely, without this, to me there is no heat under the Tropick; nor any light, though I dwelt in the body of the Sun.

> As, when the labouring Sun hath wrought his track
> Up to the top of lofty Cancers back,
> The ycie Ocean cracks, the frozen pole
> Thaws with the heat of the Celestial coale;
> So, when Thy absent beams begin t' impart
> Again a Solstice on my frozen heart,

[69] "Thereby is meant our good angel appointed us from our nativity!"—*T. B.*

My winter's ov'r, my dropping spirits sing,
And every part revives into a Spring.
But if Thy quickning beams a while decline,
And with their light bless not this Orb of mine,
A chilly frost surpriseth every member,
And in the midst of June I feel December.
O how this earthly temper doth debase
The noble Soul, in this her humble place;
Whose wingy nature ever doth aspire
To reach that place whence first it took its fire.
These flames I feel, which in my heart do dwell,
Are not Thy beams, but take their fire from Hell:
O quench them all, and let Thy Light divine
Be as the Sun to this poor Orb of mine;
And to Thy sacred Spirit convert those fires,
Whose earthly fumes choak my devout aspires.

XXXIII. Therefore for Spirits, I am so far from denying their existence, that I could easily believe, that not onely whole Countries, but particular persons, have their Tutelary and Guardian Angels. It is not a new opinion of the Church of Rome, but an old one of Pythagoras and Plato; there is no heresie in it; and if not manifestly defin'd in Scripture, yet is it an opinion of a good and wholesome use in the course and actions of a mans life, and would serve as an Hypothesis to salve many doubts, whereof common Philosophy affordeth no solution. Now, if you demand my opinion and Metaphysicks of their natures, I confess them very shallow; most of them in a negative way, like that of GOD; or in a comparative, between ourselves and fellow-creatures; for there is in this Universe a Stair, or manifest Scale of creatures, rising not disorderly, or in confusion, but with a comely method and proportion. Between creatures of meer existence, and things of life, there is a large disproportion of nature; between plants, and animals or creatures of sense, a wider difference; between them and Man, a far greater: and if the proportion hold one, between Man and Angels there should be yet a greater. We do not comprehend their natures, who retain the first definition of Porphyry, and distinguish them from our selves by immortality; for before his Fall, 'tis thought, Man also was Immortal; yet must we needs affirm that he had a different essence from the Angels. Having therefore no certain knowledge of their Natures, 'tis no bad method of the Schools, whatsoever perfection we find obscurely in our selves, in a more compleat and absolute way to ascribe unto them. I believe they have an extemporary knowledge, and upon the first motion of their reason do what we cannot without study or deliberation; that they know things by their forms, and define by specifical difference what we describe by accidents and properties; and therefore probabilities to us may be demonstrations unto them: that they have knowledge not onely of the specifical, but numerical forms of individuals, and understand by what reserved difference each single Hypostasis[70] (besides the relation to its species,) becomes its numerical self: that, as the Soul hath a power to move the body it informs, so there's a faculty to move any, though inform none: ours upon restraint of time, place, and distance; but that invisible hand that conveyed Habakkuk to the Lyons Den,[71] or Philip to Azotus,[72] infringeth this rule, and hath a secret conveyance, wherewith mortality is not acquainted. If they have that intuitive knowledge, whereby as in reflexion they behold the thoughts of one another, I cannot peremptorily deny but they know a great part of ours. They that, to refute the Invocation of Saints, have denied that they have any knowledge of our affairs below, have proceeded too far, and must pardon my opinion, till I can thoroughly answer that piece of Scripture, *At the conversion of a sinner the Angels in Heaven rejoyce.* I cannot, with those in that great Father,[73] securely interpret the work of the first day, *Fiat lux,* [Let there be light] to the creation of Angels; though I confess, there is not any creature[74] that hath so neer a glympse of their nature as light in the Sun and Elements. We stile it a bare accident; but, where it subsists alone, 'tis a spiritual Substance, and may be an Angel: in brief, conceive light invisible, and that is a Spirit.

XXXIV. These are certainly the Magisterial and masterpieces of the Creator, the Flower, or (as we may say,) the best part of nothing; actually existing, what we are but in hopes and probability. We are onely that amphibious piece between a corporal and spiritual Essence, that middle form that links those two together, and makes

---

[70] Distinct substance.   [71] Bel and the Dragon, 36.   [72] Acts viii. 40.
[73] The idea is found in both St. Chrysostom and St. Augustine.   [74] Created thing.

good the Method of God and Nature, that jumps not from extreams, but unites the incompatible distances by some middle and participating natures. That we are the breath and similitude of God, it is indisputable, and upon record of Holy Scripture; but to call ourselves a Microcosm, or little World, I thought it only a pleasant trope of Rhetorick, till my neer judgement and second thoughts told me there was a real truth therein. For first we are a rude mass, and in the rank of creatures which onely are, and have a dull kind of being, not yet priviledged with life, or preferred to sense or reason; next we live the life of Plants, the life of Animals, the life of Men, and at last the life of Spirits, running on in one mysterious nature those five kinds of existences, which comprehend the creatures not onely of the World, but of the Universe. Thus is Man that great and true *Amphibium,* whose nature is disposed to live, not onely like other creatures in divers elements, but in divided and distinguished worlds: for though there be but one to sense, there are two to reason, the one visible, the other invisible; whereof Moses seems to have left description, and of the other so obscurely, that some parts thereof are yet in controversie. And truely, for the first chapters of Genesis, I must confess a great deal of obscurity; though Divines have to the power of humane reason endeavoured to make all go in a literal meaning, yet those allegorical interpretations are also probable, and perhaps the mystical method of Moses bred up in the Hieroglyphical Schools of the Egyptians.

XXXV. Now for that immaterial world, methinks we need not wander so far as beyond the first moveable;[75] for even in this material Fabrick the Spirits walk as freely exempt from the affection of time, place, and motion, as beyond the extreamest circumference. Do but extract from the corpulency of bodies, or resolve things beyond their first matter, and you discover the habitation of Angels, which if I call the ubiquitary and omnipresent Essence of God, I hope I shall not offend Divinity: for before the Creation of the World God was really all things. For the Angels He created no new World, or determinate mansion, and therefore they are everywhere where is His Essence, and do live at a distance even in Himself. That God made all things for Man, is in some sense true, yet

[75] *Primum mobile,* the tenth sphere of the old astronomy.

not so far as to subordinate the Creation of those purer Creatures unto ours, though as *ministring Spirits* they do, and are willing to fulfill the will of GOD in these lower and sublunary affairs of Man. GOD made all things for Himself, and it is impossible He should make them for any other end than His own Glory; it is all He can receive, and all that is without Himself. For, honour being an external adjunct, and in the honourer rather than in the person honoured, it was necessary to make a Creature, from whom He might receive this homage; and that is, in the other world, Angels, in this, Man; which when we neglect, we forget the very end of our Creation, and may justly provoke GOD, not onely to repent that He hath made the World, but that He hath sworn He would not destroy it. That there is but one World, is a conclusion of Faith: Aristotle with all his Philosophy hath not been able to prove it, and as weakly that the World was eternal. That dispute much troubled the Pen of the ancient Philosophers, but Moses decided that question, and all is salved with the new term of a *Creation,* that is, a production of something out of nothing. And what is that? whatsoever is opposite to something; or more exactly, that which is truely contrary unto GOD: for He onely is, all others have an existence with dependency, and are something but by a distinction. And herein is Divinity conformant unto Philosophy, and generation not onely founded on contrarieties, but also creation; GOD, being all things, is contrary unto nothing, out of which were made all things, and so nothing became something, and Omneity informed Nullity into an Essence.

XXXVI. The whole Creation is a mystery, and particularly that of Man. At the blast of His mouth were the rest of the Creatures made, and at His bare word they started out of nothing: but in the frame of Man (as the Text describes it,) He played the sensible operator, and seemed not so much to create, as make him. When He had separated the materials of other creatures, there consequently resulted a form and soul; but, having raised the walls of Man, He was driven to a second and harder creation of a substance like Himself, an incorruptible and immortal Soul. For these two affections[76] we have the Philosophy and opinion of the Heath-

[76] Qualities.

ens, the flat affirmative of Plato, and not a negative from Aristotle. There is another scruple cast in by Divinity concerning its production, much disputed in the Germane auditories, and with that indifferency and equality of arguments, as leave the controversie undetermined. I am not of Paracelsus mind, that boldly delivers a receipt to make a man without conjunction;[77] yet cannot but wonder at the multitude of heads that do deny traduction,[78] having no other argument to confirm their belief then that Rhetorical sentence and *Antimetathesis*[79] of Augustine, *Creando infunditur, infundendo creatur*. [By creating it is poured in, by pouring in it is created.] Either opinion will consist well enough with Religion: yet I should rather incline to this, did not one objection haunt me, (not wrung from speculations and subtilties, but from common sense and observation; not pickt from the leaves of any Author, but bred amongst the weeds and tares of mine own brain;) and this is a conclusion from the equivocal and monstrous productions in the conjunction of Man with Beast: for if the Soul of man be not transmitted and transfused in the seed of the Parents, why are not those productions meerly beasts, but have also an impression and tincture of reason in as high a measure as it can evidence it self in those improper Organs? Nor, truly, can I peremptorily deny that the Soul, in this her sublunary estate, is wholly and in all acceptions[80] inorganical; but that for the performance of her ordinary actions there is required not onely a symmetry and proper disposition of Organs, but a Crasis[81] and temper correspondent to its operations: yet is not this mass of flesh and visible structure the instrument and proper corps of the Soul, but rather of Sense, and that the hand of Reason. In our study of Anatomy there is a mass of mysterious Philosophy, and such as reduced the very Heathens to Divinity: yet, amongst all those rare discoveries and curious pieces I find in the Fabrick of Man, I do not so much content my self, as in that I find not, there is no Organ or Instrument for the rational Soul; for in the brain, which we term the seat of Reason, there is not anything of moment more than I can discover in the crany[82]

[77] Sexual intercourse.   [78] Derivation (of the soul from the parents).
[79] The giving of two different meanings from two different arrangements of the same words.   [80] Acceptations.   [81] Constitution.   [82] Skull.

of a beast: and this is a sensible and no inconsiderable argument of the inorganity of the Soul, at least in that sense we usually so receive it. Thus we are men, and we know not how: there is something in us that can be without us, and will be after us; though it is strange that it hath no history what it was before us, nor cannot tell how it entred in us.

XXXVII. Now, for these walls of flesh, wherein the Soul doth seem to be immured before the Resurrection, it is nothing but an elemental composition, and a Fabrick that must fall to ashes. *All flesh is grass,* is not onely metaphorically, but litterally, true; for all those creatures we behold are but the herbs of the field, digested into flesh in them, or more remotely carnified[83] in our selves. Nay further, we are what we all abhor, *Anthropophagi* and Cannibals, devourers not onely of men, but of our selves; and that not in an allegory, but a positive truth: for all this mass of flesh which we behold, came in at our mouths; this frame we look upon, hath been upon our trenchers; in brief, we have devour'd our selves. I cannot believe the wisdom of Pythagoras did ever positively, and in a literal sense, affirm his Metempsychosis, or impossible transmigration of the Souls of men into beasts. Of all Metamorphoses or transmigrations, I believe only one, that is of Lots wife; for that of Nebuchodonosor proceeded not so far: in all others I conceive there is no further verity than is contained in their implicite sense and morality. I believe that the whole frame of a beast doth perish, and is left in the same state after death as before it was materialled unto life: that the Souls of men know neither contrary nor corruption; that they subsist beyond the body, and outlive death by the priviledge of their proper natures, and without a Miracle; that the Souls of the faithful, as they leave Earth, take possession of Heaven: that those apparitions and ghosts of departed persons are not the wandring souls of men, but the unquiet walks of Devils, prompting and suggesting us unto mischief, blood, and villany; instilling and stealing into our hearts that the blessed Spirits are not at rest in their graves, but wander sollicitous of the affairs of the World. But that those phantasms appear often, and do frequent Cœmeteries, Charnel-

[83] Made flesh.

houses, and Churches, it is because those are the dormitories of the dead, where the Devil, like an insolent Champion, beholds with pride the spoils and Trophies of his Victory over Adam.

XXXVIII. This is that dismal conquest we all deplore, that makes us so often cry, *O Adam, quid fecisti?* [O Adam, what hast thou done?] I thank God I have not those strait ligaments, or narrow obligations to the World, as to dote on life, or be convulst and tremble at the name of death. Not that I am insensible of the dread and horrour thereof; or by raking into the bowels of the deceased, continual sight of Anatomies, Skeletons, or Cadaverous reliques, like Vespilloes,[84] or Grave-makers, I am become stupid, or have forgot the apprehension of Mortality; but that, marshalling all the horrours, and contemplating the extremities thereof, I find not any thing therein able to daunt the courage of a man, much less a well-resolved Christian; and therefore am not angry at the errour of our first Parents, or unwilling to bear a part of this common fate, and like the best of them to dye, that is, to cease to breathe, to take a farewel of the elements, to be a kind of nothing for a moment, to be within one instant of a Spirit. When I take a full view and circle of my self without this reasonable moderator, and equal piece of Justice, Death, I do conceive my self the miserablest person extant. Were there not another life that I hope for, all the vanities of this World should not intreat a moments breath from me; could the Devil work my belief to imagine I could never dye, I would not outlive that very thought. I have so abject a conceit[85] of this common way of existence, this retaining to the Sun and Elements, I cannot think this is to be a Man, or to live according to the dignity of humanity. In exspectation of a better, I can with patience embrace this life, yet in my best meditations do often defie death; I honour any man that contemns it, nor can I highly love any that is afraid of it: this makes me naturally love a Souldier, and honour those tattered and contemptible Regiments that will die at the command of a Sergeant. For a Pagan there may be some motives to be in love with life; but for a Christian to be amazed at death, I see not how he can escape this Dilemma, that he is too sensible of this life, or hopeless of the life to come.

[84] Latin, corpse-bearers. [85] Idea.

XXXIX. Some Divines count Adam thirty years old at his Creation, because they suppose him created in the perfect age and stature of man. And surely we are all out of the computation of our age, and every man is some months elder than he bethinks him; for we live, move, have a being, and are subject to the actions of the elements, and the malice of diseases, in that other World, the truest Microcosm, the Womb of our Mother. For besides that general and common existence we are conceived to hold in our Chaos, and whilst we sleep within the bosome of our causes, we enjoy a being and life in three distinct worlds, wherein we receive most manifest graduations. In that obscure World and Womb of our Mother, our time is short, computed by the Moon, yet longer then the days of many creatures that behold the Sun; our selves being not yet without life, sense, and reason; though for the manifestation of its actions, it awaits the opportunity of objects, and seems to live there but in its root and soul of vegetation. Entring afterwards upon the scene of the World, we arise up and become another creature, performing the reasonable actions of man, and obscurely manifesting that part of Divinity in us; but not in complement[86] and perfection, till we have once more cast our secondine,[87] that is, this slough of flesh, and are delivered into the last World, that is, that ineffable place of Paul, that proper *ubi*[88] of Spirits. The smattering I have of the Philosophers Stone (which is something more than the perfect exaltation of gold,) hath taught me a great deal of Divinity, and instructed my belief, how that immortal spirit and incorruptible substance of my Soul may lye obscure, and sleep a while within this house of flesh. Those strange and mystical transmigrations that I have observed in Silk-worms, turned my Philosophy into Divinity. There is in these works of nature, which seem to puzzle reason, something Divine, and hath more in it then the eye of a common spectator doth discover.

XL. I am naturally bashful; nor hath conversation, age, or travel, been able to effront[89] or enharden me; yet I have one part of modesty which I have seldom discovered in another, that is, (to speak truely,) I am not so much afraid of death, as ashamed thereof. 'Tis

---

[86] Completeness. [87] After-birth. [88] Dwelling-place.
[89] Embolden.

the very disgrace and ignominy of our natures, that in a moment can so disfigure us, that our nearest friends, Wife, and Children, stand afraid and start at us: the Birds and Beasts of the field, that before in a natural fear obeyed us, forgetting all allegiance, begin to prey upon us. This very conceit hath in a tempest disposed and left me willing to be swallowed up in the abyss of waters, wherein I had perished unseen, unpitied, without wondering eyes, tears of pity, Lectures of mortality, and none had said.

Quantum mutatus ab illo!
[How changed from that man!]

Not that I am ashamed of the Anatomy of my parts, or can accuse Nature for playing the bungler in any part of me, or my own vitious life for contracting any shameful disease upon me, whereby I might not call my self as wholesome a morsel for the worms as any.

XLI. Some, upon the courage of a fruitful issue, wherein, as in the truest Chronicle, they seem to outlive themselves, can with greater patience away with death. This conceit and counterfeit subsisting in our progenies seems to me a meer fallacy, unworthy the desires of a man that can but conceive a thought of the next World; who, in a nobler ambition, should desire to live in his substance in Heaven, rather than his name and shadow in the earth. And therefore at my death I mean to take a total adieu of the World, not caring for a Monument, History or Epitaph, not so much as the bare memory of my name to be found any where but in the universal Register of GOD. I am not yet so Cynical as to approve the Testament of Diogenes,[90] nor do I altogether allow that *Rodomontado*[91] of Lucan,

——*Cælo tegitur, qui non habet urnam.*

He that unburied lies wants not his Herse,
For unto him a Tomb's the Universe.

but commend in my calmer judgement those ingenuous intentions that desire to sleep by the urns of their Fathers, and strive to go the neatest way unto corruption. I do not envy the temper of Crows

---

[90] "Who willed his friend not to bury him, but to hang him up with a staffe in his hand to fright away the crowes."—*T. B.*   [91] Boastful utterance.

and Daws,[92] nor the numerous and weary days of our Fathers before the Flood. If there be any truth in Astrology, I may outlive a Jubilee:[93] as yet I have not seen one revolution of Saturn,[94] nor hath my pulse beat thirty years; and yet, excepting one, have seen the Ashes and left under ground all the Kings of Europe; have been contemporary to three Emperours, four Grand Signiours, and as many Popes. Methinks I have outlived my self, and begin to be weary of the Sun; I have shaken hands with delight, in my warm blood and Canicular[95] days, I perceive I do anticipate the vices of age; the World to me is but a dream or mock-show, and we all therein but Pantalones and Anticks, to my severer contemplations.

XLII. It is not, I confess, an unlawful Prayer to desire to surpass the days of our Saviour, or wish to outlive that age wherein He thought fittest to dye; yet if (as Divinity affirms,) there shall be no gray hairs in Heaven, but all shall rise in the perfect state of men, we do but outlive those perfections in this World, to be recalled unto them by a greater Miracle in the next, and run on here but to be retrograde hereafter. Were there any hopes to outlive vice, or a point to be super-annuated from sin, it were worthy our knees to implore the days of Methuselah. But age doth not rectify, but incurvate[96] our natures, turning bad dispositions into worser habits, and (like diseases,) brings on incurable vices; for every day as we grow weaker in age, we grow stronger in sin, and the number of our days doth but make our sins innumerable. The same vice committed at sixteen, is not the same, though it agree in all other circumstances, at forty, but swells and doubles from the circumstance of our ages; wherein, besides the constant and inexcusable habit of transgressing, the maturity of our judgement cuts off pretence unto excuse or pardon. Every sin, the oftner it is committed, the more it acquireth in the quality of evil; as it succeeds in time, so it proceeds in degrees of badness; for as they proceed they ever multiply, and, like figures in Arithmetick, the last stands for more than all that went before it. And though I think no man can live well once, but he that could live twice, yet for my own part I would not live over my hours past, or begin again the thread of my days:

[92] These birds were supposed to live several times the length of human life.
[93] Fifty years. [94] Thirty years.
[95] Dog-days: here, figuratively, for young manhood. [96] Make crooked.

not upon Cicero's ground, because I have lived them well, but for fear I should live them worse. I find my growing Judgment daily instruct me how to be better, but my untamed affections and confirmed vitiosity makes me daily do worse. I find in my confirmed age the same sins I discovered in my youth; I committed many then, because I was a Child; and because I commit them still, I am yet an infant. Therefore I perceive a man may be twice a Child, before the days of dotage; and stand in need of Æsons Bath[97] before threescore.

XLIII. And truly there goes a great deal of providence to produce a mans life unto threescore: there is more required than an able temper for those years; though the radical humour[98] contain in it sufficient oyl for seventy, yet I perceive in some it gives no light past thirty: men assign not all the causes of long life, that write whole Books thereof. They that found themselves on the radical balsome,[99] or vital sulphur[99] of the parts, determine not why Abel lived not so long as Adam. There is therefore a secret glome[100] or bottom[100] of our days: 'twas His wisdom to determine them, but His perpetual and waking providence that fulfils and accomplisheth them; wherein the spirits, ourselves, and all the creatures of GOD in a secret and disputed way do execute His will. Let *them* not therefore complain of immaturity that die about thirty; they fall but like the whole World, whose solid and well-composed substance must not expect the duration and period of its constitution: when all things are completed in it, its age is accomplished; and the last and general fever may as naturally destroy it before six thousand, as me before forty. There is therefore some other hand that twines the thread of life than that of Nature: we are not onely ignorant in Antipathies and occult qualities; our ends are as obscure as our beginnings; the line of our days is drawn by night, and the various effects therein by a pensil that is invisible; wherein though we confess our ignorance, I am sure we do not err if we say it is the hand of GOD.

XLIV. I am much taken with two verses of Lucan, since I have been able not onely, as we do at School, to construe, but understand:

Victurosque Dei celant, ut vivere durent,
Felix esse mori.[101]

---

[97] For restoring youth. [98] The moisture essential to vitality according to the old physiology. [99] Supposed sources of longevity. [100] Ball (of worsted). [101] Lucan's "Pharsalia," iv. 510.

> We're all deluded, vainly searching ways
> To make us happy by the length of days;
> For cunningly to make 's protract this breath,
> The Gods conceal the happiness of Death.

There be many excellent strains in that Poet, wherewith his Stoical Genius hath liberally supplied him; and truely there are singular pieces in the Philosophy of Zeno, and doctrine of the Stoicks, which I perceive, delivered in a Pulpit, pass for current Divinity: yet herein are they in extreams, that can allow a man to be his own Assassine, and so highly extol the end and suicide of Cato. This is indeed not to fear death, but yet to be afraid of life. It is a brave act of valour to contemn death; but where life is more terrible than death, it is then the truest valour to dare to live. And herein Religion hath taught us a noble example; for all the valiant acts of Curtius, Scevola, or Codrus, do not parallel or match that one of Job; and sure there is no torture to the rack of a disease, nor any Ponyards in death it self like those in the way or prologue to it.

> *Emori nolo, sed me esse mortuum nihil curo.*[102]
> I would not die, but care not to be dead.

Were I of Cæsar's Religion, I should be of his desires, and wish rather to go off at one blow, then to be sawed in pieces by the grating torture of a disease. Men that look no farther than their outsides, think health an appurtenance unto life, and quarrel with their constitutions for being sick; but I, that have examined the parts of man, and know upon what tender filaments that Fabrick hangs, do wonder that we are not always so; and, considering the thousand doors that lead to death, do thank my GOD that we can die but once. 'Tis not onely the mischief of diseases, and the villany of poysons, that make an end of us; we vainly accuse the fury of Guns, and the new inventions of death; it is in the power of every hand to destroy us, and we are beholding unto every one we meet, he doth not kill us. There is therefore but one comfort left, that, though it be in the power of the weakest arm to take away life, it is not in the strongest to deprive us of death: GOD would not exempt Himself from that, the misery of immortality in the flesh, He undertook not that was im-

---
[102] Quoted by Cicero, "Tusc. Quæst." i. 8, from Epicharmus.

mortal. Certainly there is no happiness within this circle of flesh, nor is it in the Opticks of these eyes to behold felicity. The first day of our Jubilee is Death; the Devil hath therefore failed of his desires: we are happier with death than we should have been without it: there is no misery but in himself, where there is no end of misery; and so indeed, in his own sense, the Stoick[103] is in the right. He forgets that he can dye who complains of misery; we are in the power of no calamity while death is in our own.

XLV. Now, besides this literal and positive kind of death, there are others whereof Divines make mention, and those, I think, not meerly Metaphorical, as mortification, dying unto sin and the World. Therefore, I say, every man hath a double Horoscope, one of his humanity, his birth; another of his Christianity, his baptism; and from this do I compute or calculate my Nativity, not reckoning those *Horæ combustæ*[104] and odd days, or esteeming my self any thing, before I was my Saviours, and inrolled in the Register of CHRIST. Whosoever enjoys not this life, I count him but an apparition, though he wear about him the sensible affections[105] of flesh. In these moral acceptions,[106] the way to be immortal is to dye daily: nor can I think I have the true Theory of death, when I contemplate a skull, or behold a Skeleton, with those vulgar imaginations it casts upon us; I have therefore enlarged that common *Memento mori,* [Remember you must die] into a more Christian memorandum, *Memento quatuor Novissima,* [Remember the four last things] those four inevitable points of us all, Death, Judgement, Heaven, and Hell. Neither did the contemplations of the Heathens rest in their graves, without a further thought of Rhadamanth,[107] or some judicial proceeding after death, though in another way, and upon suggestion of their natural reasons. I cannot but marvail from what Sibyl or Oracle they stole the Prophesie of the Worlds destruction by fire, or whence Lucan learned to say,

> *Communis mundo superest rogus, ossibus astra Misturus.*[108]

There yet remains to th' World one common Fire,
Wherein our bones with stars shall make one Pyre.

---

[103] In holding that death is no evil.
[104] Combust hours, "when the moon is in conjunction and obscured by the sun."
[105] Qualities.   [106] Acceptations.   [107] Judge in Hades.   [108] "Pharsalia" vii. 814.

I believe the World grows near its end, yet is neither old nor decayed, nor shall ever perish upon the ruines of its own Principles. As the work of Creation was above Nature, so is its adversary, annihilation; without which the World hath not its end, but its mutation. Now what force should be able to consume it thus far, without the breath of God, which is the truest consuming flame, my Philosophy cannot inform me. Some believe there went not a minute to the Worlds creation, nor shall there go to its destruction; those six days, so punctually described, make not to them one moment, but rather seem to manifest the method and Idea of the great work of the intellect of God, than the manner how He proceeded in its operation. I cannot dream that there should be at the last day any such Judicial proceeding, or calling to the Bar, as indeed the Scripture seems to imply, and the literal Commentators do conceive: for unspeakable mysteries in the Scriptures are often delivered in a vulgar and illustrative way; and, being written unto man, are delivered, not as they truely are, but as they may be understood; wherein, notwithstanding, the different interpretations according to different capacities may stand firm with our devotion, nor be any way prejudicial to each single edification.

XLVI. Now to determine the day and year of this inevitable time, is not onely convincible[109] and statute-madness,[110] but also manifest impiety. How shall we interpret Elias six thousand years,[111] or imagine the secret communicated to a Rabbi, which God hath denyed unto His Angels? It had been an excellent Quære[112] to have posed the Devil of Delphos,[113] and must needs have forced him to some strange amphibology.[114] It hath not onely mocked the predictions of sundry Astrologers in Ages past, but the prophesies of many melancholy heads in these present; who, neither understanding reasonably things past or present, pretend a knowledge of things to come: heads ordained onely to manifest the incredible effects of melancholy, and to fulfil old prophecies rather than be the authors of new. *In those days there shall come Wars and rumours of Wars,* to me seems no prophecy, but a constant truth, in all times verified since it was pronounced. *There shall be signs in the Moon and Stars;*

---

[109] Capable of proof.   [110] Madness defined by law.   [111] The time of the existence of the world, according to a tradition ascribed to the school of Elijah in the Talmud.   [112] Question.   [113] The oracle of Apollo.   [114] Ambiguity.

how comes He then *like a Thief in the night,* when He gives an item of His Coming? That common sign drawn from the revelation of Antichrist, is as obscure as any: in our common compute He hath been come these many years: but for my own part, (to speak freely,) I am half of opinion that Antichrist is the Philosopher's stone in Divinity, for the discovery and invention whereof, though there be prescribed rules and probable inductions, yet hath hardly any man attained the perfect discovery thereof. That general opinion that the World grows near its end, hath possessed all ages past as nearly as ours. I am afraid that the Souls that now depart, cannot escape that lingring expostulation of the Saints under the Altar, Quousque, Domine? *How long,* O Lord? and groan in the expectation of that great Jubilee.

XLVII. This is the day that must make good that great attribute of God, His Justice; that must reconcile those unanswerable doubts that torment the wisest understandings; and reduce those seeming inequalities and respective distributions in this world, to an equality and recompensive Justice in the next. This is that one day, that shall include and comprehend all that went before it; wherein, as in the last scene, all the Actors must enter, to compleat and make up the Catastrophe of this great piece. This is the day whose memory hath onely power to make us honest in the dark, and to be vertuous without a witness.

Ipsa sui pretium virtus sibi,[115]

that Vertue is her own reward, is but a cold principle, and not able to maintain our variable resolutions in a constant and setled way of goodness. I have practised that honest artifice of Seneca, and in my retired and solitary imaginations, to detain me from the foulness of vice, have fancied to my self the presence of my dear and worthiest friends, before whom I should lose my head, rather than be vitious: yet herein I found that there was nought but moral honesty, and this was not to be vertuous for His sake Who must reward us at the last. I have tryed if I could reach that great resolution of his, to be honest without a thought of Heaven or Hell: and indeed I found, upon a natural inclination and inbred loyalty unto virtue,

[115] Claudian. "De Mallii Theod. Consul." v. i.

that I could serve her without a livery,[116] yet not in that resolved and venerable way, but that the frailty of my nature, upon an easie temptation, might be induced to forget her. The life, therefore, and spirit of all our actions is the resurrection, and a stable apprehension that our ashes shall enjoy the fruit of our pious endeavours: without this, all Religion is a Fallacy, and those impieties of Lucian, Euripides, and Julian, are no blasphemies, but subtle verities, and Atheists have been the onely Philosophers.

XLVIII. How shall the dead arise, is no question of my Faith; to believe only possibilities, is not Faith, but meer Philosophy. Many things are true in Divinity, which are neither inducible by reason, nor confirmable by sense; and many things in Philosophy confirmable by sense, yet not inducible by reason. Thus it is impossible by any solid or demonstrative reasons to perswade a man to believe the conversion[117] of the Needle to the North; though this be possible, and true, and easily credible, upon a single experiment unto the sense. I believe that our estranged and divided ashes shall unite again; that our separated dust, after so many Pilgrimages and transformations into the parts of Minerals, Plants, Animals, Elements, shall at the Voice of GOD return into their primitive shapes, and joyn again to make up their primary and predestinate forms. As at the Creation there was a separation of that confused mass into its species; so at the destruction thereof there shall be a separation into its distinct individuals. As at the Creation of the World, all the distinct species that we behold lay involved in one mass, till the fruitful Voice of GOD separated this united multitude into its several species; so at the last day, when those corrupted reliques shall be scattered in the Wilderness of forms, and seem to have forgot their proper habits, GOD by a powerful Voice shall command them back into their proper shapes, and call them out by their single individuals. Then shall appear the fertility of Adam, and the magick of that sperm[118] that hath dilated into so many millions. I have often beheld as a miracle, that artificial resurrection and revivification[119] of Mercury, how being mortified into a thousand shapes, it assumes again its own, and returns into its numerical[120] self. Let us speak naturally and like

---

[116] Reward. [117] Turning. [118] Seed. [119] Restoration to its own form. [120] Individual.

Philosophers, the forms of alterable bodies in these sensible corruptions perish not; nor, as we imagine, wholly quit their mansions, but retire and contract themselves into their secret and unaccessible parts, where they may best protect themselves from the action of their Antagonist. A plant or vegetable consumed to ashes to a contemplative and school-Philosopher seems utterly destroyed, and the form to have taken his leave for ever; but to a sensible Artist the forms are not perished, but withdrawn into their incombustible part, where they lie secure from the action of that devouring element. This is made good by experience, which can from the Ashes of a Plant revive the plant, and from its cinders recall it into its stalk and leaves again. What the Art of man can do in these inferiour pieces, what blasphemy is it to affirm the finger of GOD cannot do in these more perfect and sensible structures! This is that mystical Philosophy, from whence no true Scholar becomes an Atheist, but from the visible effects of nature grows up a real Divine, and beholds not in a dream, as Ezekiel, but in an ocular and visible object, the types of his resurrection.

XLIX. Now, the necessary Mansions of our restored selves are those two contrary and incompatible places we call *Heaven* and *Hell*. To define them, or strictly to determine what and where these are, surpasseth my Divinity. That elegant[121] Apostle,[122] which seemed to have a glimpse of Heaven, hath left but a negative description thereof; *which neither eye hath seen, nor ear hath heard, nor can enter into the heart of man:* he was translated out of himself to behold it; but, being returned into himself, could not express it. St. John's description by Emerals, Chrysolites, and precious Stones, is too weak to express the material Heaven we behold. Briefly therefore, where the Soul hath the full measure and complement of happiness; where the boundless appetite of that spirit remains compleatly satisfied, that it can neither desire addition nor alteration; that, I think, is truly Heaven: and this can onely be in the injoyment of that essence, whose infinite goodness is able to terminate the desires of it self, and the unsatiable wishes of ours: wherever GOD will thus manifest Himself, there is Heaven, though within the circle of this sensible world. Thus the Soul of man may be in Heaven any where,

[121] Perhaps for eloquent. [122] St. Paul.

even within the limits of his own proper body; and when it ceaseth to live in the body, it may remain in its own soul, that is, its Creator: and thus we may say that St. Paul, *whether in the body, or out of the body,* was yet in Heaven. To place it in the Empyreal, or beyond the tenth sphear, is to forget the world's destruction; for, when this sensible world shall be destroyed, all shall then be here as it is now there, an Empyreal Heaven, a *quasi* vacuity; when to ask where Heaven is, is to demand where the Presence of God is, or where we have the glory of that happy vision. Moses, that was bred up in all the learning of the Egyptians, committed a gross absurdity in Philosophy, when with these eyes of flesh he desired to see God, and petitioned his Maker, that is, Truth it self, to a contradiction. Those that imagine Heaven and Hell neighbours, and conceive a vicinity between those two extreams, upon consequence of the Parable, where Dives discoursed with Lazarus in Abraham's bosome, do too grosly conceive of those glorified creatures, whose eyes shall easily out-see the Sun, and behold without a perspective[123] the extreamest distances: for if there shall be in our glorified eyes, the faculty of sight and reception of objects, I could think the visible species there to be in as unlimitable a way as now the intellectual. I grant that two bodies placed beyond the tenth sphear, or in a vacuity, according to Aristotle's Philosophy, could not behold each other, because there wants a body or Medium to hand and transport the visible rays of the object unto the sense; but when there shall be a general defect of either Medium to convey, or light to prepare and dispose that Medium, and yet a perfect vision, we must suspend the rules of our Philosophy, and make all good by a more absolute piece of opticks.

L. I cannot tell how to say that fire is the essence of Hell: I know not what to make of Purgatory, or conceive a flame that can either prey upon, or purifie the substance of a Soul. Those flames of Sulphur mention'd in the Scriptures, I take not to be understood of this present Hell, but of that to come, where fire shall make up the complement of our tortures, and have a body or subject wherein to manifest its tyranny. Some, who have had the honour to be textuary in Divinity, are of opinion it shall be the same specifical fire with ours.

[123] Telescope.

This is hard to conceive; yet can I make good how even that may prey upon our bodies, and yet not consume us: for in this material World there are bodies that persist invincible in the powerfullest flames; and though by the action of fire they fall into ignition and liquation, yet will they never suffer a destruction. I would gladly know how Moses with an actual fire calcined or burnt the Golden Calf unto powder: for that mystical metal of Gold, whose solary[124] and celestial nature I admire, exposed unto the violence of fire, grows onely hot, and liquifies, but consumeth not; so, when the consumable and volatile pieces of our bodies shall be refined into a more impregnable and fixed temper like Gold, though they suffer from the action of flames, they shall never perish, but lye immortal in the arms of fire. And surely, if this frame must suffer onely by the action of this element, there will many bodies escape; and not onely Heaven, but Earth will not be at an end, but rather a beginning. For at present it is not earth, but a composition of fire, water, earth, and air; but at that time, spoiled of these ingredients, it shall appear in a substance more like it self, its ashes. Philosophers that opinioned the worlds destruction by fire, did never dream of annihilation, which is beyond the power of sublunary causes; for the last and proper action of that element is but vitrification, or a reduction of a body into glass; and therefore some of our Chymicks facetiously affirm, that at the last fire all shall be christallized and reverberated into glass, which is the utmost action of that element. Nor need we fear this term, *annihilation,* or wonder that GOD will destroy the works of His Creation; for man subsisting, who is, and will then truely appear, a Microcosm, the world cannot be said to be destroyed. For the eyes of GOD, and perhaps also of our glorified selves, shall as really behold and contemplate the World in its Epitome or contracted essence, as now it doth at large and in its dilated substance. In the seed of a Plant to the eyes of GOD, and to the understanding of man, there exists, though in an invisible way, the perfect leaves, flowers, and fruit thereof; for things that are *in posse* to the sense, are actually existent to the understanding. Thus GOD beholds all things, Who contemplates as fully His works in their Epitome, as in their full volume; and beheld as amply the whole world in that

[124] Solar. Astrology associated gold with the sun.

little compendium of the sixth day, as in the scattered and dilated pieces of those five before.

LI. Men commonly set forth the torments of Hell by fire, and the extremity of corporal afflictions, and describe Hell in the same method that Mahomet doth Heaven. This indeed makes a noise, and drums in popular ears: but if this be the terrible piece thereof, it is not worthy to stand in diameter[125] with Heaven, whose happiness consists in that part that is best able to comprehend it, that immortal essence, that translated divinity and colony of GOD, the Soul. Surely, though we place Hell under Earth, the Devil's walk and purlue is about it: men speak too popularly who place it in those flaming mountains, which to grosser apprehensions represent Hell. The heart of man is the place the Devils dwell in: I feel sometimes a Hell within my self; Lucifer keeps his Court in my breast, Legion is revived in me. There are as many Hells, as Anaxagoras conceited worlds.[126] There was more than one Hell in Magdalene, when there were seven Devils, for every Devil is an Hell unto himself; he holds enough of torture in his own *ubi,* and needs not the misery of circumference to afflict him: and thus a distracted Conscience here, is a shadow or introduction unto Hell hereafter. Who can but pity the merciful intention of those hands that do destroy themselves? the Devil, were it in his power, would do the like; which being impossible, his miseries are endless, and he suffers most in that attribute wherein he is impassible,[127] his immortality.

LII. I thank GOD, and with joy I mention it, I was never afraid of Hell, nor never grew pale at the description of that place. I have so fixed my contemplations on Heaven, that I have almost forgot the Idea of Hell, and am afraid rather to lose the Joys of the one, than endure the misery of the other: to be deprived of them is a perfect Hell, and needs, methinks, no addition to compleat our afflictions. That terrible term hath never detained me from sin, nor do I owe any good action to the name thereof. I fear GOD, yet am not afraid of Him: His Mercies make me ashamed of my sins, before His Judgements afraid thereof. These are the forced and secondary method of His wisdom, which He useth but as the last remedy, and

---

[125] In opposition to. [126] *I. e.,* an infinite number. The doctrine belongs to Anaxarchus. [127] Exempt from decay.

upon provocation; a course rather to deter the wicked, than incite the virtuous to His worship. I can hardly think there was ever any scared into Heaven; they go the fairest way to Heaven that would serve GOD without a Hell; other Mercenaries, that crouch into Him in fear of Hell, though they term themselves the servants, are indeed but the slaves, of the Almighty.

LIII. And to be true, and speak my soul, when I survey the occurrences of my life, and call into account the Finger of GOD, I can perceive nothing but an abyss and mass of mercies, either in general to mankind, or in particular to my self. And (whether out of the prejudice of my affection, or an inverting and partial conceit of His mercies, I know not; but) those which others term crosses, afflictions, judgements, misfortunes, to me, who inquire farther into them then their visible effects, they both appear, and in event have ever proved, the secret and dissembled favours of His affection. It is a singular piece of Wisdom to apprehend truly, and without passion the Works of GOD, and so well to distinguish His Justice from His Mercy, as not to miscall those noble Attributes: yet it is likewise an honest piece of Logick, so to dispute and argue the proceedings of GOD, as to distinguish even His judgments into mercies. For GOD is merciful unto all, because better to the worst than the best deserve; and to say He punisheth none in this World, though it be a Paradox, is no absurdity. To one that hath committed Murther, if the Judge should only ordain a Fine, it were a madness to call this a punishment, and to repine at the sentence, rather than admire the clemency of the Judge. Thus, our offences being mortal, and deserving not only Death, but Damnation, if the goodness of GOD be content to traverse and pass them over with a loss, misfortune, or disease, what frensie were it to term this a punishment, rather than an extremity of mercy, and to groan under the rod of His Judgements, rather than admire the Scepter of His Mercies! Therefore to adore, honour, and admire Him, is a debt of gratitude due from the obligation of our nature, states, and conditions; and with these thoughts, He that knows them best, will not deny that I adore Him. That I obtain Heaven, and the bliss thereof, is accidental, and not the intended work of my devotion; it being a felicity I can neither think to deserve, nor scarce in modesty to expect. For these two ends of us all, either as rewards or punishments, are mercifully ordained and disproportionably disposed unto our actions; the one being so far beyond our deserts, the other so infinitely below our demerits.

LIV. There is no Salvation to those that believe not in CHRIST, that is, say some, since His Nativity, and, as Divinity affirmeth, before also; which makes me much apprehend[128] the ends of those honest Worthies and Philosophers which dyed before His Incarnation. It is hard to place those Souls in Hell, whose worthy lives do teach us Virtue on Earth; methinks, amongst those many subdivisions of Hell, there might have been one Limbo left for these. What a strange vision will it be to see their Poetical fictions converted into Verities, and their imagined and fancied Furies into real Devils! How strange to them will sound the History of Adam, when they shall suffer for him they never heard of! when they who derive their genealogy from the Gods, shall know they are the unhappy issue of sinful man! It is an insolent part of reason, to controvert the works of GOD, or question the Justice of His proceedings. Could Humility teach others, as it hath instructed me, to contemplate the infinite and incomprehensible distance betwixt the Creator and the Creature; or did we seriously perpend that one simile of St. Paul, *Shall the Vessel say to the Potter, "Why hast thou made me thus?"* it would prevent these arrogant disputes of reason; nor would we argue the definitive sentence of GOD, either to Heaven or Hell. Men that live according to the right rule and law of reason, live but in their own kind, as beasts do in theirs; who justly obey the prescript of their natures, and therefore cannot reasonably demand a reward of their actions, as onely obeying the natural dictates of their reason. It will, therefore, and must at last appear, that all salvation is through CHRIST; which verity, I fear, these great examples of virtue must confirm, and make it good how the perfectest actions of earth have no title or claim unto Heaven.

LV. Nor truly do I think the lives of these, or of any other, were ever correspondent, or in all points conformable, unto their doctrines. It is evident that Aristotle transgressed the rule of his own Ethicks. The Stoicks that condemn passion, and command a man

[128] Contemplate with fear.

to laugh in Phalaris[129] his Bull, could not endure without a groan a fit of the Stone or Colick. The Scepticks that affirmed they knew nothing, even in that opinion confute themselves, and thought they knew more than all the World beside. Diogenes I hold to be the most vain-glorious man of his time, and more ambitious in refusing all Honours, than Alexander in rejecting none. Vice and the Devil put a Fallacy upon our Reasons, and, provoking us too hastily to run from it, entangle and profound us deeper in it. The Duke of Venice, that weds himself unto the Sea by a Ring of Gold, I will not argue of prodigality, because it is a solemnity of good use and consequence in the State; but the Philosopher that threw his money into the Sea to avoid Avarice, was a notorious prodigal. There is no road or ready way to virtue: it is not an easie point of art to disentangle our selves from this riddle, or web of Sin. To perfect virtue, as to Religion, there is required a *Panoplia,* or compleat armour; that, whilst we lye at close ward against one Vice, we lye not open to the venny[130] of another. And indeed wiser discretions that have the thred of reason to conduct them, offend without pardon; whereas under-heads may stumble without dishonour. There go so many circumstances to piece up one good action, that it is a lesson to be good, and we are forced to be virtuous by the book. Again, the Practice of men holds not an equal pace, yea, and often runs counter to their Theory: we naturally know what is good, but naturally pursue what is evil: the Rhetorick wherewith I perswade another, cannot perswade my self. There is a depraved appetite in us, that will with patience hear the learned instructions of Reason, but yet perform no farther than agrees to its own irregular humour. In brief, we all are monsters, that is, a composition of Man and Beast, wherein we must endeavor to be as the Poets fancy that wise man Chiron,[131] that is, to have the Region of Man above that of Beast, and Sense to sit but at the feet of Reason. Lastly, I do desire with GOD that all, but yet affirm with men that few, shall know Salvation; that the bridge is narrow, the passage strait, unto life: yet those who do confine the Church of GOD, either to particular Nations, Churches, or Families, have made it far narrower than our Saviour ever meant it.

---

[129] A Sicilian tyrant of the 6th century B. C., who sacrificed human beings in a heated brazen bull.   [130] Assault.   [131] The Centaur.

LVI. The vulgarity of those judgements that wrap the Church of GOD in Strabo's *cloak*,[132] and restrain it unto Europe, seem to me as bad Geographers as Alexander, who thought he had Conquer'd all the World, when he had not subdued the half of any part thereof. For we cannot deny the Church of GOD both in Asia and Africa, if we do not forget the Peregrinations of the Apostles, the deaths of the Martyrs, the Sessions of many and (even in our reformed judgement) lawful Councils, held in those parts in the minority and nonage of ours. Nor must a few differences, more remarkable in the eyes of man than perhaps in the judgement of GOD, excommunicate from Heaven one another; much less those Christians who are in a manner all Martyrs, maintaining their Faith in the noble way of persecution, and serving GOD in the Fire, whereas we honour him but in the Sunshine. 'Tis true we all hold there is a number of Elect, and many to be saved; yet, take our Opinions together, and from the confusion thereof there will be no such thing as salvation, nor shall any one be saved. For first, the Church of Rome condemneth us, we likewise them; the Subreformists and Sectaries sentence the Doctrine of our Church as damnable; the Atomist,[133] or Familist,[134] reprobates all these; and all these, them again. Thus, whilst the Mercies of GOD do promise us Heaven, our conceits and opinions exclude us from that place. There must be, therefore, more than one St. Peter: particular Churches and Sects usurp the gates of Heaven, and turn the key against each other; and thus we go to Heaven against each others wills, conceits, and opinions, and, with as much uncharity as ignorance, do err, I fear, in points not only of our own, but one anothers salvation.

LVII. I believe many are saved, who to man seem reprobated; and many are reprobated, who, in the opinion and sentence of man, stand elected. There will appear at the Last day strange and unexpected examples both of His Justice and His Mercy; and therefore to define either, is folly in man, and insolency even in the Devils. Those acute and subtil spirits, in all their sagacity, can hardly divine who shall be saved; which if they could Prognostick, their labour were at an end, nor need they compass the earth *seeking whom they may*

---

[132] Strabo compared the known world of his time to a cloak.
[133] Apparently a sect of Browne's time.
[134] One of the sect called "The Family of Love."

devour. Those who, upon a rigid application of the Law, sentence Solomon unto damnation, condemn not onely him, but themselves, and the whole World: for, by the Letter and written Word of God, we are without exception in the state of Death; but there is a prerogative of God, and an arbitrary pleasure above the Letter of His own Law, by which alone we can pretend unto Salvation, and through which Solomon might be as easily saved as those who condemn him.

LVIII. The number of those who pretend unto Salvation, and those infinite swarms who think to pass through the eye of this Needle, have much amazed me. That name and compellation of *little Flock,* doth not comfort, but deject, my Devotion; especially when I reflect upon mine own unworthiness, wherein, according to my humble apprehensions, I am below them all. I believe there shall never be an Anarchy in Heaven; but, as there are Hierarchies amongst the Angels, so shall there be degrees of priority amongst the Saints. Yet is it (I protest,) beyond my ambition to aspire unto the first ranks; my desires onely are (and I shall be happy therein,) to be but the last man, and bring up the Rere in Heaven.

LIX. Again, I am confident and fully perswaded, yet dare not take my oath, of my Salvation. I am as it were sure, and do believe without all doubt, that there is such a City as Constantinople; yet for me to take my Oath thereon were a kind of Perjury, because I hold no infallible warrant from my own sense to confirm me in the certainty thereof. And truly, though many pretend an absolute certainty of their Salvation, yet, when an humble Soul shall contemplate her own unworthiness, she shall meet with many doubts, and suddenly find how little we stand in need of the Precept of St. Paul, *Work out your salvation with fear and trembling.* That which is the cause of my Election, I hold to be the cause of my Salvation, which was the mercy and beneplacit[135] of God, before I was, or the foundation of the World. *Before Abraham was, I am,* is the saying of Christ; yet is it true in some sense, if I say it of my self; for I was not onely before my self, but Adam, that is, in the Idea of God, and the decree of that Synod held from all Eternity. And in this sense, I say, the World was before the Creation, and at an end

[135] Good pleasure.

before it had a beginning; and thus was I dead before I was alive: though my grave be England, my dying place was Paradise: and Eve miscarried of me before she conceiv'd of Cain.

LX. Insolent zeals,[136] that do decry good Works and rely onely upon Faith, take not away merit: for, depending upon the efficacy of their Faith, they enforce the condition of GOD, and in a more sophistical way do seem to challenge Heaven. It was decreed by GOD, that only those that lapt in the water like Dogs, should have the honour to destroy the Midianites; yet could none of those justly challenge, or imagine he deserved, that honour thereupon. I do not deny but that true Faith, and such as GOD requires, is not onely a mark or token, but also a means, of our Salvation; but where to find this, is as obscure to me as my last end. And if our Saviour could object unto His own Disciples and Favourites, a Faith, that, to the quantity of a grain of Mustard-seed, is able to remove Mountains; surely, that which we boast of, is not any thing, or at the most, but a remove from nothing. This is the Tenor of my belief; wherein though there be many things singular, and to the humour of my irregular self, yet, if they square not with maturer Judgements, I disclaim them, and do no further father them, than the learned and best judgements shall authorize them.

[136] Zealots.

RELIGIO MEDICI

THE SECOND PART

NOW for that other Virtue of Charity, without which Faith is a meer notion, and of no existence, I have ever endeavoured to nourish the merciful disposition and humane inclination I borrowed from my Parents, and regulate it to the written and prescribed Laws of Charity. And if I hold the true Anatomy of my self, I am delineated and naturally framed to such a piece of virtue; for I am of a constitution so general, that it consorts and sympathiseth with all things. I have no antipathy, or rather Idiosyncrasie, in dyet, humour, air, any thing. I wonder not at the French for their dishes of Frogs, Snails and Toadstools, nor at the Jews for Locusts and Grasshoppers; but being amongst them, make them my common Viands, and I find they agree with my Stomach as well as theirs. I could digest a Salad gathered in a Church-yard, as well as in a Garden. I cannot start at the presence of a Serpent, Scorpion, Lizard, or Salamander: at the sight of a Toad or Viper, I find in me no desire to take up a stone to destroy them. I feel not in my self those common Antipathies that I can discover in others: those National repugnances do not touch me, nor do I behold with prejudice the French, Italian, Spaniard, or Dutch: but where I find their actions in balance with my Country-men's, I honour, love, and embrace them in the same degree. I was born in the eighth Climate,[1] but seem for to be framed and constellated unto all. I am no Plant that will not prosper out of a Garden. All places, all airs, make unto me one Countrey; I am in England every where, and under any Meridian. I have been shipwrackt, yet am not enemy with the Sea or Winds; I can study, play, or sleep in a Tempest. In brief, I am averse from nothing: my Conscience would give me the lye if I should say I absolutely detest or hate any essence but the Devil; or

[1] Region of the earth's surface, used like our degrees of latitude.

so at least abhor any thing, but that we might come to composition. If there be any among those common objects of hatred I do contemn and laugh at, it is that great enemy of Reason, Virtue and Religion, the Multitude: that numerous piece of monstrosity, which, taken asunder, seem men, and the reasonable creatures of God; but, confused together, make but one great beast, and a monstrosity more prodigious than Hydra. It is no breach of Charity to call these *Fools;* it is the style all holy Writers have afforded them, set down by Solomon in Canonical Scripture, and a point of our Faith to believe so. Neither in the name of *Multitude* do I onely include the base and minor sort of people; there is a rabble even amongst the Gentry, a sort of Plebeian heads, whose fancy moves with the same wheel as these; men in the same Level with Mechanicks, though their fortunes do somewhat guild their infirmities, and their purses compound for their follies. But as, in casting account, three or four men together come short in account of one man placed by himself below them; so neither are a troop of these ignorant *Doradoes*[2] of that true esteem and value, as many a forlorn person, whose condition doth place him below their feet. Let us speak like Politicians:[3] there is a Nobility without Heraldry, a natural dignity, whereby one man is ranked with another, another filed before him, according to the quality of his Desert, and preheminence of his good parts. Though the corruption of these times and the byas of present practice wheel another way, thus it was in the first and primitive Commonwealths, and is yet in the integrity and Cradle of well-order'd Polities, till corruption getteth ground; ruder desires labouring after that which wiser considerations contemn, every one having a liberty to amass and heap up riches, and they a licence or faculty to do or purchase any thing.

II. This general and indifferent temper of mine doth more neerly dispose me to this noble virtue. It is a happiness to be born and framed unto virtue, and to grow up from the seeds of nature, rather than the inoculation and forced graffs of education: yet if we are directed only by our particular Natures, and regulate our inclinations by no higher rule than that of our reasons, we are but Moralists; Divinity will still call us Heathens. Therefore this great work of

[2] Spanish, the name of a fish: here=fools.   [3] Statesmen.

charity must have other motives, ends, and impulsions. I give no alms only to satisfie the hunger of my Brother, but to fulfil and accomplish the Will and Command of my GOD: I draw not my purse for his sake that demands it, but His That enjoyed it: I relieve no man upon the Rhetorick of his miseries, nor to content mine own commiserating disposition; for this is still but moral charity, and an act that oweth more to passion than reason. He that relieves another upon the bare suggestion and bowels of pity, doth not this, so much for his sake as for his own; for by compassion we make others misery our own, and so, by relieving them, we relieve our selves also. It is as erroneous a conceit to redress other Mens misfortunes upon the common considerations of merciful natures, that it may be one day our own case; for this is a sinister and politick kind of charity, whereby we seem to bespeak the pities of men in the like occasions. And truly I have observed that those professed Eleemosynaries, though in a croud or multitude, do yet direct and place their petitions on a few and selected persons: there is surely a Physiognomy, which those experienced and Master Mendicants observe, whereby they instantly discover a merciful aspect, and will single out a face wherein they spy the signatures and marks of Mercy. For there are mystically in our faces certain Characters which carry in them the motto of our Souls, wherein he that cannot read A. B. C. may read our natures. I hold moreover that there is a Phytognomy, or Physiognomy, not only of Men, but of Plants and Vegetables; and in every one of them some outward figures which hang as signs or bushes[4] of their inward forms. The Finger of GOD hath left an Inscription upon all His works, not graphical or composed of Letters, but of their several forms, constitutions, parts, and operations, which, aptly joyned together, do make one word that doth express their natures. By these Letters GOD calls the Stars by their names; and by this Alphabet Adam assigned to every creature a name peculiar to its Nature. Now there are, besides these Characters in our Faces, certain mystical figures in our Hands, which I dare not call meer dashes, strokes *à la volée,* or at random, because delineated by a Pencil that never works in vain; and hereof I take more particular notice, because I carry that in mine own hand which I could never read

[4] Bushes were hung out as signs before tavern doors.

of nor discover in another. Aristotle, I confess, in his acute and singular Book of *Physiognomy,* hath made no mention of Chiromancy; yet I believe the Egyptians, who were neerer addicted to those abstruse and mystical sciences, had a knowledge therein, to which those vagabond and counterfeit Egyptians[5] did after pretend, and perhaps retained a few corrupted principles, which sometimes might verifie their prognosticks.

It is the common wonder of all men, how among so many millions of faces, there should be none alike: now contrary, I wonder as much how there should be any. He that shall consider how many thousand several words have been carelessly and without study composed out of twenty-four Letters; withal, how many hundred lines there are to be drawn in the Fabrick of one Man, shall easily find that this variety is necessary; and it will be very hard that they shall so concur as to make one portract like another. Let a Painter carelesly limb out a million of Faces, and you shall find them all different; yea, let him have his Copy before him, yet after all his art there will remain a sensible distinction; for the pattern or example of every thing is the perfectest in that kind, whereof we still come short, though we transcend or go beyond it, because herein it is wide, and agrees not in all points unto the copy. Nor doth the similitude of Creatures disparage the variety of Nature, nor any way confound the Works of God. For even in things alike there is diversity; and those that do seem to accord do manifestly disagree. And thus is man like God; for in the same things that we resemble Him, we are utterly different from Him. There was never anything so like another as in all points to concur: there will ever some reserved difference slip in, to prevent the identity; without which, two several things would not be alike, but the same, which is impossible.

III. But to return from Philosophy to Charity: I hold not so narrow a conceit of this virtue, as to conceive that to give Alms is onely to be Charitable, or think a piece of Liberality can comprehend the Total of Charity. Divinity hath wisely divided the act thereof into many branches, and hath taught us in this narrow way many paths unto goodness; as many ways as we may do good, so many ways we may be charitable. There are infirmities not onely of Body,

[5] Gipsies.

but of Soul, and Fortunes, which do require the merciful hand of our abilities. I cannot contemn a man for ignorance, but behold him with as much pity as I do Lazarus. It is no greater Charity to cloath his body, than apparel the nakedness of his Soul. It is an honourable object to see the reasons of other men wear our Liveries, and their borrowed understandings do homage to the bounty of ours: it is the cheapest way of beneficence, and, like the natural charity of the Sun, illuminates another without obscuring itself. To be reserved and caitiff in this part of goodness, is the sordidest piece of covetousness, and more contemptible than pecuniary Avarice. To this (as calling my self a Scholar,) I am obliged by the duty of my condition: I make not therefore my head a grave, but a treasure, of knowledge; I intend no Monopoly, but a community, in learning; I study not for my own sake only, but for theirs that study not for themselves. I envy no man that knows more than my self, but pity them that know less. I instruct no man as an exercise of my knowledge, or with intent rather to nourish and keep it alive in mine own head then beget and propagate it in his: and in the midst of all my endeavours there is but one thought that dejects me, that my acquired parts must perish with my self, nor can be Legacied among my honoured Friends. I cannot fall out or contemn a man for an errour, or conceive why a difference in Opinion should divide an affection; for Controversies, Disputes, and Argumentations, both in Philosophy and in Divinity, if they meet with discreet and peaceable natures, do not infringe the Laws of Charity. In all disputes, so much as there is of passion, so much there is of nothing to the purpose; for then Reason, like a bad Hound, spends upon a false Scent, and forsakes the question first started. And this is one reason why Controversies are never determined; for, though they be amply proposed, they are scarce at all handled, they do so swell with unnecessary Digressions; and the Parenthesis on the party is often as large as the main discourse upon the subject. The Foundations of Religion are already established, and the Principles of Salvation subscribed unto by all: there remains not many controversies worth a Passion; and yet never any disputed without, not only in Divinity, but inferiour Arts. What a $βατραχομυομαχία$[6] and hot skirmish is betwixt S. and

---

[6] Battle of the Frogs and Mice.

T. in Lucian![7] How do Grammarians hack and slash for the Genitive case in *Jupiter!*[8] How do they break their own pates to salve that of Priscian!

> *Si foret in terris, rideret Democritus.*
>
> [If he were on earth, Democritus would laugh.]

Yea, even amongst wiser militants, how many wounds have been given, and credits slain, for the poor victory of an opinion or beggerly conquest of a distinction! Scholars are men of Peace, they bear no Arms, but their tongues are sharper than Actius his razor;[9] their Pens carry farther, and give a louder report than Thunder: I had rather stand the shock of a Basilisco,[10] than the fury of a merciless Pen. It is not meer Zeal to Learning, or Devotion to the Muses, that wiser Princes Patron the Arts, and carry an indulgent aspect unto Scholars; but a desire to have their names eternized by the memory of their writings, and a fear of the revengeful Pen of succeeding ages; for these are the men, that, when they have played their parts, and had their *exits,* must step out and give the moral of their Scenes, and deliver unto Posterity an Inventory of their Virtues and Vices. And surely there goes a great deal of Conscience to the compiling of an History: there is no reproach[11] to the scandal of a Story; it is such an authentick kind of falshood that with authority belies our good names to all Nations and Posterity.

IV. There is another offence unto Charity, which no Author hath ever written of, and few take notice of; and that's the reproach, not of whole professions, mysteries, and conditions, but of whole Nations, wherein by opprobrious Epithets we miscall each other, and by an uncharitable Logick, from a disposition in a few, conclude a habit in all.

> *Le mutin Anglois, et le bravache Escossois,*
> *Et le fol François,*
> *Le poultron Romain, le larron de Gascongne,*
> *L'Espagnol superbe, et l'Aleman yvrongne.*

[The stubborn Englishman, the swaggering Scot, the foolish Frenchman, the coward Roman, the Gascon thief, the proud Spaniard, and the drunken German.]

---

[7] In Lucian's "Judicium Vocalium," where the letter S accuses T of interference with the other consonants.   [8] Whether Jupiteris or Jovis.   [9] Which cut through a whetstone.   [10] A kind of cannon.   [11] Because it is believed.

St. Paul, that calls the Cretians *lyars*,[12] doth it but indirectly, and upon quotation of their own Poet.[13] It is as bloody a thought in one way, as Nero's[14] was in another; for by a word we wound a thousand, and at one blow assassine the honour of a Nation. It is as compleat a piece of madness to miscal and rave against the times, or think to recal men to reason by a fit of passion. Democritus, that thought to laugh the times into goodness, seems to me as deeply Hypochondriack as Heraclitus, that bewailed them. It moves not my spleen to behold the multitude in their proper humours, that is, in their fits of folly and madness; as well understanding that wisdom is not prophan'd unto the World, and 'tis the priviledge of a few to be Vertuous. They that endeavour to abolish Vice, destroy also Virtue; for contraries, though they destroy one another, are yet the life of one another. Thus Virtue (abolish vice,) is an Idea. Again, the community[15] of sin doth not disparage goodness; for when Vice gains upon the major part, Virtue, in whom it remains, becomes more excellent; and being lost in some, multiplies its goodness in others which remain untouched and persist intire in the general inundation. I can therefore behold Vice without a Satyr, content only with an admonition, or instructive reprehension; for Noble Natures, and such as are capable of goodness, are railed into vice, that might as easily be admonished into virtue; and we should be all so far the Orators of goodness, as to protect her from the power of Vice, and maintain the cause of injured truth. No man can justly censure or condemn another, because indeed no man truly knows another. This I perceive in my self; for I am in the dark to all the world, and my nearest friends beheld me but in a cloud. Those that know me but superficially, think less of me than I do of my self; those of my neer acquaintance think more; GOD, Who truly knows me, knows that I am nothing; for He only beholds me and all the world, Who looks not on us through a derived ray, or a trajection[16] of a sensible species, but beholds the substance without the helps of accidents, and the forms of things as we their operations. Further, no man can judge another, because no man knows himself: for we

---

[12] "Titus" i. 12. [13] Epimenides.
[14] Perhaps a confusion with Caligula, who wished that the whole Roman people had one neck. [15] Prevalence. [16] Emission.

censure others but as they disagree from that humour which we fancy laudable in our selves, and commend others but for that wherein they seem to quadrate[17] and consent with us. So that, in conclusion, all is but that we all condemn, Self-love. 'Tis the general complaint of these times, and perhaps of those past, that charity grows cold; which I perceive most verified in those which most do manifest the fires and flames of zeal; for it is a virtue that best agrees with coldest natures, and such as are complexioned for humility. But how shall we expect Charity towards others, when we are uncharitable to our selves? *Charity begins at home,* is the voice of the World; yet is every man his greatest enemy, and, as it were, his own Executioner. *Non occides,* [Thou shalt not kill] is the Commandment of GOD, yet scarce observed by any man; for I perceive every man is his own *Atropos,*[18] and lends a hand to cut the thred of his own days. Cain was not therefore the first Murtherer, but Adam, who brought in death; whereof he beheld the practice and example in his own son Abel, and saw that verified in the experience of another, which faith could not perswade him in the Theory of himself.

V. There is, I think, no man that apprehends his own miseries less than my self, and no man that so neerly apprehends anothers. I could lose an arm without a tear, and with few groans, methinks; be quartered into pieces; yet can I weep most seriously at a Play, and receive with true passion the counterfeit grief of those known and professed Impostures. It is a barbarous part of inhumanity to add unto any afflicted parties misery, or indeavour to multiply in any man a passion whose single nature is already above his patience. This was the greatest affliction of Job, and those oblique expostulations of his Friends a deeper injury than the down-right blows of the Devil. It is not the tears of our own eyes only, but of our friends also, that do exhaust the current of our sorrows; which, falling into many streams, runs more peaceably, and is contented with a narrower channel. It is an act within the power of charity, to translate a passion out of one breast into another, and to divide a sorrow almost out of it self; for an affliction, like a dimension, may be so divided, as, if not indivisible, at least to become insensible. Now

[17] Square. [18] The Fate who cuts the thread of life.

with my friend I desire not to share or participate, but to engross, his sorrows; that, by making them mine own, I may more easily discuss them; for in mine own reason, and within my self, I can command that which I cannot intreat without my self, and within the circle of another. I have often thought those noble pairs and examples of friendship not so truly Histories of what had been, as fictions of what should be; but I now perceive nothing in them but possibilities, nor anything in the Heroick examples of Damon and Pythias, Achilles and Patroclus, which methinks upon some grounds I could not perform within the narrow compass of my self. That a man should lay down his life for his Friend, seems strange to vulgar affections, and such as confine themselves within that Worldly principle, *Charity begins at home*. For mine own part I could never remember the relations that I held unto my self, nor the respect that I owe unto my own nature, in the cause of God, my Country, and my Friends. Next to these three, I do embrace my self. I confess I do not observe that order that the Schools ordain our affections, to love our Parents, Wives, Children, and then our Friends; for, excepting the injunctions of Religion, I do not find in my self such a necessary and indissoluble Sympathy to all those of my blood. I hope I do not break the fifth Commandment, if I conceive I may love my friend before the nearest of my blood, even those to whom I owe the principles of life. I never yet cast a true affection on a woman; but I have loved my friend as I do virtue, my soul, my God. From hence me thinks I do conceive how God loves man, what happiness there is in the love of God. Omitting all other, there are three most mystical unions: 1. two natures in one person; 2. three persons in one nature; 3. one soul in two bodies; for though indeed they be really divided, yet are they so united, as they seem but one, and make rather a duality than two distinct souls.

VI. There are wonders in true affection: it is a body of *Enigma's,* mysteries, and riddles; wherein two so become one, as they both become two. I love my friend before my self, and yet methinks I do not love him enough: some few months hence my multiplied affection will make me believe I have not loved him at all. When I am from him, I am dead till I be with him; when I am with him, I am not satisfied, but would still be nearer him. United souls are not satisfied with imbraces, but desire to be truly each other; which being impossible, their desires are infinite, and must proceed without a possibility of satisfaction. Another misery there is in affection, that whom we truly love like our own selves, we forget their looks, nor can our memory retain the Idea of their faces; and it is no wonder, for they are our selves, and our affection makes their looks our own. This noble affection falls not on vulgar and common constitutions, but on such as are mark'd for virtue: he that can love his friend with this noble ardour, will in a competent degree affect all. Now, if we can bring our affections to look beyond the body, and cast an eye upon the soul, we have found out the true object, not only of friendship, but Charity; and the greatest happiness that we can bequeath the soul, is that wherein we all do place our last felicity, Salvation; which though it be not in our power to bestow, it is in our charity and pious invocations to desire, if not procure and further. I cannot contentedly frame a prayer for my self in particular, without a catalogue for my friends; nor request a happiness, wherein my sociable disposition doth not desire the fellowship of my neighbour. I never hear the Toll of a passing Bell, though in my mirth, with out my prayers and best wishes for the departing spirit; I cannot go to cure the body of my patient, but I forget my profession, and call unto GOD for his soul; I cannot see one say his prayers, but, in stead of imitating him, I fall into a supplication for him, who perhaps is no more to me than a common nature: and if GOD hath vouchsafed an ear to my supplications, there are surely many happy that never saw me, and enjoy the blessing of mine unknown devotions. To pray for Enemies, that is, for their salvation, is no harsh precept, but the practice of our daily and ordinary devotions. I cannot believe the story of the Italian:[19] our bad wishes and uncharitable desires proceed no further than this life; it is the Devil, and the uncharitable votes of Hell, that desire our misery in the world to come.

VII. To do no injury, nor take none, was a principle, which to my former years and impatient affections seemed to contain enough of Morality; but my more setled years and Christian constitution have

[19] Who killed his enemy after inducing him to blaspheme, that he might go to hell.

fallen upon severer resolutions. I can hold there is no such thing as injury; that, if there be, there is no such injury as revenge, and no such revenge as the contempt of an injury; that to hate another, is to malign himself; that the truest way to love another, is to despise our selves. I were unjust unto mine own Conscience, if I should say I am at variance with any thing like my self. I find there are many pieces in this one fabrick of man; this frame is raised upon a mass of Antipathies. I am one methinks, but as the World; wherein notwithstanding there are a swarm of distinct essences, and in them another World of contrarieties; we carry private and domestic enemies within, publick and more hostile adversaries without. The Devil, that did but buffet St. Paul, plays methinks at sharp[20] with me. Let me be nothing, if within the compass of my self I do not find the battail of Lepanto,[21] Passion against Reason, Reason against Faith, Faith against the Devil, and my Conscience against all. There is another man within me, that's angry with me, rebukes, commands, and dastards me. I have no Conscience of Marble to resist the hammer of more heavy offences; nor yet so soft and waxen, as to take the impression of each single peccadillo or scape of infirmity. I am of a strange belief, that it is as easie to be forgiven some sins, as to commit some others. For my Original sin, I hold it to be washed away in my Baptism: for my actual transgressions, I compute and reckon with GOD but from my last repentance, Sacrament, or general absolution; and therefore am not terrified with the sins or madness of my youth. I thank the goodness of GOD, I have no sins that want a name; I am not singular in offences; my transgressions are Epidemical, and from the common breath of our corruption. For there are certain tempers of body, which, matcht with an humorous depravity of mind, do hatch and produce vitiosities, whose newness and monstrosity of nature admits no name: this was the temper of that Lecher that fell in love with a Statua, and the constitution of Nero in his Spintrian[22] recreations. For the Heavens are not only fruitful in new and unheard-of stars, the Earth in plants and animals, but mens minds also in villany and vices. Now the dulness of my reason, and the vulgarity[23] of my disposition, never prompted my

[20] Fights in earnest.   [21] "Used for a deadly contest."   [22] Obscene.
[23] Commonplaceness.

invention, nor solicited my affection unto any of these; yet even those common and quotidian infirmities that so necessarily attend me, and do seem to be my very nature, have so dejected me, so broken the estimation that I should have otherwise of my self, that I repute my self the most abjectest piece of mortality. Divines prescribe a fit of sorrow to repentance: there goes indignation, anger, sorrow, hatred, into mine; passions of a contrary nature, which neither seem to sute with this action, nor my proper constitution. It is no breach of charity to our selves, to be at variance with our Vices, nor to abhor that part of us which is an enemy to the ground of charity, our GOD; wherein we do but imitate our great selves, the world, whose divided Antipathies and contrary faces do yet carry a charitable regard unto the whole, by their particular discords preserving the common harmony, and keeping in fetters those powers, whose rebellions, once Masters, might be the ruine of all.

VIII. I thank GOD, amongst those millions of Vices I do inherit and hold from Adam, I have escaped one, and that a mortal enemy to Charity, the first and father-sin, not onely of man, but of the devil, Pride: a vice whose name is comprehended in a Monosyllable, but in its nature not circumscribed with a World. I have escaped it in a condition that can hardly avoid it. Those petty acquisitions and reputed perfections that advance and elevate the conceits of other men, add no feathers unto mine. I have seen a Grammarian towr and plume himself over a single line in Horace, and shew more pride in the construction of one Ode, than the Author in the composure of the whole book. For my own part, besides the *Jargon* and *Patois* of several Provinces, I understand no less than six Languages; yet I protest I have no higher conceit of my self, than had our Fathers before the confusion of Babel, when there was but one Language in the World, and none to boast himself either Linguist or Critick. I have not onely seen several Countries, beheld the nature of their Climes, the Chorography[24] of their Provinces, Topography of their Cities, but understood their several Laws, Customs, and Policies; yet cannot all this perswade the dulness of my spirit unto such an opinion of my self, as I behold in nimbler and conceited heads, that never looked a degree beyond their Nests. I know

[24] Description.

the names, and somewhat more, of all the constellations in my Horizon; yet I have seen a prating Mariner, that could onely name the pointers and the North Star, out-talk me, and conceit himself a whole Sphere above me. I know most of the Plants of my Countrey, and of those about me; yet methinks I do not know so many as when I did but know a hundred, and had scarcely ever Simpled[25] further than *Cheap-side*.[26] For, indeed, heads of capacity, and such as are not full with a handful or easie measure of knowledge, think they know nothing till they know all; which being impossible, they fall upon the opinion of Socrates, and only know they know not anything. I cannot think that Homer pin'd away upon the riddle of the fishermen; or that Aristotle, who understood the uncertainty of knowledge, and confessed so often the reason of man too weak for the works of nature, did ever drown himself upon the flux and reflux of Euripus. We do but learn to-day what our better advanced judgements will unteach to morrow; and Aristotle doth but instruct us, as Plato did him; that is, to confute himself. I have run through all sorts, yet find no rest in any: though our first studies and *junior* endeavours may style us Peripateticks, Stoicks, or Academicks; yet I perceive the wisest heads prove, at last, almost all Scepticks, and stand like Janus[27] in the field of knowledge. I have therefore one common and authentick Philosophy I learned in the Schools, whereby I discourse and satisfy the reason of other men; another more reserved, and drawn from experience, whereby I content mine own. Solomon, that complained of ignorance in the height of knowledge, hath not only humbled my conceits, but discouraged my endeavours. There is yet another conceit[28] that hath sometimes made me shut my books, which tells me it is a vanity to waste our days in the blind pursuit of knowledge; it is but attending a little longer, and we shall enjoy that by instinct and infusion, which we endeavour at here by labour and inquisition. It is better to sit down in a modest ignorance, and rest contented with the natural blessing of our own reasons, than buy the uncertain knowledge of this life with sweat and vexation, which Death gives every fool *gratis,* and is an accessary of our glorification.

[25] Botanized.   [26] A great herb market in the 17th century.   [27] A Roman deity whose statues had two faces looking in opposite directions.   [28] Idea.

IX. I was never yet once, and commend their resolutions who never marry twice: not that I disallow of second marriage; as neither, in all cases, of Polygamy, which, considering some times, and the unequal number of both sexes, may be also necessary. The whole World was made for man, but the twelfth part of man for woman: Man is the whole World, and the Breath of GOD; Woman the Rib and crooked piece of man. I could be content that we might procreate like trees, without conjunction, or that there were any way to perpetuate the World without this trivial and vulgar way of union: it is the foolishest act a wise man commits in all his life; nor is there any thing that will more deject his cool'd imagination, when he shall consider what an odd and unworthy piece of folly he hath committed. I speak not in prejudice, nor am averse from that sweet Sex, but naturally amorous of all that is beautiful. I can look a whole day with delight upon a handsome Picture, though it be but of an Horse. It is my temper, and I like it the better, to affect all harmony; and sure there is musick even in the beauty, and the silent note which Cupid strikes, far sweeter than the sound of an instrument. For there is a musick where ever there is a harmony, order, or proportion: and thus far we may maintain the music of the Sphears; for those well-ordered motions, and regular paces, though they give no sound unto the ear, yet to the understanding they strike a note most full of harmony. Whatsoever is harmonically composed delights in harmony; which makes me much distrust the symmetry of those heads which declaim against all Church-Musick. For my self, not only for my obedience, but my particular Genius, I do embrace it: for even that vulgar and Tavern-Musick, which makes one man merry, another mad, strikes in me a deep fit of devotion, and a profound contemplation of the First Composer. There is something in it of Divinity more than the ear discovers: it is an Hieroglyphical and shadowed lesson of the whole World, and creatures of GOD; such a melody to the ear, as the whole World, well understood, would afford the understanding. In brief, it is a sensible fit of that harmony which intellectually sounds in the ears of GOD. I will not say, with Plato, the soul is an harmony, but harmonical, and hath its nearest sympathy unto Musick: thus some, whose temper of body agrees, and humours the constitution of their souls, are born

Poets, though indeed all are naturally inclined unto Rhythme. This made Tacitus, in the very first line of his Story, fall upon a verse; and Cicero, the worst of Poets, but declaiming for a Poet, falls in the very first sentence upon a perfect Hexameter. I feel not in me those sordid and unchristian desires of my profession; I do not secretly implore and wish for Plagues, rejoyce at Famines, revolve Ephemerides[29] and Almanacks in expectation of malignant Aspects,[30] fatal Conjunctions,[30] and Eclipses.[30] I rejoyce not at unwholesome Springs, nor unseasonable Winters: my Prayer goes with the Husbandman's; I desire every thing in its proper season, that neither men nor the times be put out of temper. Let me be sick my self if sometimes the malady of my patient be not a disease unto me. I desire rather to cure his infirmities than my own necessities. Where I do him no good, methinks it is scarce honest gain; though I confess, 'tis but the worthy salary of our well-intended endeavours. I am not only ashamed, but heartily sorry, that, besides death, there are diseases incurable: yet not for my own sake, or that they be beyond my Art, but for the general cause and sake of humanity, whose common cause I apprehend as mine own. And to speak more generally, those three Noble Professions which all civil Commonwealths do honour, are raised upon the fall of Adam, and are not any way exempt from their infirmities; there are not only diseases incurable in Physick, but cases indissolvable in Laws, Vices incorrigible in Divinity. If General Councils may err, I do not see why particular Courts should be infallible; their perfectest rules are raised upon the erroneous reasons of Man, and the Laws of one do but condemn the rules of another; as Aristotle oft-times the opinions of his Predecessours, because, though agreeable to reason, yet were not consonant to his own rules, and the Logick of his proper Principles. Again, (to speak nothing of the Sin against the HOLY GHOST, whose cure not onely but whose nature is unknown,) I can cure the Gout or Stone in some, sooner than Divinity, Pride or Avarice in others. I can cure Vices by Physick when they remain incurable by Divinity, and shall obey my Pills when they contemn their precepts. I boast nothing, but plainly say, we all labour against our own cure; for

[29] Tables showing the daily state of the heavens.
[30] Astronomical conditions supposed to presage disaster.

death is the cure of all diseases. There is no *Catholicon* or universal remedy I know, but this; which, though nauseous to queasie stomachs, yet to prepared appetites is Nectar, and a pleasant potion of immortality.

X. For my Conversation,[31] it is like the Sun's, with all men, and with a friendly aspect to good and bad. Methinks there is no man bad, and the worst, best; that is, while they are kept within the circle of those qualities wherein they are good: there is no man's mind of such discordant and jarring a temper, to which a tunable disposition may not strike a harmony. *Magnæ virtutes, nec minora vitia* [Great virtues, nor less vices]; it is the posie of the best natures, and may be inverted on the worst; there are in the most depraved and venemous dispositions, certain pieces that remain untoucht, which by an *Antiperistasis*[32] become more excellent, or by the excellency of their antipathies are able to preserve themselves from the contagion of their enemy vices, and persist intire beyond the general corruption. For it is also thus in nature: the greatest Balsomes do lie enveloped in the bodies of most powerful Corrosives.[33] I say, moreover, and I ground upon experience, that poisons contain within themselves their own Antidote, and that which preserves them from the venome of themselves, without which they were not deleterious to others onely, but to themselves also. But it is the corruption that I fear within me, not the contagion of commerce[34] without me. 'Tis that unruly regiment[35] within me, that will destroy me; 'tis I that do infect my self; the man without a Navel[36] yet lives in me; I feel that original canker corrode and devour me; and therefore *Defenda me* Dios *de me,* "Lord deliver me from my self," is a part of my Letany, and the first voice of my retired imaginations. There is no man alone, because every man is a Microcosm, and carries the whole World about him. *Nunquam minus solus quam cum solus* [Never less alone than when alone], though it be the Apothegme of a wise man, is yet true in the mouth of a fool. Indeed, though in a Wilderness, a man is never alone, not only because he is with himself and his own thoughts, but because he is with the Devil, who ever consorts with our solitude, and is that

---

[31] Intercourse.   [32] Heightening by contrast.   [33] Poisons.   [34] Intercourse.
[35] Company of evil impulses.   [36] Adam, as not being born of woman.

unruly rebel that musters up those disordered motions which accompany our sequestred imaginations. And to speak more narrowly, there is no such thing as solitude, nor any thing that can be said to be alone and by itself, but GOD, Who is His own circle, and can subsist by Himself; all others, besides their dissimilary and Heterogeneous parts, which in a manner multiply their natures, cannot subsist without the concourse[37] of GOD, and the society of that hand which doth uphold their natures. In brief, there can be nothing truly alone and by it self, which is not truly one; and such is only GOD: all others do transcend an unity, and so by consequence are many.

XI. Now for my life, it is a miracle of thirty years, which to relate, were not a History, but a piece of Poetry, and would sound to common ears like a Fable. For the World, I count it not an Inn, but an Hospital; and a place not to live, but to dye in. The world that I regard is my self; it is the Microcosm of my own frame that I cast mine eye on; for the other, I use it but like my Globe, and turn it round sometimes for my recreation. Men that look upon my outside, perusing only my condition and Fortunes, do err in my Altitude; for I am above Atlas his shoulders. The earth is a point not only in respect of the Heavens above us, but of that heavenly and celestial part within us: that mass of Flesh that circumscribes me, limits not my mind: that surface that tells the Heavens it hath an end, cannot persuade me I have any: I take my circle to be above three hundred and sixty; though the number of the Ark[38] do measure my body, it comprehendeth not my mind: whilst I study to find how I am a Microcosm, or little World, I find my self something more than the great. There is surely a piece of Divinity in us, something that was before the Elements, and owes no homage unto the Sun. Nature tells me I am the Image of GOD, as well as Scripture: he that understands not thus much, hath not his introduction or first lesson, and is yet to begin the Alphabet of man. Let me not injure the felicity of others, if I say I am as happy as any: *Ruat cælum, fiat voluntas Tua* [Let Thy will be done, though the heavens fall], salveth all; so that whatsoever happens, it is but what our daily prayers desire. In brief, I am content; and what should

---

[37] Cooperation.   [38] Here, circumference of a circle.

Providence add more? Surely this is it we call Happiness, and this do I enjoy; with this I am happy in a dream, and as content to enjoy a happiness in a fancy, as others in a more apparent truth and realty. There is surely a neerer apprehension of any thing that delights us in our dreams, than in our waked senses: without this I were unhappy; for my awaked judgment discontents me, ever whispering unto me, that I am from my friend; but my friendly dreams in the night requite me, and make me think I am within his arms. I thank God for my happy dreams, as I do for my good rest; for there is a satisfaction in them unto reasonable desires, and such as can be content with a fit of happiness: and surely it is not a melancholy conceit to think we are all asleep in this World, and that the conceits of this life are as meer dreams to those of the next; as the Phantasms of the night, to the conceits of the day. There is an equal delusion in both, and the one doth but seem to be the embleme or picture of the other: we are somewhat more than our selves in our sleeps, and the slumber of the body seems to be but the waking of the soul. It is the ligation[39] of sense, but the liberty of reason; and our waking conceptions do not match the Fancies of our sleeps. At my Nativity my Ascendant was the watery sign of Scorpius; I was born in the Planetary hour of Saturn, and I think I have a piece of that Leaden Planet in me. I am no way facetious, nor disposed for the mirth and galliardize[40] of company; yet in one dream I can compose a whole Comedy, behold the action, apprehend the jests, and laugh my self awake at the conceits thereof. Were my memory as faithful as my reason is then fruitful, I would never study but in my dreams; and this time also would I chuse for my devotions: but our grosser memories have then so little hold of our abstracted understandings, that they forget the story, and can only relate to our awaked souls, a confused and broken tale of that that hath passed. Aristotle, who hath written a singular Tract *Of Sleep,* hath not, methinks, throughly defined it; nor yet Galen, though he seem to have corrected it; for those Noctambuloes and night-walkers, though in their sleep, do yet injoy the action of their senses. We must therefore say that there is something in us that is not in the jurisdiction of Morpheus; and that those abstracted and ecstatick souls do walk about in their

[39] Binding. [40] Merriment.

own corps, as spirits with the bodies they assume, wherein they seem to hear, see, and feel, though indeed the Organs are destitute of sense, and their natures of those faculties that should inform them. Thus it is observed, that men sometimes, upon the hour of their departure, do speak and reason above themselves; for then the soul, beginning to be freed from the ligaments of the body, begins to reason like her self, and to discourse in a strain above mortality.

XII. We term sleep a death; and yet it is waking that kills us, and destroys those spirits that are the house of life. 'Tis indeed a part of life that best expresseth death; for every man truely lives, so long as he acts his nature, or some way makes good the faculties of himself. Themistocles, therefore, that slew his Soldier in his sleep, was a merciful Executioner: 'tis a kind of punishment the mildness of no laws hath invented: I wonder the fancy of Lucan and Seneca did not discover it. It is that death by which we may be literally said to dye daily; a death which Adam dyed before his mortality; a death whereby we live a middle and moderating point between life and death: in fine, so like death, I dare not trust it without my prayers, and an half adieu unto the World, and take my farwel in a Colloquy with GOD.

> The night is come, like to the day,
> Depart not Thou, great GOD, away.
> Let not my sins, black as the night,
> Eclipse the lustre of Thy light:
> Keep still in my Horizon; for to me
> The Sun makes not the day, but Thee.
> Thou, Whose nature cannot sleep,
> On my temples Centry keep;
> Guard me 'gainst those watchful foes,
> Whose eyes are open while mine close.
> Let no dreams my head infest,
> But such as Jacob's temples blest.
> While I do rest, my Soul advance;
> Make my sleep a holy trance;
> That I may, my rest being wrought,
> Awake into some holy thought;
> And with as active vigour run
> My course, as doth the nimble Sun.
> Sleep is a death; O make me try,
> By sleeping, what it is to die;

> And as gently lay my head
> On my grave, as now my bed.
> However I rest, great GOD, let me
> Awake again at last with Thee;
> And thus assur'd, behold I lie
> Securely, or to awake or die.
> These are my drowsie days; in vain
> I do not wake to sleep again:
> O come that hour, when I shall never
> Sleep again, but wake for ever.

This is the Dormative[41] I take to bedward; I need no other Laudanum than this to make me sleep; after which I close mine eyes in security, content to take my leave of the Sun, and sleep unto the Resurrection.

XIII. The method I should use in distributive Justice,[42] I often observe in commutative;[43] and keep a Geometrical proportion in both, whereby becoming equable to others, I become unjust to my self, and supererogate[44] in that common principle, *Do unto others as thou wouldst be done unto thy self*. I was not born unto riches, neither is it, I think, my Star to be wealthy; or, if it were, the freedom of my mind, and frankness of my disposition, were able to contradict and cross my fates: for to me, avarice seems not so much a vice, as a deplorable piece of madness; to conceive ourselves pipkins, or be perswaded that we are dead, is not so ridiculous, nor so many degrees beyond the power of Hellebore,[45] as this. The opinions of Theory, and positions of men, are not so void of reason as their practised conclusions. Some have held that Snow is black, that the earth moves, that the Soul is air, fire, water; but all this is Philosophy, and there is no delirium, if we do but speculate[46] the folly and indisputable dotage of avarice. To that subterraneous Idol and God of the Earth I do confess I am an Atheist; I cannot perswade myself to honour that the World adores; whatsoever virtue its prepared substance[47] may have within my body, it hath no influence nor operation without. I would not entertain a base design, or an action that

[41] Sleeping draft.
[42] Distribution of rewards and punishments according to the desert of each.
[43] The justice which is corrective in transactions between man and man, exercised in arithmetical proportion. The distinction is made by Aristotle.
[44] Do more than is necessary. [45] Used as a remedy for madness. [46] Consider.
[47] Gold was commonly used as a medicine.

should call me villain, for the Indies; and for this only do I love and honour my own soul, and have methinks two arms too few to embrace myself. Aristotle is too severe, that will not allow us to be truely liberal without wealth, and the bountiful hand of Fortune. If this be true, I must confess I am charitable only in my liberal intentions, and bountiful well-wishes; but if the example of the Mite be not only an act of wonder, but an example of the noblest Charity, surely poor men may also build Hospitals, and the rich alone have not erected Cathedrals. I have a private method which others observe not; I take the opportunity of my self to do good; I borrow occasion of Charity from mine own necessities, and supply the wants of others, when I am in most need my self: for it is an honest stratagem to take advantage of our selves, and so to husband the acts of vertue, that, where they are defective in one circumstance, they may repay their want and multiply their goodness in another. I have not Peru[48] in my desires, but a competence, and ability to perform those good works to which He hath inclined my nature. He is rich, who hath enough to be charitable; and it is hard to be so poor, that a noble mind may not find a way to this piece of goodness. *He that giveth to the poor, lendeth to the* Lord: there is more Rhetorick in that one sentence, than in a Library of Sermons; and indeed, if those Sentences were understood by the Reader, with the same Emphasis as they are delivered by the Author, we needed not those Volumes of instructions, but might be honest by an Epitome. Upon this motive only I cannot behold a Beggar without relieving his Necessities with my Purse, or his Soul with my Prayers; these scenical and accidental differences between us, cannot make me forget that common and untouch't part of us both: there is under these *Centoes*[49] and miserable outsides, these mutilate and semi-bodies, a soul of the same alloy with our own, whose Genealogy is God as well as ours, and in as fair a way to Salvation as our selves. Statists that labour to contrive a Common-wealth without poverty, take away the object of charity, not understanding only the Commonwealth of a Christian, but forgetting the prophecie of Christ.[50]

XIV. Now, there is another part of charity, which is the Basis and

[48] A symbol of vast wealth. [49] Masses of patches.
[50] "The poor ye have always with ye."

Pillar of this, and that is the love of GOD, for Whom we love our neighbour; for this I think charity, to love GOD for Himself, and our neighbour for GOD. All that is truly amiable is GOD, or as it were a divided piece of Him, that retains a reflex or shadow of Himself. Nor is it strange that we should place affection on that which is invisible: all that we truly love is thus; what we adore under affection of our senses, deserves not the honour of so pure a title. Thus we adore Virtue, though to the eyes of sense she be invisible: thus that part of our noble friends that we love, is not that part that we imbrace, but that insensible part that our arms cannot embrace. GOD, being all goodness, can love nothing but Himself; He loves us but for that part which is as it were Himself, and the traduction[51] of His Holy Spirit. Let us call to assize the loves of our parents, the affection of our wives and children, and they are all dumb shows and dreams, without reality, truth, or constancy. For first there is a strong bond of affection between us and our Parents; yet how easily dissolved! We betake our selves to a woman, forget our mother in a wife, and the womb that bare us, in that that shall bear our Image. This woman blessing us with children, our affection leaves the level it held before, and sinks from our bed unto our issue and picture of Posterity, where affection holds no steady mansion. They, growing up in years, desire our ends; or applying themselves to a woman, take a lawful way to love another better than our selves. Thus I perceive a man may be buried alive, and behold his grave in his own issue.

XV. I conclude therefore, and say, there is no happiness under (or, as Copernicus will have it, *above*) the Sun, nor any Crambe[52] in that repeated verity and burthen of all the wisdom of Solomon, *All is vanity and vexation of Spirit.* There is no felicity in that the World adores. Aristotle, whilst he labours to refute the Idea's of Plato, falls upon one himself; for his *summum bonum* is a Chimæra, and there is no such thing as his Felicity. That wherein GOD Himself is happy, the holy Angels are happy, in whose defect the Devils are unhappy, that dare I call happiness: whatsoever conduceth unto this, may with an easy Metaphor deserve that name; whatsoever else the World terms Happiness, is to me a story out of Pliny, a tale of Boccace or Malizspini, an apparition, or neat delusion, wherein there

[51] Derivative.   [52] "Tiresome repetition."

is no more of Happiness than the name. Bless me in this life with but peace of my Conscience, command of my affections, the love of Thy self and my dearest friends, and I shall be happy enough to pity Cæsar. These are, O Lord, the humble desires of my most reasonable ambition, and all I dare call happiness on earth; wherein I set no rule or limit to Thy Hand or Providence. Dispose of me according to the wisdom of Thy pleasure: Thy will be done, though in my own undoing.

FINIS